BACKSTORY 3

Books by Patrick McGilligan

Cagney: The Actor as Auteur
Robert Altman: Jumping off the Cliff
George Cukor: A Double Life
Jack's Life: A Biography of Jack Nicholson
Fritz Lang: The Nature of the Beast

As editor:

Backstory: Interviews with Screenwriters of Hollywood's Golden Age
Backstory 2: Interviews with Screenwriters of the 1940s and 1950s
Backstory 3: Interviews with Screenwriters of the 1960s
Screenplays, with Introduction:
Yankee Doodle Dandy
White Heat
Six Scripts by Robert Riskin

BACKSTORY 3

Interviews with Screenwriters of the 1960s

Pat McGilligan

University of California Press

Berkeley   Los Angeles   London

University of California Press
Berkeley and Los Angeles, California

University of California Press, Ltd.
London, England

© 1997 by
The Regents of the University of California

Library of Congress Cataloging-in-Publication Data

Backstory 3 : interviews with screenwriters of the 1960s / Pat
    McGilligan.
        p.   cm.
    Includes bibliographical references and indexes.
        ISBN 0-520-20426-3 (cloth : alk. paper).—ISBN 0-520-20427-1
    (pbk. : alk. paper)
        1. Screenwriters—California—Los Angeles—Interviews.
    I. McGilligan, Patrick.
    PN1998.2.B34   1997
    812'.03'09—dc20   96-44753
    [B]   CIP

Printed in the United States of America
9 8 7 6 5 4 3 2 1

This book is for Todd McCarthy,
friend and colleague

Contents

Acknowledgments

The portrait photography is by William B. Winburn, who kindly devoted himself to taking the exceptional photographs that are part of the *Backstory* tradition.

Other photographs appear courtesy of the following individuals and institutions: George Axelrod, Ted Post, Irving Ravetch, Arnold Schulman, Joseph Mehling, Nat Segaloff, Stirling Silliphant, Barry Strugatz, Academy of Motion Picture Arts and Sciences, British Film Institute, Collectors Bookstore, Pat McCarver's Collector's Originals, Eddie Brandt's Saturday Matinee, Museum of Modern Art, Wisconsin Center for Film and Theater Research, and the University of Southern California, Special Collections.

The George Axelrod interview was excerpted in the November–December 1995 issue of *Film Comment.* An edited version of the Walon Green interview appeared as "Greenland" in the January–February 1993 issue of *Film Comment.* The Charles B. Griffith interview was initially published in the fall 1984 issue of *Midnight Marquee.* The Ring Lardner Jr. interview was originally conducted by Barry Strugatz for a filmed documentary, its transcript published in the October 1888 issue of *Film Comment.* (The *Film Comment* version is augmented here by an interview I conducted with Lardner.) A version of the Wendell Mayes interview was first published as "Writing for the Movies: Wendell Mayes" in issue number 7 of *Focus on Film* in 1972. An extract of the interview with Irving Ravetch and Harriet Frank Jr. was published in the summer 1990 issue of *Sight and Sound.* All interviews are published here courtesy of the authors.

Special thanks to Richard Jameson of *Film Comment,* who not only kept me going by occasionally publishing my pieces but also chipped in some editing improvements. And a grateful nod to Bertrand Tavernier, a follower of the *Backstory* series, who rekindles my energy and devotion with his perpetual curiosity about screenwriters.

Introduction

Backstory began as a single volume devoted to the life stories, behind-the-scenes reminiscences, craft methodology, and professional point of view of the best screenwriters of the once-upon-a-time Golden Age of Hollywood. It has evolved into a running series, a stateside *Paris Review* devoted to screenwriters.

The first *Backstory* (1986) presented a collection of transcribed interviews with illustrious scriptwriters who began their careers and earned their reputations during the era of early talkies and the heyday of the 1930s. *Backstory 2* (1991) grouped together interviews with the next generation of Hollywood writers who rose to prominence in the studio system of the 1940s and 1950s.

Backstory 3 continues the chronology with close-ups of expert scenarists who reigned in their field during one of Hollywood's rockiest periods, the decade of the 1960s, when the studios were undergoing a process of collapse and renovation, when turmoil in the world meant extreme changes in narrative style and screen values, when events in Hollywood, as elsewhere, sometimes seemed a confusing, delirious stampede. Screenwriters were as ever part of and integral to what was happening on- and offscreen.

The word *backstory* is a tried-and-true screenwriter's expression for what happens in the plot of a movie before the story on the screen unfolds. In the oral tradition of this series, the designated subjects speak into a whirring tape recorder (or, in one case, a fax machine served as the medium), answering questions about themselves, their scripts and film credits, their modus operandi, and life and activities in the motion picture capital. The result is part biography, part historical record, part anecdotage, and part instructional seminar.

*   *   *

1

The screenwriters of the 1960s were not a youth movement. Typically, the people interviewed for this volume were born into the first age of motion pictures—long before 1960. Actually, most of the fifteen writers in this book were born before the depression and, in one or two cases, during the time of World War 1.

They spent long years learning to write, developing their skills, and making professional progress before they peaked—some are still peaking—in the 1960s. Some cut their teeth in low-budget filmmaking and also in television, radio, theater, newspapers, magazines, and publicity. Walter Bernstein had only one Hollywood job before being blacklisted in the late 1940s; Ring Lardner Jr. already possessed his first Oscar. Irving Ravetch and Harriet Frank Jr. started at Metro-Goldwyn-Mayer (MGM) under the studio's apprentice writing program in the 1940s. But most of the first credits of the screenwriters interviewed here begin in the middle to late 1950s, and by 1960, most of the people in this volume were already into their forties.

These screenwriters grew up, therefore, in the shadow of motion pictures, as fans since childhood. They developed fewer prejudices against movies than their pioneer forebears had possessed. Some screenwriters represented in the earlier *Backstory* books were oppressed by their ambivalence—a love-hate attitude. For some of them, movies weren't serious, and some yearned to write novels or plays. In general, however, the screenwriters of the 1960s did not have any hostility toward film. Their passion was wholehearted. They may not always have liked the way they were treated as screenwriters and they may not have liked Hollywood when they finally arrived there, but they did love movies.

The screenwriters of the 1960s did not carry any grudge against television. In contrast, many older screenwriters, among those profiled in *Backstory* and *Backstory 2*, had seen television, when it first swept the nation in the late 1940s and early 1950s, as a sinister rival; and from their perspective, this view was reasonable. However, coming from outside the studio apparatus, the relative newcomers of *Backstory 3* took television more in stride. Early television was a legitimate stepping stone for many of them. Writing for television could be a grind, but it could also be "different" in ways that Hollywood wouldn't dare. Many screenwriters of the 1960s learned useful dos and don'ts in television. For some, television was more than a laboratory: it was a creative refuge.

From the late 1940s on, the once-vaunted studios began to crumble under attack. The disarray seemed systemic. The "consent decree actions" that forced the sale of studio-owned theater chains meant cutbacks in production and personnel. The cold war witchhunt for Communists and left-wing sympathizers ignited a purge of Hollywood citizens. (The ranks of writers probably suffered most.) Television, in its novelty phase, soared in popularity.

For writers, there was work, and plenty of it, in television. Blacklisted writers could hide behind "fronts" and operate with impunity there. Aspiring writers could learn from senior writers, many of them old hands on sabbatical or layoff from Hollywood. Thus, the torch was passed.

To some extent, the new writers also learned from each other and from people who knew nothing about Hollywood verities. Inexperience and brashness, even boldness, contributed to an infusion of fresh ideas and points of view. Much of the work of the first generation of television writers is lost forever. (A book about the writers and scripts of the Golden Age of Television would be a precious act of archaeology.) But these interviews show that writers benefited from the hurly-burly of early television: passing through, they learned expedient methods during "live" broadcast. They practiced workups of eventual films (more than one writer went on to write one of his or her television episodes for the bigger screen in Hollywood); they developed close relationships with directors, producers, and collaborators that tended to continue throughout their careers.

Television was a mixed bag, but it was undeniably an outlet for the budding talents of many of the screenwriters of the 1960s. Ironically, some established screenwriters have returned to television. Nowadays the wide-open territory of cable and pay channels provides a closing of the circle. Certain screenwriters, like Walter Bernstein and Arnold Schulman—both of whom came to Hollywood at the twilight of the studio era—have rounded out their long, productive careers by returning to the small screen with high-profile projects.

It is true that, dating from the silent era, the vast majority of screenwriters have hailed from the East Coast, especially New York. That city's scenes, vitality, humor, and point of view (sometimes an eastern point of view about the West) have enriched and, in effect, dominated motion pictures. Partly because of television but also because of Broadway and Manhattan publishing, that is also the case with the screenwriters of the 1960s (at least among those represented in this volume). There are occasional westerners (in *Backstory* 3, two hail from Texas, one from California, and one was born in the Pacific Northwest), but most are New Yorkers and transplanted New Yorkers. As George Axelrod points out in his interview, in the so-called good old days, if a screenwriter came to Hollywood a successful novelist or Broadway playwright, he or she arrived with a cachet among studio executives.

With the breakdown of the contract system, however, it became more acceptable, even vital, to accept scripts from outside the studio radius—from outside Hollywood. The 1960s screenwriters were the first genuinely bicoastal generation, to the point where many of the people represented in this volume never did settle down on the West Coast and chose to live elsewhere—even, in Stirling Silliphant's case, as far away as Thailand. Perhaps for those off-site the flow of assignments suffered. Perhaps, as Walter Bernstein comments, the production heads preferred to assign scripts to a "local."

In the long run, though, living elsewhere had some advantages. And in both cases the long-term survivors were those writers who could roll with the punches or even lurch back to their feet after a knockout (nothing has changed about this truism).

The number of motion pictures filmed and released by the major film companies plunged from 391 in 1951 to 131 in 1961. In 1951, for example, MGM produced 41 films; however, the MGM total for 1961 was 21 (in 1969, the last year of the decade, MGM produced only 16). Columbia went from 63 movies produced in 1951 to 28 in 1961, and by 1958, RKO (36 movies in 1951) had ceased to exist altogether. There was a corresponding drop in regular attendance, from an average 87,500,000 weekly in 1949 to 42,000,000 in 1959. By the end of the 1960s, this figure had dropped to 17,500,000 weekly, and moviegoing looked passé.[*]

Less movies meant less movie writers. There was a distinct change in the screenwriter population. It was as if a long, cruel winter had set in. Most of the veterans from the early sound era had retired; a few, the hardiest of the breed, hung in there. During this period, the studios understandably did not recruit many young screenwriters. The vast majority of the screenwriters interviewed in this volume already had a foot in the door by 1960, whereas afterward, it was hard for newcomers to break in.

Very few young women broke in, for example. Ironically, there had been female screenwriters galore under the old contract system because women were sought out and hired with regularity—often by female scouts, agents, and story editors. "Women's subjects" were a staple of the old studio lineup. There was no longer a proliferation of teams formed by studio dictate (the only bona fide team in this book is the married couple Irving Ravetch and Harriet Frank Jr.). Shared script credits, symptomatic in the 1930s, became again epidemic in the 1960s. But this time there were no writers' tables in the studio commissaries (the commissaries were shutting down too), and a screenwriter might never glimpse a colleague, who was also off the lot. Because of the shrinking rolls, there are a high number of coincidentally shared credits among the subjects in *Backstory* 3: writers who collaborated (never in the same place at the same time) on *The Cincinnati Kid* (1965), *Barbarella* (1968), *The Poseidon Adventure* (1972), and *Funny Lady* (1975).

The era of Writers Guild of America (WGA)[†] muscle, escalating bidding on high-concept scripts and chunky profit-percentage clauses, was still far in

---

[*] Cobbett Steinberg, *Reel Facts: The Movie Book of Records* (New York: Vintage, 1978).

[†] The WGA, in effect the labor union of Hollywood screenwriters, has a long, complicated history that is chronicled in *The Hollywood Writers' Wars*, by Nancy Lynn Schwartz (New York: Knopf, 1982).

the future at the dawn of the 1960s. Screenwriters made a good living, but their fees were nowhere in the neighborhood of those of stars and directors. Writer-directors, other than those handful already firmly established (Billy Wilder is mentioned by more than one subject of *Backstory 3* as an inspirational figure), were not encouraged. Of the writers in this book, only George Axelrod tried film directing during the decade of the 1960s, and only Axelrod, Walter Bernstein, and Charles B. Griffith made a sideline out of it.

When the studio setups became dysfunctional, most of the screenwriters of the 1960s had to learn to function as their own career gurus. They had to keep alert, scrambling from teetering studio to studio, playing tag with hopeful projects, keeping track of fleetingly important people. It was a period that called for luck and fortitude, as well as initiative. Although screenwriters had more than the usual job insecurity, they also had unusual independence and were able to push personal and passionately believed-in material. Taking advantage of studio vicissitudes, they were able to usher their stories out of the office of the man of the hour and onto the screen with surprising speed and lack of interference. Sometimes.

There was maneuvering room in the 1960s. In the first *Backstory,* the screenwriter Julius J. Epstein sounded a typical complaint that he specialized in adaptations because in the 1930s and 1940s, producers did not welcome or value original scripts, and anyway, "in those days you soon found out that no matter what you wrote, original or adaptation, it never wound up the way you wanted." The pendulum swung the other way in the 1960s. Without the studio story departments to ferret out properties, there was more of a market for original ideas. Every writer in *Backstory 3* has both adaptations and originals in his or her filmography. The opportunities were such that, more often than in the past, screenwriters could also act as producers of a cherished project themselves, which proved the case at least once for nearly every screenwriter in this volume.

The quantity of films may have dropped in the 1960s, but thanks to screenwriters, at the same time the range of subjects widened. There were old-fashioned dramas and comedies, musicals and westerns, historical epics and thrillers, but also clever new hybrid genres, breakthroughs in form and substance, changes in filmmaking that were challenging as well as liberating.

The civil rights and black power struggles, the anti-Vietnam War protests, the feminist movement and ecological awareness were rattling the foundations of society. Screenwriters were Hollywood's shock troops, obliged to confront the times. Social upheaval was transformed into integrationist stories, alienated characters and pre-feminist heroines, anti-war and anti-establishment themes. The accepted frontiers of sex, violence, and language changed swiftly, continuously, and radically.

Even the most "far out" of 1960s films may look tasteful by today's standards. Because of censorship and outdated taboos, the vast majority of 1960s' films remained unaffected by the social upheaval going on around Hollywood. The Production Code and Legion of Decency (to name two bastions) managed to withstand repeated assault before finally withering away in the period from the late 1960s to the early 1970s.[*]

The 1970s brought the real youthquake, a delayed reaction to the 1960s. Films such as *Easy Rider* and its many imitations opened the floodgates to the first wave of post-film school, pre-MTV filmmaking. In a Hollywood that prized youth more than ever, the changing marketplace was mirrored by ever younger people in charge, behind-the-scenes and behind-the-camera, including (though still at the bottom of the totem pole) a new generation of up-and-climbing, hard-charging screenwriters and another new species of "hyphen-ates," the screenwriter-directors. These came out of film schools, the first generation to take film self-consciously and sometimes pretentiously as art. For American film and scriptwriting, the 1970s was a decade of sharp contrasts and distinctions, of highpoints as well as of flash-in-the-pan excitement and overall blandness. It was a decade of doddering old genres (star-laden disaster movies, inflated in expense and importance; a last hurrah of musicals and westerns) and invigorated, startlingly revamped ones (some stellar gangster films, action-adventure, and science fiction). Talented newcomers made show-offy moves, while venerable figures of the 1930s and 1940s, those handful still in the game, notched final credits. Veteran screenwriters came under pressure, like everyone else. Many abdicated.

After the 1960s, screen credits spread out. They were more likely than ever to be shared, often with a youthful writer added at the end of a process begun by a veteran. Another passing of the torch. By 1981, the majority of the people featured in *Backstory 3* had been squeezed out of the profession. The new management style, the youth orientation and generation gap, the radical shift in screen values—as well as personal problems and ambivalences—made careers tenuous. People moved farther and farther away, not just back to New York City. The few in this volume who continue to write screenplays are the exception, exemplars tilting against the odds. Too often there are strikingly

---

[*] The Production Code was established by the motion picture industry to regulate the presentation of sex, violence, and other social mores on the screen. The Legion of Decency was a similar organization, independently operated by the Catholic Church. For additional background on their history, see Leonard J. Leff and Jerold L. Simmons's *Dame in the Kimono: Hollywood, Censorship and the Production Code from the 1920s to the 1960s* (New York: Grove Weidenfeld, 1990); James M. Skinner's *Cross and the Cinema: The Legion of Decency and the National Catholic Office for Motion Pictures* (Westport, Conn.: Praeger, 1993); and Gregory D. Black's *Hollywood Censored: Morality Codes, Catholics, and the Movies* (Cambridge: Cambridge University Press, 1994).

concise careers that seemed to have reached their peak in and been set off in time by the 1960s.

If there is a continuing theme of the *Backstory* series, it is that Hollywood extracts a price, a piece of the soul, from the writer. Screenwriting is fraught with anecdotes about the studio system, but some of the worst horror stories for screenwriters come in the 1970s and the 1980s. In these interviews, the 1960s appear almost idyllic, a dreamland by contrast. But the high-handedness and vacillation, job uncertainty, the arrogant director and meddling producer, were constants. Only the most resolute screenwriters stuck it out with any integrity and self-esteem. Only the most fortunate manage to guard their souls.

The people interviewed in the *Backstory* series are among the most prolific and most accomplished scriptwriters. But they are also those who were willing to submit to lengthy grilling. In most cases, they have acknowledged status, but others have had relatively quiet careers or are cult figures who are not instantly recognizable but who wrote admirable films.

Originally from Texas, **Jay Presson Allen** may be considered almost a quintessential East Coast screenwriter by virtue of never having lived anywhere else for very long (certainly not Hollywood). She specializes in New York types of things—hardboiled characters, crackling dialogue and repartee, streetwise material like *Prince of the City.* She has had success in television and on Broadway, as well as in motion pictures. She helped turn one of her several plays and one of her two novels into motion pictures. Her reputation is guaranteed by prestigious 1960s and 1970s credits—a collaboration with the director Alfred Hitchcock, the adaptation of *The Prime of Miss Jean Brodie,* the film version of *Cabaret* directed by Bob Fosse, an adaptation of Graham Greene's *Travels with My Aunt* for the director George Cukor (with Katharine Hepburn busy behind the scenes), and several high-profile projects in close association with the director Sidney Lumet. Few women in her day and age have had her success as a scriptwriter while remaining aloof from the Hollywood mill. Few film writers, Jay Presson Allen says, without a pinch of modesty, have her versatility and range.

George Axelrod is well known for his sex-obsessed comedies such as *The Seven Year Itch* and *Will Success Spoil Rock Hunter?,* high romantic comedy like *Breakfast at Tiffany's*, scathing black comedy such as *The Manchurian Candidate,* no-holds-barred, absurdist comedy like *Lord Love a Duck*—and, well, just comedy. Like Jay Presson Allen, Axelrod has adapted his own plays and contributed original stories and scripts to motion pictures, as well as churning out some sterling adaptations. He is a child of show business: his mother was a silent-screen actress; and his father, someone whose show business aspirations were thwarted and whose influence haunts his son's life story. From alienated adolescence to World War II trenches to radio and TV jokesmithing to Broadway and Hollywood heights, Axelrod's life touches common as well as uncommon chords. Nobody threw more extravagant and glittering parties in the twilight of the Golden Age of Hollywood, no screenwriter had a more brilliant career, and none fell off the map, after the 1960s, more completely and dramatically. Axelrod is candid about the reasons, and hopeful for a comeback in the 1990s.

Walter Bernstein has come back once, twice—who's counting? After service in World War II and a nonfiction book of his reportage, he is one of the few writers in this volume who set foot in Hollywood in the 1940s; however, Bernstein was blacklisted, after his first screen credit, for steadfast political beliefs. Early television sustained him. After slipping the noose of the blacklist, Bernstein had colorful and eye-opening jobs with the directors Michael Curtiz and George Cukor, including the last, unfinished film starring Marilyn Monroe, *Something's Got to Give.* But his more reliable experiences were with his director friends Sidney Lumet and Martin Ritt, with whom he worked in television, and with whom he built a string of solid, usually intensely dramatic, often socially conscious screen credits including *That Kind of Woman* (1959), *Paris Blues* (1961), *Fail-Safe* (1964), and *The Molly Maguires* (1970). Starting in 1976 with the quasi-autobiographical *The Front* (still the most truthful film about the blacklist), Bernstein found fulfillment in "serious comedy" in the 1980s. He made a stab at directing and after slowing down with film credits, like some other screenwriters in *Backstory 3*, took work regularly behind the scenes as a script doctor. An unregenerate New Yorker, he has returned to television to write and sometimes direct significant telefilms.

One of the foremost American playwrights of our time is **Horton Foote,** who has had a steady and impressive parallel career as a scenarist for motion pictures. A Texan, Horton Foote writes about the small town where he grew up, imagined into drama. He has adapted his plays into novels, teleplays, and films with surprising frequency and success. He is quite capable of adapting other people's work into film also, usually kindred small-towners, southerners, or ruralists. The list of his script credits includes adaptations of popular works by Harper Lee, William Faulkner, and John Steinbeck. Foremost, Horton Foote writes about people who—though they are scarred by family, society, or harsh experience—remain admirably indomitable. He has the distinction of having twice received an Oscar for Best Screenplay: in 1962 for *To Kill a Mockingbird* and again in 1983 for *Tender Mercies.* Foote has a new play in production, which he is also directing, and at the age of eighty, he shows no signs of slowing down.

A Johnny-come-lately compared to others in *Backstory 3*, is **Walon Green.** His first script credits come in the early 1960s, in television, where he won awards writing an assortment of documentaries for the producer David L. Wolper. His first motion picture screenplay credit, *The Wild Bunch* directed by Sam Peckinpah in 1969, was a watershed film that set the fashion for future westerns, stylistically and in terms of graphic violence. He received an Oscar for his documentary *The Hellstrom Chronicle.* In the early 1970s, Green formed a strong collaboration with the director William Friedkin (*Sorcerer* and *The Brink's Job*), and for Friedkin and others, he has specialized in hardboiled characters, fatalistic situations and exotic climes. He continues to work regularly for the most prestigious and cutting-edge dramatic television series (*Hill Street Blues, Law and Order,* and *N.Y.P.D. Blue*). At sixty, Green is the youngest of the screenwriters included in this volume, and *The Wild Bunch* is the last "first credit" among those represented in the book.

Roger Corman, as producer-director-entrepreneur, is a name to reckon with, yet it is fair to say that without **Charles B. Griffith** there would be a smaller Corman body of work and less of a Corman mystique. Griffith was one of Corman's key lieutenants. Like Curt Siodmak (who was interviewed in *Backstory 2*), Griffith proved a catchpenny master of the macabre and of all subjects absurd or fantastical. His scripts for so-called exploitation films livened up the popular culture of the 1950s and 1960s, packing audiences in at double bills and drive-ins, appealing mostly to young people and cineasts. Today, the best and worst of these films (sometimes the line between them is thin) still seem eternally young and raw, their stories as wonderfully weird as ever. Griffith always worked outside the mainstream and the major studios, but in this volume he is the only example of a writer with family ties to Hollywood and a California upbringing.

John Michael Hayes wrote four features for Alfred Hitchcock in the mid-1950s, which set his career in motion and placed his name forever in film reference books. A onetime crime reporter and radio mystery writer, Hayes seemed perfectly attuned to Hitchcock, writing the scripts for *Rear Window* (1954), *To Catch a Thief* (1955), *The Trouble with Harry* (1955), and the remake of *The Man Who Knew Too Much* (1956). But their relationship was complicated by rivalry, and they parted bitterly. Hayes went on accumulate solid credits in the 1960s, working with the directors Mark Robson, Henry Hathaway, William Wyler, and Edward Dmytryk, among others; but his script work dwindled for personal reasons in the 1970s. His life story includes repeated setbacks and tragedy, as well as an unusual twilight comeback in the 1990s.

Ring Lardner Jr. also has received Oscars for Best Screenplay in two separate decades, under unique circumstances. The eldest of the writers gathered in *Backstory 3* (he was born in 1914), he is the son and namesake of the famed humorist and sportswriter Ring Lardner. In Hollywood since 1936, he came under the wing of the producer David O. Selznick and made his mark, at a young age, sharing an Oscar for the script of *Woman of the Year* (1942). Other respectable credits followed, but like Walter Bernstein, Lardner had his career momentum interrupted by the blacklist. He speaks candidly in this interview about his activity in the Communist Party, his experience as one of the jailed Hollywood Ten, and his nom de plume years of the 1950s. One of those screenwriters who clawed his way back to prominence, Lardner earned his second Oscar for Best Screenplay for his adaptation of *M*A*S*H,* the seminal sixties' film (actually released in 1970) that launched the director Robert Altman.

Another master of fear and fantasy, and another veteran of close encounters with Roger Corman, is **Richard Matheson.** Matheson is well known in his own right as the author of numerous, oft-reprinted short stories and novels straddling science fiction, fantasy, horror, and western genres. In Hollywood since the late 1950s, Matheson is responsible for classic television episodes, a cycle of stylish horror films for Corman in the 1960s, a number of collaborations with the director Steven Spielberg, landmark telefilms, and memorable science fiction and fantasy films, some of which are based on Matheson's fiction. His odyssey as a writer—his years of anonymity and his struggle to make a living and achieve recognition—is reflected in a highly personal body of work that emphasizes ordinary people trapped by fate or in peculiar circumstances of terror.

In the 1950s, **Wendell Mayes** was one of the respected writers of teleplays who was drafted by Hollywood, where he stayed much in demand for two decades. He worked with the director Billy Wilder on *The Spirit of St. Louis* (1957), with Henry Hathaway on *From Hell to Texas* (1958), and *North to Alaska* (1960), with Dick Powell on *The Enemy Below* (1957) and *The Hunters* (1958), with Delmer Daves on *The Hanging Tree* (1959), with Otto Preminger on *Anatomy of a Murder* (1959), and *Advise and Consent* (1962), and *In Harm's Way* (1965). Mayes was known for his tightly structured plotting and complex characterizations. Like others in this volume, Mayes was sidetracked in the late 1960s and moved into producing and writing glossy, big-budget films. But in 1978, he topped off his career with one of the first and finest of the anti–Vietnam War films, *Go Tell the Spartans,* a project he shepherded into existence.

The only pure team represented in *Backstory 3* is also the only married couple, **Irving Ravetch** and **Harriet Frank Jr.** Harriet is the daughter of one of MGM's Scheherazades, who was duly employed to regale Louis B. Mayer and other executives with synopses of prospective screen stories.* As a boy, Irving, the son of a rabbi, came west to maintain his health, a move that had the side effect of nurturing his love of movies and westerns. Ravetch and Frank

---

* According to Norman Zierold, *The Moguls* (New York: Coward-McCann, 1969), "Harriet Frank was herself a sound actress. When she recited a story for [Louis B.] Mayer, a table lamp was carefully arranged to highlight her face, especially to show a single tear rolling down her cheek. Almost always the tear, which she had an uncanny ability to produce, made Mayer buy the property."

met as junior writers in MGM corridors, married, and for a while pursued separate bylines. Their films took a leap in quality and prestige when, out of loneliness, they began to work together. They made a habit of adapting William Faulkner, wrote gritty westerns, returned again and again to the social tapestry of the South, occasionally taking up a cause, as in their moving, pro-union *Norma Rae* (1979). Their friend Martin Ritt was usually their director and close collaborator, and they did not work very often without him. Like Horton Foote and Ring Lardner Jr., they have been honored with the Writers Guild Laurel Award, the highest citation of the Guild, for their lifetime achievement of intelligent films with integrity.

Arnold Schulman has had a checkered career, as he is the first to admit. Hollywood has exacted a toll from him. He started as an aspiring playwright and author of prime-time teleplays. His career in motion pictures began in the twilight of the Golden Age with an offbeat project for the director George Cukor and the producer Hal Wallis. Then his first serious play was tinkered with repeatedly before it was finally adapted into a comedy, transformed almost beyond recognition, by Schulman himself and the director Frank Capra. Schulman had a winning streak in the 1960s with an original, *Love with a Proper Stranger* (1963), and the adaptation of Philip Roth's novel *Goodbye, Columbus* (1969), both much-lauded screenplays. The 1970s were a professional nightmare he can laugh about now, because Schulman bounced back in the 1980s and 1990s with richly textured scripts for the quixotic *Tucker: The Man and His Dream* (1988, directed by Francis Coppola) and the critically acclaimed telefilm of Randy Shilts's book about the history of AIDS, *And the Band Played On* (1993).

The phenomenal **Stirling Silliphant** retreated to Thailand, where he managed to keep up an active Hollywood career. Arguably one of the most produced scriptwriters of his generation, Silliphant started in journalism and studio publicity, then began writing movies in 1955. In the 1960s, he wrote (often as adaptations) *Village of the Damned* (1960), *The Slender Thread* (1965), *In the Heat of the Night* (1967), *Charly* (1968), *Marlowe* (1969), *A Walk in the Spring Rain* (1970), and *The Liberation of L. B. Jones* (1970). Silliphant spent almost as much time in television and wrote dozens of original teleplays for *Route 66, Naked City, Alfred Hitchcock Presents,* and many other noteworthy series. Continuing to write films with regularity in the 1970s, 1980s, and early 1990s, Silliphant contributed to disaster films, the *Shaft* and *Dirty Harry* films, and more.

Two of the quintessential films of the 1960s are *Dr. Strangelove; or, How I Learned to Stop Worrying and Love the Bomb* (1964) and *Easy Rider* (1969). **Terry Southern** left his imprint on both, although these films' respective directors, Stanley Kubrick and Dennis Hopper, have promoted a more auteurist view of how these modern classics were created. Southern seemed everywhere at once in the 1960s, hanging out with the cool crowd and making all the hip scenes, a friend to trendy artists and influential people. He was involved with the development of curious and curiouser 1960s and 1970s film projects. It may seem that the coauthor of the novel and the screenplay *Candy* kept a low profile and had an unfulfilled screenwriting career since his 1960s heyday; however, the reasons are fascinating, and his story is a sympathetic one.

Here it might be appropriate to quote from the introduction to the first *Backstory:* "Taken together, these interviews comprise an affectionate group portrait of the movie writers of a bygone era—of their lives and lifestyles, of their vast body of work, of their differing approaches to the challenge of writing motion pictures. This book is not meant to be a scholarly or historical work, a purely factual study, or even a complete representation of the profession. Names and faces are missing. It would take six hundred such interviews to reflect the diversity of writers who wrote our favorite movies."

And here it might be appropriate to quote from the introduction to *Backstory 2*: "Oral history is not, strictly speaking, factual. Fact is increasingly presumptive in the realm of Hollywood history and hard to pin down amid so much conflicting rumor, gossip, legend, folklore and reminiscence. Naturally, screenwriters get the benefit of the doubt here, and that may be cause, for some, for skepticism. Although the editor admits siding passionately with the writers' points of view and their generally unsung contributions, he also tries to be fair. Where an obvious or glaring error of fact has been detected, the correction has been noted in the text or footnoted."

Both of the above statements continue to be part of the *Backstory* credo. There are dozens upon dozens of books about famous stars and directors, producers and studios, but not as nearly as many as there ought to be about the people who are fundamental to the creation of films, yet who rank as, in the words of Albert Hackett in the first *Backstory,* "less than dust" in the Hollywood hierarchy.

It is startling how long ago the 1960s seem and how few of the screenwriters interviewed here are still screenwriting. Hollywood has a short memory for them and their accomplishments. This series continues to be not only a backstory of individuals and their classic (as well as negligible) film credits but also an informal backstory of the profession and a wishful corrective to film history.

A Note on Credits

It is not a simple job to compile the filmography of a screenwriter, for as Richard Corliss has written in his indispensable book *Talking Pictures,* "A writer may be given screen credit for work he didn't do (as with Sidney Buchman on *Holiday*), or be denied credit for work he did do (as with Sidney Buchman on *The Awful Truth*)." Therefore, there are irresolvable gaps and inaccuracies in the best sources.

The *American Film Institute's Catalog of Feature Films* (1921–1930, 1961–1970) (New York: Bowker, 1971) is incomplete and not always reliable. *Who Wrote the Movie (And What Else Did He Write)?* (1936–1969) (Los Angeles: AMPAS and WGA-West, 1970), the joint project of the Academy of Motion Picture Arts and Sciences and the Writers Guild of America-West, is less than authoritative. It overlooks movies written before the inception of the Guild and toes the official Guild line of accreditation thereafter. Consequently, many famous and not-so-famous instances of uncredited complicity are omitted. The blacklist years are riddled with aliases and omissions. And the Guild maintains rules (disallowing screen credit to any director who has not contributed at least 50 percent of the dialogue, for example) that, while they may protect screenwriters, do not promote a full accounting of the screenplay.

The credits for this book were cross-referenced from several sources—those cited above, the *New York Times* and *Variety* film reviews, *International Motion Picture Almanac* and *Motion Picture Daily* yearbooks, *A Guide to American Screenwriters: The Sound Era, 1929–1982,* by Larry Langman (New

York and London: Garland Publishing, 1984), and *The Film Encyclopedia,* by Ephraim Katz, rev. ed. (New York: HarperCollins, 1994). In individual cases, there was additional spadework by the interviewers. As a final resort, whenever possible, the interview subjects were confronted with the results of research and asked to add to or subtract from the list. Jay Presson Allen, George Axelrod, Walter Bernstein, Horton Foote, Walon Green, John Michael Hayes, Ring Lardner Jr., Richard Matheson, Irving Ravetche and Harriet Frank Jr., Arnold Schulman, Stirling Silliphant, and Terry Southern—all reviewed their transcripts and filmographies, clarifying aspects of their interviews.

As to specific claims and counterclaims concerning who wrote exactly what, there is another kind of cross-referencing to be done. The oral historian cannot always separate fact from factoid or having an opinion from having an ax to grind. Likely, there is much in this collection of reminiscences that contradicts, or is contradicted by, material in other books. Partly, such conflicting tales are to be expected of a branch of the film industry that has been relatively untapped for its perspective, and where egos and careers have been so trampled. And partly, such differences arise inevitably from individual points of view on a group enterprise.

Jay Presson Allen: Writer by Default

Interview by Pat McGilligan

The "Jay" is actually Jacqueline. "Never particularly fond of her given name, she decided to use her first initial when writing (the more elaborate form, Jay, is the work of a Social Security Clerk, she says)," according to the *Dictionary of Literary Biography.*

Presson is her maiden name, mostly for byline purposes and long ago abandoned in routine introductions and everyday conversation. (More than once I have answered the phone and been surprised to hear her announce herself, "This is Jay Allen.")

Allen is the surname she took from her husband, the stage and screen producer Lewis Maitland Allen. For film, he has sponsored such unusual and rewarding fare as as *The Balcony* (1963), *Lord of the Flies* (1963), *Farenheit 451* (1967), *Fortune and Men's Eyes* (1971), *Never Cry Wolf* (1983), and *Swimming to Cambodia* (1987); on Broadway, his eclectic résumé includes productions of *Ballad of the Sad Café, Annie, I'm Not Rappaport, A Few Good Men, Tru, Vita & Virginia,* and *Master Class.* The Allens have been married since 1955.

Born in San Angelo, Texas, she moved to New York in the mid-1940s with the goal of becoming an actress. She married, lived for a while in Los Angeles, wrote a first novel, *Spring Riot,* divorced. Moving back to New York, she realized she preferred a career on the other side of the footlights. Partly "by default," as she modestly puts it, because she was a good talker, devoted reader, and facile writer, Jay Presson Allen became a working scenarist, starting out in live television and graduating by degrees to Broadway, before being summoned to Hollywood by Alfred Hitchcock, in 1963, to toil on *Marnie.*

Since then, her career, divided between Broadway and Hollywood (mixing in a little television of the best sort), has been stellar. Any list of preeminent screenwriters who got started in the 1960s would have to include her. It helped that she usually worked with outstanding directors—Hitchcock, Cukor, Bob Fosse, Sidney Lumet. She earned Writers Guild nominations for Best Screenplay for her adaptation of *The Prime of Miss Jean Brodie* (based on her play), *Travels with My Aunt* (although in this interview she blithely discounts her contribution), and *Prince of the City,* for which she was also nominated for an Academy Award for Best Screenplay. She won the Writers Guild top adaptation award for *Cabaret* in 1971. She also won the Donatello Award (Italy's equivalent of the Oscar) for the screenplay of her novel *Just Tell Me What You Want.*

She is one of a handful of first-rank screenwriters of the post-1960s who also happens to be female. This has figured into her trademark of flamboyant female characters, stories that often focus on divorce and marriage or explosive relationships, family matters (including the pilot episode of the prestigious television series *Family*), or occasional subjects with the interests of children at heart. But she hates being typed, can't be typed, and reminds you that she writes compelling male characters too; after all, she wrote and produced *Prince of the City,* one of the quintessential, New York true-life street stories about police and corruption, with nary a female character worth mentioning.

In general, her characters, male or female, are like herself—smart, tough, funny, slippery, resilient in life situations. I first met Jay Presson Allen several years ago when I talked to her about the director George Cukor for my biography of Cukor; and some of that material is incorporated into this interview. In that conversation, she surprised me by stating unequivocally that she had decided to quit writing motion pictures, that all the grief of coping with "development" and present-day studio procedures was not worth it. When I came back to see her some time later for *Backstory 3,* she had kept her vow, and therefore, all of her movie work since the mid-1980s has been invisible, rewriting scripts at the last minute for high pay and no credit. This is a lamentable trend among screenwriters of her generation.

She continues to write under her name for the stage. After years of independence from each other, she and her husband began to work together occasionally in recent years—he served as producer of her 1989, one-person hit play about Truman Capote, *Tru,* which she also directed.

Even though she is an easy talker, Jay Presson Allen does not enjoy giving extended interviews, and there are not many on the record. Like some of the other writers in *Backstory 3,* she wanted to polish her words before committing them to posterity. As part of our agreement, I let her read and hone the transcript. She took out nothing juicy. Her penciled touches, all in the direction of accuracy or crispness, only improved the text.

Jay Presson Allen in New York City, 1994. (Photo by William B. Winburn.)

Jay Presson Allen (1922–   )

1963   *Wives and Lovers* (John Rich). Adaptation from Allen's play *Rich and Famous*.

1964   *Marnie* (Alfred Hitchcock). Script.

1969   *The Prime of Miss Jean Brodie* (Ronald Neame). Script, based on Allen's play.

1972   *Cabaret* (Bob Fosse). Script.

1972   *Travels with My Aunt* (George Cukor). Co-script.

1975   *Funny Lady* (Herbert Ross). Co-script.

1980   *Just Tell Me What You Want* (Sidney Lumet). Coproducer, script, based on Allen's novel.

1981   *Prince of the City* (Sidney Lumet). Co-script.

1982   *Deathtrap* (Sidney Lumet). Script.

Television credits include contributions to *Philco Playhouse, Playhouse 90, Hallmark Hall of Fame, The Borrowers* (1973 telefilm, script), and *Family* (1976–1980, creator and story consultant).

Plays include *The First Wife, The Prime of Miss Jean Brodie, Forty Carats, The Big Love,* and *Tru.*

Novels include *Spring Riot* and *Just Tell Me What You Want.*

Academy Award honors include Oscar nominations for Best Adapted Screenplays for *Cabaret* and *Prince of the City.*

Writers Guild honors include nominations for Best Script for *The Prime of Miss Jean Brodie, Travels with My Aunt,* and *Prince of the City;* and the award for Best-Written Comedy Adapted from Another Medium for *Cabaret.*

I was surprised, reading a thumbnail sketch of your career, to be confronted by the information that you were born and raised in Texas. I had never paid that much attention to that interesting fact before.
Well, why should you?
Is there a Texas strain in your work?
Nothing—except maybe a kind of insouciance. I grew up in a little town called San Angelo, ranching country, later oil. A prosperous little town, not very far from the Mexican border. My father was a merchant, not very prosperous, coming out of the depression.
In those days there was still a kind of frontier mentality—a belief that you not only could do anything but that you *had* to. I don't mean literally, but it was certainly part of the psychological makeup of the people I knew. At the same time, I was an only child and was given a great deal of self-confidence by my parents—a lot of approval—and a lot of responsibility for an only child.
What was the nature of your education, growing up?
No education to speak of. Texas public schools and a couple of years in a place called, in those days, Miss Hockaday's School for Young Ladies.
Were your parents readers or writers?
Nah. Not at all.
What sort of interest did you have in theater and movies? Did you ever go to New York to see a play?
Oh no! (*Laughs.*) We did go to Dallas to see whatever came on tour. The Metropolitan came every year, so I saw opera too. The Lunts toured every-

where, so we saw the Lunts in Dallas every two or three years. That was enormously exciting.

The movies were every Saturday and Sunday from one o'clock until somebody dragged you out at seven. That was literally how one's winter weekends were spent—in the moviehouse. Movies were very, very important. I remember seeing—I must have been eight to nine years old—one movie, and realizing how green other places were and how many trees there were elsewhere. I knew from that time that I would not be staying in Texas.

Did you travel as a child?

No. People from West Texas didn't travel. A wonderful friend of mine, Popsie Whittaker, one of the original editors of the *New Yorker,* went to Texas for the first time in his later years. This must have been in the 1950s. It was in the worst part of summer, and Dallas is a hellhole in the summer. He used to tell this story: He was being entertained by rich people, and sitting at a dinner table between two bejeweled women, he turned to one of these obviously rich, rich women, and said, "What I cannot understand about you people is that you could go anywhere to get out of this heat . . . why do you stay in Dallas?" And the woman said, "Well, Mr. Whittaker, it's hot all *over* Texas!" (*Laughs.*) I only knew two people, growing up, who had ever been to Europe.

When did you first know you wanted to be a writer?

I don't think I ever wanted to be a writer. I became a writer by default. I was a show-off kid who got a lot of encouragement. I wanted to be an actress, from the earliest age, and I never presumed to be anything else. I came to New York at the first opportunity and discovered rather quickly that I only liked rehearsal. I discovered I didn't like to *perform.* It was a shock.

So I married the first grown man who asked me.* Then I lived in southern California during the Second World War, in a small academic town called Claremont. I had two friends who were in the movie business, but it never occurred to me to aspire to that world. It was exotic. It was not a *business* as far as I knew. My innocence was profound and sublime.

When I chose to leave that marriage, I felt guilty because my husband's big fault was marrying someone too young. I'd always read an enormous amount of trash, and I couldn't imagine not being able to write as well as a great deal of the stuff I was reading. I'd always written facilely, in school and letters. So I decided to write my way out of that marriage, and I did.

You mean you realized that writing would give you a necessary financial foothold? You consciously set about becoming a writer, so you could break free and become independent of your husband?

Yes.

---

* Allen declined to name her first husband.

What did you write?

I wrote a novel. It was published by a well-known house in '46 to '47. The name of it was *Spring Riot.*[*] Don't ask me what the title means. I haven't a clue.

Was it any good?

I certainly wouldn't think so! (*Laughs.*)

Was it hard to get published for the first time?

No. Easy. I was so ignorant—I thought if you *wrote* a book, it got published. It never occured to me that you could write a book which nobody would pay you for. The ignorance was breathtaking.

Was it a genre novel, coming-of-age? . . .

It was smart-ass: what I'd seen of Hollywood—and what I'd seen I didn't understand. There's nothing as dumb as a smart girl.

My agent was Marsha Powers, who had been Sinclair Lewis's teenage mistress, and whom he had set up in an agency. She was clever and active. I can't remember who sent me to her, but she took the book and sold it instantly.

What was the critical reaction?

Oh, I got mixed notices, which astonished me. I didn't really know much about notices. I was dumbfounded by all of it. Everything was a surprise.

Did it sell?

Some.

You didn't write another novel for thirty years. Did that experience temporarily quash your literary ambitions?

I don't believe I ever thought about literary ambitions. I just wanted to make some money and have some fun.

How did you progress?

I came back to New York, marginally divorced, and performed on radio and in cabaret. For my sins. Agony! It never occurred to me when I woke up most mornings, that some great grisly thing wouldn't happen—like my parents would be killed in an automobile accident—and that I wouldn't have to perform that night. Around four o'clock every day, it would become clear that I *was* going to perform. Then I'd go through the whole show, weeping. I hated it. But they wouldn't fire me.

You started writing again, little by little . . .

By that time, television existed, and once again, I didn't see how I couldn't do *that* well. My sights were never set very high. (*Laughs.*) So I did—sold some stuff to television, *Philco Playhouse,* etcetera. About four shows, and they all sold to good programs. I knew I could make a living at it. I hoped I wouldn't have to.

Why? What did you hope would happen?

Something lovely—with chiffon and feathers.

---

*   *Spring Riot* (New York: Rinehart, 1948).

Was the work of writing too hard?

No. But it wasn't wonderful. It always seemed like an exercise—like you were doing homework. Writing wasn't terrible, but you'd rather be out shopping, or playing tennis or poker, or something.

Did you feel you were falling short of what you were trying to do?

No. I don't think there was ever any question of setting my sights above what I was able to do facilely.

Don't you think there was something in your personality or character, in your personal circumstances, that helped make you a writer?

Well, I am a chronic reader. Compulsive, chronic reader. I could never get enough of books. I was and am a bookworm. And I've always been interested in the *why* of human behavior. I think most dramatic writers are natural psychologists.

What about inside of you—something that drew you, inevitably, to the act of writing?

Who knows? My God, that's an imponderable, isn't it? Do people ever know that?

Sometimes people have an inkling. Like: "I was a failure as an actress—an extrovert—therefore, I became a writer . . ."

I *wasn't* a failure. I could have been an actress. I obviously was going to be able to work. But the profession was alarming. I found the life so unsatisfactory so quickly that I backed off. Maybe I was frightened. I didn't think I was, but maybe I was.

Had you gotten as far as Broadway?

I was getting there. I did some road shows.

Then you wrote a play . . .

Then I wrote a play, which was optioned by producer Bob Whitehead. I was ambitious for that play. I think that was the first real ambition I ever experienced. I liked that play and was proud of it. I picked out this particular producer because he had produced *Member of the Wedding,* which I loved, and my play was also about a child. I thought he would like my play, so I sent it to his office. Ere long, I got it back, rejected, and was astonished.

I didn't send it anywhere else for a couple of months. Finally, I came to this conclusion; "I bet some reader rejected my play. I bet Mr. Whitehead never read it." So I sent it back. And I had guessed right. The reader who had read the play and rejected it had now gone off to Mexico with a beautiful actress. This time Bob read the play himself and instantly optioned it. The reader who had rejected my play came back in a couple of years, and I married him. (*Laughs.*) That was Lewis Allen, my husband.

Was the play produced?

It was never produced. We had a very difficult time casting it. Mostly, the problem was with the child, but sometimes, it was with the lead actress. Bob was a fairly young producer, and he wouldn't go near anybody whose work he didn't know. Among the people he didn't know—who I thought was absolutely wonderful, but she gave a bad reading, and he wouldn't even talk about her afterwards—was Geraldine Page. If we got an actress, he wouldn't go with the child; if we got a child, he wouldn't go with the actress.

Finally, Bob let it go, and I gave it to [producer] Fred Coe, whom I had worked for in television.* It was optioned again—and again—but never done. By the time it would have been done, that kind of play—very small, very domestic—had become a television genre. It no longer had the size for Broadway. I lost that play.

How were you able to make a living while all this was going on?

One way or another. It wasn't so hard to make a living in those days. It didn't cost much to live. And don't forget unemployment insurance. It was certainly important to me. I was young, I was healthy. If worst came to absolute worst, I could always take a real job. But I never did.

How long was it before you wrote your second play?

Well, I wrote *Prime of Miss Jean Brodie* when my daughter was . . . I think, six? She was born in '56—so about '63.

What had happened in the meantime?

I grew up a little. I got married and had a child and entered a very different world. When Lewis and I first got married, we both decided we wouldn't work anymore. Lewis had a pittance of income. We decided we would go to the country and live—he wanted to write, and I didn't want to do anything. So that's what we did. I had a baby and spent two and a half absolutely wonderful years in the country.

Lewis is a natural scholar. He's never had to be conventionally employed to be occupied. He is extremely creative . . . much more creative than I am. He always has extraordinary ideas for stories. He would do a wonderful draft, and then he wouldn't do the donkey's work. But he's gifted.

Anyway, one day Lewis came to me and said, "Let's go back to the city. I want to go back to work." So that was that.

What made you start writing again, specifically on Miss Brodie?

Because Bob Whitehead had become a good friend, and he was very encouraging. He pushed me: "Do a play, do a play, do a play." One day I picked up this little book [*The Prime of Miss Jean Brodie,* by Muriel Spark (London: Macmillan, 1961)] and read it and thought it was wonderful. I could see a play, instantly, in that book. I called Bob and said I had found this book which I wanted to adapt into a play. He read it and said, "Do you *really* want to do this?" I said yes. He really did not think it would make a play. However,

---

* The producer-director Fred Coe is remembered warmly by several writers in *Backstory 3*. He produced more than five hundred television shows, including NBC's *Philco-Goodyear Playhouse,* the Mary Martin *Peter Pan,* and *Playhouse 90* shows for CBS. On Broadway, he produced *The Miracle Worker,* and *A Trip to Bountiful, A Thousand Clowns,* and other noteworthy plays.

he was very generous, and insisted that I go to Scotland and do some research, which never would have occurred to me. I did; then I wrote the play.

That seems a great leap of faith.

When I wanted to do *Brodie,* nobody I spoke to about it thought it would make a play—except Lillian Hellman. Lillian said, "God, yes." But I always thought I was a very good judge of what worked in theater. We used to put a little bit of money into plays, here and there. I took a little flyer whenever there was something around I liked, with not much money. My batting average was very high, even before my husband.

You weren't deterred by people's skepticism?

You clearly want validation and approbation, but if you don't get it, it's not the end of the world. Nobody's writing it but you, so nobody can make the judgment but you.

During this period of time, leading up to Brodie, *were you paying any attention to the possibilities of writing for movies?*

No. It never entered my mind. I never heard of a screenwriter. That was the most esoteric thing I could imagine.

What is the first you heard of Hollywood or the first Hollywood heard of you?

People like [Alfred] Hitchcock have always had their finger in the agencies. Stuff is sent to them early. Preproduction. Hitch read *Brodie,* called me, and asked me to do *Marnie.*

"A very flawed movie": Tippi Hedren and Sean Connery in Alfred Hitchcock's *Marnie.*

You went out to Hollywood . . .

I don't think I would have gone if it had been anybody but him. I didn't know how to write a movie. I wasn't ambitious to do a movie. I certainly didn't want to spend any time in California. I had a child. I was going to have a play produced. There was every reason in the world not to go. I went out of curiosity as much as anything else.

Hitchcock guided you through the experience?

He was a great teacher. He did it naturally, easily, and unself-consciously. In that little bit of time that I worked for him, he taught me more about screenwriting than I learned in all the rest of my career. There was one scene in *Marnie,* for example, where this girl is forced into marriage with this guy. I only knew how to write absolutely linear scenes. So I wrote the wedding and the reception and leaving the reception and going to the boat and getting on the boat and the boat leaving . . . I mean, you know, I kept plodding, plodding, plodding. Hitch said, "Why don't we cut some of that out, Jay? Why don't we shoot the church and hear the bells ring and see them begin to leave the church. Then why don't we cut to a large vase of flowers, and there is a note pinned to the flowers that says, 'Congratulations.' And the water in the vase is sloshing, sloshing, sloshing."

Lovely shorthand. I often think of that. When I get verbose, I suddenly stop and say to myself, "The vase of water."

How literate was Hitchcock in terms of the script and his general education?

Hitch was certainly literate. He had no education but had read a lot. People like that are sponges and learn a lot from educated conversations.

What stopped him, then, from writing his own scripts?

I think a sense of being uneducated. He was very defensive about that. He was extremely defensive about class.

He was wonderful to me. So was his wife, Alma. She was very influential in everything Hitch did. She had been a successful editor before they were married, and she contributed a lot to his films. She was around a lot, though not for script sessions. But it was all very easy and open. Alma was knowledgeable, more sophisticated than Hitch. We were together all the time and got along well.

I should say they *tried* to teach me to write a script. I couldn't learn fast enough to make a first-rate movie, although *Marnie* did have some good scenes in it.

If you were getting along so wonderfully, what went wrong?

It is a very flawed movie, for which I have to take a lot of the responsibility—it was my first script. Hitch certainly didn't breathe on me. He loved the script I did, so that he did not make as good a movie as he should have made. I think one of the reasons that Hitch was fond of me and filmed a lot of the stuff I wrote was that I am frequently almost crippled by making everything rational. There always has to be a reason for everything. And he loved that.

Another reason is that Hitch was very concerned with characterization when he could get it, and basically, that's what I do.

That's scarcely what people think of when they think of Hitchcock . . .

I know, but that's what he loved. Maybe because his stuff was usually so plotty and convoluted, characterization escaped him more than he would have wished it to. He loved to talk about the characters. We talked endlessly. In fact, he wouldn't let me begin to write for almost two months. We just played and chatted, day after day after day. He got very involved in trying to get some reality in the relationship between the two people in the story, and he kind of got bogged down in that relationship. God knows, I did.

Maybe his interest in characterization was something relatively recent in his career—having something to do with growing older and maturing as a director.

Maybe. Hitch was enormously permissive with me. He fell in love with my endless linear scenes and shot them. In point of fact, he loved what I wrote, he shot what I wrote, and he shouldn't have.

People say he loved script sessions and the preproduction of a film, but that he hated the actual job of filming. I visited the set of his last production, The Family Plot, *and it certainly appeared that he was bored.*

I think he was totally bored during the filmmaking. He storyboarded every single, solitary thing. There was a drawing of every shot. By the time he got to the set, the work was done. He was no longer interested. He had done it all. What he responded to, the visual and creative work, was all finished in his head.

Was it at all odd or uncomfortable, in the 1960s, being the rare female screenwriter in Hollywood?

No. I never knew the difference.

Did Hitchcock ever say anything to you—like, he had come to you because Marnie was a female character, and it was a female-oriented story?

Nope. Nope. Looking back in light of the sixties, women's lib, and all the historical things one reads, I know there were women writers at the beginning in Hollywood, but then there was a long period of time when there weren't any. Yet I never ever felt discriminated against. If anything, I felt that I was promoted. Almost all of the men I worked with were supportive. If I was getting a bum rap somewhere, I didn't know it.

Why do you think it is that there were so few women screenwriters?

Well, there was that period after World War II and coming out of the fifties where women were supposed to be in the kitchen or doing their nails. There was a sense of psychological and even physical weakness about women—and therefore executives and directors maybe felt it would not be suitable to grind a woman writer down the way they would another man.

It's not a business for sensitive souls. I think the minute they figured you weren't going to cry, you were on track.

I had a very powerful man [in Hollywood] tell me shocking stories of criminal behavior, and I know it was because: one, the writer is a lowly thing, and two, a woman writer is a doubly lowly thing, perceived as being so unthreatening that they can say anything in front of you.

What was your impression of Hollywood this time around? Now that you were much closer to the business . . .

I *still* wasn't in the business. I was with Hitchcock, and he wasn't in the business either.

You were around soundstages, stars . . .

It didn't seem any different from what you'd expect. A star is a star is a star. They have stars in small towns, you know.

Well, does the Hollywood of today seem different from the Hollywood of those days?

Very. Very. Hollywood seemed leisured. Expected. Very organized. Everybody knew what was expected, and they pretty much did it. Now, it seems wild, frenetic. There's a lot of fear now, with good reason: everything costs too much. If some executive says yes to a movie, it's forty million dollars—bang. It's scary, and people are nervous. Scared.

Prime of Miss Jean Brodie *really hit the jackpot.*

I thoroughly expected it to . . .

Up to that time, however, your career had been relatively modest.

I never thought of myself as having a career. The term *career* was not all that applicable. I never set out to be a writer. I had no serious ambitions to continue as a writer. It's only in the last seven or eight years, as I've grown older, that I think of this as my *career.* Writing was just something I could do, with a little bit of talent and considerable skill.

What was the particular challenge of turning your play into a film?

When producers pay a great deal of money for a project, which they did for *Brodie,* they want what they buy. I thought the play could have been opened up an enormous amount. I was a little disappointed that we couldn't have made it richer. But they wanted what they bought, and the film was very successful. And it is a charming film.

Was there much involved in taking Cabaret *from stage to screen?*

Initially, I was approached by Cy Feuer, who was the producer, simply saying, "We do not want to do the book of the musical. We want to go back to [Christopher] Isherwood's book [*Goodbye to Berlin* (London: Hogarth Press, 1939)], and start all over again."

That seems a brave decision.

Onstage, *Cabaret* was a brilliant production with a wonderful score, but really the book was rather bland. The book of the musical didn't even suggest that he [the English tutor, Brian, played by Michael York in the film] was a

Joel Grey and chorus in the film *Cabaret,* directed by Bob Fosse.

homosexual, so in the end, the play made no sense. I had read Isherwood, of course, so I said I'd love to try.

Did you ever talk to Isherwood about it?

No. I never met him.

Of course, I had the benefit of starting out with that wonderful score, and I had the great joy of being able to work with [John] Kander and [Fred] Ebb on new stuff.* We worked together on it, I thought and they thought, most happily.

What about [the director] Bob Fosse—was he around much?

He was around to a degree. During the actual writing, he was busy working on something else. I didn't find him the happiest collaborator I ever had. For a man who dealt with women as much as he was obliged to, let's say he had an extremely parochial view of women.

---

* Kander and Ebb are the composer-lyricist team best known for *Cabaret* and other Broadway musicals, as well as for the title track for Martin Scorsese's 1977 film *New York, New York.*

Did he hurt the principal female character? What was lost by his direction?

The film had less humor than the script. It's always very hard for me to see humor go down the drain. It's always an agonizing loss.

What did he bring on the plus side?

Oh, visual brilliance. He brought his enormous visual talent to the project. I just personally didn't like Bobby. We didn't like each other.

At a certain point, didn't you drop out of the writing?

I had another project to do. Then when they went to Germany and had to have some scenes, I suggested they take on a friend of mine, Hugh Wheeler.*

Was what Wheeler wrote congenial to your script?

Entirely congenial. The loss of humor was not Hugh, because Hugh was very humorous.

How did you get involved with Travels with My Aunt*?*

The inception of that particular project, I am almost certain, was Kate [Hepburn] wanting to give [the director] George [Cukor] a job. He was not getting work, he wanted to work, and there was no reason in the world why he shouldn't work. So he and Hepburn had teamed up with Bobby Fryer [who had produced *Brodie* as a film] to do *Travels.*

They called me, and I was involved in something else. I suggested Hugh Wheeler. To tell you the truth, I wasn't all that crazy about the material. The characters were wonderful, but I didn't really know how you were going to string all that into a movie. Bobby called me back several months later. They were unhappy with what Hugh had done. I agreed to take a shot at it.

I went and met George, and just adored him. I did a pretty straightforward, quite a competent script. At the beginning, George was very reasonable to deal with. We only locked horns on a couple of things. For one, George wanted to show Kate as a young woman in a flashback, but I thought it was a disservice to her and to the film. I believe in the film they show Maggie [Maggie Smith, who took over the role] as a young woman—which is more reasonable—but I desperately thought they shouldn't with Kate, and George was very, very determined to do that.

I don't think George was great with script. Storytelling was instinctive with Hitch. George was great with feeling and with the mood he wanted, but structurally, he didn't have Hitch's knack. However, George was a creature of the theater, and he was wonderful with actors. Hitch wasn't all that good with

---

* Hugh Wheeler wrote mystery novels under the names Patrick Quentin, Quentin Patrick, and Jonathan Stagge. The British-born playwright, novelist, and screenwriter contributed the books of the broadway musicals *A Little Night Music, Candide, Pacific Overtures,* and *Sweeney Todd*—all in collaboration with the composer Stephen Sondheim and the producer-director Harold Prince. Hugh Wheeler's screenplay credits include several adaptations of his mystery novels, *Something for Everyone* (directed by Harold Prince), and two co-scripts with Jay Presson Allen (*Travels with My Aunt* and *Cabaret*).

actors, whereas George was wonderful with them. He was a cunning psychologist.

What happened between the cup and the lip is that Kate went into *The Madwoman of Challiot* [1969], and it was a kind of disaster for her. By the time I came out with my script, she didn't want to do *Travels* anymore. She didn't want to play another crazy old lady, not an unreasonable position. However, she would never admit it. She was loyal to George and reluctant to let him down.

George wanted desperately to work, and as she began to withdraw or find problems, he became frantic—like a boiling pot. He couldn't afford to deal with Kate, the real problem, because he would lose the project. He was genuinely devoted to Kate. They were bosom buddies; they laughed a lot and comforted one another. As we began to flounder, I think he panicked.

I rewrote and rewrote, trying to satisfy Kate, but I knew it was not going to work out. What she really wanted was to get the hell out of the project, and she was unable to face that. At some point, she had worked on parts of the script herself. I had once, a couple of years before all this, read a screenplay that she had written. It was pretty good. Now, I read what she was trying to do with *Travels*. It was talented and interesting, and I felt I had run my course; so I spoke to George, then to her: "Kate, you ought to write it yourself." So she did, and I went merrily on my way, happy to escape.

Kate wrote and wrote. My guess is that she was happy enough writing it, but she *still* didn't want to play it. Everybody was made very nervous. Jim Aubrey, who was running MGM at the time, had a very rough reputation, and he got a bellyful of all the toing and froing. So Aubrey called Kate up and said, in effect, "Miss Hepburn, report to work on script number fourteen on Monday morning." And she said exactly what he knew she would say, "Get yourself another girl." Of course, Bobby [Fryer, the producer] had Maggie Smith, who had done *Brodie,* standing by, and they were very compatible. So MGM gave George about thirty-seven dollars and sent him to Spain to make the movie.

Did any of it turn out to be your script?

The script they went with had one big speech of mine. Otherwise, it was all Kate's. It had nothing of Hugh's. One big speech of mine. I got a call from Bobby in the middle of the night from Spain, and he said, "We've run out of money, and we're only on page—something—what the hell do I do?" I said, "Just say, 'Cut.' " (*Laughs.*)

But when I saw the movie, I thought it was pretty darned good. George's work, considering the circumstances, was pretty darned good. It's a nice picture.

When credit time came up, I got a call from the Guild, asking me what I wished to claim. I said, "Oh, I didn't write anything in that movie. I don't want any credit. That is Miss Hepburn's script." The Guild's attitude was, in effect: So what? She's not a member of the Guild, no credit. Hugh was furious that I

Jay Presson Allen and director Sidney Lumet, her frequent collaborator in the 1970s.

wanted to take my credit off. Hugh was furious anyway. He wanted that credit. Bobby said he'd paid me a lot of money, and he wanted my credit on the picture. Everybody seemed mad at *me,* so I just shrugged and left my credit on. But I've never made any bones about writing that movie.

Kate got screwed on the credit. And did you see what she wrote in her book [*Me: Stories of My Life,* by Katharine Hepburn (New York: Knopf, 1991)]?* She got to the part about *Travels with My Aunt* and wrote, "It was not a very good script . . ." But she didn't ascribe the writing to herself! (*Laughs.*) So I have taken the rap for it. That's all right. I *did* get paid a lot of money.

When and where did you meet Sidney Lumet?

New York is a small community, theatrically. I had met Sidney, on and off over the years, and we had once flirted briefly with doing a version of *Pal Joey*—not a musical version—with Al Pacino. I knew him to that extent.

All these years later, I had terrible trouble getting together a production of *Just Tell Me What You Want.* The studio had snapped up the book [*Just Tell Me What You Want,* by Jay Presson Allen (New York: Dutton, 1975)], but it hadn't got done

---

* Hepburn writes, "George Cukor wanted to quit as director because he felt that it was our property. I persuaded him that that would be senseless—that he should stay on as director. We might need the money. They had fired me because they felt I was holding up the project. That was true—I was holding it up because I thought the script could be improved. Actually, I was right—and the movie was not a success."

for a number of reasons. Finally, although I didn't think that Sidney was the ideal director for *Just Tell Me What You Want,* we took it to him. We didn't hear for months and months, a very long time; then one night, I got a telephone call from him. He had just read it and wanted to do it. That is how our partnership began.

How do Cukor and Hitchcock compare as directors in their approaches with someone more contemporary, like Sidney Lumet?

Sidney is a wonderful structuralist, great with structure. Sidney has his most difficult time with humorous dialogue. It's not that he doesn't get it—he does; he has got a lovely sense of humor. But he hasn't found a way to shoot humorous dialogue as brilliantly as he shoots everything else. Like dramatic scenes—Sidney goes after drama and gets it by the throat.

That must not always be to your advantage, since one of your strengths is smart-ass comedy.

It is possible that someone else would have served that script better, but I think he served it wonderfully. We lost some humor in *Just Tell Me What You Want* and also in *Deathtrap. Just Tell Me What You Want* was partly a terrible circumstance—we lost the voice-over of Myrna Loy. Her voice turned out to be weak, shaky. Instead of letting me restructure the piece—Sidney is always in such a hurry—he gave the voice-over to the girl, and it was wrong.

Ali MacGraw and Alan King in *Just Tell Me What You Want.*

We lost the very first scene, a *key* scene, at the beginning of *Deathtrap,* because an actress didn't pan out, and Sidney wouldn't shoot it over with somebody else. He just cut it. Sidney's abiding sin is speed, which I empathize with. We're speeders, both of us. We like to go fast. The speed is thrilling. It's wonderful to work with someone that sure. I adored working with Sidney, and one of the things I loved was his speed. But you pay a little price for it.

Do you have other things in common—do you start to think alike—when you are working together?

With casting, for example, we are always so close together, just on the nose. I went into my first meeting with Sidney for *Just Tell Me What You Want* with a secret agenda, which was Alan King to play Max—but extremely diffident about the suggestion. We talked for a couple of hours, at which point Sidney said, "I've got an off-the-wall suggestion for Max." I said, "Who is that?" He said, "Alan King?" We just fell on each other.

We cast *Prince of the City,* all the many parts—a very large cast—hardly discussing the casting. One of us would say a name, and the other would say yes. It was like that throughout our work—all three movies.

Do you have a favorite film, among those you did with Sidney?

Of all my work, *Prince of the City* is my absolute all-time favorite. I like *scenes* from everything else. That's the only one that I like in totality.

How did that project get started—with you as producer?

The book [*Prince of the City,* by Robert Daley (New York: Dutton, 1975)] was reviewed very late in the game. I read the review, and went and bought the book. I thought, "Oh yeah. This *is* Lumet!" Instantly, I called the publisher to see who the agent was, but the book had already been sold. It had been sold to Orion for David Rabe as screenwriter and Brian De Palma as director. I didn't think that two men who leave their prints so richly on material would be able to do this book, because there wasn't any room for the screenwriter and not all that much room for the director. The material just *dictated* what was to be there.

I didn't think they would ever come out with the film, so I called John Calley at Warner Brothers—at that time Warner Brothers umbrellaed Orion—and said, "If this falls through, I would like to get this for Sidney, and I want to produce it, *not* write it." He said, "If it falls through, it's yours." At that point, I showed the book to Sidney, and he just flipped. We had to wait to see what would happen. Well, we waited and waited and waited, and it seemed as if nothing would come of it. And Sidney was within twenty-four hours of signing up for another movie when we got the call.

But I didn't want to write that movie. I was tired. I just wanted to produce it. I thought it seemed like a hair-raising job to find a line, get a skeleton out of the book, which went back and forth . . . all over the place. I thought it was too big a job. I told Sidney there were other writers we could get. But Sidney said he wouldn't do it if I didn't write it. He said, "Would you write it if I do an outline first?" I said, "Do the outline, and we'll see." So we sat down together and went over the book and the scenes, and agreed on the scenes and characters that we felt we absolutely had to have, as well as a general thrust for the movie.

We were sharing an office, and he would come in every day with a legal pad, and sit at his desk: scribble, scribble, scribble, Mr. Gibbons. I was horrified because I knew he had to be writing scenes. I thought, "Well, this is the end of a beautiful friendship, because he's going to turn this stuff in, I'm going to read it, and I'm going to be forced to reject it." Anyway, two or three weeks pass, and he hands the pages to me. If memory serves, something in the neighborhood of one-hundred handwritten pages. My heart really, really sank. I went home and read the pages, and he *had* written scenes, and most of them were *not* right. But the outline was just wonderful. I went back to him and said exactly that. Then I took what he had done, and went to work.

It was the first time I had ever written anything about living people—so I interviewed almost everybody in the book. And I had right next to me—the minute I was stuck on anything—all those phone numbers to dial. I could dial the *real* characters and say, "This doesn't sound right to me . . ." Mr. Daley,

"My absolute all-time favorite": Treat Williams in *Prince of the City.*

a good Catholic boy, was more a believer than I was. Eventually, I sat down with my interviews, what Sidney had done, the book and the telephone numbers, and turned out a three-hundred-and-some-page script in ten days.

The studio was so generous. A three-hour movie is very, very hard to sell. But we didn't know any other way to do the movie. We said, going in, "We're going to have a three-hour movie. Do you want to do it—if we can make it for ten million dollars?" They let us do it.

Afterwards, you continued to function as your own producer. Why?

It seemed easier than the alternative, dealing with someone new to the projects, somebody else to argue with. Producing is not a job I normally seek. With Sidney, it was easy. Sidney and John Calley made it easy.

You and Sidney seem to have been very fortunate, in general, at Warner Brothers.

Sidney and I never had any trouble. We were always under Calley's wing. John was the head of production at Warner Brothers. He is bloody smart and so funny. And a facilitator. Unlike most studio executives, he *personally* knows how to produce. He makes your job easy. He's still a very good friend.

It was Calley who gave you and Sidney the green light to do so many films?

Yes, he did, and he would have given me a green light to do more—I think I disappointed him. I have just never been very ambitious.

Why did the partnership between you and Sidney end?

Everything ends. Sidney wanted very much to work with David Mamet, which was right for him, exactly what he should have done. John quit, not long after that. He stopped having fun. And by that time I was exhausted.

How detailed are your scripts?

Very. Maybe overdetailed. I overwrite, so most of my scripts need a lot of cutting. I've been lucky in that I've been in on the cutting of almost all of them. Which I like to do—I've had directors order me to stop cutting.

Do you write much description?

I loathe writing description, but I do a lot of it.

Camera direction?

Oh, good heavens, no. No director wants to be told where to put the camera, unless it's specific to a line of dialogue. I don't dictate to a director. I work *for* a director. If you don't work very closely with a director, you're not going to see anything you want up on the screen. There's no way. So you had better invite the gentleman to piss a little on the script. Put his mark on it. Make it *his*.

To what percentage?

To the percentage that is necessary.

What percentage is unacceptable?

I don't have that option, do I?

You have the option of quitting or taking your name off the script.

They don't care if you quit! (*Laughs.*) I've worked with a couple of directors I wouldn't work with again for absolutely personal reasons. One of them had no humor, and that's death for me. Another one was a kind of depressive, and working to get him up to a state where he could contribute took all of my energy. I was in those situations before I could get out. Once in, I saw them through. But those two people I would never want to work with again. Otherwise, I've had very good experiences with directors.

Do you put in any blocking suggestions?

Not much, unless it's necessary physical business.

Do you contribute either in the script or discussions to visual ideas in the film?

Sometimes. I think something turned out wonderfully in *Cabaret* that was mine, which was when the camera pulls back, from a young boy singing solo to show the chorus of Nazi voices rising around him. That was mine. I suggest something every now and then. It's not something that I normally want to do, because that really is the director's job, and I don't have a great talent for that. If I wanted to do that, I'd try to be a director.

What are the hardest elements of the story for you?

For me? Plot.

The easiest?

Dialogue. Because I'm naturally articulate. Also, I think because of that little bit of theater training I had, all those years of wanting to be an actress, when I was a child and when I was in plays. I did virtually nothing else from the time I was about fourteen.

Do you feel you have a particular strength with female characters?

Yes, but I also think I have a particular strength with male characters. I've written a lot of good male characters. Male characters are easier to write. They're simpler. I think women are generally more psychologically complicated. You have to put a little more effort into writing a woman.

Therefore, women are twice as hard for men to write?

I'll say. Men keep writing themselves. Or else they write fantasies of women.

Do you feel that in your career you have tended at all to specialize in writing female characters, either by chance or otherwise?

I am attracted to a piece if it's exciting, theatrically exciting. Or if it has a marvelous character. I specialize in writing characters that interest me. I don't care whether the character is a man or a woman. I couldn't care less.

Yet quite often they turn out to be women . . .

They send me that stuff. I seldom go after anything. I never go after assignments. I almost never initiate anything. That's not quite true—I did initiate *Prime of Miss Jean Brodie, Just Tell Me What You Want,* and *Prince of the City.* But that's about it.

It occurs to me that you are also attracted frequently to stories involving parent-child relationships, or children—child characters.

I love writing children.

Why?

Because they're fun. It's almost impossible to write a dull kid.

Does your interest in writing children have anything to do with being a woman or a mother?

You bet.

The Borrowers *is one I wish they'd put out on video—for my children to see.*

I myself never saw it. I had totally forgotten *The Borrowers* until you mentioned it just now. I was out of that project at an early stage. I would love to see it.[*]

Writing children?—that's an only-child syndrome. I'm an only child, I have an only child. Only children think a lot about their childhood, and it maintains interest. In any case, I find itty-bitty babies the most riveting things on earth. They are little learning machines, and there's a kind of violence in their madness to take everything in. Children are fascinating. It's exciting to be around them. Exhausting but exciting.

Tell me a little bit about your writing regimen.

I don't do anything but write.

All day?

I get up and I write and I write, until I have to go to sleep; then, I get up, eat something, then go back to work. I do a script very fast, because I don't stop. All day. All night, until I'm too sleepy.

As a result, you can do a script in ten days?

Sure I can. So could you—if you wrote eighteen hours a day. Of course, I do a lot of rewriting. A tremendous amount of rewriting.

Do you drink coffee, smoke cigarettes while you are writing?

No. I don't have any vices. (*Laughs.*) I take a little exercise now and then, a little run. I use an old Underwood 1949 typewriter, which takes a lot of pounding and gets a lot of aerobic stuff going for you.

Do you invite or suffer any distractions—phone calls from friends, dinner parties?

If I have any distractions, the game's up.

What's the hardest part for you?

Getting started. Making up my mind to do it. In effect, it's a sink full of dirty dishes. You know you're going to be sitting at a typewriter for eighteen hours a day for however as long as it takes. That's not an enthralling prospect.

What's the easiest part?

The easiest part is going into some kind of overture. When you come out, you don't know who wrote it. That's kind of wonderful. You start writing at eight

---

[*] Based on Mary Norton's children's classic *The Borrowers*, first published by Harcourt, Brace in 1953, this film is about a miniature family living underneath the floorboards of a Victorian house. Since this interview was conducted, *The Borrowers* has become available on videocassette.

o'clock in the morning. The first thing you know it's two, and you don't remember that time. That's when all the good stuff happens. If I have to labor and sweat, it's never any good.

Reluctantly, I went back and read *Just Tell Me What You Want* recently—I hadn't read it since I wrote the screenplay. It was much better than I had thought it was. It's really funny. The good parts of it I have no recollection at all of having written. The doppelgänger effect. Wherever it went inert, *that* part I remember.

Do you ever experience writer's block?

I got writer's block one time and never again. It's a funny story, do you want to hear it? After I got Bob Whitehead to buy *Brodie* and he sent me to Scotland, I came home and I never looked at the book or thought about it again, for almost a year. The option was almost up. I didn't do any work. I wasn't worried—I didn't even know I had writer's block. I just thought I wasn't *ready* to do it. As I am a great procrastinator, this didn't alarm me. Finally, with not much time left, I had to sit down and say to myself, "My God, I'm not going to write this thing." My shame was profound.

I had a friend—Bill Gibson's wife, Margaret Brenman Gibson, who is a therapeutic hypnotist, an analyst[*]—who once gave me some book to read on hypnosis. I decided I would be a marvelous subject—I'm so suggestible. So I went to my doctor in New York and told him I wanted to try hypnotism. My doctor said the best guy on the East Coast was here in New York, and was doing a paper on writer's block. His name was Lewis Wolberg.

So I made an appointment with Dr. Wolberg. Now, I'm always on time—I'm not early or late; it's an inner clock, I don't even have to check my watch—but I got to this appointment about forty minutes early. I had to question that. What I was doing was checking out the pictures on the wall, the magazines, the decor of his office, and finding everything lacking. It was such a comical psychological ploy—trying to put down the doctor before I saw him, while at the same time I really did think I wanted to be helped. So I went in.

Dr. Wolberg was a very unthreatening man. He was very, very smart and I liked him instantly. I told him, "Listen, I think I would be a good subject. I have this problem . . . I come to you with an open mind, but at the same time, this is what I did while I was in your waiting room . . ." He laughed. Then he gave me some tests and asked me what kind of problem, specifically, I was having and what I thought was causing it. I had a fairly good idea and told him. "Well," he said, "that is a highly sophisticated idea of what the problem might be, and you might be right . . ."

What was the specific problem?

---

[*] Margaret Brenman-Gibson is also the author of *Clifford Odets, American Playwright: The Years from 1906 to 1940* (New York: Atheneum, 1981).

I don't want to tell you. (*Laughs.*) He said, "Why don't we do several sessions? Meanwhile, I will teach you to hypnotize yourself, and you can do it at least twice a day at home. I think you're going to be a breeze." He also warned me, "Don't expect a deep trance, because it's not necessary. You'll hear traffic and noise, etcetera . . ."

He told me the name of the trance that he was going to put me into—which was hilarious. He was going to put me into what they called a hypnagogic reverie. So I submitted myself to a hypnagogic reverie. It was very relaxing. Though clearly I wasn't hypnotized, I kind of felt sorry for Dr. Wolberg because he seemed so sure of himself, and I liked him. But the trance obviously wasn't working. So when he told me to raise my hand, I raised my hand—like in the movies. Then he said he was going to count to twenty, and after that time, he wanted me to fantasize for about twenty minutes. I should have known what was happening, because what I had wasn't a fantasy; it was more like a dream.

I was in Mexico in a cathedral where the walls were all covered with beaten gold. Down at the altar, there was a bishop wearing a bishop's miter with a face very like Dr. Wolberg's. I went down to take the wine and the host—mind you, I am not only not a Catholic, I am a stone atheist. I knelt down, and when the bishop with Dr. Wolberg's face came to me with the wine, I spit it out and said, "Don't guess! Bless!" I got up and went to the wall and rolled down a big sheet of gold and hugged it to me. It was very lightweight. I carried the gold outside, sat on the steps in the sunshine, watched the peasants go by, and was very happy. I had to laugh at the dream. Any fool could figure it out. It was so obvious: Help me if you can, but I prefer to help myself.

Afterwards, I told Dr. Wolberg I hadn't been hypnotized. He said, "Oh, it was as good as . . . don't worry about it. Next time it'll work better . . . trust me." Then I walked home. His office was on the upper East Side, and I found myself standing on the corner on Eighty-sixth and Lexington, waiting for the light to change. I became aware of a woman standing next to me, staring very rudely at me. I whipped my head around in a confrontational manner, then suddenly realized I was singing, quite loudly, "I'll Get by, As Long As I Have You!" I went home and called my husband and said, "I think I was hypnotized."

In any event, I did begin to do the exercises at home while continuing to see Dr. Wolberg. He kept insisting I was dreaming about the book, but I never dreamed about the book. I didn't even open the book. I didn't do a speck of work, though I was having obvious success with the hypnosis. So much so that one day Dr. Wolberg said to me, "You're doing so well, is there anything else you'd like to work on?" I said, "Yes, I don't go out very much, I'm not very gregarious, and I think my husband suffers from this. I would like to go out more spontaneously than I do." He said, "Well, we can do that."

A couple of weeks later, my husband was getting ready to go out. By this time, I was getting quite good at hypnotizing myself, and I said, "Where are you going?" He said, "I promised two guys downtown I'd take a look at their film." Lewis had, by that time, produced *The Connection* [1961] and *The Balcony* [1963], and he attracted avant-garde and amateur filmmakers. I said, "Well, I'll go with you." He said, "You're not going to enjoy it." I said, "Sure, I will. I'll go." I got up and got dressed and said, "See, it's working!"

One of the two guys was a poet, the other a filmmaker; and they showed us this appalling film, very sixties stuff, about a naked, three hundred pound woman. I thought to myself, This is a good time for one of my exercises, and I put myself out. The first thing I remember hearing was the film winding down. I came out, smiling and cheerful. Then I realized they were loading up the machine again. I asked one of the guys if they were going to show another film. He said, "Yeah." I said, "Gee, I really hated that one. Is there any place I can go and read?" The guy was cool. "Sure," he said, "go into the library. There's plenty to read." So I went into the library, and there were about twenty-five hundred volumes of poetry. I have no poetry in my soul. But I cheerfully picked up a book and started to read.

After a while, I began to hear some quite alarming sounds from the other room—dozens of people talking and partying. They had really set Lewis up, sandbagged him, invited everybody they knew to come down and see the film. At that point, the star of the first movie came into the library. She was very rowdy. I thought, "Well, I'll journey on." I went up to Lewis and said, "Do you think I could go home?" He said, "Nobody's going to notice if you go . . ." As I sidled up to the door, a heavy hand hit me on the shoulder. This enormous, fat woman accosted me. She said, "What's the matter, aren't we good enough for you?" I said, "Actually, no . . ." I understood how horribly rude I had been, that I had disgraced my husband, and yet I was euphoric, very high.

The next day, I went to see Dr. Wolberg and told him what had happened. He said, "My God, what suggestion did you give yourself when you put yourself under?" I said, "I told myself that I would find some way to enjoy the evening." He said, "Jay, that doesn't even *begin* to be specific enough!" (*Laughs.*)

In any event, after my sessions with Dr. Wolberg concluded, a friend of mine loaned me his house up the Hudson, and Lewis drove me up. I always have to be by myself to write, and I didn't have a studio in New York at that time. I *knew* I couldn't write the play. There was no question of writing the play. Not only had I *not* dreamed about it, I hadn't even thought about it, marked the book, nothing. I thought, "Well, I will sit at the typewriter eight hours a day for the three weeks I have left, and I will be able to tell Bob that I tried."

I went into this house, and before I went to bed that night, I went through my hypnotic exercises again because, apart from everything else, I had been to the dentist recently, and on that level, the hypnosis was wonderful. The next morning I went through my little drill again, then sat down at the typewriter and wrote the only thing I knew to write—which was "Act 1, Scene 1." I came to eighteen hours later with the play over a third written. I finished writing it in three days. And what I wrote was 95 percent of what went on the stage. It was like pulling the plug out of a tub. I knew I would never, ever experience writer's block again.

I'm struck by how flexible you seem in your approach and the broad range of interests evidenced by the disparate subjects of your scripts.
I may not be the best writer in Hollywood, but I think I have the greatest stretch. I can write about more different things than anybody else I can think of.
You can say that definitively?
I say that without a pinch of modesty.
Does the price tag, or how much somebody invests in your work, affect your attitude towards the work?
Oh yes. Absolutely. You feel terribly guilty if you don't deliver. I took a job, a few years ago, the first time I ever took a job where I was worried about not liking the material enough. It was a very big book, and there was some wonderful stuff in it, certainly enough to make a movie. But there was a world of garbage in it too, and I knew the producers were going to want a lot of that left in. I really shouldn't have taken the job. Somebody told me they overheard one of the producers saying, "Be careful . . . I think she's taken an *assignment*." It was the first time I had ever heard that expression, and it absolutely shocked me. Because I can't imagine anything as dreadful as to have to work on something for which you have no sympathy, no feeling.
Now there may have been people who did movies and TV in the past who really did hack work and never tried to rise above it, but I've never known any of them. I always try to do my best. (*Laughs.*) And the more it pays, the harder I try. I like to earn my money. At the same time, I don't know anybody who doesn't write except the best they can, almost always—the best they know how to write—no matter what they are paid.
When I talked to you a couple of years ago, you shocked me by saying you thought you weren't going to write a movie from beginning to end ever again.
It really stopped being fun. Movies cost too much. When an executive green-lights a project, he may be risking his own job. So something has been thrown up to protect the executives from the talent. The talent is, almost by definition, *persuasive.* Consequently, dangerous. The barrier that has been thrown up is called Development. So today, most scripts are developed: which means "writing by committee." No fun. But there's an upside: "developed" scripts tend to need rewrites—from outside the "development circle." A production rewrite means that the project is in production. Big money elements—directors, actors—are pay or play. There is a *shooting* date. The shit is in the fan.
And that's where writers like me come in. Writers who are fast and reliable. We are nicely paid to do these production rewrites . . . and we *love* these jobs.
Without credit?

Never with credit. If you go for credit on somebody else's work, you have to completely dismantle the structure. Who wants a job where you have to completely dismantle the structure? I only take things that I think are in reasonable shape. The director and the producer and the studio may not necessarily agree with me, but *I* think the script is in reasonable shape. Besides, no one but the writer ever knows how much trouble any one piece of work will be. Only the *writer* knows that. *Only* the writer. So I take what looks to me like something that is in good enough shape, yet which I can contribute to and make it worth the pay they are going to give me.

Do you ever talk to the original scriptwriter?

No. Well, once. I was once asked to do something on a David Mamet script. Not an original. An adaptation. I thought his script was great. The woman character was weak but easily corrected. It was called *The Verdict.* I told the producers—David Brown and Dick Zanuck, who had produced *Brodie*—the script was wonderful. They said, "Yes, but we want certain things from the book he's written out, and he doesn't want to go on with it." So I called David Mamet and said, "Do you really not want to go on with it?" He agreed that was the case. I said, "Then I'm going to take the job." He said, "Be my guest."

I did a draft and did make the woman strong, and the producers were thrilled with it. I said, "Get Paul Newman for the lead and get Robert Redford to direct, and you'll have both of their names up there." Before anything could happen, Bob Redford came to look at our house in Connecticut at a time when we thought we were maybe moving. He saw a copy of the script in the house. He said, "I've heard about that script. Is it for me?" I said, "No, you're too young." He said, "What do you mean, I'm too young?" I said, "You're still radiant, Bob. This guy's really beat up." He asked, "Can I read it?" I said, "Sure, but I'll have to tell David and Dick that you've got it." He said, "No problem," and took it away. The next thing I hear, he's signed to act in it.

For one year, he jerked them around. Redford has a pattern of finding something that he thinks is well written and trying to make it fit for him. He did that with another script of mine, the only script I ever wrote from scratch that was never produced, a western. In any event, he drove Dick and David crazy. Finally, they did a very bold thing: they fired Redford. This was at the peak of his career. Then they hired [Paul] Newman, provided they could get a director.

David [Brown] called me and said, "Do you think Sidney would direct this movie?" I said, "I think he would love this movie." He said, "Will you ask him?" I said, "Sure." I went into his office—we were still partners—and said, "There is a script called *The Verdict* that I have been working on . . ." He said, "I know that script. That's David Mamet's script . . . I read that script once." I said, "Well, he did the first draft, and I have done the second draft, and David and Dick want to know if you will direct it." He said, "Yes! I want to direct David Mamet's script!" I said, "Dump my script?" He said, "Jay, do you want to do a rewrite on what you've already done, just to please me? Do you want to go through all that?" I said, "No." He said, "You've got all the money, haven't you? All you're going to get?" I said, "Yes." He said, "Then, what do you care if I do David Mamet's script?" I said, "I don't." (*Laughs.*)

You didn't?

I didn't. Mamet's script won an Academy Award. But the woman character went back to being weak! (*Laughs.*)

Aren't people amazed that someone like yourself, with all of your background and career, is willing to do this kind of discreet work?

There are more than one of us out there. These jobs are quick, sometimes they're even fun, and you don't have to take the terrible meetings. They're not breathing on you. They're just desperate to get a script. I've never taken anything that I knew I couldn't help. They pay good money. I need the money. We've built a house in Italy, and you can't imagine how soft the dollar was during construction.

You're willing to do production rewrites because the alternative is so harrowing—seeing a movie through from beginning to end?

Oh, I don't think I would ever want to do that again.

That's definite—you won't do another movie of your own?

Never say never, but that's generally more work than I want to do now. I'm tired of a certain kind of writing. I'm tired of the terrible responsibility of a script from scratch and of the terrible price it costs to make the movies today, so that nobody is having much fun. I used always to have myself joined at the hip of a director who could protect me. That's not going on as much now as it was. It's not as easy a job as it used to be, just on the level of the word *Development*. I just don't want to do it.

That's so mysterious to me.

Listen, it's more complicated now. Less amusing. I'm ancient, and there are other things I'd rather do.[*]

---

[*] At this writing, Jay Presson Allen's play *Breaking and Entering* is scheduled to creep into Broadway sometime during the 1996–1997 season.

George Axelrod: Irony!

Interview by Pat McGilligan

Good comedy, George Axelrod once said, is bitter; great comedy, angry. He should know. In the Hollywood of the fifties and sixties, it was mostly comedies that put him at the top of the screenwriting profession: *Phffft!, The Seven Year Itch, Bus Stop, Breakfast at Tiffany's, The Manchurian Candidate*—as ferocious in its political satire as in its paranoid-thriller plot—and the cult classic *Lord Love a Duck.* His name became synonymous with craft and sophistication. He became a hyphenate, a living legend, and an entry in most film encyclopedias. Then it was mostly downhill, and admittedly, Axelrod has been off the A list for twenty-five years.

His comedy could be exceedingly angry. His sex-obsessed farces aggressively attack the sacrosanct. Extramarital affairs are seen not as illicit so much as aphrodisiac prescriptions for stale marriages. Monogamy is dull. Sex is fun, not sinful. The Production Code Administration and the Catholic Legion of Decency—Axelrod's twin nemeses in his golden years—didn't think his humor was very funny, and relentlessly lobbied to water down his scripts. Hardly anybody thought *The Manchurian Candidate* was funny when it was first released; it was pilloried across the spectrum by groups ranging from the American Legion to the Communist Party. It took time for people to realize just how funny it was. But the anger came through.

Axelrod had not only a wildly prominent but also a prematurely aborted, misunderstood career. The playwright-gone-Hollywood never experienced one of his plays happily transferred to the screen: Working with Billy Wilder was a joy, but *The Seven Year Itch,* a hit on Broadway (and in summer stock forever after), was half a botch on film. The Frank Tashlin movie of *Will Success Spoil Rock Hunter?,* based on Axelrod's play of the same name, Axelrod has never seen; ditto Vincente Minnelli's version of *Goodbye Charlie.* The films in which Axelrod enjoyed the highest degree of success were not his trademark "boobs and boobs" comedies, and they tend to show the writer in a different, more complicated light.

Bus Stop, an adaptation of a William Inge play, provides the cinema's fondest window on Marilyn Monroe. Axelrod viewed Monroe, a close friend, tragically, and so does the movie. Among the actress's dramatic vehicles, only *The Misfits* approaches its insight and compassion. But *Bus Stop* also has Axelrod's wicked sense of humor.

Breakfast at Tiffany's, loosely drawn from Truman Capote's novella, was another triumph of adaptation, a heart-on-its-sleeve romantic comedy that revealed the rarely indulged flip side of Axelrod's cynicism. *Tiffany's* is usually given short shrift in discussions of the scriptwriter's career, as if it were somehow an impersonal project. Capote, too, was a close friend, and staying faithful inside of the restrictions of the day without bowdlerizing the source material was a challenge that whetted the writer's appetite. Axelrod's reteaming with Audrey Hepburn, *Paris When It Sizzles,* turned out to be "Paris When It Fizzles," but the sweetness, sentimentality, and high-toned comedy of *Tiffany's* stands the test of time.

The Manchurian Candidate—well, how many movies enjoy a revival and national re-release twenty-seven years after their first exhibition? How many movies of that era were so far ahead of their audience that their comedy and *politique* are still on the cutting edge today? Richard Condon's novel was a pet project, ingeniously adapted, then cast and coproduced by Axelrod and the director John Frankenheimer. Its polished blend of black comedy, high-octane thriller, and cautionary political parable remains unique.

It may be as novel to appreciate Axelrod as a first-rank adapter as it is to call him romantic and compassionate—but that is how it stacks up. *Lord Love a Duck,* his screen directorial debut and his Waterloo, is also an adaptation, Axelrod's co-script of the Al Hine novel is unromantic, dispassionate, yet distinctively Axelrod, and in many ways a category unto itself. Perhaps Axelrod, viciously satirizing almost everything he could think of—teenage-dom, mother-sonhood, pop religion, laid-back California culture—bit off more than he could chew. Perhaps the coarse, black-and-white, handheld camera rubbed salt in wounds. Perhaps, as with *Manchurian,* Axelrod was too far in front of the demographics. Perhaps the movie is not as slashingly brilliant as cultists think. ("His best script," declares David Thomson in *A Biographical Dictionary of Film.*) However, isn't it more the point that Axelrod really relished the risk taking and saw courting risk and rejection as part of the job?

Axelrod's life story, far from happy go lucky, tells us where the edge and risk taking came from. While he was growing up, there was misery. Then, grindingly hard work paid off, as he turned thirty, in over-the-top success. (After Axelrod's first play was written, in 1953 the *New York Times* reported that his taxes that year would rise close to $100,000, "almost single-handedly paying the President's salary.") Hollywood offers followed, and unlike some

George Axelrod in New York City, 1995. (Photo by William B. Winburn.)

writers—though he continued to live on the East Coast for a long time and later shifted to London—Axelrod embraced Hollywood, became well integrated in the community (a fabulous host and party giver), loved the lifestyle (and loved ridiculing it). And then came a series of professional heartbreaks and missteps, long spells of ill-advised work, and years of too much Russian vodka on crushed ice.

George Axelrod (1922–   )

1954   *Phffft!* (Mark Robson). Story, script.

1955   *The Seven Year Itch* (Billy Wilder). Co-script, based on Axelrod's play.

1956   *Bus Stop* (Joshua Logan). Script.

1957   *Will Success Spoil Rock Hunter?* (Frank Tashlin). Based on
        Axelrod's play.

1958   *Rally 'Round the Flag, Boys!* (Leo McCarey). Uncredited contribution.

1961   *Breakfast at Tiffany's* (Blake Edwards). Script.

1962   *The Manchurian Candidate* (John Frankenheimer). Coproducer,
        script.

1964   *Paris When It Sizzles* (Richard Quine). Coproducer, script.
        Goodbye Charlie (Vincente Minnelli). Based on Axelrod's play.

1965   *How to Murder Your Wife* (Richard Quine). Producer, story, script.

1966   *Lord Love a Duck* (George Axelrod). Producer, director, co-script.

1968   *The Secret Life of an American Wife* (George Axelrod). Producer,
        director, story, script.

1979   *The Lady Vanishes* (Anthony Page). Script.

1985   *The Holcroft Covenant* (John Frankenheimer). Co-script.
        The Fourth Protocol (John Mackenzie). Adaptation.

Television credits include numerous script contributions to episodes of *The Colgate Comedy Hour, The Boris Karloff Mystery Playhouse, The Peter Lind Hayes Show,* and others.

Plays include contributions to *Small Wonder, The Seven Year Itch, Will Success Spoil Rock Hunter?* and *Goodbye Charlie.*

Novels include *Beggar's Choice, Blackmailer,* and *Where Am I Now—When I Need Me?*

Academy Award honors include an Oscar nomination for Best Screenplay Based on Material from Another Medium for *Breakfast at Tiffany's.*

Writers Guild honors include nominations for Best Script for *Phffft!, The Seven Year Itch,* and *Bus Stop.* Axelrod won Best Written American Comedy for *Breakfast at Tiffany's.*

Tell me a little bit about your background . . .
    Let me say a couple of things first—worries that I have about your books. Sometimes what I don't like about the interviews is they are so self-serving. I cannot stand self-serving in anybody—particularly writers. *Screen*writers.

I guess I'm proud they are self-serving. In your world, the world of screen-writing, they must look extremely self-serving. But in the larger scheme of things, in and out of Hollywood, I hope they redress some balance.

Redress the great wrongs? (*Chuckles.*) An example of which: Just last week, during the Academy Awards, they saluted the people behind the camera in a montage at the beginning of the show. They showed only one writer, and that was Robert Redford, typing at the typewriter in a scene from *The Way We Were* [1973]. That was the only writer!

In the larger scheme of things, there aren't too many books like the Back-story *series. I know they are self-serving for screenwriters, and I'm proud of that. I like the sameness of the stories: people saying, "I really thought of that . . . the director is the one who screwed it up . . . and it would have been great if only they had done it my way."*

That sounds so childish.

On the one hand. On the other hand, these are time-honored complaints from writers about Hollywood . . . not just clichés.

It's the nature of the job. In the theater, the writer is God. You can't change a line without the author's permission. But that's because in the theater, you're given one set, five characters, and two hours; and you've got to hold the stage with just talk. Here, talk is considered kind of more wordage.

Another problem I have with your books is that everybody out here [in Hollywood] is so literal. When people say something ironical in one of your books and it comes out in cold print, you can't convey any irony. I'm always misquoted in books, and the irony doesn't show up.

Irony is a dirty word out here. Just the other day, a kid agent, one of these intense lunatics from CAA [Creative Artists Agency] who regards agenting as a religious calling—they go on retreats and everything nowadays—asked me why I was doing something [in one of my scripts]. I said it was ironical. He tried to bring me up to date and launch me into the new world. He said, "We don't do irony anymore. It's elitist."

He said that with a straight face? That's depressing.

Terrifying. So, irony is difficult to do out here, and it's difficult to do in one of these interviews.

For example, I might say to somebody, and there's a germ of truth in this, "I'm no longer interested in seeing movies about anybody less socially well placed than myself. I don't want to see poor people or sick people. I want to see rich, beautiful people saying witty things and screwing." When you print that out flat, it looks godawful. But it's kind of funny when you say it. I don't actually mean it—I'm just trying to convey the idea that I prefer old-fashioned high comedy.

Which almost doesn't exist anymore. Except maybe from [the writer-director] Blake Edwards.

God, no. Comedies of manners don't exist because there are no more manners, and drawing-room comedies don't exist because there are no more drawing rooms. And Blake Edwards, God love him, doesn't have a clue about high anything. What he does, and does brilliantly, is slapstick.

Just to balance the scales, what I love about the books you are doing are the specifics. I am interested in the process of screenwriting. Is that what people who buy these books are interested in? Or do they just want to hear gossip—you know, what was Marilyn Monroe *really* like?

Let's try again. Back up. Start with a little biography.
Very briefly, I was born in 1922. I was born in New York City in a hotel, the Cambridge Hotel. My mother was a movie starlet, although they didn't really call them starlets then. Her name was Betty Carpenter. She appeared in a series of films called the Sunshine Comedies, a rival group to Mack Sennett's bathing beauties. She was in one picture with Slim Summerville, the comedian, a short called *A High-Diver's Last Kiss* [1918], in which she was a high diver on a diving board, and he comes along in an autogiro, as they were called then—a helicopter—and her bathing suit gets all tangled up in the blades.
So you yourself are a child of slapstick . . .
Kind of. My mother had pretensions as well. She made a couple of serious pictures with Dick Barthelmess and Buster Collier. Then she married my father, Herman Axelrod. He was Russian Jewish; my mother was Scottish English—kind of a heady mixture. My father had gone to Columbia University with Oscar Hammerstein. They had written varsity shows and other material together. He and Larry Hart, who was their age—Dick Rodgers was the young kid of the group—were all in the same circle. Like them, my father was going to make his career in the theater.

His father, my grandfather, was a domineering, tyrannical, very interesting man—a self-made millionaire who arrived in this country with only a pair of glasses, and made millions building buildings and buying real estate. When my father wanted to marry this blond, Hollywood shiksa, my grandfather said, "Okay, but I'll make a deal with you. You've got to join the business and not screw around in the theater." So my father copped out and made a deal which ruined his life. He and my mother had to make enormous sacrifices to this little tin god, my grandfather. Shortly thereafter, my mother and he were divorced. Oh, there were disastrous goings-on.

I had no respect for my father whatsoever because of that decision. So what I did in my career was partly related to the tense feelings I had about him.
Reaction against him?
Showing him, shoving it at him. Interestingly enough, I suppose, although I don't hold with Freudian stuff—it's too simpleminded—when he died, finally, in 1967, I sort of lost interest in my career. I lost the drive. I had nobody to show anymore. I haven't really done a lot since then, only odds and ends.

In your mind, you really make that connection?

Either that, or it's a remarkable coincidence.

Were you raised by your mother?

Sort of. I lived with her. She was pretty haphazard.

You didn't see your father very much.

No, not often.

Did you reconcile with him before he died?

Unfortunately not. I'm sorry about that. When I'm uncomfortable sometimes in a situation and I hear myself saying truly stupid things, I recognize my father's voice. So I know that he must have been uncomfortable most of his life, in any special or interpersonal relationship. He couldn't deal with people, yet he had a great surface charm. He was a very complicated man.

He must have had a wellspring of creativity that was all bottled up.

He was a big man at Columbia. He was the editor of the humor magazine *The Jester.* He wrote and starred in two of the college varsity shows, and earned a letter as a high jumper in track, which was a feat for this Jewish boy, in those times when there was quite a bit of anti-Semitism. Later on, he was a lieutenant officer in the First World War. He started off in life like a fire-cracker, then just fizzled.

Did he become a dull, gray businessman?

And a bitter one.

So you never witnessed any demonstration of his youthful, show-business flair?

He was a hanger-on to Oscar Hammerstein's behind for years. As a friend, kind of.

As an investor in shows, too?

As a friend. He was too chicken to invest. He was too chicken to do anything. I've actually made money investing, which is a rare boast. Mr. [George] Abbott once asked me if I would write the book for the musical $7\frac{1}{2}c$ [based on Richard Bissell's comic novel]. I read it and went to a meeting with Mr. Abbott. I said I didn't know how to write a musical about a strike in a pajama factory. But I felt guilty about it, so I put some money into the production. I still get money from *Pajama Game*. Oh!

Leland Hayward, who I worked with and who produced a play of mine called *Goodbye Charlie,* told me once that a little piece of *Sound of Music* was dropping out. He said, "You could have that if you want." I said, "I'll take it, provided I never, ever, have to see it in any form." I put some money in, and I never have seen it. And I am still getting money.

The idea of The Sound of Music *is too schmaltzy for you?*

Oh! Also, I have a lifelong hatred of Oscar Hammerstein, which is all mixed up with the feelings for my father.

His reputation is a saintly one.

I know! Beware of saints. Beware of the arrogance of the do-gooder. Saintly?!! Oscar Hammerstein was a miserable son of a bitch, at least I thought so. He was terrible to my father, and he was kind of snotty to me too. What a sanctimonious guy!

Later on in life, when I was going to do *The Seven Year Itch* in London, I had Howard Rhineheimer as my lawyer because I did not know any better. He was Oscar Hammerstein's lawyer as well. He convinced me, because Rodgers and Hammerstein had blocked money in England, to let them coproduce *Itch* there with Binky Beaumont and H. M. Tennant. I said, "Why not?" I didn't know what I was doing. I didn't realize there is too little money to be made producing shows in England to split it with anyone. The production was kind of botched, anyway. It ran a year in London, but it was not the hit it should have been. Oscar told me, "Don't worry, kid. You'll write another play someday." He was so patronizing about it. I had a smash goddamn hit, which ran 1,141 performances on Broadway. Talk about self-serving! And I had to take crap from Oscar Hammerstein—urban, Jewish guy writing rural stuff. "The corn is as high as an elephant's eye! . . ." For Chrissake.

Did your mother pass on a love of show business?

She gave show business up altogether and didn't do anything with her life for a while. She had a series of gentlemen friends who contributed to her general well-being. Later on, she got into the wallpaper business and proved herself a driving and ambitious lady. I made peace with her toward the end, but I got out of the house as fast as I could.

After high school?

Actually, I'm prematurely Holden Caulfield. I got kicked out of Hill, Lawrenceville, Collegiate . . . I never finished high school.

And you never went to college?

Nah.

What did you end up doing?

In the summer of 1940, after I got kicked out of Collegiate, through a kind of nepotism I was introduced to [the director-producer] Dick Aldrich, who ran the Cape Playhouse at Dennis, Massachusetts—a good summer theater, one of the best. I got hired on as an apprentice. Mel Ferrer was the stage manager that season. But, by the end of the season, I had become the stage manager because Mel was playing in a production of *Kind Lady* with Grace George, which Bill Brady, the producer, then decided to bring into New York as a revival. So, at the age of eighteen, I became an assistant stage manager on Broadway.

Then I did some summer stock and went into the Walgreen's kid-actor business for a while. What I really wanted to be was a writer. I knew that. But I also realized that nobody wanted to read anything an eighteen-year-old boy wrote, so acting would be my way into show business.

What made you decide to be a writer?

I have no idea. It never occurred to me to do anything else. I guess I realized I could make a living as a writer during the period when I was miserable at the Hill, a boarding school in Pennsylvania. One afternoon in the winter, when I was supposed to be in the gym, I was goofing off in the library and pulled down a book I had also seen on my father's bookshelf—[Ernest Hemingway's novel] *The Sun Also Rises.* I read it in two afternoons, two sittings, and it changed my life. I said to myself, "My God, writing is about conversation. Is this how you do it? I could do this . . ." It was a revelation.

Very shortly thereafter, I encountered the short stories of William Saroyan—the early, wonderful ones where he's in a hotel in New York, with his hair freezing because there's no heat, with all the romance of being a young writer in New York. I thought, "Christ, that's for me . . ."

When I was eighteen, I wrote a play that actually Dick Aldrich considered for a while. It wasn't any good, but it had something . . . and I spent some time trying to write short stories for preposterous magazines. Then I sold a half-hour radio play when I was twenty, the first big thing I sold and the first thing I wrote for radio.

I knew a guy in an ad agency who produced radio shows, and he let me go to a rehearsal. I had never seen a radio script before I got a copy of one. The phrase "music up and down" is how they used to do the bridges. That was the "fade in and fade out." I read that and thought, "Oh, that's how they do that!" I went home and wrote a radio script, and I sold it.

Were you being supported at all by your parents at this point? Were you well heeled?

No. My father and grandfather survived the Crash very well, but what put them out of business was rent control. They owned these apartment buildings where the rent had to be frozen. My grandfather had elevator boys and doormen and all the facade—he was not going to give up the service and the elegance, right to the end, though he kept losing building after building after building. He was down to his last one—he lived to be ninety-one—and at ninety-one, he jumped off the roof of his last building.

Oh, really?

If I ever digressed like this in a movie script, I would have lost the audience already.

So you sold your first radio script when you were twenty . . .

I sold maybe a half dozen of them. I wrote a couple of *The Shadows*—they paid me $250 each. The ones I couldn't sell here I sold to *Canadian Theater of the Air,* where they would pay $100.

Then, of course, the war came along and three years in the army. I wrote a novel while I was in the army, which Simon and Schuster was going to publish if I would revise it. I typed a lot of the first draft at Camp Crowder [in Missouri], where they had a typewriter in the recreation hall, which you could use if you put a quarter in. But I was in a foxhole in Normandy, and there was no way I was going to be able to finish rewriting it. I kept getting letters from Simon and Schuster and notes from the editor while I was stuck in this foxhole. My rewrites were in V-letter.[*]

It was a mystery-spy story actually, and part of the premise was cracking the code. Hilarious! I said to myself, "I can't just say, 'He sat and sweated all night and cracked the code.' I have to show people how he cracked it." So first I had to figure out a code. I sent some revisions off to Simon and Schuster, and along came two guys in a jeep to where the foxhole was and brought me back to a place called Ramrod Advance. Because they were censoring the mail, and had figured out I was developing a code. Try to explain you're writing a mystery novel for Simon and Schuster! I feared I would be shot out of hand.

Was it a comic mystery novel?

No. It was deadly serious. I wasn't sure about the comedy yet. Comedy kept creeping in. The only good stuff in it was the funny stuff. But I was just feeling my way.

One of the reasons I knew I could make people laugh—in person—was because that's how I survived the war. I was in with a bunch of hillbillies in the Signal Corps—with those Bell Telephone Company guys who were officers. Oh, boy! During the Battle of the Bulge, when I found myself out in the snow with those guys, I figured, "Jesus, I'm not going to make it through this one . . ."

I had this one horrible sergeant—Sergeant Gilstrap was his name—I'll never forget Sergeant Gilstrap. His brother was a sheriff down south in Georgia who was famous for beating a black guy to death with a lead pipe, and everybody in my unit thought that was pretty neat. I used to say, "Sergeant Gilstrap, you need me out here because I'm the only guy who can walk through this snow and not leave tracks . . ." "You what?" "My ass is dragging so low it wipes them out." Ho, ho, ho! Sergeant Gilstrap'd slap his thick knees and repeat my jokes to everyone. I realized I could make him laugh—rather primitively, albeit. Those kinds of jokes stood me in good stead later on when I wrote for the *Grand Ole Opry.*

No kidding?

For two years. That was my Guggenheim Fellowship. At a certain point in my career, indeed toward the very end of my radio and television writing career—I'm jumping ahead of myself—I had to write forty cow jokes a week for Rod Brasfield and Minnie Pearl.[†]

This was when you were back living in New York?

---

[*] Shorthand for Armed Services mail—or Victory-letter.

[†] Rod Brasfield was a hillbilly comic who starred for many years on the radio station WSM's famed *Grand Ole Opry* broadcast from Nashville. Minnie Pearl was another *Grand Ole Opry* regular.

In New York, sending them down to Nashville. Rod was wonderful to write for. It wasn't really writing; it was anthologizing, because Rod really wouldn't do jokes that he didn't know and love, so you had to keep finding new ways of doing the old jokes. I know more cow jokes than any living human being. "Why did the cow jump over the moon? The farmer had such cold hands" kind of jokes. "What is a cow's favorite song? 'The Yanks Are Coming.'" I would try to slip some of my own in occasionally. I could write pretty good ones, but he wouldn't do them if they were too uptown. I remember one wonderful, uptown cow joke. "Did you hear about the cow that swallowed a bottle of blue ink and mooed indigo?" Rod would say, "That's too uptown . . ."

In a way, that's the story of your life.

Yeah, I'm too uptown. Irony! Anyway, to get back chronologically, then came the turning point.

When I finished the manuscript of the mystery novel I had written at Camp Crowder, I sent it to Frannie Pindyke, whom I had heard of—she was running Leland Hayward's literary department. Frannie loved it, so I became a client of Leland Hayward's office. Then Leland sold out to MCA [Music Corporation of America], so I became an MCA client. This was approximately 1947. MCA absorbed Leland's literary clients; they had two departments at MCA in those days—talent and writers.

Then, this is what happened: CBS was attempting to build some in-house comedies because they were always being forced to buy packages and getting screwed on the deals, and also because they felt tyrannized by Arthur Godfrey. So they had a double mission: create in-house comedy packages while building a new star that would threaten the tyrannical powers of Arthur Godfrey, who was bleeding them of money and had become a total monster running rampant. They wanted to create a countermonster, a house personality.

In a flight of sanity, they hired a guy named Goodman Ace, from *Easy Aces,* an old strip radio show,* who was a comic genius—a true, natural comic genius—as the head of a development program of young writers. By "young," they meant "inexpensive." They had a name for the new star; they wanted to call him Robert Q. Lewis; and they had several candidates for the guy that they were going to build into the countermonster. Written by a bunch of kids that Goody Ace would teach how to write comedy. The whole thing was going to cost nothing, and it was going to be a triumph.

Well, about one hundred kids came in—college kids, all types of young kids. Word had gotten out that there was going to be an opening. Goody Ace was going to pick ten guys—five guys to work on a strip, an across-the-board show for this Robert Q. Lewis that we were going to discover; and five guys to work on big Saturday night specials. MCA sent me in. Goody gave us assign-

---

* A serial program with continuing characters.

ments: "Write a telephone conversation. Robert Q. Lewis gets a telephone call from a fan. One page, no more."

What kind of personality was Robert Q. Lewis supposed to have?

We didn't know yet. That was part of what we were going to create. So, maybe one hundred guys wrote a one-page sketch, and out of these submissions, Goody picked Doc and Danny Simon as a team; Paddy Chayefsky, who had not written anything at that point; Ernest Lehman; a guy named Bobby Cohen, who was killed in an accident—he was maybe the most talented of all—and four or five other people. Goody hit paydirt with five, six counting me, which suggests he was a rather perceptive personality.

Goody was a primitive, in a way. He had been a general critic on a Kansas City newspaper, and used to review the vaudeville acts that came through town. He began selling jokes to some of the vaudeville acts, and among other people, he sold a joke to Jack Benny, when Benny was in vaudeville. I remember the joke, because he told it to me proudly. In those days, vaudeville had to have acrobats to open. Usually Oriental acts. Jack Benny had a Filipino tumbling act. Goody's joke was: "I thought we had to have Japs or better to open." Benny bought this joke, and that started Goody on his career.

Goody started writing for early radio. Then he brought his wife in, Jane Ace, who was a kind of thinking-man's Gracie Allen. Jane did exquisite malaprops. Goody and Jane developed a strip show, fifteen minutes daily, five times a week. They moved to Chicago, then to New York. *Easy Aces* was the show. It was hilarious. I grew up on it. I was a big fan. During the war, for example, Jane would get a job in a war plant, but somehow or other, her knitting instructions would get mixed up with bombing plans, so she'd be knitting this thing that grew bigger and bigger, which developed wings on it. Meanwhile, the war plant was turning out thousands of tiny aluminum sweaters. Wild ideas!

I was hired with Doc and Danny to work on the Saturday night special. R. Q. Lewis was selected. It came down to two disc jockeys, including one named Bob Goldberg, who became R. Q. Lewis. We labored for eight months, ten months a year, on those Robert Q. Lewis special shows and for two or three years on the strip, and Robert Q. Lewis never did become a household name, I tell you. We did not succeed!

So they abandoned Robert Q. Lewis, and Goody went on to do a half-hour version of the *Easy Aces* called *Mr. Ace and Jane of the "Easy Aces."* I worked on that one.

What were you learning, working with Goody?

How to write comedy. Comedy is so delicate. The words have got to be in the right order, or it's not funny. I learned a lot from Goody. At the same time, I taught him a lot, because he had never heard of irony, which I seemed to know about, or satire. He started to do parodies of stuff, which—parody—he had never heard of before. Talk about self-serving!

Are there a million practical suggestions for writing comedy?

Absolutely none. But you can learn by doing. Funny is really built in the way you think. A really pompous thing to say is "I think funny." But most things *do* strike me as funny.

How did you go from writing jokes and being funny in person to learning structure and storytelling for an entire script?

By degrees, I guess. Trial and error. But I was born with a pretty good sense of structure.

You never took classes or workshops?

God, no. I never spoke to other writers except when I was working.

Were you sometimes writing with other people?

I was never a very good collaborator. Sometimes we used to do round-table stuff on the big comedy shows, but mostly I worked alone.

When you're working alone, how do you think up the jokes?

I tell you, I think funny. I sit there and laugh—if it's going good. Paddy Chayefsky used to say, "I sit there and cry, with tears streaming down my face."

You never come up empty?

Yeah. A lot, over the years. But you make it on the percentages.

Did this illustrious group continue for very long with Goodman Ace?

Doc and Danny branched off to Sid Caesar; Chayefsky started writing for real; Ernie Lehman, who had been a press agent selling jokes to columnists, went on and did great adaptations out here and one terrific, original screenplay, *Sweet Smell of Success.* Meanwhile, while I was still doing radio shows, I started doing early, early television . . .

At that time I was extremely disciplined and always doing two or three things at once, radio and television. I was married by then, with a child, a son. So I also needed the money, boy.

Money was always a big motivation?

Oh yeah. But I wanted to write, and I loved what I was doing and felt that I was very good at it.

If I went back and looked at the radio and TV shows, were some of them good, and would they hold up?

We'll never know, because they were on kinescope. They didn't have tape then. It was all live television. Kind of a joke—irony! Indeed, in my first movie script, I almost left time for the costume changes, I was so used to live television. Kind of a joke—irony!

The sex comedy? Was it cropping up on radio?

You could do a lot on radio if you were very judicious, because people couldn't see it, and a lot of times, the insinuation wouldn't catch. It could be in the readings and it was live, so once you did it, they couldn't do a goddamn thing about it. I got a tremendous laugh from Rod Brasfield on the *Grand Ole Opry* once on a joke that was the closest we came ever to being rowdy. He was talking about having bought his girlfriend a pair of full-length stockings—she wanted them to be very high. He said, "They came up to her expectations. Indeed, they almost tickled her fancy." People roared, laughing.

The same with early television? Could you also get away with murder?

I was never in TV when it wasn't live. Oh, I did shabby stuff. I had such contempt for the sponsors and all the ad agency guys. I loathed them. In those days, and I guess still, there were shady people around who would bribe writers to get products into scripts. Plugaroos. You had to mention the product's name. The idea being, you were making the product sound like it was such a universal thing, a household word. With each mention of the product, you got either sixty dollars, or a case of scotch or whiskey. A lot of my time was spent trying to figure out how to work this scam, and the ad agencies were out to stymie it, because their clients were paying good money to be advertised in these shows. So it was a war of wits. On one of the shows, I had a running character who was a silent movie star called Maybelline Mascara. They didn't catch on to that for a long time. And I got my case of liquor every time they said, "Maybelline Mascara."

Did some of the stuff from this period, some of these jokes, some of the sketches, get recycled later on?

Oh, sure. A scene from a novel I never finished is intact in *Itch*—it's the psychiatrist scene where the guy is attempting to commit criminal assault on a piano bench. I had to fix it, so it fit into the context, but the scene itself played right out of the book. And I have jokes that have appeared in fifty different things and been cut out because they aren't any good, but I keep sticking them back in.

I was doing the maddest stuff in those days. One of the shows I was writing was *The Eddie Albert Show*—a five-a-week show with Eddie that was broadcast all over the country but not in New York—it did not have a New York outlet. It was an early morning show, so nobody in New York ever heard it. It was a variety show which I turned into an experimental show. Nobody listened to it, so we could do anything. Real fun and free-flow stuff. We didn't have any sponsor to worry about. We were just filling in our time, and nobody at CBS in New York ever heard the show. One time I had Eddie up there inveighing against the March of Dimes. Eddie was playing in a play in New York at the time, so he'd stagger in—we had to record this show at eight o'clock in the morning—and he'd read anything you put in front of him. Anything! We had a marvelous time and invented all kinds of stuff. Oh, Eddie's a great guy!

One of the fellows working on the show became a producer at [the advertising agency] William Este. One of his clients was the *Grand Ole Opry*. When Eddie finally wanted to get out of the show, he said to me, "Why don't you take a crack at these goddamn cow jokes? You're versatile . . ." So that's when I started writing the cow jokes, and I wrote them for two years, 104 consecutive shows, where you had to come up with forty cow jokes a week.

You worked in television from '47 to?—

Fifty-two. I escaped in '52. They used to let one television writer out over the wall every year to keep the courage of the others up. They let Sam Taylor out first, then me, Doc Simon a couple of years later . . . but the poor schmucks—irony!—who stayed, like Norman Lear, just ended up as billionaires. Poor Norman—he was part of [Ed] Simmons and Lear at that time.* They were doing Martin and Lewis shows. I replaced Simmons and Lear, writing the old *Colgate Comedy Hour* with [Dean] Martin and [Jerry] Lewis [as guest hosts].

From '47 to '52 must have been chaotic as well as productive.

It was wild. I wrote, or contributed to, or collaborated on, over four hundred radio and television scripts, everything from the *Grand Ole Opry* to *The Boris Karloff Mystery Playhouse* to *The Peter Lind Hayes Show.* I remember *The Peter Lind Hayes Show* as being great fun—because again, like Eddie, Peter would do anything.

Did you get any sleep?

No.

Did you have any quality of life?

No. Nothing. I was a lousy father to my two children by then—and a terrible husband.

Yet you look back on that period warmly?

Yes. It was very exciting. And in the mornings, between eight and nine, which is when I had to leave to go to work, I would work on my play.

You had time left over to work on a play?

That's what I always wanted to do: write plays. I was going to escape. Television was a means to support myself and learn my craft. I had the idea for *The Seven Year Itch.* I wrote it—not in fifteen days—but in fifteen hour, hour and a half sessions at the typewriter. I started on an Easter Sunday, when I didn't have to do anything, and finished it on the Fourth of July in '52. I'd taken cracks at plays, but I never could get one that seemed to come . . . together. This one came in one piece.

Were you going to the theater a lot?

Always. But in those days I was poor, and there were hundreds of shows—Broadway was booming—an opening every night. I never saw a first act, not for a long time. I'd go in after the first act and mingle with the crowd going into the second act. I saw a lot of second and third acts.

Consequently, your openings are always mysteriously weak . . . but your endings are strong? That's irony!

Irony! Yeah, right. We don't do irony here.

Were you an omnivorous reader?

---

* Ed Simmons stayed in television and was later associated with *The Carol Burnett Show.* Norman Lear co-created the television series *All in the Family.*

Omnivorous reader. I read endlessly to make up for my lack of formal education.

You wrote Itch *so quickly. Then what happened?*

I gave the play to [the producer] Courtney Burr, who was a friend of my father's. Although by this time I was not without reputation—not in the theater but in my own racket. Courtney read it and liked it. I wanted Elliott Nugent to play the lead. Elliott, who was just about to play in the revival of *The Male Animal,* said he wouldn't be able to and, "I'm too old for it anyway." Later on, that decision drove him crazy when *Itch* became a hit. So Elliott enlisted his son-in-law, Johnny Gerstad, who was a pretty good actor, and who wanted to be a director. Elliott said he would oversee the production when he could. I didn't give a shit. I just wanted to get it on, man. And, indeed, I finished the play on the Fourth of July, and by September, we were in rehearsal.

Well, Nugent turned out to be a monster. Gerstad was great because he was willing to listen to me. Where my chutzpah came from I don't know, but I stood up to Nugent when he wanted to change scenes and rewrite. For one thing, he hated the title. He said he wanted to take out an ad in *Variety* which said he loved the play he was producing but hated the title because it was vulgar: "I think the title is vulgar, and I don't want to be associated with it." But, fortunately, he was involved with *The Male Animal.* Johnny Gerstad and I used to say, "Let's try to keep the grown-ups out of this . . ."

Courtney Burr was no help. I learned a lot from Courtney about how to live, but in terms of standing up to Nugent, well, I invented a dish called Chicken Courtney. I did learn how you stay at the Ritz in Boston and get the corner suite with a fireplace and send over to S.S. Perce for booze. I learned a lot about life and high living from Courtney.

We managed to bring the play in unscathed. I had not wanted Tommy Ewell for the lead, really, but he was wonderful in it. You cannot fault something that worked. My original choice, after Elliott couldn't do it, would have been Keenan Wynn, who was a good stage actor before he hardened into a film actor. I wanted Keenan, but they were firm about Tommy.

In those days, Keenan was almost good looking enough to get the girl, certainly as good looking as Tommy—a superb comic actor. I came out to see him in Hollywood when we were casting the national company, but it didn't work out. Keenan was happily ensconced at MGM, making his twenty-five hundred dollars a week. He was in a picture called *Kiss Me Kate* [1953], playing one of the gangsters, and I remember him sitting there on the lot, happily reading his motorcycle magazines.

That was the first time you were in Hollywood?

Yeah. I came out to talk to Keenan but also to see Billy [Wilder], because he was going to do the movie of *Itch.*

Was that the first time you met Billy? What was that like?

Oh, Billy! I lobbied for Billy for the movie. When the play was up for sale, I said, "I want Billy Wilder." I *longed* to meet Billy Wilder. [The agent] Irving Lazar got into the act, and he put the package together and offered it to [the agent-producer] Charlie Feldman and Billy Wilder. I was sitting in my kitchen one night and the phone rings and it's Billy Wilder. He said (*Billy Wilder imitation*), "You are putting me in the impossible position of bidding against Loew's Incorporated!" He said, "You will do the following: you will get on the airplane in the morning; then you will come out here and . . ." Right away, he started running my life.

I was so in awe of Billy. But we didn't really make a very good picture. In addition to having a horrible Breen Office problem,* the play just didn't adapt. The claustrophic element of the play is what makes it work—the guy trapped in the little apartment, his imagination soaring out of the apartment. When you open the play up, it loses its tension. Certain stories God doesn't mean to be movies. Every story has its form, its ideal form. The trick of doing an adaptation is to see if you can take the heart—the genetic code of the play— and transport that code, into another medium.

Into a new code.

While retaining the integrity of the original code and recoding it into a movie. I have a certain gift for that sometimes. Sometimes, I can see right into a thing and see what the genetic code is. Sometimes, you get touched on the shoulder, and then you can see how to transport it.

What's amazing to me is that nowadays everybody in the world is writing a screenplay. A screenplay is the hardest single form there is. You can't make any mistakes. Because it's not like a book where you can turn back the pages and say, "Oh, that's what he said!" It's continuous, razor-edge-of-now action. You aren't allowed any mistakes, because the audience is a fantastic entity. You can have 1,100 morons sitting in the audience, but when they come together in the darkness, an almost mystical thing happens, a kind of mass unconscious that is smarter than you are. They can spot a phony a mile off.

The first part of a movie has got to be not only engaging their attention in some way but building their trust. If you lose their trust, you can never get it back. They've got to feel that they're in good hands, that the guy who's telling the story knows what he is doing. They'll give you ten minutes. They'll accept any premise. They've gone out of the house—or, nowadays, rented the video—in any case, they've paid their money, and they're ready. Tell them a

---

* The Breen Office was also known as the Hays Office, the unofficial name of the Motion Picture Production Code organization regulating film industry censorship. Joseph Breen, long associated with code enforcement, took over Hollywood supervision when the chairman Will H. Hays retired in 1945.

story, and they will listen for ten minutes. Tell them Martians are about to invade, or any goddamn thing, for ten minutes—

About the length of a pitch meeting—

It's a pitch meeting, exactly. That's what it is. Very often, once they get the idea, they say, "Oh, I don't like that." You've lost them. But they'll give you that ten minutes . . . then, you have to be true to your premise. Any deviation, they don't know why, they're made uneasy. They're unforgiving, and they're almost always right.

With Billy, you were the sitter; he was the walker?

I'm the typer; he's the walker. English is Billy's third language. He doesn't physically write. He's always the walker and the talker. He *can't* type. I made him use the typewriter once when we finished *Itch.* I turned the typewriter around and said, "You've got to type 'The End.'"

Billy has a foreigner's love for American idiom—he is a master of American idiom. But, in overall sentence structure, English is still his third language. It comes out sounding not quite right. Izzy [I.A.L.] Diamond, rest his dear soul, used to say, "I'm a $150,000 secretary."* Which was not true. That was irony!

When I say Billy was the walker, we really *walked*—because Billy loves to go shopping. We'd work at [20th Century-Fox] in the mornings, then go over to Warners for lunch, because Mr. Blau, in the executive dining room, was Billy's favorite cook. We'd work a little bit in the afternoon, then go to Beverly Hills and go shopping—for anything. Billy is a compulsive buyer.

I learned so much about everything from Billy. Billy was, is, a wonderful teacher. I learned about art, food, everything. I didn't learn about writing so much. I learned about real life. Culture. Look around this room. That painting . . . that one-hundred-year-old figure, which Billy gave me . . . Billy's influence is everywhere.

But with *Itch,* we were attempting to do something impossible.

In spite of that, did Billy teach you anything at all about writing?

Yes. Billy has certain rules that are inviolate. Thou Shalt Not Bore. And, Anything Is Permitted—narration, anything you want to do, whatever gets the story across. Billy gave me the courage to do some of the nutty stuff we did in *The Manchurian Candidate.* If it works, do it.

What about tricks to get past the problems?

There are a lot of those. There are certain audience-delight kinds of things that you learn as you go along, like "the duchess trucks."

---

* I.A.L. Diamond, born Itek Dommnici in Romania in 1920, died in 1988. Diamond started out as a junior writer at Paramount from 1941 to 1943, and accumulated modest comedy credits, including *Monkey Business* for the director Howard Hawks, before affiliating with Billy Wilder. Starting with *Love in the Afternoon* in 1957, Diamond collaborated almost exclusively with Wilder—on twelve films in all—often as associate producer as well as co-screenwriter.

The duchess trucks?

Yeah, the audience loves it when the sinister character turns out to be lovable: "The duchess breaks into a jazz dance." There are dozens of those tricks.

How long did it take you to write the script for Itch?

A while. We wrote part of it in New York at the St. Regis, because we made a deal that Billy would come to New York to do part of it, and I'd come to California to do part of it. Part of it at the St. Regis, part at his office at 20th and part at his office at Warners, because he was preparing two different pictures at the same time, *Itch* and the Charles Lindbergh picture [*The Spirit of St. Louis*, 1957].

Did you realize all the time you were writing that the script was doomed to fail?

Only in retrospect. We thought it was working, and that it would be wonderful. I was in love with the work and Billy was terrific and all I knew was how lucky I was.

I think Billy needs friction in a collaborator.

He does, and he didn't get any from me. I didn't stand up to him the way I stood up to Elliott Nugent, because I had no respect for Elliott Nugent. Not only did I have respect for Billy, but I had awe. And I just thought everything he said was hilarious. You do need friction. If you collaborate with someone, you have to have a bounce. Otherwise, what's the point?

But we had such fun. We became very close friends, laughing and shopping and having lunch with Mr. Blau.

Billy was thinking of doing something last year—at eighty-six. He had a funny idea, and he had the money from France to do it, but he couldn't quite solve the story. So I went in and sat with him for a couple of weeks to see if we could put it together, but it didn't work out. Also, by this time, I'm so used to working alone that I don't like to say an idea out loud, because an idea's so fragile; and Billy's hard of hearing now, so you not only have to say it out loud, you have to shout it out loud.

Billy was in earnest . . . working on this new script, at age eighty-six?

Very much so.

Itch *went on so long, playing on stage and then being developed for film, that by this point in time, you had already tucked away another picture, your first picture . . . Phffft!*

That was an original. But I had a sweet, dear, darling man, [the director] Mark Robson, who hadn't a clue how to do comedy. Not a clue. I had Judy Holliday, one of the finest comedy technicians in the world, and Jack Carson, another great comedy technician, and Jack Lemmon too, but the director was miscast.

Judy had a terrible time. She understood how to do the material, but Mark crushed the scenes up all the time. We were fighting the director and censorship. The seduction scene with Judy and Jack Carson—a brilliantly funny scene with these two masters—and Jack made it so erotic. In the case of that scene, we had it on film right. The two of them were left to their own devices with the camera. Afterwards, they cut the shit out of it. The censorship destroyed it, so it wasn't even funny.

Mark was an editor. He didn't understand his own limitations. Good directors come in various ways, but editors are the worst because they are interested in editing. They don't know about story. They don't know about comedy. Or even acting. They only know about having a "match."

I had no say, really. I was at Columbia with Harry Cohn and Jerry Wald. Mark Robson had done some wonderful films. I said, "Does he know how to do comedy?" They said, "Sure, comedy." I knew pretty much from the time we started that he was inept at comedy, that he didn't quite understand what was funny, but he was so sweet, and I didn't have any control over what we were doing. I was an employee.

Was Jerry Wald of any use as a producer?

Yeah. I learned a lot from Jerry. Some of the nuts and bolts. I loved Jerry.

People tell me he was a frantic personality . . .

He was frantic, but he was a fountain of energy and ideas. He'd say, "George, I've got a wonderful idea. No? Okay, I've got another wonderful idea . . ." And about the fifth idea would be great. He was just a dynamo.

On the other hand, he gave you Mark Robson.

On the other hand, he gave me Mark Robson. What Jerry giveth, Jerry taketh away.

Starting with Phffft! *and* Itch, *you developed such a reputation for sex comedy. Where did the preoccupation with sex come in for you?*

Wishful thinking, I suppose. I invented a name for what I used to write: Boobs and boobs. Dumb guys and sexy girls. I remember meeting Jimmy Stewart—who was going to play Charles Lindbergh for Billy Wilder—when I came out to work on *Itch* with Billy. Stewart was interested in doing *Itch*—the movie. He said (*Jimmy Stewart voice*), "I'm in the boob business, you know. You wrote a pretty good boob. I can play the hell out of that boob."

It was totally wishful thinking. Not an extension of your private life?

Wishful thinking. *Itch* is really heartfelt in a way. It was written seriously. It was a comedy, but I was madly in love with a young actress while I was married, and I used to go through agonies about it. I took a lot of her dialogue, her chatter, almost word for word, and put it into the play. Later, this lady played *Itch* on a national tour, and she told me, "God, that dialogue is so real." She had no idea it was stuff she had said.

In addition to being self-serving, these interviews have a lot of cop-outs. I'll give you a real cop-out. The bulk of my sex-comedy career was done with this enormous handicap: not being allowed to have any sex. I was trying to write these so-called sex comedies in the fifties when we had to deal with the Breen Office. *The Seven Year Itch* was a funny, funny play that still plays today. It plays all over the world today. I make quite a bit of money in royalties on it—it's been translated into a number of foreign languages. But the premise of *Seven Year Itch* is that a guy has an affair with a girl while his wife is away, and [he] feels guilty about it. And the guilt is *funny.* In the movie, he couldn't have the affair, but he felt guilty anyway; so the goddamn premise didn't make any sense.

Okay, self-serving. In the case of *Bus Stop,* I believe the movie of *Bus Stop* is a better movie than the play of *Bus Stop* is a play. Because *Bus Stop* is not a particularly good play of Bill Inge's, but it had two unforgettable characters—the chanteuse and the cowboy.

The play just plays in one set, at the bus stop, and I had to open it up. I had a brilliant scene in the screenplay for *Bus Stop,* which the Breen Office just murdered. In the play, the cowboy is bragging about how literate he is—that he can recite the Gettysburg Address. In the movie, I had him break into the girl's room in the morning, while she is asleep, just to prove how literate he is. As he's screwing her, he is reciting the Gettysburg Address. It went on and on: "We are met on a great battlefield . . ." The longer it went on, the funnier it was, but he has to be screwing her while he's doing it. Hilarious scene. But, of course, the Breen Office didn't allow them to screw. So it was a botch.

Whatever deluded you into writing it?

Perversity. I hoped Josh [Logan] would figure some way to make it work—film it on their faces, or something.

Were you hoping for a breakthrough in the Production Code?

The breakthroughs weren't anywhere near. Years later, with *Lord Love a Duck,* they still hadn't broken through. The last scene, where Roddy [McDowall] goes off triumphantly, screaming? I had him mouth "Fuck you!" and they cut it out.

Did these things drive you crazy?

Oh, mad. Not only did I have to cope with the Breen Office, but I had the Legion of Decency. Frank McCarthy, who was in charge of getting stuff through the Legion of Decency at 20th, used to say, "George, for Chrisake, why do you fight the system? Monsignor Biddle"—who was the movie guy for the Legion of Decency—"will be more than happy to sit down and write the scene with you . . ." (*Laughs.* Long pause.)

Irony?

Irony! The fact is that I would not sit down with Monsignor Biddle to write sex comedy scenes.

Then, unfortunately, after you wrote them, he went ahead and rewrote them.

Yeah, he just blue-penciled them out.

You told me that Itch *was inspired by a real person. How often do you do that—take dialogue from real people?*

I do listen to people. Almost all my original stuff is based on a real person; most, loosely. Almost everything starts with a person. Something about that person which gets me thinking—and, mostly, it's a woman.

Why?

I don't know why. A lot of stuff was written for Marilyn. I had a big, professional, emotional hang-up with Marilyn.

When did you meet Marilyn?

When I first came out and started working with Billy in '53. She was rehearsing a musical at 20th—I remember she was doing a dance routine

Axelrod and Marilyn Monroe on the set of *Bus Stop,* directed by Joshua Logan. (Courtesy of George Axelrod.)

with [the choreographer] Jack Cole on a hot, sweaty soundstage in grungy rehearsal clothes, all covered with sweat, and she was just edible—glorious.

Poor Marilyn. I did two pictures with her and got to know her pretty well. She was a sad, sad, sad creature. She was sick. In a rightly ordered world, she would have been in a nuthouse. She was psychotic. Once you got to know her, one couldn't feel sexy about her. She was pathetic, sad. You just wanted to comfort her, cuddle her, father her, say, "It's going to be all right, child."

Did she ever involve herself, critically or otherwise, in the process of writing?

No.

Did she make script suggestions?

Not that I ever heard.

She would read the lines as written?

If she could remember them, and she couldn't.

If she couldn't, then she might do some interpolation?

No. She'd burst into tears and run off. The scene on the bus in *Bus Stop,* where she's pouring her heart out to Hope Lange, was a nightmare to shoot. "Rear projection" wasn't as good as it is now, so they kept running out of film. We had this rickety insert of a bus, and a rear projection screen, and Hope and Marilyn with a big, long speech, and Marilyn couldn't remember the words. Josh's dialogue director was propped up just outside of the screen, feeding her the lines, which she would parrot back. She had reached a point in her neurosis where if anybody said, "Cut!" she took it as an affront, burst into tears, and ran into her dressing room. So Josh never said cut. He'd run the whole nine hundred feet, keep running it and running it while he talked to her.

He was a huge man, Josh, so most of the time the screen was filled with Josh's behind and Marilyn's face, with this voice coming from the sky reading the lines that Marilyn would parrot. It took four days to shoot this scene, but it cut together like a dream, partly because Hope Lange is a professional actress and we'd cut to her. Little pieces of what Marilyn would do were inspired, magical, but interspersed with tears and "oh, shit!" and "what the fuck!" and getting her back together—all of it with the camera running because you couldn't say cut. God, the goings-on!

Is there any way to compare working with Josh Logan to Billy Wilder?

They were both very strong, very powerful idea people, and Josh again was a writer of sorts—again, a writer who never actually set words to paper. He dictated. He dictated scenes to Joe Curtis, his assistant, the dialogue director whose voice was heard coming from above Marilyn on the bus. He was Josh's writing tool.

Was Josh involved at all in the adaptation of Bus Stop*?*

Oh yes. He took my first draft, and we really worked on it together for another two to four months. He was very important to that script. He channeled it.

Tell me about Frank Tashlin.

I never knew Frank Tashlin. I never worked with him. I had nothing to do with the film of *Will Success Spoil Rock Hunter?* I never saw the movie. Not to this day.

Why not?

They didn't use my story, my play, or my script.

You know that without having seen it?

I know what they did. I made it about the movies—they made it about television.

So, why did they buy it?

I was hot as a pistol. Buddy Adler bought it. Buddy and I were good friends, socially. He was the producer of *Bus Stop,* as well as being head of the studio. He was very supportive. He was going to be the producer of *Rally 'Round the Flag*—which is why I agreed to do it—then he got [the director] Leo McCarey, who chose to produce it himself.

Were you angry about Rock Hunter?

I'm never angry. Just saddened. Why do I want to torture myself by seeing it?

Are there other movies of yours you have never seen?

Well, I don't think I ever sat through the movie of *Goodbye Charlie.* I saw a couple of minutes of it on television once.

Why? . . .

Hmmm . . . Debbie Reynolds?

But on the other hand, Vincente Minnelli [as director] . . .

I like Vincente, but they completely changed *Goodbye Charlie* right from the start. And I know I never saw *Rally 'Round the Flag,* after I took my name off.

What happened in the case of Rally 'Round the Flag?

Leo was a kind of genius, although I caught him at the end of his career. *Rally 'Round* was a very hard book [*Rally 'Round the Flag, Boys!* by Max Shulman (New York: Doubleday, 1957)] to beat, and I was never really able to beat it; neither was anybody else. I had a radical way I wanted to do it, and Leo went along with it for a while, but the studio wouldn't hear of it. The novel was not very good, but it did have the author, Max Shulman's, voice, as the narrator of the book. I thought the author's voice was so strong the picture should be narrated by somebody like Fred Allen, someone with a really dry, intelligent voice, and then we could do the film like an old Pete Smith specialty.* It worked very well that way, I thought, and Leo liked that approach. But Buddy Adler and the people running Fox at the time wouldn't hear of it. They couldn't understand my script. To them, it was all talk, talk, talk. Leo

---

* Peter Smith produced hundreds of folksy and humorous short subjects—which won numerous Academy Awards—from 1931–1955.

eventually had to go the other way. I thought the final script had nothing to do with what I wrote, so I took my name off.

Did Leo actually write?

He wrote in the Billy Wilder sense. He also never touched a typewriter or a pen or any writing utensil of any kind. They both liked to talk. Oh, sure, Leo was a writer. A writer-director. He worked so closely with writers that he was very much a writer.

His writing credits are usually co-credits.

He was a verbal guy—one of the great Irish charmers of the world, a sales-man. He was famous for going in and selling *The Cowboy and the Lady* to Goldwyn without having written a word. Goldwyn said, "I love it." They made a deal, and Leo left it to someone else to write. Two, three years went by while they were trying to figure out how to make *The Cowboy and the Lady.* Finally, they did manage to do it with Gary Cooper.

McCarey hadn't been driven too crazy by his paranoia about Hollywood communists by this time?

"Jesus and Mary and Leo McCarey" was his nickname, actually. Because of the Catholic films he did, he was always besieged by priests. Like everyone else in the world, there is no priest who hasn't got a screenplay under his frock.

My impression is that by this stage of his career, he was pretty dissolute.

Oh, he was pretty beat up. But interestingly beat up. No, Leo was a nice guy, and our differences were quite truly artistic only. We became good friends. When he was compelled to change the script, there was no reason for me to keep my name on it. He wanted me to keep my name on. I had to plead to get it off.

And you weren't angry about that experience, either?

Not angry. Even then, I was beyond getting angry about any of those things. It wasn't that important. It was only a movie.

I'll tell you a worse tale. I was working for Hecht-Hill-Lancaster* around the time Ernie Lehman was writing *Sweet Smell of Success.* [Clifford] Odets worked on that too. I know, because [the producer] Jim Hill had Odets locked upstairs, and me locked downstairs. Ernie was going to write *and* direct *Sweet Smell,* but he panicked and went to Hawaii.

I was working on another one of those projects that never came to fruition, an adaptation of Jim Thurber's story "The Catbird Seat." I was never allowed to write; I became a frustrated writer. Jim Hill—the middle name of Hecht-Hill-Lancaster—loved to have story conferences. I used to sit in his office and

---

* Hecht-Hill-Lancaster was the film production company—from the early 1950s until the early 1960s—of the former agent Harold Hecht, the producer Jim Hill, and the actor Burt Lan-caster.

bullshit with him, endlessly. He used sports analogies. "Now, you see, in the first scene"—he acted out the pitching—"you throw the fastball and dust him off . . ." I eventually brought a golf club in and practiced my chip shot over the couches. Never did a goddamn thing all summer. I finally gave back what I had collected by that time, around $175,000. I gave it all back. I said I'd never write another screenplay unless it was written into the contract that I never had to speak to Jim Hill again—even at a party. By this time, I wanted to kill him. Kill, kill!

What did Harold Hecht do in that partnership?

Hecht was the business guy. Kind of a genius that way and a big drunk. He liked to claim that he developed and produced *Cat Ballou* [1965], then opened it [in theaters]—but couldn't remember anything about it at all. Never remembered doing it!

Who was the brains behind the company? Lancaster?

Indicate in script "no comment."

Someone had to be the brains. It was an interesting company, yes?

It was. It shows you that these things are kind of self-generating. Look at the morons who are running this business today, and every once in a while, a pretty good picture comes out.

So the answer is, there was no brains running the company?

No discernible brains. But they also hired good people. Ernie [Lehman] wrote stuff, and eventually stuff came out.

You're saying, production companies are a dime a dozen, and what happens inside of them is sometimes a mystery? . . .

I'm the least New Age person you are ever going to find, but there is something mysterious about how a movie gets made. There is a mystery. That's why I think screenplays are so hard. It's not that there are no rules; there are, but nobody knows what they are, and they change with each picture. So you're trying to play the game according to a very rigid set of rules which nobody has explained to you. Any violation, you lose. Go directly to jail. Do not pass Go.

Once you think you've got the rules, they change. It's like doing a crossword puzzle; every day there's a new theme. This morning in the *L.A. Times,* the clue was "Planes from NY." The answer was "JFK's SSTs." Once you've got the idea that in this puzzle the trick is initials, it begins to come together. But if you try that with tomorrow's puzzle, it's not going to work.

Each picture is like a crossword puzzle in a funny way. Every story has rules that govern it—you don't know what they are, but you've got to solve them.

For a long time, you refused to settle down in Hollywood. You lived more than half of the time in New York and concentrated on theater. Did you have negative feelings about being here, at first, in the 1950s?

Oh no, I loved it. I thought it was terrific. Hooray for Hollywood. It was fun in those days. I, unlike a lot of other writers, was a hit New York playwright. I went boom, bang, bam, right from the airplane into the Goetzes' living room.* I was treated like royalty. I had it made. We gave great parties. I was an outrageous host. I'd do wild stuff . . .

We had a theory—my wife and I—that if you had the head of the studio to your house for dinner to meet important people, he's going to think twice about offering you small amounts of money for your next script, because he knows it costs a lot to live like this. He'll want to help you maintain your standard of living.

So . . . Harry Cohn came to dinner?

Not Harry Cohn. Never Harry Cohn! The line had to be drawn somewhere. But Darryl Zanuck, Buddy Adler, Sam Goldwyn, who was like a father to me for a while . . .

You'd set Sam up next to some incongruous personality?

Sam was a gent. He did say those things. They were not just press agent manufactured. The very first one he ever said to me, when I was just getting to know him—he was trying to make conversation—he said, "I ran into your friend Billy Wilder the other day." I said, "Oh, where?" He said, "At my house." That's not a real Goldwynism, but it shows you how his mind worked.

You never worked with him, though.

He asked me to write the sequel to *The Secret Life of Walter Mitty* [1947] because I was the okay-dream-sequence writer for that year. We could never get it to work really, because the first picture wasn't any good anyway. In his alleged correspondence to [James] Thurber, Goldwyn supposedly said, "I hope you won't find the movie too blood and thirsty," and Thurber is alleged to have replied, "No, I was horror and struck."

There are still dinner parties in Hollywood. Maybe the conversation isn't as sparkling. Were the parties so much different then from now?

Oh yes. In the first place, movie stars lived here. They don't now. The producers are no longer colorful. They're lawyers and accountants and business people. They're all yuppies, and they have kids. It's a whole other world. It's still glamorous, though.

It was just as inbred before.

Oh yes. And it was very, very structured. It was a caste system. There were above-the-line people and below-the-line people, and they never met socially.

Fortunately, you were above the line.

Very much so. Irony!

Can you give me an example of one of your sterling dinner party guest lists?

We used to call it the Jewish A-group, although you didn't have to be Jewish.

Well, you just had to be Jewish in some way.

---

* The erstwhile producer and studio executive William Goetz and his wife, Edith, one of Louis B. Mayer's daughters, were famed for their social gatherings.

Irony! Right. Gary Cooper was an honorary member of the Jewish A-group. He was always there.

He was witty?

No, but he was charming. Coop was a truly elegant man. The regulars would include the Goetzes and the Goldwyns. Everybody loved them. We were minor hosts compared to them; they were the great hosts. There would be Danny Kaye, David Niven when he was here, the Wilders, the Wylers, [Fred] Astaire . . .

You'd pepper the group with writers and directors?

Top, top writers and directors. Novelists—which were more acceptable than Hollywood writers—Hollywood writers were considered below the line. Odets might be there, for example. He was a regular guest and maybe not a very good guest, because he got loaded all the time. But visiting novelists, visiting playwrights, were acceptable.

When did you break down and come out here to live?

For a long time, I commuted, but my base was still in New York. I didn't come out here to live until '61. Again, Billy Wilder had an influence. I had raised hell with Blake [Edwards] about *Breakfast at Tiffany's*. Billy said, "Look, the time has come. You cannot sit in New York, see the finished product, then raise hell about it. If you want to be involved in the making of the picture, you've got to be out here to do it."

I had a tremendous row with Blake and persuaded Audrey [Hepburn] to give us a three-day shoot [for free], so we could reshoot the Mickey Rooney scenes. I hated that Jap routine that Mickey Rooney does in the film. It was all solo stuff except the one scene at the end of the film where he brings the police in. Audrey agreed to come in for nothing to reshoot that scene with another actor. Blake violently disagreed, so Mickey Rooney's still in the picture, boy, to the great detriment of the picture. Blake said, "I love it. It gives a big lift to the picture." It's the one lapse in taste in the picture.

I'd come out for crises before, but I was still doing most of my work in New York. I had plays going on. I was a playwright who took the loot and scooted, as people say. But, by the time Billy said this, the climate had changed a little bit. I had had a series of hits both as a writer and director and producer. I had *Itch*, then *Will Success Spoil Rock Hunter?*; then I produced Gore Vidal's play *Visit to a Small Planet*, which was a hit; then I started to direct my own plays and other peoples', including Harry Kurnitz's play *Once More with Feeling* with Arlene Francis and Joe Cotten . . .

Then, things changed. I directed my play *Goodbye Charlie* with Lauren Bacall, which didn't get very good notices. It turned out well over the stretch—it plays all over the world—in fact, I just got a check out of the blue for fifty thousand dollars for the Japanese television rights, so they can do the play on television in Japan. But it didn't do very well on Broadway. It got poor notices. And I remember the drama critic Walter Kerr, in one of his reviews, saying it read as though it was written by a swimming pool.

I said to myself, "Walter, you've given me an idea. That sounds pretty good to me." Because at the same time that *Goodbye Charlie* was receiving poor notices in New York, I was getting nominated for an Academy Award for the script for *Breakfast at Tiffany's*. I had built up enough clout that I could produce my films. Also, I thought it would be maybe a good idea not to bring the kids up in New York. Big mistake!

So you weren't happy with Breakfast at Tiffany's*? . . .*

No, it was a completely happy collaboration. Except for the Mickey Rooney scenes.

Did Blake have anything to do with the writing?

No, Blake was brought in at the last minute. Johnny Frankenheimer was going to direct. I developed it with Johnny.

I didn't realize that. Hmm, it doesn't sound like a Frankenheimer film.

No. Audrey Hepburn didn't think so either. When she became involved in the film, she had director okay, and he was not on her list. Blake was acceptable and available.

Had you known Blake previously?

No. Blake arrived so late he didn't touch a line. The only thing he did do was some improvisation in the party scenes. He *loved* the party scenes.

Blake's very good. He's a student of slapstick, while I'm more word oriented. We've been tempted to work together several different times. He asked me to write the screenplay of *Victor/Victoria* [1982] with him.

Why didn't you?

I didn't like the idea. Blake Edwards did this curious thing, recently. With *Switch* [1991], he did the same story as *Goodbye Charlie*. And it was pretty good. All of Blake's films have wonderful stuff in them. Although I think he reached his pinnacle with the *Pink Panther* films. Some of those were really, really funny. Peter Sellers was a major artist.

Sellers and I worked for about a year once, trying to get a project together. We had a very good idea. Douglas Fairbanks Jr. had a manservant, a butler who, he discovered, had been a war hero and flight commander during World War II. Also, he was extravagantly, screamingly gay. He had been a saloon singer in Marseilles in the south of France, and because he was fluent in French and German, he was recruited into MI5 and became a gay spy. He slept his way up through the whole SS and ended up screwing an SS colonel. They finally caught on to him and beat the shit out of him—which he loved. Afterwards, he became a big hero. Sellers and I were going to do his story—a gay James Bond.

What stopped you?

Oh, it was too outrageous for its day.

Was Truman Capote involved in adapting Breakfast at Tiffany's *at all?*

No. I knew Truman before and after, because he, my wife, and I were good friends, but he had nothing to do with the script. He was quite put out because I got more money for writing the screenplay than he got for selling the book rights!

I've got one funny story, which is about the only time I got the better of that very witty man. One day I had lunch with him. I said, "Tru, baby, I just want you to know this is not my fault . . . I fought this thing. I have done everything I could. But I cannot win this war." Tru said (*Truman Capote imitation*), "What's the matter?" I said, "It's the goddamn title! Truman, you know how they test these things. Nobody outside of New York knows what Tiffany's is. And *Breakfast* at Tiffany's . . . what does *that* mean?" Truman said, "They're going to change the title?" "Yeah." "What are they going to call it?" "Follow that Blond." He screamed and screamed. I had him going.

Truman didn't have much to do with the film. Again, it was such a loose adaptation. I tried to keep the gene pool of the novella. I couldn't use the structure at all, because it's the same story as *I Am a Camera* [The dramatization of Christopher Isherwood's *Goodbye to Berlin* by John Van Druten], just a homosexual or asexual man observing a sexy girl. You can't make a love story out of that—and they wanted a love story.

You couldn't mention the homosexuality either.

Nor, in those days, could you mention the homosexuality. So I just eliminated it. The trick was to find a hero and some reason why they just didn't fall into bed, or the picture would be over. What I came up with was the idea that he was in the same line of work: she was a hooker, he was a kept man, and they couldn't afford each other. The parallel lines couldn't meet until the end. That worked, kind of.

How did you meet Frankenheimer?

I met him when he was going to do *Breakfast at Tiffany's* . . . when I finally managed to get myself hired to write the script. First I had to sell myself to [the producer] Marty Jurow.

That's a project you went after?

Actually, *Breakfast* was something Josh [Logan] and I wanted to do, but for a long time, we couldn't figure out how to do it; then, one morning, I figured it out.

It started with Josh, moved to Frankenheimer, and ended up with Blake Edwards.

Yes.

But you had to sell yourself as the screenwriter? . . .

Marty Jurow, for some reason, didn't think I was uptown enough.

What was his idea of uptown?

Audrey Hepburn, not Jayne Mansfield. He associated me with Jayne Mansfield, because I had launched Jayne. She was in the play *Will Success*

Spoil Rock Hunter? As a matter of fact, I directed her first screen test, and sold her contract to 20th.

It sounds as though you were always a very good businessman as well as writer.

I did very well.

Tell me more about how you put Manchurian *together.*

Johnny [Frankenheimer] and I had become friends and were looking around for something else to do. I read a review of *The Manchurian Candidate* in the *New Yorker* and bought the book [by Richard Condon (New York: McGraw-Hill, 1959)] the next day. I thought, "Jesus Christ, what a fucking movie!" There was a lot of resistance. It was everything the studios didn't want—*political* satire, worse than regular satire. It was not easy, but [Frank] Sinatra made it all possible. Sinatra agreed to play [Bennett] Marco, and that's the only way United Artists would let us do it.

I was good friends with Frank anyway. I met Frank through Goody Ace. He had wanted to do *Seven Year Itch,* back when his career was on its ass. I had known Frank for years. We were very close friends.

"The best adaptation I ever did": Frank Sinatra and Laurence Harvey in *The Manchurian Candidate,* directed by John Frankenheimer.

Was Condon or Frankenheimer involved in the script?
I worked with Frankenheimer on it from the beginning.
Was he helpful?
Very much so. Condon was not involved, although Dick became a very good friend. I wrote the first draft of *The Manchurian Candidate* in New York, in a house in Bedford Village, in the summer. Then I came out here in August or September of '61 to work with Frankenheimer, who produced *Manchurian* with me, and to prepare the film. I stayed here until '68, when we moved to London.

For film, I do two very specifically different things. I'm a pretty good adapter, and I can do the odd original. They're two very different techniques. The very best adaptation I ever did was *The Manchurian Candidate.* It is a brilliant, wildly chaotic novel. Wonderful voice. To take the essence of that and try to make it so that it worked for a film was a challenge.

A very good example of breaking the rules of the craft is *The Manchurian Candidate* screenplay: it breaks every single known rule. It's got dream sequences, flashbacks, narration out of nowhere. When we got in trouble, it had just a voice explaining stuff. Everything in the world that you're told not to do. But that was part of its genetic code, the secret of the crossword puzzle. It worked for this script.

For example, one scene: When the book describes the reading matter of the hero, it says his library consists of books which have been picked out for him at random by a guy in a bookstore in San Francisco from a list of titles he happens to have on hand at the moment. What I did was transpose that, so when the colonel [played by Douglas Henderson] comes in to fire Marco, he notices that Marco has a lot of books. I had Frank read off the titles of all his books: "*The Ethnic Choices of Arabs, The Jurisdictional Practices of the Mafia* . . ." With Frank saying the titles, it makes an excellent scene. But it was not a scene in the book—I had to make a scene out of a piece of description by Condon. That's what I mean by transposing the gene.

The main trick of *Manchurian* was to make the brainwashing believable. What I did was dramatize the way the prisoners were brainwashed into believing they were attending a meeting of a lady's garden society. I had the further idea of making Corporal Melvin [played by James Edwards] black and doing the whole second half of the dream with black ladies. I remember we shot for days, getting all the different angles—front and back, black and white. At the time, we weren't entirely sure how it was going to fit together. We had miles of film. It was bewildering.

Meanwhile, we had to screw the [production] board all up and schedule all Frank's scenes up front. We had to shoot all his stuff in fifteen days—because he has the attention span of a gnat—to keep his interest. Then he was set to leave. He was going off to Europe or some place.

Before he left, he announced, "I want to see every foot of film that I'm in before I leave." Johnny Frankenheimer said, "You can see everything except the brainwashing sequence." Frank said, "Oh, no, no, no. I want to see *everything*," in a voice where you felt kneecaps were going to be broken. Now, this is *totally* self-serving but absolutely true: I said, "Let me take a crack at it because I really understand what I am trying to do . . ." The editor, Ferris Webster, and I went back to my office, and we got the script out. I just penciled the script where the shots were—cut, cut, cut—then he went back and put it together, and we never changed the sequence. That's how it was cut, that magical sequence.

Was Frank a good actor, acting out of continuity?

Frank is one of the best screen actors in the world. He's magic. Like Marilyn. But you have to understand how he works. When he won't do many takes, it's because he can't. He has no technical vocabulary as an actor. Something magical happens the first time, and sometimes, he can do it a second time. After that, it's gone.

But can he work out of continuity?

He understands how to do each scene—what it's about. He's a musical genius, and he's lyrically sensitive. He knows that each scene tells a little story. He never tries to change a line. He has enormous respect for the dialogue. He was just a dream to work with.

Did he always work in one take?

We had one tragedy. In the scene where he is shuffling the cards, with fifty-two queens of diamonds—with Larry Harvey—big, tense scene. We shot it. Frank was brilliant. We looked at the rushes. His face was soft. It was not the camera operator's fault. Frank had gone off his marks. He knew he had done it great, but he had to do it again. I was the one who had to tell him.

It was all very expensive. Of course, we shot his hours—starting at eleven. Eleven o'clock, Frank wasn't there. Twelve o'clock, one o'clock, Frank's still not there. Larry Harvey was waiting. Everybody was waiting. Silence. Nothing. No one said a word. Suddenly, you felt this black cloud coming up Santa Monica [Boulevard], turning on Formosa [Avenue], coming onto the set. Frank strides onto the set. Speaks to no one. Goes into his trailer. You could hear him slamming things around. His dresser comes running out in terror. Around two o'clock in the afternoon, Frank comes out, black with rage. And Larry Harvey, who was a fearless man, speaks up: "My dear, we're having our period today? . . ." Frank started to laugh. It broke the tension. We had the shot in ten minutes.

Why did you decide to become a movie director?

The same reason I became a stage director—to protect my stuff. I couldn't bear having someone else mangle my stuff. I write a very delicate thing. To me. Self-serving!—like everybody.

Did it feel like everything had been mangled?
To a point.
Anything not mangled?
Manchurian Candidate, Bus Stop—which Josh and I fought through.
Not Breakfast at Tiffany's?

Not really. It's a little off. I wanted a high romantic comedy. The Mickey Rooney stuff and other stuff brings it down. There are lovely things in it. There's an actor named John McGiver, who I then used in *Manchurian Candidate* as the senator, who is a genius at high comedy. My favorite scene, if I say so myself, is the scene in Tiffany's with the Tiffany clerk. That's not in the book. Oh, it's a very free adaptation. I took a little delicate part of the book, a small enzyme, and turned it into that scene.

You don't get angry, but the frustration was accumulating.

Yes, the dissatisfaction. You don't get much satisfaction from something you don't think is right. I love, for all its mistakes and dumbness, *Lord Love a Duck.*

In the beginning, you said a lot of your career was about making money. So a lot of it was about satisfaction, too?

Yeah. One wouldn't confess that at the time.

So, ultimately, you get more satisfaction from your plays.

Sure. Because you have some control. And, even then, I had the Nugent and Gerstad situation—which isn't exactly what I wanted—so little things about each play still irritate me.

When I moved out, the first thing I did was become producer, so with *Manchurian,* theoretically I would have more control. After *Manchurian,* I kept control, but I got involved with [the director] Dick Quine. He was also on Audrey Hepburn's okay list. He had been a kid actor, playing Dick Powell as a child in *Dames* (1934). He was sweet and highly talented, but totally insane, which made him exactly my kind of person. He and I produced a totally insane picture called *Paris When It Sizzles.*

You worked with him twice.

He was a close friend. But we had a rocky time. After *Paris,* he talked me into letting him direct *How to Murder Your Wife,* which I should have directed myself. I was ready then but too frightened. I waited until *Lord Love a Duck.* Had *Duck* been a hit, my life would have changed.

For the better?

Differently.

It wasn't a hit, because nobody understood the humor?

I can't imagine why it wasn't a hit. It got no reaction. I couldn't get anybody into the theaters to see it. It was one of those pictures that died. United Artists sold the shit out of it. I went on the road with it. I got reams of press. I ran what I thought was a clever ad campaign, parodying all the other cam-

Audrey Hepburn and George Axelrod on the set of *Paris When It Sizzles*.
(Courtesy of George Axelrod.)

paigns. "Suddenly last summer, United Artists realized it was being used for
something evil . . . *Lord Love a Duck*!"

Did you enjoy directing?

Oh yeah. I adored it. I was learning to be a pretty good director. Indeed,
when you see *Duck* now, the problems with it are in the script, not the directing. It is very well directed. I never quite solved the script. I was a little bit
overconfident and thought I could wing it.

How'd you solve for yourself the scary hurdle of the technology?

That's a myth, a great myth, like the myth rich people foist on poor people
by saying it's lonely at the top. It's lonelier at the bottom, I've got news for
you. You get yourself a good cameraman . . . and of course, I'd been around
for a long time. All a director has to know, only one thing, is how to tell a
story, and all the rest of it you pick up as you go along. Sure, there are virtu-
oso cameramen, and I had a very good one—Danny Fapp, a competent one
for what I did—but I didn't duck the job. I fought for black-and-white [pho-
tography]. I made it for $1.2 million in six and one-half weeks. And I loved
doing it.

I saw it in college, where it played over and over.

"I adored directing": George Axelrod in the director's seat for *Lord Love a Duck.*

Where were you when I needed you? Gene Siskel, he was out here for the Academy Awards last year, told me, "God, I love *Lord Love a Duck.*" I said, "Where were all you guys when I couldn't sell any tickets?"

Hollywood was kind to you, at least. You got a second chance with Secret Life of an American Wife.

You get two. Then I screwed up the second one. Remember, I said earlier, that stories have their natural form. That was a play, it was going to be a play, and it should have stayed a play. It was a two-character play, two sets, in a

Ruth Gordon, Roddy McDowall, and Tuesday Weld in *Lord Love a Duck.*

hotel. But I had a bust-up with United Artists, I needed a movie, and Dick Zanuck at 20th wanted to buy *Secret Life* and go with it. Someone says, "You can write and direct and produce"—*and* it's your own material? Who could say no? I should have said no. Because it was meant to be a play.

Besides, I had written it for Frank Sinatra and Shirley MacLaine, and I ended up with Walter Matthau and Anne Jackson, both talented people, but not right for this film . . . which was meant to be a play.

Once again, it needed more writing than directing.

The directing is not bad . . . it's just that it's a play. It talks itself to death.

Did its failure drive you to London?

It drove me, so that nobody would let me direct anymore.

How long a period of time elapsed before its failure precipitated your move to London?

Very shortly thereafter.

How long were you living in London?

We lived in London for '68, '69, '70, '71, '72, '73, and '74. We came back for a while in '74; then we went back in '79 and '80.

Were you consciously giving up writing?

No, I wrote another novel, *Where Am I Now—When I Need Me?* [New York: Viking, 1971]. I have written three novels in all. Right after the war, I wrote a novel called *Beggar's Choice,* which Howell-Soskin published [New York: 1947]. And some time later, I wrote *Blackmailer,* which I had called "Lipstick" [New York: Gold Medal, 1952]. That was done by Pocket Books, just a paperback.

I settled into being an Englishman. I wrote for *Punch,* reviewed books for the *New Statesman,* wrote the restaurant column for British *Vogue.*

You didn't miss the life in Hollywood?

No. I loved London. I was tired too. I needed a break.

What brought you back?

The tax laws changed. When we first went over, we had a wonderful tax break, living there. We came back in '74 when they were threatening to change the tax laws. It became dangerous to live there at that point. We thought we would come back to America and touch base.

Were you out of the loop by this time?

Oh no. I wrote some stuff. I wrote a misbegotten remake of [Alfred Hitchcock's film] *The Lady Vanishes* [1938], which was a disaster; then, I did a terrible picture with Frankenheimer called *The Holcroft Covenant.* And with Freddie Forsyth I wrote the screenplay of *The Fourth Protocol,* which he then rewrote.

With your track record, why did you agree to do such, as you say, misbegotten projects?

I needed the money.

But these films were ill advised . . .

Oh yeah. I got paid for all this stuff, but I really haven't had a movie made where I could hear my own dialogue, my own voice, for a long time.

Is that frustrating?

Yes!

At the same time, booze played a part in your downfall, right?

Drink played a great big part in my life. I finally had to cool it.

Did drink help you to write?

In the beginning, it did. I'll tell you why. It was a method for getting inside. The real writing comes when you are getting inside. When you write and write and write, and two hours pass and you have no recollection whatever of what you have written and it's all there on the page and it's all perfect. Those golden moments that happen occasionally. It's very hard to produce the climate that produces the work. Very difficult. For a time, drink helped. It got me relaxed and ready.

Even in the morning?

Yes, that was the beginning of the downfall.

Aren't there other ways?

I used to be able to do it by just doing it—when I was younger.

Later on—

I tried to induce it. By any means. Drink, drugs. Even speed, although speed was never any good. Speed was all right. Dexamil was something everybody took for a time, but that was no good because it had Amytal, and it made everything seem funny even if it wasn't.

I have painkillers for occasional head- or backaches, which are quite effective now and then against a deadline.

I understand.

Although sometimes it ruins the day afterwards.

Oh, afterwards. But if you get two hours inside, you're in good shape.

Some people see that sort of thing as addictive, whereas writers see it as—

A tool. A way to get inside. A means to an end.

Writers are willing to sacrifice their health and everything else for what they are writing. Eventually, of course, it turns on you.

Oh yeah, I had to cool it. I was never an alcoholic. I was a drunk. There's a big difference. Drunks don't have to go to meetings. Irony!

Is that part of why your output slacked off? Why the writing went bad?

Oh sure. Booze. The energy level was shot. Bad judgment. Judgment calls got crazier and crazier. I finally had to go to [the] Betty Ford [Clinic].

When did you finally kick the booze?

In '87.

How did the realization dawn on you?

It was either that or die. It was a toss-up. I didn't really care.

I used Ford to help me get through the physical addiction, because I was very sick. They used that AA method, which works with some people who like to sit around a room talking about how they used to drink. What insanity! But I desperately needed help to get through the interlude of change under controlled conditions, just to get through the harrowing, physical withdrawal. Then it took me a couple of years really, before I could function again.

Getting inside is tough under the best circumstances. Some days you feel like it. Other days . . .

It only happens at the typewriter.

What about on a train . . . on a notepad?

Metaphorically speaking, at the typewriter. Wherever you happen to work, but you have to be *working*. And suddenly, it takes off.

That's an oppressive thought some days. And it's arduous to get to that point.

Terrible sometimes, and the tricks and devices you have to use, and it's harder as you get older.

Some days coffee will do it.

I'm beyond coffee.

What personal tricks do you have?

The first and best one is the alternative of total humiliation. You've taken the money, and the deadline is now approaching. The or-else method. I function better if the heat is on . . . yet I hate to take the money up front, because that way you don't own anything. On the other hand, it's very hard to get producers to let you write something on your own.

I wouldn't think you needed any money . . .

I don't need the money, but I need it to embarrass me.

Like a carrot on a stick?

To beat me into writing.

Also, maybe to know that the project has a chance of being real, getting made.

I still have the illusion that anything I write is going to get done. It's turning into more and more of an illusion.

It makes you almost a Pollyanna.

The odds are tougher and tougher, Comedy dates. Comedy is very, very dated. A lot of my stuff is fifties-ish still—I can't deny it. I concede the fact that fashions change. I can't write social comedy anymore, because I don't know how yuppies talk.

Do you have tricks or habits with pencils and pens?

I play solitaire.

Until you're ready.

Until I'm ready. It's not just solitaire. It's involved with solitaire, but it's almost fortune-telling. I fantasize off the solitaire.

You're getting some message from the cards?

Yeah. It's also because I don't drink anymore. I don't smoke anymore. I've got to do something with my hands. I wear out decks of cards. It looks like I'm doing nothing, but my mind is going furiously.

Writing is such a mysterious process for me. For example, I don't use a computer, because I like the manual feeling of building something with my hands. Someone said to me recently, "Computers are wonderful. You can just push a button and change a character's name." Change a character's name! In my opinion, you've got to go to court and throw the whole script out if you have to change a character's name. The name is part of his identity. When I want to make a change, I retype the whole page. Each time I put something through the typewriter, it gets tighter and cleaner—and better. The first half of any script of mine has been rewritten forty—fifty times. That's the way you begin to get the stuff to jump off the page.

How long do you play solitaire before you start to write?

Sometimes all day.

How long do you do it before you give up?

I'm not as persevering as I used to be. That's why a deadline is so helpful.

Solitaire is a unique trick, in my experience.

You'd be amazed at the number of things you find on a writer's desk.

Where did solitaire come in? After the alcohol?

After the alcohol.

It wasn't there in the alcohol days?

No, no, no.

It's been seven years since you kicked booze. Have you been able to get back inside?

It's just beginning to come back.

That same, youthful energy?

Getting inside on my own. I just finished two marvelous scripts.

These two new scripts—

They are really the first products done without booze.

And the first things you're proud of since '68?

I know I'm writing well again. I've been able to get inside again, although I can't get them made.

Why?

I don't know why. The world has changed. Nobody can get a movie made. I have one that is in "turnaround" at Fox and one that is in turnaround at Disney.

You can get them in turnaround easy enough.

Boy, I can get them in turnaround, and I can get handsomely paid for doing it. But so far, I haven't been able to get either of them made.

The one in turnaround at Disney is marvelous. Somebody is going to make it, eventually. It's an adaptation of a minor, 1930s British classic called *His Monkey Wife,* by John Collier [*His Monkey Wife; or, Married to a Chimp* (New York: D. Appleton, 1931)].* I did a very loose adaptation. It's a love story between a guy and a chimpanzee. He's a schoolteacher in Africa, who brings his monkey to class, and the chimpanzee learns to read as he's teaching kids to read. Because he starts off with Jane Austen and the Brontës, the monkey's head gets filled with romantic nonsense until the monkey realizes this emotion she feels for her owner is love. It's very sophisticated and rather touching, not a kid's story. It's an outlandish story.

Can anyone in the Hollywood of today appreciate it?

No. Disney owns it. I had always wanted to do *His Monkey Wife* but didn't know how to beat it until, again, one day a couple of years ago I woke up in the morning, and I realized how. I tried to buy it and discovered that, not only did Disney own it, but they had been working on it for three years but didn't know how to beat it. I said, "You own it, I know how to beat it; maybe we should get together?" So I went over there, explained my ideas, and they said all right. I did all the required drafts. I loved it, they loved it. It went right up to the finish line before they decided no . . . and it went into turnaround.

---

* The British novelist and screenwriter John Collier moved to Hollywood and wrote the scripts for *I Am a Camera* and *Deception,* as well as collaborating on *Sylvia Scarlett* and *The African Queen.* Among his writings is a published screenplay based on John Milton's *Paradise Lost* called *Screenplay for Cinema of the Mind.*

Thinking over your career, I'm struck by how often things don't work out and by all the films that didn't come to fruition the way you hoped.

That's why it's such a narrow body of work. It isn't from lack of trying. You miss much more often than you succeed. I've been a professional writer, from 1940 until now—over fifty years—and I have a relatively small body of work, because a lot of it doesn't work out. I have maybe five or six pictures that I'm proud of, three plays that I'm proud of, and a lot of stuff that didn't materialize, maybe because I misread the rules.

Don't some of these experiences break your heart?

They all break your heart a little bit. But I've got a big heart.

Walter Bernstein:
A Moral Center

Interview by Pat McGilligan

The first time I met Walter Bernstein was at a socialist film festival in Burlington, Vermont. On the schedule was a revival showing of *The Front,* the 1976 standout comedy with a message—written by Bernstein, directed by his long-time friend and associate Martin Ritt—about the blacklist period in show business, with Woody Allen as the schlemiel who doesn't back down when bullied by the House Un-American Activities Committee (HUAC). After this and other programs about the blacklist, a panel of former blacklistees convened, which included the animator Faith Hubley, the documentary filmmaker Leo Hurwitz, and the screenwriters Maurice Rapf and Walter Bernstein.

Afterward, Faith Hubley introduced me to Bernstein. Faith knew Walter from days of youth, and from her and other people, I already knew that he was a person of enormous warmth and likability, as well as an iconoclastic fire-brand with a slashing comic sensibility. One of the reasons for his long, continuing career and his early breakout from the blacklist may be his likability. More than most screenwriters, Bernstein has persistently managed to get away with social statements in his produced scripts. His candor, sense of humor, and easy rapport with directors and producers has worked to his advantage.

One of the last of the blacklist era who is still active writing scripts, Bernstein began his career in the late 1940s with a Hollywood stint, which was interrupted by the blacklist (though he kept more than busy in television and with "fronts"), and his career reached a zenith in the 1960s and 1970s, with films such as *Fail-Safe, The Molly Maguires, The Front, Semi-Tough,* and *Yanks.* These are his best and most personal credits and, not coincidentally, are the ones most faithful to his scripts. In 1980, Bernstein took a detour into directing the remake of *Little Miss Marker.* Although the work officially slowed down, he did a lot of script doctoring in the 1980s and, between Hollywood credits, kept up a strategic presence (like many another refugee from the Golden Age) in the relatively open-minded field of cable television, where he found a temporary haven for his kind of films—stories with stance, troubling themes, and a moral center.

"Return to Kansas City" (1992), one-third of the *Women and Men 2* series, gave Bernstein an opportunity to adapt and direct a short story written by an old friend, Irwin Shaw. *Doomsday Gun* (1994), a true-life tale about a Reagan era arms merchant gone amok, was a compelling extension of topical ideas first explored in Bernstein's adaptation of *Fail-Safe.*

Throughout his career, Bernstein has written short stories and reportage (including a book of his columns from the *New Yorker* during World War II called *Keep Your Head Down!*). His "Marilyn Monroe's Last Picture Show," published in the July 1983 *Esquire*—Bernstein was the finishing writer on her last and unfinished film *Something's Got to Give*—is definitive journalism on Monroe. His critique of Elia Kazan's memoir, *A Life* ("Elia Kazan: A Stool Pigeon Named Desire," *In These Times,* July 6 – 19, 1988), is an equally conclusive character study of opportunism and deviousness. "He is not dirt," Bernstein wrote of Kazan. "No one is. But he soiled himself, and the stain remains."

The blacklist remains a live grenade for Bernstein. At the Barcelona Film Festival in 1988, he found himself involved in a panel discussion on the McCarthy era witchhunt with the director Edward Dmytryk and his wife among those, quite unexpectedly, in attendance. Dmytryk, who cooperated with the HUAC inquisitors after an initial term in jail as one of the Hollywood Ten, told the audience, "I never regretted anything I did. I feel myself a free man. McCarthy had nothing to do with it." Jules Dassin was one of the panel members who took the occasion to vehemently attack Dmytryk. Bernstein was another. "Mr. Dmytryk is scum," Bernstein told the audience. "It's not a debatable subject. I'm not interested if he's free or not." By the end of the nearly two-hour session, *Variety* reported, "Dmytryk's wife was in tears."*

Not only did Bernstein write *The Front* and *The House on Carroll Street* (1988)—a less successful but still rewarding Hitchcock-style mystery-drama, set in the McCarthy era, peppered with Nazis and spies and anti-Commie fanatics—but there is also his other blacklist script. This serious comedy is based on an unproduced play of Woody Allen's, and was originally intended to star Martin Ritt as a vulgar TV producer. After Ritt died, the film project was temporarily set aside, but now and then, Woody Allen talks of reviving it.

After I met and got to know Bernstein, I also met and got to know his wife, Gloria Loomis, who is now my agent. People who would like to know more,

---

* Peter Besas, "Old Wounds Reopened during Symposium on McCarthy Era," *Variety* (July 6, 1988).

Walter Bernstein in New York City, 1994. (Photo by William B. Winburn.)

after reading this interview, about Walter Bernstein's richly eventful life and career, will be happy to learn that he recently completed *Inside Out: A Memoir of the Blacklist,* which was published in late 1996 by Alfred A. Knopf.

Walter Bernstein (1919–   )

1948   *Kiss the Blood off My Hands* (Norman Foster). Coadaptation.

1959   *That Kind of Woman* (Sidney Lumet). Script.
        The Wonderful Country (Robert Parrish). Uncredited contribution.

1960   *Heller in Pink Tights* (George Cukor). Co-script.
        A Breath of Scandal (Michael Curtiz). Uncredited contribution.

1961   *Paris Blues* (Martin Ritt). Co-script.

1964   *Fail-Safe* (Sidney Lumet). Script.

1965   *The Train* (John Frankenheimer). Co-script.

1966   *The Money Trap* (Burt Kennedy). Script.

1970   *The Molly Maguires* (Martin Ritt). Producer, script.

1976   *The Front* (Martin Ritt). Script.

1977   *Semi-Tough* (Michael Ritchie). Script.
        Annie Hall (Woody Allen). Actor.

1978   *The Betsy* (Daniel Petrie). Co-script.

1979   *Yanks* (John Schlesinger). Co-script.
        An Almost Perfect Affair (Michael Ritchie). Co-script.

1980   *Little Miss Marker* (Walter Bernstein). Director, Script.

1985   *The Legend of Billie Jean* (Matthew Robbins). Co-script.

1988   *The House on Carroll Street* (Peter Yates). Producer, script.

Television credits include numerous script contributions to episodic television including *The Somerset Maugham Theatre; Danger; Charlie Wild, Private Eye; Colonel March of Scotland Yard; You Are There; Studio One; Westinghouse Playhouse;* and *Philco Playhouse;* and "Return to Kansas City," *Women and Men 2* (1992, adaptation and direction); *Doomsday Gun* (1994, telefilm, co-script); and *Miss Evers' Boys* (1997, telefilm, script).

Nonfiction books include *Keep Your Head Down!*

Academy Award honors include an Oscar nomination for Best Original Screenplay for *The Front*.

Writers Guild honors include nominations for Best Script for *The Front* and *Semi-Tough*. He also received the Ian McLellan Hunter Memorial Award for Lifetime Achievement presented by the Writers Guild-East in 1994.

Am I right? Did you start out as a newspaperman?
I started out as a fiction writer. I sold a story to the *New Yorker* when I was in Dartmouth. They published another story of mine, and then the war came along. I went into the army and started writing nonfiction: "Reporters-at-Large" for the *New Yorker*. Also I was on the army magazine called *Yank*.
After the war, the *New Yorker* pieces were published in a book that Viking put out called *Keep Your Head Down!* [New York: 1945]. It's a collection of all

the "Reporters-at-Large," I wrote over the four years I was in the army. It's a book about me, really.

Oh, is it a good book?

I think two or three of the pieces would stand up—the combat pieces would stand up. There's a long, three-parter at the end of the book about my getting into Yugoslavia . . . a kind of very gung-ho, lefty piece . . . that I don't know about. The rest I think would be very dated.

Was it hard for you to switch to nonfiction?

No, I liked doing it right away. After I got out of the army, I went to work for the *New Yorker* for about a year, writing other "Reporters-at-Large" and that kind of thing. I tried to write fiction again. I wrote a couple of stories which the *New Yorker* published during that time.

I didn't quite know what I was going to do after the war, actually. When I came back from overseas, I found myself a father with a year-old daughter. It was tough to get adjusted. But what I really wanted to do was to go to Hollywood. Movies had always been very important to me.

Why?

That's where I lived my real life. My fantasy life was at home. Starting Friday evening, after school and going through till Sunday afternoon, I lived in the movies. There was always this sense of weight dropping off me when they took the ticket and I walked into a moviehouse. It was very palpable, very important. I loved the movies.

Was that because your home life was so unhappy?

It wasn't happy. It wasn't unhappy. My father was a schoolteacher. We weren't affected by the Depression. The Depression was happening all around us, but we weren't affected.

You had to be solidly middle class to end up going to Dartmouth.

It was my father's dream that I go to Dartmouth. All I cared about was getting out of town. He knew somebody who was a prominent alumnus [of Dartmouth], and that's how I got in. My marks weren't particularly good. But Dartmouth was an experience. Going up to New Hampshire and New England was wonderful. I loved it.

Could you keep up with movies at Dartmouth?

There was a student there named Lester Koenig, a senior, who later became an associate producer for Willy Wyler.* He was [eventually] blacklisted also. When he was blacklisted, Lester went into the record business—jazz

---

* Lester Koenig met the director William Wyler while producing training films during World War II, and later served as his associate on films including *The Best Years of Our Lives* and *Roman Holiday*. Later, he formed the Good Time Jazz and Contemporary labels, recording top jazz artists such as Art Pepper, Ornette Coleman, and Benny Carter.

records—where he was quite successful until he had a heart attack and died. At that time, Lester was the movie critic for the *Dartmouth*. When Lester left, he bequeathed the job of movie reviewer to me, so I would see the movies that came up, a few times a week.

I got into trouble for panning *Lost Horizon* [1937]. I wrote a scathing review of it. For some reason, that caused a big commotion on campus. The man who defended me was a very interesting man named William Remington, who later, in the early fifties, lost his government job in a big Red purge and was sent to jail. He was killed in jail, bludgeoned to death.

Anyway, I was kicked off the newspaper. The only other movie experience I had at Dartmouth was when director Leo Hurwitz and [the photographer] Paul Strand came up to photograph *Native Land* [1942], and I drove them around while they were shooting.

Hollywood sent a number of their people to Dartmouth for some reason. Budd Schulberg, Maurice Rapf, Peter Viertel . . . Walter Wanger, who had been an alumnus, was very active in trying to set up a film department at Dartmouth.

It was this isolated, Republican, very reactionary, and very beautiful school. I liked it there. Of course, I knew, being a poor student and coming from Erasmus Hall High School in Brooklyn, with five thousand battling students, that I wouldn't have to work hard. I would get through okay.

All these kids from prep schools! I was very awed socially because I had never seen people wearing jackets that didn't match their pants. Where I came from, you wore a sweater, or you wore a suit. There was no such thing as sport jackets or odd pants.

Did you arrive at Dartmouth with a social conscience?

I had graduated from high school in the middle of the year—in January–February of '36; in those days, they had so many kids that they graduated them twice a year. My father had some idea of me that I was trying to fulfill, so he sent me to France with my high school French. I was terrified.

It was very exciting to be in France at the time. This was during the period of the sitdown strikes and the Popular Front. I fell in with a group of English kids who were also studying there, some older than I. They were very left wing. One of them was a big, hot Communist youth named Robert Conquest, who later became an avid right-wing anti-Communist and expert on the Gulag. Then the Spanish Civil War broke out. Conquest went down to Spain and wanted me to come with him—they were having an alternative workers' Olympics in Barcelona. I didn't have enough money and had to go home. But that started my political consciousness, the Spanish Civil War and anti-fascism . . .

Your politics didn't come out of your home situation?

No. I had a Communist aunt, a charter member of the Communist Party. But she was the black sheep of the family, and I didn't hardly talk to her until I was sixteen.

So, you're not a Red-diaper baby?

Not at all. Then, when I was at Dartmouth, from '36 to '4o, it was a very active time politically, because of the Spanish Civil War. Budd Schulberg had just left campus, and he had been a big left-wing editor of the daily paper. There was a lot of activity going on amongst a small group of us.

Beyond that, the war really formed me. I was lucky in that I went overseas for *Yank,* was able to move around; I got into Yugoslavia surreptitiously, interviewed Tito, and spent some time with the partisans in Italy. That really made me what I am, essentially, still.

Anyway, after I got out of the army, I had my book published. I met an agent through a friend by the name of Jerome Chodorov, the writer. Jerry's agent was Harold Hecht. Hecht got me a job working for Bob Rossen, who had the idea of making a movie out of a Chekhov story called "Grasshopper," about this flighty woman.* Rossen had a deal with Columbia, then. He had just finished directing *Body and Soul* [1947], and was hot.

Had you known Rossen previously?

No. I didn't know anybody at all in Hollywood.

Except through Dartmouth connections . . .

Well, Schulberg is the only one I really knew—only from visiting. He had come back my freshman year to work on [the novel] *What Makes Sammy Run?* He was very nice to me, by the way.

Anyway, I went out to Hollywood in July or August of '47 with this ten-week deal at Columbia, and I stayed for six months. Rossen and I talked and quickly discarded "Grasshopper." He was working on *All the King's Men* [1949], so I worked on that with him. But I didn't really work. I really sat and listened to him. He would use me as a kind of political barometer.

Why? He thought you had correct politics?

Yeah. It was a very funny time. One day he wanted to move the desk in his office from one place to another. He look one end and I took the other. All of a sudden, this man appeared in the doorway—tough-looking, bald-headed man. "What are you doing?" "Moving the desk." "It shouldn't go there, it should go here. C'mere." He took the other end of the desk. He looked at me and said to Rossen, "Who's that? One of your Commie writers from New York?" Rossen laughed and said, "Yeah." It was Harry Cohn.

---

* Robert Rossen was a veteran Warner Brothers screenwriter (*Marked Woman, The Sea Wolf, The Roaring Twenties,* etc.) who graduated to directing in the late 1940s with hard-hitting films, which he sometimes scripted, including *Johnny O'Clock, Body and Soul, All the King's Men* (which won the Oscar for Best Picture in 1949), and *The Hustler* (which won the Oscar for Best Picture in 1961).

Rossen knew my politics, and I knew his. He'd go down for meetings with Cohn and come back after having sold out some important political point, and we'd talk. (*Laughs.*) He was doing a juggling act, trying to make things work. But I learned a lot from him, just sitting and listening to him. He was very much a Warners product, that 1930s ethic. He was very ambitious, feisty. I rather liked him. And I got him to tell me stories about the Warner Brothers days . . .

Can you characterize what you learned from him in terms of script?

I learned about moving a story in terms of action—a kind of movie storytelling. At one particular point [in the script of *All the King's Men*]—it sticks in my mind—Rossen was trying to figure out how to tell the audience that the Huey Long character was not just a marvelous idealist. He wrote a scene—he didn't like it; it was too wordy. Then he came up with some idea of a scene with no dialogue, where Broderick Crawford is eating a piece of chicken as people are extolling him—cutting to him and his indifferent reaction—so that we know that he's not buying any of it. Things like that—visual detail, not dialogue—I learned that from Rossen.

Why did Rossen need you at that stage of his career?

He didn't need me. I think he liked me, and he liked having me around. I served as a sounding board for him, not just politically but in other ways.

He ended up writing that script himself, right?

Actually, the one who did a great deal of work and wrote a complete script, whom I always think got screwed on the credit, was Norman Corwin.

He did? He isn't credited on the screen.

Somehow Norman got screwed, because the script I read—afterwards, with his name on it—was not that far off from the script that was shot.

Anyway, the ten weeks were going to be up, and Rossen asked if I would stay on. But Hecht had just formed his company with [Burt] Lancaster at Universal, and their first film was going to be a thing called *Kiss the Blood off My Hands*.

I was getting $250 a week from Columbia, and Harold said he could get me $500. Besides being the producer, he was also my agent; so he took his percentage. I went to Rossen and told him they were doubling my salary at Universal. He said good-bye and good luck. I went over there, and they put me together with Ben Maddow, who had no experience.[*] I spent another four to five months, very happy months, working with Ben on that script.

Again, I learned a lot. Ben was the best pure screenwriter that I've ever met—really—in the sense of knowing that medium, understanding it, and working in it.

---

[*] Ben Maddow's long, fascinating career as a poet, documentarist, photography critic-essayist, and screenwriter is treated in *Backstory* 2.

We wrote what I always thought was a very interesting, odd, Hitchcockian kind of script, that I liked. Our script was never filmed. On the basis of our script, they got the director [Norman Foster], [the cinematographer] Gregg Toland, and Joan Fontaine to play opposite Lancaster. Then they did what they usually do. They hired another writer [Leonardo Bercovicci] who, I felt, made it much more ordinary than it was. I think the structure is still ours but very little else.

It's true ours was a kind of strange script, but I liked working on it with Ben, and I got to know Lancaster, because I didn't have a car and lived in Beverly Hills. He was shooting *All My Sons* [1948] at Universal at the time, so he would pick me up in the morning and drive me to the studio and talk.

Did Lancaster have any political convictions or affiliations?

I don't think so. He was very unformed still. He would ask me questions about what books to read or what music to listen to. He wanted to take acting lessons to be a better actor, but Harold wouldn't let him. In the story conferences, I always had learned to listen to what Lancaster had to say, even when I didn't agree with him, because his concerns always came out of something real. They came out of intelligence and looking for something. I liked him, though he was a strange man in many ways.

I finished that picture, and I had to make a decision whether to stay in California. I had two kids by then, but my marriage was foundering. So I went back to New York, at Christmas of '47, for domestic reasons, essentially. I had had a very good time in California, the kind of good time I would have later on in Los Angeles. But I was unsure where I wanted to live.

After I went back, the marriage broke up. The divorce was a difficult, messy one. I had intentions of continuing to work in movies. But I felt I had to stay in New York. I was just beginning to work in live television when I got blacklisted, and that put a stop to movies.

Tell me how you first met Marty Ritt and Sidney Lumet, how far back you go with them, and why you proved so compatible with them as friends and collaborators.

Marty and I met first. Marty I met shortly after the war—'45 or '46. I'm vague about how we met or through whom, but we became friends. We used to play ball together in the park on Sundays, softball in the spring and summer, then touch football in the fall. My happiest memory of those days—which doesn't involve Marty, although he was in the game—is blocking out Irwin Shaw, who weighed about one hundred pounds more than I did, so that John Cheever could run for a touchdown. Irwin was astonished, and I was pleased.

Then, in the late forties, Marty and his wife practically supported me. I lived with them after my marriage had broken up. I lived on their couch. They had a little one-bedroom apartment on West Twenty-second Street. His wife was working for the Yellow Pages, selling space, making very little money, so Marty supported us by gambling.

We first started working together in television. Marty got a job directing something called *The Somerset Maugham Theatre,* a half-hour dramatic show based on Maugham's stories. I wrote some of those for him. And Sidney and I first met on a half-hour show at CBS called *Danger.* Marty had been the producer and Yul Brynner was the director and Sidney was Yul's assistant. When Marty and Yul left the show, Sidney became the director, and that's when our friendship started.

Marty and Sidney and I all came from the same kind of background—New York, Jewish. Sidney and Marty had both acted in the Group Theatre. Sidney had been a child actor; his father had been an actor in the Yiddish stage. So we all came out of a certain, naturalist thirties tradition—Clifford Odets and those kinds of plays. We tended to relate to the same kind of material, apart from whatever our personal feelings were about each other.

What was your attitude toward television?

Television was just starting. Live television was very attractive because it was dramatic writing. It wasn't really movies, more like the stage. You were making it up as you went along. Nobody knew what it was supposed to be. And a lot of very talented people were involved in it—like Marty and Sidney.

Those *Danger* shows were actually quite good, as I remember them, although they were done quickly. One of the early *Danger* shows I wrote, which was called "The Paper Box Kid" and based on a Mark Hellinger story, starred Marty as an actor. It was a half-hour show in which Marty played a hoodlum who goes to the electric chair. Marty hadn't acted for eight years or something like that, and he just exploded. He was wonderful, just wonderful—the show was an incredible success. People would stop us in the street or at the racetrack for weeks afterwards and talk about it.

There was also a show for Herb Brodkin called *Charlie Wild, Private Eye,* a half-hour show. I forget what we got for a script in those days—$200, maybe. That whole show was done for $5,000, in which the packager took $1,500, I remember. But the show was kind of fun.

I gather this was just on the cusp of the blacklist. How did you find out that you were going to be blacklisted?

Well, the producer of *Danger* was a man named Charles Russell, who had been an actor under contract to Sam Spiegel at a time when he was "S. P. Eagle." Charlie had given acting up and become a producer—he was a very nice, totally apolitical guy. Anyway, Charlie came in one day and said, "I can't use you." I said, "Why not?" He said, "They just told me you're on some sort of list. I'm supposed to tell you we're using different writers . . . or we're changing the style of the show . . . or something like that." I said, "Oh." He said, "Just put another name on the script." He was really sticking his neck out, because if they found out about him, he would have gotten in trouble.

So I did that. I wrote a few shows under a pseudonym. Then they were kind of getting wise and began demanding real people, fronts, so I had to get fronts.

Did you have any alternatives besides writing for television?

I did a few magazine pieces under my own name before the television thing got started—that was still a little area that I could work in. I wrote a piece for *Argosy,* for example, on the life of a jockey. But I couldn't make a living.

Why were you blacklisted, how were you named, in the first place?

I was blacklisted because my name was in *Red Channels.* That's the only thing. I was never named, at least publicly. I was subpoenaed later on, but I never appeared.

Why were you in Red Channels?*

Six or eight listings—Russian war relief, anti-fascist appeal, Spanish refugees, an article for the *New Masses,* something for a black veterans' organization . . . oh, they were all true.

Could you go and confront anyone in television about it?

Nah. Because they would always deny it—either deny it, or the networks had someone then—some vice president of affairs—who dealt with that sort of thing, and who would ask you for a statement to clear yourself. Or you could go to George Sokolsky or Frederic Woltman in the *World-Telegram* . . . one of those things. Since I wasn't about to do that, it was academic.

For the next eight years, it was a question of getting different fronts and working that way. Around that time, Abe Polonsky came east, and along with another man I had become friends with, named Arnold Manoff, we formed a kind of group, the three of us, trying to get fronts and helping each other get work.† We wrote many of the subsequent *Danger* shows. Then they started a show called *You Are There,* and we wrote almost all of those under various names.

---

* According to Larry Ceplair and Steven Englund's authoritative *The Inquisition in Hollywood: Politics in the Film Community, 1930–1960* (Garden City, N.Y.: Anchor Press, 1980), "Taking up where HUAC left off, the American Legion and a private firm called American Business Consultants culled HUAC and Tenney Committee reports, appendices, and hearing transcripts, back issues of the *Daily Worker,* letterheads of defunct Popular Front organizations, etc., to compile a list of people who could not be accused of 'Communism' but who had, at one time or another, dallied with liberal politics or causes. The Legion published two magazines, *Firing Line* and *American Legion Magazine,* and ABC put out a periodical entitled *Counterattack* and an index called *Red Channels;* all these publications carried attacks on individuals, organizations, and industries, as well as long lists of names of 'subversives.' "

† Abraham Polonsky is best known for his Academy Award–nominated script for *Body and Soul,* and for writing and directing *Force of Evil* in 1948; then, over twenty years later, after the interlude of the blacklist, for the writing and direction of *Tell Them Willie Boy Is Here* in 1970. The screenwriter, playwright, and novelist Arnold Manoff, whose career was abbreviated by the blacklist, had several 1940s screen credits, including *Man from Frisco, Casbah,* and *No Minor Vices,* for which he received a Writers Guild Award nomination. He worked for television and films under several noms de plume in the 1950s. His wife was the actress Lee Grant.

I also worked on *Studio One, Westinghouse, Philco Playhouse*—mostly the one-hour dramatic shows. I did everything from Thornton Wilder's *The Bridge of San Luis Rey* to, I remember, an adaptation of F. Scott Fitzgerald's short story "Rich Boy," which starred Grace Kelly and was a very successful show.

Did the three of you have anything to do with the Robin Hood series?

Ring [Lardner Jr.] and Ian Hunter did most of those. Abe and I did a show for that same woman, [the producer] Hannah Weinstein—*Colonel March of Scotland Yard,* with Boris Karloff. We wrote a bunch of those together.

Did the three of you actually pool your money?

No. The group had very strict rules. Whoever found a job, that was his job, and it was up to him if he wanted to share it. If I was working on something and heard about something else, I could then bring it into the group, and we might decide among us who needed to do it. But whoever did the work, that was their money. The money was never shared. What the group had was an obligation to help anybody on a script. If I was having problems on a script— on *You Are There* particularly, we were always trying to figure them out—we'd do them together.

The thing that made it work is we were all on the same level of competence. Since producers never knew what style was—one person's style—we could get away with it. For example, on the *You Are There*s, I did all the Civil War stuff; Abe took the weighty subjects, like Savonarola and Galileo and Beethoven; Arnie did the philosophical stuff like the death of Socrates. We did what interested us, and it was a very happy arrangement.

Did you talk about the ideas you were putting into the work, consciously? Did the three of you get in a room and chortle over some political parable you were writing?

No. Never. The only thing we chortled over—and chortle is really not the word—is the *You Are There* shows. At that particular time, it was right in the middle of the McCarthy era, and a lot of the shows were very strong civil liberties shows, about Galileo or Milton. Some were quite tough and very good. They were a strange combination of camp and closely reasoned, dramatic stuff that we felt very good about and were conscious of doing. The other stuff, no.

On the other hand, I was talking to Sidney Lumet once about the *Danger* shows we did in the 1950s—those half-hour melodramas—and we realized, talking about them, that they were all about betrayal, all quite grim. I suppose that's the way I felt at that time . . . and it's true that sometimes the things I felt closest to were the stories about people doing rotten things to each other.

Where would you get your fronts?

They came from all kinds of places—from people who wanted the credit because they were trying to get ahead; from people who wanted the money. Some people did it out of friendship—those were the ones who lasted. The ones that did it for the other reasons never really lasted. They'd get worried. Ego would interfere in some way.

I remember there was a very nice man, a good writer, who let me use his name for a couple of shows. It was a bad time of my life. They were comedy shows and not very good. He got very upset I was letting him down with his name on them. In a very nice way, he detached himself from it. I couldn't blame him.

The front that worked the best for me was an old friend of my brother's, someone I had known since I was ten years old, who had a job on a trade paper, didn't want to take any money for being a front, and kind of liked the whole idea of going up to story conferences—the playacting part of it. He was the one I used mostly. He was very helpful.

You think of that period as being such an awful period, and it was. But within that, that sense of friendship and helping each other—which we all did, not just the three of us—was very real.

One of the things that was sad after the blacklist was that everybody went back to the same, old, dog-eat-dog kind of thing. People remained friends, but the whole camaraderie, that whole sense of helping each other, as part of your existence, disappeared. I missed that.

Your partnership with Abe and Arnie was happily sustained for eight years?

Yes. It was very important. Of course, we all did things outside the partnership. Abe went and did a movie in Canada, *Oedipus Rex* [1957], with Tyrone Guthrie, I think. Abe also wrote a movie for Harry Belafonte and Bob Ryan, a grim melodrama called *Odds against Tomorrow* [1959] . . .

But you yourself didn't do anything in motion pictures for eight years, from '50 to '58.

No. Only television. My contacts in movies were very limited. Until, in '58, Sidney Lumet got a movie to direct [*That Kind of Woman*]. The producer was Carlo Ponti. They needed the script rewritten, and Sidney called me. Ponti didn't know from American politics, and he hired me with, I assume, Paramount paying my salary. Since I wasn't known out in Hollywood at all, since I hadn't been active at all politically out there, I was able to work. I did the script and in fact went out to Hollywood to finish it up.

My agent, Irving Lazar—he was introduced to me by Irwin Shaw, and became my agent on this movie—got me a lot of money. Lazar told me he could always get more money for someone who was new than for someone who had been around a long time. Funny, I went to Europe later on to do films for George Cukor and other people, and when I came back—it was less than a year later—I found I couldn't get a job. I called Lazar and asked what was happening. He said, "Look, someone like you makes a lot of money, so it's hard for me to get you a job . . ." This was less than a year later! I guess I had stopped being new.

Anyway, Paramount liked what I was doing, and they were talking about me working for Ponti again. As I was finishing the script, Lazar called me and said Paramount had decided not to make a new deal, because there was a subpoena out for me. The House Un-American Committee was having what turned out to be their last hearings—this was in '58, I guess. I said, "Thank you very much," packed my bags, left, and flew back home.

I went to stay with a marvelous pair of people named Harvey and Jesse O'Connor, an old radical journalist and his wife. They had a great house in Rhode Island. I hid out there and finished *That Kind of Woman*. Leonard Boudin was my lawyer. He got in touch with the committee, who confirmed there was a subpoena out for me. The hearings were held in New York, and I wasn't served. That was the end of it.

It was very funny, because around that time I had a meeting with Ponti—Ponti, an interpreter, Boudin, and me. Leonard explained what had happened, what my position would be, that I was not going to be a cooperative witness. The interpreter translated everything. Ponti said something to the interpreter in Italian. The interpreter turned to us and said, "Mr. Ponti would like to know who has to be fixed and for how much . . ." It was all politics, bullshit, to him. Making a movie—now, that was serious. His attitude was, let's just pay somebody off and get to work.

Was there ever any question that you might not get your screen credit on That Kind of Woman?

No. That issue never came up.

Wasn't that sort of unreal at the time?

I didn't know. Everything was going so fast then.

When Sidney first talked to you about That Kind of Woman, *he had a political background, he must have been aware that he was heading into unknown territory by employing you?*

Oh, sure. He had known about me working all those years with a front. It was no secret. He was complicitous in that.

Most sources say Dalton Trumbo broke the blacklist with Exodus *in 1960. That means you came up with a screen credit almost two years before. That puts you at least two years in the vanguard. At the time, you were not particularly aware of it?*

No, Marty Ritt had gone out to Hollywood, and the impression he had was that the blacklist wasn't as firm as before . . .

Was there a sense of there being more loopholes on the East Coast?

No. But by '58, there were cracks in the blacklist. Although, at that last hearing, Lee Grant, who was married to Arnie Manoff, was called to testify, and several other people too . . .

Your relative anonymity in Hollywood served you well at this juncture.

I think so. Otherwise, I wouldn't have been hired. But after I finished the first script, I couldn't get another job. Paramount was still insisting I testify.

There was this writer, Robert Alan Aurthur, who had helped Marty get his first directing job.* Now, Aurthur was going to write *The Magnificent Seven* [1960] for United Artists. Marty [Ritt] was involved in some fashion. They were also involved together in planning the movie about Spartacus.

Originally, they had asked me to write *The Magnificent Seven* script, but I had chosen the Ponti deal instead. When the second Ponti script fell through, Robert Alan Aurthur went to Marty and said, "I'm not blacklisted. I can work anywhere. I know you offered this to Walter before. So I'll back out. Give it to him now." Marty and Yul [Brynner, one of the stars of *The Magnificent Seven*] went to United Artists and took the position with [the executives Arthur B.] Krim and [Robert S.] Benjamin and the others that they didn't know anything about any subpoena; all they knew was that I had just finished a script with Paramount, so therefore I was employable. I was hired and did a draft of *The Magnificent Seven.*

Yul was supposed to direct it, but then Tyrone Power died, and they asked Yul to replace him in whatever movie he was doing in Spain [*Solomon and Sheba,* 1959], offering him a lot of money. Yul chickened out of directing, I think. He would have been an interesting director.

After that I went to Lazar and said, "Look, I can work. I've just done this and the other thing . . ." Lazar called Paramount, and they said, "Nope, he's got to go testify . . ."

Then I got a call from one of the executives at Paramount, asking if I would come in and meet with the head of Paramount—a man named Y. Frank Freeman. Very, very reactionary southern gentleman. I said, "Sure"; I went in. He was a very courtly combination of shrewdness and idiocy. He started off telling me a long story about a technician's strike in Hollywood with all of "his boys" out on the picket line. He said he could have settled the strike by going out and talking to them, but "Russian-looking" men kept interfering. (*Laughs.*)

He had my whole dossier on his desk, going back to college. He said, "Would you mind if I asked you some questions?" He went down the complete list of everything I had ever done. I answered honestly. By that time, I knew I wasn't going to be destroyed—I'd been through the blacklist—and I wanted to work. I said, "Yeah, I still believe in this . . . I'd still do this . . . maybe I wouldn't do this anymore . . . but it's all true." He liked me. He said, "I've helped people like you in your situation," and he proceeded to name a

---

*   The writer-producer Robert Alan Aurthur was a prolific writer of articles, short stories, books, plays, teleplays, and motion picture scripts. His adaptation of Arthur Koestler's *Darkness at Noon* won an Emmy. His story "A Man Is Ten Feet Tall" was adapted by him for the director Martin Ritt's feature film debut, *Edge of the City.* Aurthur's other screen credits, alone or in collaboration, include *Warlock, Grand Prix, For the Love of Ivy, The Lost Man* (in which Aurthur doubled as director), and *All That Jazz.*

couple of the stool pigeons—Sterling Hayden, I forget who else. He said, "I want to help you. Be honest with me. If you get subpoenaed, what are you going to do?" I told him what I was going to do—be an unfriendly witness who wouldn't name names. He said, "Well, don't go then. There's no point in going if that's what you're going to do." He said, "Let me think about this. Let me consult with my good friend Jim O'Neill, who is head of the American Legion, who I talk to about things like this, and I'll get back to you." I said, "Fine." Two weeks later, they called me and said, "You can work." That's how I got cleared. Because Y. Frank Freeman liked me, and also because I had a kind of I-don't-give-a-shit attitude. I wasn't interested in arguing.

By that time, I think, the end was beginning, although I still could not work in television for two or three years afterward. The irony of it is, the next television I did was much later on when they tried to revive *You Are There* as a Saturday afternoon children's show. The producer called me and asked me to do a couple. I said, "Sure," as long as I could put my own name on it this time.

The second script that Ponti wanted you to do was Heller in Pink Tights, *for director George Cukor, right?*

Right. Dudley Nichols had written a script or a treatment, but he was very sick and couldn't go on with it. I was introduced to Nichols once, I think, when I first came to work on the script, but I never saw him again. I knew who he was, of course. I was very impressed by him.

They had a start date, and they had Tony Quinn. Since I was under contract to Paramount, they put me on the script, and I wrote that picture about a week ahead of shooting . . . sometimes they would catch up to me, so that I'd be bringing in the pages in the mornings they were supposed to shoot that very day. It was both a good and a terrible position to be in—if you could bring them something they could shoot, you were a hero.

Was director George Cukor involved at all in the scriptwriting process?

Yes, but everything was so hectic. George was much more involved with [the art directors George] Hoyningen-Huene and Gene Allen, and the style of the picture, really. It was not his kind of movie really, a western. What interested him was the idea of this theatrical troupe in the West—this kind of picaresque, crazy bunch of people.

Tony was dreadfully miscast in the part. He was too heavy for it; it required a much lighter touch. It was a part that Jack Lemmon or James Garner should have played, essentially. Cukor wanted a young English actor nobody had ever heard of by the name of Roger Moore. Of course, no one was going to give him Roger Moore.

In fairness to Tony, he didn't have the pages. He couldn't go home and read the script and work on his character. Nobody knew what they were getting the next day. That was very tough on everybody.

I suppose Tony did do a very good job, considering; but he was a big pain in the ass during the shooting. Taking issue with this, not liking what he had to do there. I remember at one point during a script conference with him, Sophia [Loren], George, and I don't know who else, George got so angry that he got down on his knees and started to *salaam* in front of Tony, because he was just so angry he didn't know what else to do. That defused the situation. It also defused George's own anger.

On the other hand, George was very courtly and very nice with Sophia, who was still not yet a star and very uncertain of the language.

What was your impression of Cukor?

I was enamored of George. I thought he was a wonderful man—a gent, extremely generous, funny, and bitchy.

I was entranced by that trio of Cukor, Huene, and Allen—Huene was a very elegant baron; Gene Allen was an ex–LA cop that Cukor found somewhere and brought to work for him, and was of a considerably developed aesthetic sensibility. Allen looked like a cop, talked like a cop, but Cukor was able to see what he had to contribute, and Gene was very, very valuable. Gene did all the camera setups; he walked through them and laid them out.

Did that strike you as unusual?

Not in that context, really. Because you never felt that he was doing something that Cukor couldn't do, particularly. Cukor was very smart that way; he didn't have an ego in that sense—he used whatever he could.

The best moment in the picture—when the Indians raid the trunk of costumes, a marvelous scene—that's really what George was interested in in the film. I wrote a lot of scenes that were shot but cut out of the movie, because when he finished it, Paramount didn't know what to do with it. It wasn't a typical western. I know they made George shoot a couple of action scenes that weren't in the original script. He had no interest in doing that, but he was very much a company guy: he knew he didn't have control; that was it and on to the next thing. Then Paramount cut it their way—which was to cut out all the quality and the character, and go to plot. The plot was ridiculous!

So I've always felt that picture—apart from the fact that what was really shot was, in script terms, first draft—fell between two schools. It wasn't really a straight, bang-up western, yet I'm very fond of the movie . . . when I look back on it, with my own subjectivity, I was so happy at the time. I had just recently been cleared of the blacklist, I was working on something I loved, and there I was on a movie set! I just saw everything in a glowing kind of way.

After Heller, *you worked with Cukor twice again.*

After *Heller,* I went to Europe for Ponti and got stuck in Vienna, rewriting some terrible, terrible thing [*A Breath of Scandal*]—I think the only movie I ever took my name off—it was just awful. Michael Curtiz was the director, but [Vittorio] De Sica was really directing it, afterwards. Ring Lardner [Jr.] had just finished a version and left, so I got put on it. Every ten minutes, a very nice man who was Ponti's partner—Marcello Gerosi—would come to me and say, "Now, look, you've got to write in a part here for an Italian actress

. . ." I'd say, "Listen, this is taking place in the Vienna of the Austro-Hungarian Empire. How am I going to do that?" He'd say, "Never mind how. If you put the part in, we'll get six million lire from Italy . . ." They were putting the picture together that way. Curtiz was kind of in his dotage. He would leave the set, and De Sica would come in and direct behind his back. Also, De Sica had to be paid in cash at the end of every day for his gambling. It was just a terrible, ridiculous mess, and I couldn't wait to get out of Vienna.

Then the [Charles] Vidor company came to Vienna to film *Song without End* [1960], and Vidor died. Then George came to replace Vidor. I found out that George was in Vienna and called him just to say hello. He said, "As long as you're here, why don't you read this script?" He sent over the script, and I read it. I remember I said to him—he had Dirk Bogarde playing the lead— "My best advice to you is to get rid of Dirk Bogarde and get Sid Caesar. Then, just film the script." It was like a parody, just a terrible script. He said, "Would you stay and do some work on it?" I said, "No, I can't. I've got to get out of here, or I'll go crazy . . ." My wife-to-be was waiting for me in Paris.

The picture was being partly produced by Charles Feldman, the agent. Feldman's mistress, Capucine, was playing the lead in it, one of her first movies. George said to Feldman, "I want Walter. I need him to work on this picture. Go get him." Feldman came to Paris, found out where I was—turns out he was an old friend of the lady I was going to marry—and for the first and only time in my life, I was subjected to this great Hollywood wooing. Every night he took us out to the best restaurants, saying things like "Just do two weeks for me; I'll get you twice your pay"—the whole *schmear.* What's fascinating about it is that 99 percent of you is laughing at what is happening, but there's another one percent in the back of your mind that is saying, "Well, maybe, who knows? . . " Finally, I said yes to the two weeks.

It was very funny because we were supposed to have dinner with Feldman that night, which was a Friday, and as soon as I told him yes, two hours later I got a call back from him saying, "Geez, something has come up. I can't have dinner with you tonight . . ." The wooing was all over, finished.

Anyway, I went back to Vienna and met with George. I said, "Look, there's nothing much we can do in two weeks . . . let's just go through the script step-by-step on the basis of what you have to shoot first, and we'll just fix the scenes as best we can, and make them less egregiously awful." He said, "Absolutely."

I remember the first scene I started on was a scene between Wagner and Liszt. I rewrote the scene and brought it to him. He said, "It's not right." I said, "I know it's not right, but it's better, isn't it?" He said, "It's better, but it's not right." I said, "But it's better; let's keep going." I ended up spending two weeks on that one scene—really, in this terrible picture where there is only this one very well-written scene. George couldn't let it go. He was fascinated by it. It hurt him to let it go.

We would meet in the morning in his hotel room. I remember getting a big basket of marvelous fruitcakes—he would eat all of his and then take mine—talking about that scene. Maybe one reason why actors liked George so much is that he was marvelous with a scene, getting all the values out of that scene, whereas he was not great in the overall conception or arc of the script. That may be one of the reasons why he was so good in the studio setup. The studios knew how to use him; he did his best work under the aegis of the studio. As soon as he had to choose his own material and become a producer-director or something else, I think he was a little bit lost.

The only other time I worked with George was on the last Marilyn Monroe movie, *Something's Got to Give.* I was on the picture about six weeks. I was rewriting it when it shut down. Although the original that it was based on was such a good movie [*My Favorite Wife*, 1940] that you wondered why they wanted to change anything.

I had read somewhere that they were looking for writers for this project at Fox. I called Lazar and said, "How about this situation?" He said, "I'll call Zanuck and get on it right away," but then I never heard anything from Lazar. So finally I just picked up the phone and called George. He said, "Are you free? That's great. Absolutely." I asked, "Didn't Lazar call you?" He said, "No." I called Lazar, and the deal was made.

Again, it was an impossible situation. What was interesting is that nobody really liked Monroe. I didn't like her, particularly; the one I liked was Dean Martin, who I thought behaved terribly well. He liked to swing his golf clubs, and I had heard about his drinking; but when he had to do something on the set, he was very professional. He wasn't an actor of the sort that Cukor was used to dealing with—Cary Grant and Jimmy Stewart, people like that—but I liked him.

Whereas Monroe was totally unreliable. Nobody knew what she was going to do. Cukor was very calm about her. Just terribly nice, always. Courteous. And optimistic. "It's gonna work, we're gonna do it . . ." I never saw the other side.

How was Cukor when it all came down?

Fatalistic. He'd been in that mill for a long time. I remember what [the director] Lewis Milestone said to me once—he was a great raconteur—he had one terrible story after another about Hollywood. I asked him, "How can you take this abuse? How can you live with this?" He looked at me with his marvelous hooded eyes and said, "How does an alley cat live in the alley?" Cukor had a little bit of that. He'd seen it all. He did his job and lived in his nice house . . .

After the blacklist ended and your credits resumed, you could have moved back to Los Angeles.

I had made the decision to live in New York. In certain ways, in terms of career, it was not a good decision. Perhaps I would have had a stronger career if I had stayed in Los Angeles. I wanted to live in New York—it isn't just having grown up here—I guess it's that old cliché-feeling about living in Los Angeles. I don't know if I'd make the same decision now.

There weren't that many films that originated in New York. Most of them came from Los Angeles. But I always managed to get enough work. And those were the days when they would fly you back and forth for a story conference. I liked going out there and living for a month and playing tennis with my friends.

When I did *The Molly Maguires,* which I coproduced with Marty [Ritt], I went out there for cutting and postproduction, and was in California for six to eight months. When I did *Little Miss Marker,* I was there for a year and a half. So I've spent a lot of time there. But I was never *of* the place, and probably that didn't do me any good.

Because, ultimately, they realize that and resent it?

I think they do, in some kind of way. They want to know you're there. They want to know they can call your agent, and you'll be in the office in an hour. They want to know they have that kind of control over you: that you are part of their labor pool. Especially in those days. Less so, now.

Sidney Lumet (looking through viewfinder) with Henry Fonda, filming *Fail-Safe.*

Apart from Cukor, for a long time in the 1960s and 1970s, it seemed as if you were virtually alternating films between Marty Ritt and Sidney Lumet. Was that deliberate . . . or coincidence?

Coincidence, really. Sidney works continuously, one thing after another, and basically, he doesn't tie himself to any one particular writer for very long. Whatever comes along that attracts him, or that he likes, he does.

Marty was, I think, much more politically oriented, as was I. I think that was the basis for Marty and I working together. Sidney would also do socially oriented movies, but Marty was always looking for material that had some kind of strong political or moral base. That is also a side of the street that I work—I like to do entertainment films that have some kind of social content.

Did you consciously choose that venue for yourself after the blacklist? Or is that just the way things developed?

It's the way things developed, but also the way I was. The way I am. And after a while, people chose me for that, if indeed they ever wanted that particularly, which they never did.

I remember visiting a prison art class once and speaking to the teacher. He told me that when prisoners are first learning and feeling their way as artists, they draw very harsh and realistic scenes of their daily lives: prison walls and steel bars, fellow convicts. Then, when they get past that stage and begin to explore their talent, they cut loose and draw almost any fantastical thing they can imagine. Can it be that, after the long years of the blacklist and writing under fronts, you were slowly emerging from a kind of mental prison?

It may have been. I never thought about it that way, particularly. I probably felt that is what I *should* be doing—that kind of material.

Were films like Paris Blues, Fail-Safe, *and* The Molly Maguires *a struggle to get made, or was the struggle somehow easier in the 1960s, when it came to socially conscious films? Did the political context of the 1960s make those subjects more feasible?*

I think so. But in the cases of both *The Molly Maguires* and *The Front,* those films wouldn't have gotten done unless we attached stars to them.

I saw Fail-Safe *again recently and was struck by how breathtaking it is stylistically. Was it written that way?*

That's Sidney. I wrote the script very quickly; then, Sidney directed it a lot like a television show. Sidney was always enormously adept technically, much more so than Marty really, much quicker with the camera. He tended to think in terms of the camera.

Sidney's camerawork can be bravura, whereas Marty's is more self-effacing.

Sidney is much more related to the camera than Marty was. Marty's style was very unostentatious. Really, he was totally interested in and believed in the primacy of content. He was also very related, as was Sidney, to actors. Marty liked to put the scene up and let the actors go to work.

Did those differences affect how you wrote for one, as opposed to the other?

No. In Marty's case, how he worked tied in a lot to how I felt. Perhaps because my relationship has always been more to words than to the camera, I tend to write that way, concentrating on scenes for actors. I tend to write a very lean script. I very rarely put in a camera direction, mainly because what I found out rapidly—early on—was that the director paid no attention to my camera directions anyway.

Working with Marty and Sidney, two old friends, also guaranteed the integrity of the script. They usually knew how to get around the obstacles— whether the obstacles were the studio or some star.

Certainly. Sidney was always very resourceful, and Marty was a fighter. He fought for what he believed in. He wouldn't do anything that in some way he didn't believe in.

Whereas, when you worked away from them, you didn't always have the same success, scriptwise. I am thinking of The Train. *Another Burt Lancaster situation . . .*

Well, Burt was running that show. It was a very unhappy experience. [The director] Arthur [Penn] and I were working on what we thought would be a very interesting movie about the tail end of a war and people who were fighting in the back lines. Then Lancaster fired Arthur after the first days of shooting. It was very unfair. It wasn't based on anything except whatever's Burt's feeling about Arthur may have been.

A personality conflict?

I think so, basically. I remember Lancaster coming over to Paris, where Arthur and I had a script meeting with him. He had read what I was doing, and he had ideas about the script and professed himself to be pleased with what was going on. I remember after I left the meeting, I was feeling very up about it, and Arthur said, "He [Lancaster] doesn't like me." I said, "What? He loves the script and . . ." Arthur had picked up on something I had not.

Unfortunately for the scheduling of the picture, the first scene that Burt had to do was a rather emotional scene with Michel Simon. I was there when they were shooting it, and Arthur was pushing him, as an actor, to go for certain things. Burt was resisting. At one point—I'll never forget this—Burt turned to Arthur and said, "Here, I'll give it the grin." He was saying, I'm not going to do what you want me to do. And shortly after, Burt fired him.

Was your script honored?

I'd been working on the script. By no means was it finished. Burt called me and said he would like me to stay on. I said I really didn't want to and finished out the week. He got some other writers working on it after that.[*] It was always the same story, and it's a good movie in certain ways, although Arthur

---

[*] Franklin Coen and Frank Davis are also credited for the screenplay of *The Train*.

"One of the rare, pure experiences": Sean Connery (center) in *The Molly Maguires.*

had really set up all the scenes. But the film was disappointing. We were after something else, and as I say, I thought it was really unfair to fire Arthur not based on anything.

The Molly Maguires, * *coming at the end of the decade, was really a high-water mark—and one of the few, serious films from Hollywood about organized labor—another being* Norma Rae, *also directed by Martin Ritt. What was the genesis of* Molly Maguires?

I had always wanted to do something about the Molly Maguires, ever since I first read about them in college. I found there was very little written about them at all. They always intrigued me. I always had in the back of my mind the idea that the subject would make a great movie. I had talked to Marty about it. Then, when the opportunity came, we just grabbed it. At that time, Marty had clout, and we were able to make a deal.

---

* The Molly Maguires were "a secret society of Irish anthracite miners in east Pennsylvania (c. 1854–77), which terrorized management and workers until with the help of Pinkerton's, the leaders were arrested and then hanged for murder" (*The Merriam-Webster Pocket Dictionary of Proper Names* [New York: Pocket Books, 1970]).

That's the most surprising thing to me. It didn't take a big effort to persuade the studio?

No. Paramount did it at a time when money was around. Where we got hurt was, Paramount produced several big-budget films around the same time; ours was the smallest, about a ten million dollar budget, I think. The others included *On a Clear Day You Can See Forever* [1970], *Paint Your Wagon* [1969], and a Harold Robbins film, *The Adventurers* [1970]. They were all initially unsuccessful at the box office, and Paramount made the corporate decision to dump them all, including *Molly Maguires.* It was never really allowed to find its audience, although over the course of time it has, of course, attracted a following. And I am certainly proud of the film. It was one of the rare, pure experiences.

All along, you had a hankering to write comedy. Why did you put it off so long? At what point, after your long string of serious dramatic credits, did you feel a lessening of the dramatic impulse?

Well, you're right, I had always wanted to do a comedy. Humor was very much a part of me. In college I was editor of the humor magazine. Even in high school, I wrote a humor column for the school newspaper. It was always there. I just kept it down. I didn't think it was serious, just as nobody thought going to Hollywood was serious. If you were going to be a writer, you should write plays or novels.

But for a long time, Marty and I had been talking about doing something about the blacklist. We wanted to do a straight dramatic story about someone who was blacklisted. We could never get anybody interested at all. It wasn't until we came up with the idea of a front and making it as a comedy that we were able to get the film done. *The Front* became my first true comedy.

When I spoke to Marty, he seemed to feel the film should have been done dramatically, and that the comedy aspect was a compromise.

I don't agree with him, really. The idea that you can't be serious in a comedy, I don't agree with.

I think what he actually said is that you and he were having some trouble licking it as a drama.

I don't think that was the question. I think we could have licked it in a formal sense, in a conventional sense; but it soon became apparent that nobody was going to produce it. We couldn't get anything going there. I'm glad we did what we did.

Did the idea of writing it as a comedy come before the idea of putting Woody Allen in the film as the star?

Yes. We went to David Begelman, who was the head of Columbia then. Being the kind of perverse guy that he is, David gave us some money to do a first draft. It was only after we had a first draft that discussions began about a star. We talked about Dustin Hoffman, Al Pacino, or Warren Beatty. Certainly, I saw somebody in the role who was not a conventional leading man. I remember, we were talking about it, and Marty said, "What about that . . . kid?" I said, "What kid?" He said, "Woody Allen." I said, "What a very interesting idea." So we sent the script to Woody, and he said yes.

It was a very happy experience for all of us. Whether he would acknowledge it or not, Woody got a great deal from Marty in terms of his acting. He was on the film purely as an actor. He didn't write anything. He only contributed a couple of jokes. The one time he tried something on the picture was the sequence at the end [of the film] where he's testifying before the committee. We shot the scene and looked at the dailies, then decided we should make it funnier than it was. Woody said, "Let's shoot it again, and let me improvise." Marty set up the camera, and Woody improvised. He was hilarious. Only it had nothing to do with the picture. It was like ten minutes of stand-up comedy. Reluctantly, we couldn't use it.

In some way, I think that picture released me, because I could do comedy after that. I loved doing *Semi-Tough,* which was really a social satire—not just about football. Things like *The Molly Maguires* and *The Front,* which came from scratch, are very important to me and mean a lot to me. But so does *Semi-Tough,* although it came from a book [*Semi-Tough,* by Dan Jenkins (New York: Atheneum, 1972)]. [The director] Michael [Ritchie] and I threw out the story and wrote one of our own. Michael and I did our own movie, just like Marty and I did our own movies.

"My first true comedy": Walter Bernstein and Woody Allen on the set of *The Front.*

Burt Reynolds and Kris Kristofferson in a scene from *Semi-Tough*.

Michael and I developed a good relationship and wrote other comedy scripts—one was an anti-FBI satire; another was a satire on radio psychologists. But we couldn't get them produced.

How do you feel about Yanks?

I love *Yanks.* I wish it had been twenty minutes shorter. The texture of the movie is what the movie is about—the look of it, the sense of it. The story itself is commonplace, soap operaish. [The writer] Colin Welland had worked for a number of years getting the film made. The story is about where he was coming from; he's really the kid in the story. I did the American stuff; essentially, that is all I did.

I think it has one piece of bad casting in it: William Devane, who is a good actor. He's not right for the part. But everybody else is so good.

Why did they come to you to help on the script?

I think because I had been in the war and had those credentials. I did use a lot of my own experience although I had not been in England. And I liked working with [the director John] Schlesinger. I thought he was very much like Cukor—in his sensibility and in something which they shared: for both of them, the total arc of the picture was where they were weakest. On the details, the scene itself, the visualization of the scene, the texture, they were wonderful.

When I see that picture, *Yanks,* I'm always moved by it. I don't know how much of it is my own nostalgia. But there's something lovely about it.

Why did you end up directing Little Miss Marker? *An offer you couldn't refuse?*

Essentially that's what happened. There were a lot of personal reasons that went into it. I was asked to write the script. I didn't think there was a chance to direct, but I said I would write it if I could direct it.

Is that something you had been saying again and again for years?

No. I'd been thinking it, never saying it.

Who did you say it to this time—who answered yes?

Jennings Lang—lovely, lovely man. His attitude was, I've set a lot of first-time directors loose in the business; you may as well be another one.

Before I started directing, I called all my director friends and asked their advice. I got all kinds of totally different advice. I called Cukor, and he said, "Ah, don't worry. It's nothing . . ." I said to Michael Ritchie, "I don't know where to put the camera. Where do I put the camera?" He said, "Ah, don't worry about it. Wherever you put it, it will be all right." I called Schlesinger, and he said, "Coverage! Coverage! Just be sure you get enough coverage." None of the advice helped.

Were you insecure about directing?

Yes, I was very tentative about it, in part because it coincided with a difficult time in my personal life. I was never able to emancipate myself from that. But I didn't think it through enough. I winged it too much. I made a lot of mistakes. I look at it now, and I'd like to start that picture all over again. It was the kind of picture that needed a lot more style than I was prepared to give it.

Theatrical style? Visual style?

Both. It needed a very strong style imposed on that picture—a Preston Sturges style. I did it much too conventionally.

Did you make the major casting decisions?

Not totally. I had [Walter] Matthau to begin with, which was wonderful. For the female lead, I chose Julie Andrews because I thought I could get something from her which in fact I was unable to get. I thought I could get some kind of mix between her and Matthau, but it didn't work, possibly my fault or possibly because there wasn't any chemistry there.

Was it also a failure on your part to relate to the actors?

No. I feel that I can relate to actors, but I think I cast it wrong. I cast Tony Curtis where I should have cast Jack Palance. I cast Julie Andrews where I should have cast Angie Dickinson. I went the wrong way. Both Tony and Julie were quite good but not quite right.

The House on Carroll Street was another partial failure. I like it, but it should have worked better. It's a good idea—a blacklist drama with Hitchcockian overtones. What went wrong?

Like *The Molly Maguires* and *The Front,* it was an original and meant a lot to me. But you're right; it didn't turn out so well. I'm not happy about it.

I gather your script was different from the eventual movie.

The original script was good—and it was the script that I started out to write. The script that was shot was also my script, however. There's nothing in it that isn't mine, so I can't very well say they took it and changed it. But it got unfortunately watered-down and became kind of a one-note thing that happens to have unfelicitous casting. It doesn't work.

In general, I've been very lucky with directors about my scripts. None of them ever wanted to write or to direct their own stuff. With Sidney, he'd read the script, he'd have very strong ideas about certain things, and that would be it. Marty would always spend more introspective time on a script. The difference is also in their personalities and their characters. Michael's full of ideas. Sidney's responses are very quick. Marty was always slower, he thought more, chewed it around.

On *The House on Carroll Street,* I am tempted to say to people . . . there was more to the original script . . . there was a scene that should have been there and is out . . . and there's a scene they shot, which they didn't use. But I feel terrible doing that. I hate myself for it.

A complicated question: After 1972, you did not work with either Sidney or Marty again. Or, at least, nothing came to fruition. Why?

It just happened. With Sidney, as I say, he goes from one project to another very quickly. But Marty and I were always talking about doing something. We were always in process. It was not that easy for us to find material, or rather, the kind of material we wanted to do was not that easy to get produced. But we were always talking about something, and in fact, before he died we were talking about a particular project—a complicated political story about the end of communism. I'm sorry about the things we never did do.

The 1990s is actually your fifth decade of writing movies. Do you find a Hollywood that you can relate to, receding from grasp?

I really try not to fall into the nostalgia trap and say, "Gee, it was better twenty years ago." One of the last times I had dinner with Marty, he was saying that he felt, in his experience there of the last thirty years, that he has never seen studio executives more incompetent, venal, or corrupt than now. But I don't have that much to do with people in Hollywood. I find it depressing when I have to go out there and meet with them. I never found it exhilarating, particularly. I do find the standards lower. I really do. I find the standards of literacy lower—film literacy, let alone intellectual literacy. There was never, in my experience, this marvelous Golden Age where all that was done was so sacred. And I feel Hollywood today reflects where this country has been going for the last eight, ten, fifteen years. Why shouldn't it?

The old-boy networks and executive relationships have sure changed.

Oh yeah. Also, they're all interchangeable. It's fascinating. Some years ago, I went out to Los Angeles to pitch story ideas. My agent set up meetings with Mike Medavoy, Jeff Katzenberg, and Ned Tanen—whoever. You have these meetings with them and always their two assistants. At the end of the day, I couldn't remember who was who of the assistants. With beards, without beards—whatever. Depressing. They're bright but interchangeable . . .

Yet you persist in the field . . .

It's where I make my living . . .

Is that the only reason? You could do a Sidney Sheldon and write novels?
. . .

I love movies. I *love* movies. I still get that frisson when I go on a movie set—the most boring business in the world—but I feel that same thing I felt when I walked on the lot of Columbia in '47: I'm here! It's always meant that to me. I've always wanted to be part of making movies.

Which movies are enduringly happy memories for you—more successfully yours?

The originals—*The Molly Maguires* and *The Front; Semi-Tough;* even though the credit is shared with Collin [Welland], *Yanks,* which I feel very strongly about; and *Fail-Safe.* The good ones. But the ones that are not so good I feel are mine too, in the sense that I can't point to any of the ones I've done and say, Well, somebody crapped up my script, because that's not me up there.

I accept the cooperative nature of filmmaking. It's one of the things that attracts me to movies, that idea. I love working with other people, so that I never feel, or have never felt—maybe it's a lack of ego—bitter. I accept the nature of that beast—not just accept it, I *like* it. When I'm working with people I respect, who add creatively to the whole of the thing, I find it exhilarating. I'm a sucker for any kind of communality or community, anywhere but especially, when it's working well, within a film.

Horton Foote:
The Trip from Wharton

Interview by Joseph A. Cincotti

The bench is Pilgrim century. The paintings, about two dozen of them, are early primitives, mostly New England. The subjects don't so much pose as stare. Though the apartment is in New York City's Greenwich Village, a short stroll from the Hudson River, the feel is that of a decorous front room, a room you might find in one of the better homes of a small rural town, like, say, Wharton, Texas. The Two Academy Awards won by the resident of the apartment are not in evidence.

A number of years ago, Albert Horton Foote bought the last two available grave sites in the Wharton cemetery. In 1993, his wife, Lillian, his sometime producer and constant confidante, was laid to rest in one of them.

In Wharton, the live theater is confined to pageants at the local church. There is no movie theater. The last picture show unspooled awhile back. However, thanks to the ubiquity of the video store, most of the Foote oeuvre is available, even there, for rent.

But for the breadth of his acclaim, Horton Foote, the most famous son of Wharton, Texas, might be classified as a regional writer. The affinities are obvious between Foote and William Faulkner, Eudora Welty, Flannery O'Connor. Foote has fictionalized Wharton into Harrison, his Faulknerian demesne, his Yoknapatawpha County, yet his territory is both broader and narrower, the landscape of the human heart. He is a chronicler of foibles, petty tyrannies, crossed purposes, intentions thwarted and realized in stories spun out in a novel, 34 produced plays, at least 29 teleplays stretching from television's golden age to the era of the miniseries, and 14 films, including *To Kill a Mockingbird* and *Tender Mercies,* both of which won him Academy Awards.

His reputation as a screenwriter is secure on the strength of those Academy-honored efforts, and of the films *The Trip to Bountiful* (which also earned him an Oscar nomination) and *Of Mice and Men,* directed by and starring Gary Sinise.

He is an actor's writer. His films find their power in the confluence of text and performance. Offhand, you may not recall, in any of Foote's films, a big moment or an immortal line. He eschews the obviously clever line, the overtly theatrical declamation, the profane outburst, the writer's wink. He doesn't write clips for the highlight reel. What he gives actors is the opportunity to build a performance moment to moment. Some take it. Gregory Peck, Robert Duvall, and Geraldine Page—all won Academy Awards for their performances in films he wrote.

As a young man, Foote left Wharton to become an actor. He bounced around Los Angeles, Washington, D.C., and New York, training in the standard American style of the day, before discovering Stanislavski through an émigré disciple, Tamara Daykarhanova. He wrote a scene for an acting class.

Horton Foote in New York City, 1995. (Photo by William B. Winburn.)

The scene eventually became a play and in 1941 was produced as *Wharton Dance*. Foote traded grease paint for a fountain pen. He still writes with a fountain pen today.

Until recently, he has been a quiet but perennial presence in New York theater, the important off-Broadway houses providing a constant if temporary shelter for his work. Then, in 1995, his *Young Man from Atlanta* won the Pulitzer Prize in Drama. Another play is scheduled to open in New York in 1996, after a circuit through several regional theaters. Although Horton Foote is eighty years old, he has three screenplays in development. Every day, in notebooks or on long legal pads, he writes.

Horton Foote (1916–)

1956   *Storm Fear* (Cornel Wilde). Script.

1962   *To Kill a Mockingbird* (Robert Mulligan). Script.

1965   *The Chase* (Arthur Penn). Adapted from Foote's play and novel.
          Baby, the Rain Must Fall (Robert Mulligan). Script, based on
              Foote's play *Traveling Lady*.

1966   *Hurry Sundown* (Otto Preminger). Co-script.

1968   *The Stalking Moon* (Robert Mulligan). Uncredited contribution.

1971   *Tomorrow* (Joseph Anthony). Script.

1983   *Tender Mercies* (Bruce Beresford). Script.

1985   *1918* (Ken Harrison). Script.
          The Trip to Bountiful (Peter Masterson). Coproducer, script based
              on Foote's play.

1986   *On Valentine's Day* (Ken Harrison). Script, based on Foote's play.

1991   *Convicts* (Peter Masterson). Script, based on Foote's play.

1992   *Of Mice and Men* (Gary Sinise). Script.

Television credits for *Philco-Goodyear Playhouse, Studio One, Playhouse 90, DuPont Play of the Month,* and *U.S. Steel Hour* include "Only the Heart" (1947); "Ludie Brooks" (1951); "The Travelers" (1952); "The Old Beginning" (1952); "The Trip to Bountiful" (1953); "A Young Lady of Property" (1953); "The Oil Well" (1953); "Rocking Chair" (1953); "Expectant Relations" (1953); "Death of an Old Man" (1953); "The Tears of My Sister" (1953); "John Turner Davis" (1953); "The Midnight Caller" (1953); "The Dancers" (1954); "Shadow of Willie Greer" (1954); "The Roads to Home" (1955);

"Flight" (1956); "Drugstore, Sunday Noon" (1956); "Member of the Family" (1957); "Traveling Lady" (1957); "The Old Man" (1959); "Tomorrow" (1959); "The Shape of the River" (1960); "The Night of the Storm" (1961); "The Gambling Heart" (1964). In addition, Foote's television work includes Flannery O'Connor's "The Displaced Person" (1977); William Faulkner's "Barn Burning" (1980); "The Story of a Marriage, Part 1, Courtship" (1987); and "The Habitation of Dragons" (1992).

Plays include *Texas Town, Only the Heart, Celebration, The Chase, The Trip to Bountiful, Traveling Lady, The Midnight Caller, John Turner Davis, Tomorrow, A Young Lady of Property, Gone with the Wind* (play, with lyrics), *Night Seasons, Courtship, 1918, Valentine's Day, In a Coffin in Egypt, The Man Who Climbed Pecan Trees, The Roads to Home* (three one-act plays: *Nightingale, The Dearest of Friends,* and *Spring Dance*), *The Old Friends, Cousin, Road to the Graveyard, Blind Date, One-Armed Man, The Prisoner's Song, Lily Dale, The Widow Claire, The Habitation of Dragons, Dividing the Estate, Talking Pictures, The Young Man from Atlanta,* and *Laura Dennis.*

Published screenplays include *Three Screenplays* (*To Kill a Mockingbird, Tender Mercies,* and *The Trip to Bountiful*).

Novels include *The Chase.*

Academy Award honors include Oscars for Best Screenplay Based on Material from Another Medium for *To Kill a Mockingbird* and Best Original Screenplay for *Tender Mercies;* and an Oscar nomination for Best Screenplay for *The Trip to Bountiful* (Adaptation).

Writers Guild Awards include Best Script for *To Kill a Mockingbird* (Adaptation) and Tender Mercies (Original); and a nomination for Best Script for *The Trip to Bountiful.* He received the Writers Guild Laurel Award for Lifetime Achievement in 1993.

You said once, when speaking of Harrison, Texas, "I did not chose this task, this place or these people."
No. They chose me. That's absolutely true. I no more consciously chose that than I flew to the moon. The kind of writers that I like, I have a hunch that's mostly true of: that their material chooses them, rather than vice versa. I have tried to write some things about other places, some of them pretty good I hope.
What things are you thinking of?
Assignments. Like adapting a book for a movie, or something like that.
You consider that just an assignment?
Because it isn't something that comes from inside. I try to take assignments very seriously, but they aren't something coming organically from me.

How does it happen that a place chooses you?

I don't know what makes a certain kind of writer interested in a sense of place or time. I only know that it's true of people whom I admire very much: Reynolds Price, who is of course a great novelist, writes about his little patch of North Carolina; Eudora [Welty] writes about Jackson, Mississippi; and Flannery O'Connor wrote about Georgia.

It has nothing to do with good or bad writing. There are certainly wonderful writers that write very differently. But look at Joyce; he lived in Paris and was obsessed with Dublin. He indeed wrote back constantly [to Dublin], asking what happened on this day at this place at this hour—"Can you remember and tell me right away?" Gertrude Stein was very abstract, but even her abstractions, if you understand and know enough about Gertrude Stein, have a basis of some kind of reality, which is often Baltimore and America.

When did you know that Harrison, Texas—or Wharton—was going to have a claim on your imagination?

I always knew that. I think the first thing I ever wrote was called *Wharton Dance,* and the second thing was called *Texas Town.* I didn't decide on the name Harrison until later because I really wanted to get away completely from people asking, "Is this about so-and-so, or this or that person?" It helped a little bit to give the place a fictional name.

Is there an element that is oedipal in your writing so much about your mother and your father?

I couldn't really answer that, could I? That's something *you* would have to decide. I haven't thought about it. It's just what I seem to know. Certainly, I seem to be fascinated with trying to find a pattern or some kind of order to all this.

On the one hand, you have a great affection for your parents. On the other hand, as a writer, you have an absolute duty to be as honest as possible.

Absolutely. It helps that my parents are not here. I can be objective in a way you couldn't be otherwise. Some writers have no feeling for that, but I do; it would worry me. My mother and father openly admitted that these stories were based on them, and I did it because I was very fascinated with their particular journey, but in truth, you know, they're much more of a collage than anything else. I think this is what you do when you're writing. I don't think you're out to just specifically copy. Somehow, the material goes through a transformation.

I understand that after you left home your mother wrote to you every day until the day she died.

Well, not every day, but for a long period of her life, she did. After I got married, it was less—maybe three to four letters a week—but up until then, it was every day. She had a remarkable knack for letter writing. She kept me in touch with that whole world down there.

You've been prolific in your career. Hearing that about your mother, people might think they understand something about your prolificness.

(*Laughs.*) I hadn't thought about that. It's true, though my mother had no ambitions as a writer. She was just a natural-born letter writer.

Were you a natural-born letter writer?

No. I didn't like to write letters. I've learned to. I have a daughter who is a natural-born letter writer, and I've realized it's very important to write letters.

When you were in California as a young man—then in New York and Washington—what effect did her letters have on you, coming so frequently, as a developing writer?

I think they had a great effect on me because I was able to keep in touch with people and things that I wouldn't have known about ordinarily. Without any strain, they just kept me in touch with the dailiness of their lives and the lives of that town; and it was that dailiness that always interested me. She didn't necessarily write me a sensational, gossipy letter, although once in a while, she'd tell me something out of the ordinary, but mostly, it was a kind of record of their day-by-day living and the living of people around them—we had a large, extended family.

Do you ever pull these letters out to help you with your writing?

Unfortunately, no. Unfortunately, many of them are gone. I'm sick about it.

What happened to them?

When you're young and you're living from hand to mouth and you don't know where your next meal is coming from and you're moving around a lot—because you can't pay the rent—you just don't hold on to things. I wish I had them, but I don't. But they're all in here somewhere. (*Points to his head.*) That's the important thing. They were an enormous help to me.

Did you get to the point where you could discern the subtext of your mother's letters? Were there things unwritten in your mother's letters?

I haven't ever thought about it. Actually, I wouldn't think so, because she was very explicit, nothing veiled or hidden at all. That's one thing I learned as an actor: to search for the subtext in the material. I never think about it while I'm writing, but later on, I'm delighted if one senses a subtext.

I know you studied for a long time as an actor and were influenced by the Method. Can you tell me a little bit about Tamara Daykarhanova?

I stumbled on her early when I was a young actor. A very well-known actress of the 1930s, named Rosamond Pinchot, met me on the street in New York and told me she would pay me to be her scene partner, working with Tamara. That's how I met Tamara. Tamara Daykarhanova was a student of Stanislavski's, who had been with a very famous revue called Balieff's *Chauve Souris,* which toured Europe. Her husband [the aeronautical engineer Sergius Vassiliev] got into deep political trouble with the interim government before the Communist government, so they had to leave Russia. They came over here and first worked with [Maria] Ouspenskaya, who had started the American Laboratory Theatre and was a very famous teacher of the method. When Ouspenskaya went to Hollywood, Tamara started her own studio [the Tamar Daykarhanova School for the Stage]. She brought into the studio Andrius Jilinsky and [his wife] Vera Soloviova, both from the Moscow Art Theater, who had been members of Michael Chekhov's company. They taught the Stanislavski system, which I am very indebted to because it taught me a great deal about play structure. I worked in Tarmara's studio with Vera for about two years, out of which we started a company called the American Actors Company [in 1938]. I guess, you'd call it an off-off-Broadway company now, but it was over a garage. That is where I first started writing.

Vera was really a great influence. I kept in touch with her through the years. She had been in Stanlislavski's famous production of [Charles Dickens's] *Cricket on the Hearth,* playing the blind sister, and then she was the second Nina in *The Cherry Orchard,* replacing the original Nina. She and Andrius Jilinsky were both members of [Eugene] Vaktahngov's first studio and of course were very steeped in the Method. Having also worked with Michael Chekhov, they had their own approach to acting.[*]

What did she teach you?

First of all, for me there was a whole period of unlearning the bad habits I had picked up in my conventional training as an actor, which was to be very vocal and to work things out vocally rather than to find my inner life. They gave us a whole series of exercises for actors—

Including the circles of attention?

Jilinsky taught that technique. We really did scene study with Vera.

Are you still, these fifty or more years later, influenced by the Method? Do you still find yourself writing in the beat?

Absolutely. The whole sense of the through-line, the sense of actions, what people *want* on stage.

Can you explain what the 'beat' is?

It's just an arbitrary term. It's like, what is the beginning of an action and the end of an action, you might say. The first beat of the play might be any moment that begins and ends.

The smallest unit of acting?

It could be. As you work on, you try to make the beats larger. At first, you might break them down into infinitesimal beats; then you try to make them larger. Some people use the term 'beats.' Other people use the term 'actions.' It

---

[*]   Additional background on Stanislavski's disciples in America can be found in Christine Edwards's *Stanislavsky Heritage: Its Contribution to the Russian and American Theatre* (New York: New York University Press, 1965), which makes mention of the American Actors Company and Horton Foote.

all means the same thing, really. The reason I like to use the word 'beat' is it's almost a musical term. It's like a musical phrase.

How did the Stanislavski system or method help you as a writer?

It applied to me wonderfully as a writer, because in my work as an actor, I would break a play down so that, without really knowing it, I was studying its structure in the sense of what it was the characters wanted. That's really much more important than the result of the character: what do they want, what causes the conflict between them, what is the structure of the scene, what is the overall through-line of the play, what is the spine, what does everything kind of hold on to. That was one way in which I could instinctually, as an actor, work on trying to understand the play.

Can you think of any other writers you would consider Method or system writers?

Oh, I don't think anybody in the modern theater has escaped it. They may think they have. They may disallow it or think it's tiresome or unnecessary. But you can't be in our theater and not have been, on some level, influenced either for or against the system or the Method. How is that possible?

What kind of career do you think you would have had as an actor if you hadn't become a writer?

Oh, my God, I don't know. I shudder to think of it, because I don't think I could take the pressure an actor has to go through. I loved acting, but I wasn't happy acting like I am happy writing. I loved it, and certain parts were very easy for me, but then other parts were very difficult. There are some actors that just enjoy taking on any role and finding certain things in it for them. I had to take roles that I felt instinctively in sympathy with. But I didn't act for very long, and we are talking about a long time ago.

Can you tell me about the gestation and incarnations of The Trip to Bountiful—*from Lillian Gish to Geraldine Page?*

Oh, well! Fred Coe was a remarkable man and remarkable producer.[*] He had started the *Philco-Goodyear Playhouse,* and was commissioning people to write television plays. I had done one for him, and he was anxious that I do another. You had to go in and tell him just a few lines of the script, which I have always felt was a horrendous experience.

Sort of a pitch?

We'd call it a pitch today. It was a sort of gentle, mild one, but that's exactly what it was.

I had an idea based on a certain situation in my family that haunted me. Originally, I had tried to start the story of *The Trip to Bountiful* on the day that Mrs. Watts was forced by her father to marry her husband—emotionally, if not

---

[*] See the Jay Presson Allen and Arnold Schulman interviews for additional *Backstory 3* reminiscences about the producer-director Fred Coe.

physically, forced—and the story just wasn't working. By that time, I knew enough to know that you can't use your well if it's not working. So I just put the work aside, and I don't know how or why—what the mechanics were—but a couple of days later, I realized I had started the story all wrong. I decided I had to start at the end of her life. When I did that, I wrote the script very quickly.

I could never tell one of my stories until after it was written, because it would ruin it for me. After I wrote it, I went down to see Fred and told him the story. He used to say that all I told him was something about this old lady who wanted to get back home. I don't believe that; maybe it's true. Then, he used to say—he always laughed about this—"Two days later, you sent me a full script." Of course, the script was already written.

Well, we did the play on television, and of course, it was 'live'. None of us realized the power and phenomenon of the play, but that night we began to sense it, because after the show the phones in the studio started to ring, and they rang and rang. People were calling and talking about Lillian Gish [who played the leading role of Mrs. Carrie Watts]. They had seen her performance and were excited because they had not seen her for years. The response was so emotional.

Then the Theatre Guild asked me if I would turn it into a full-length play, and I did.

It only ran thirty-nine performances, right?

No, more than that. First, we did it at Westport [a theater in Connecticut] for a week. Then we took it to Wilmington and Philadelphia before we brought it into New York. Lillian had an enormous success in it, and Jo Van Fleet [as Jessie Mae Watts, the daughter-in-law who hates Mrs. Watts] won the Tony that year. The out-of-town notices had been just stunning, but the New York notices were disappointing—okay, but not what we hoped. Then we had a newspaper strike, and it was rough. But the play had great partisans, even then. People would come to it three times to see it. People who liked the play liked it a lot. It was [Brooks] Atkinson whom we expected to just fling his hat in the air, because he had been very kind to me in other reviews. He loved Lillian Gish and was kind to the play, but dismissive.[*]

So the play began to have a legend. People remembered the production with fondness. Over the years, I had many movie offers, but I kept turning them down because I wanted Lillian, very badly, to play the part; and in those days, Hollywood felt she wasn't bankable. People tried to talk me into all

---

[*] Brooks Atkinson, in his *New York Times* review of November 4, 1953, praised Lillian Gish's performance as a "masterpiece," but said of the play that it did "not make for a very substantial play for a whole evening. Nor does Mr. Foote make things any better by underwriting. He is a scrupulous author who does not want easy victories, and that is to his credit morally. But he might also do a little more for the theatre by going to Bountiful himself as a writer, providing his play with more substance and varying his literary style."

kinds of other actresses they felt were bankable—like [Katharine] Hepburn—all very interesting women. But I just said, "No, this role belongs to Lillian Gish." When she hit ninety, I realized it was a losing cause, and I couldn't do anything about it any longer.

That's when [the director] Peter Masterson called me up and said he wanted to do a film and this was his choice. I said, "First thing, Pete, the stumbling block is, who is going to play the part?" He said, "What about Lillian?" I said, "I have to tell you. I think she's too old now. The whole point of Mrs. Watts is that she isn't really a very old woman—[they] have put her into that category. And secondly, I don't think, physically, she can take the job. If you ask her, she'll say yes; so don't dare ask her." I never saw Lillian after that. I hope she forgave me, but she knew how loyal I had been up until that time. It must have been hard on her, because she loved the part.

Did you rewrite the play in those intervening years?

No, never.

Did you do some rewriting for the film?

For the film, I added things, of course. You had to. It was the first time I could actually take the trip, because in the days of live television, the restrictions of television were much like theater. Peter said, "Who do you want in the part, then?" I said, "I want Geraldine Page." He said, "I absolutely agree." That was it. Except nobody wanted Geraldine Page. People suggested Anne

Rebecca De Mornay (left) and Geraldine Page in the film *The Trip to Bountiful.*

Bancroft or Jessica Tandy—I can't tell you who all they wanted. But I can be stubborn. I just bulled my neck and said, "Well, we're not going to do it unless . . ." Peter and Sterling [Van Wagenen], who was by then the coproducer [with Foote], backed me up. Of course, once we got Geraldine, they were all happy, as well they should have been.

How was Geraldine Page's Carrie Watts different from Lillian Gish's?

Oh, I know how. I'll tell you one thing that everybody says: "Lillian was very ethereal." That's not so. Lillian had certain qualities that *seemed* ethereal, and at moments, she had great spirituality, but she was as tough as a pine knot. She really was *strong* and had as much strength as Geraldine Page. Geraldine didn't play it quite as purposefully belligerent; she played it more slyly than Lillian. But they were both wonderful.

I'll tell you who was also remarkable in it just recently—Ellen Burstyn. She was in a revival of the play almost two years ago. She was extraordinary. The root was the same, but she was different. So I've had three remarkable actresses, very different from each other.

Where do you think that piece of work works best—on television, on the stage, or in film?

In all three, it worked well in its own time. Certainly, Lillian was more effective in some ways in the theater, because she had more space to work with and she had a wonderful company. Geraldine, of course, gave a landmark performance. For this last production, the play also had real vitality, and the audiences just ate it up. I never tire of watching it. I'm very impersonal about it. It's almost as though I didn't write it.

Tell me a little bit about your first screen credit, Storm Fear.

It was a learning experience because I knew nothing about the movies. I took the job because I rather liked certain things about the book [*Storm Fear,* by Clinton Seeley (New York: Holt, 1954)], and I liked Cornel Wilde.

Why did he come to you?

I think because someone had seen my play *Traveling Lady* and told him about it. He, in those days, was doing films for little money, and since this was my first film, I think he thought he could get a good writer for little money, if you want me to be truthful about it.

Did you go out to Hollywood for a time?

Yes, I did. Not during the shooting but just to work on the script.

Was Cornel Wilde helpful to you at all in terms of the script?

No, but he didn't interfere in any way. I liked working with him. I worked with Cornel at his house and at Columbia. There were certain things we talked about, but in the end, I just plunged in and did it.

Did you have contact with any other Hollywood writers?

Mostly people that I had known before, mostly theater or live television writers. And there were some actors I'd known that I was in touch with. But I was on my own with that script.

Did you have any particular impression of Hollywood at that time?

Not too much, except to save my money and get out of there as quickly as I could.

Why "quickly"?

I just didn't feel that it was a place for writers to be, and I still don't think so.

I think when people hear your name, what immediately comes to mind is the big three or four films: To Kill a Mockingbird, Tender Mercies, The Trip to Bountiful, *and* Of Mice and Men. *Perhaps they are less familiar with your plays. How do you feel about that?*

I can't help it. Nothing I can do about it. Those things right themselves. My plays are being done now a great deal outside of New York.

Can we talk about To Kill a Mockingbird *and* Of Mice and Men? *When your telephone rings and someone asks you to adapt a work of literature, what is your reaction?*

Well, I don't like to adapt, to begin with. It's a very painful process—a big responsibility—particularly if you like something, which I usually have to do. In the case of *Mockingbird,* it was sent to me, and I said, "I'm not going to read it because I don't want to do it." My wife read it—she's passed on now—but she had enormous influence on me. She said to me, "You'd better stop and read this book." So I read it and felt I could really do something with it. [The producer] Alan [Pakula] and [the director] Bob [Mulligan] had offered it to Harper [Lee, the book's author] to adapt, and she didn't want to do it. They felt she and I should meet, so they brought Harper out to Nyack, and we had an evening together and kind of fell in love. That script was a very happy experience.

Was it harder or easier to adapt than you thought it would be?

Not hard, because first of all, Alan Pakula was the producer, and he's very skillful. I have to find ways to get into things. I had read R. P. Blackmur, a critic I admired, and he wrote a review-essay about it called "A Scout in the Wilderness," comparing the novel to *Huck Finn.* That meant a lot to me because *Huck Finn* was something I always wanted to do and still would like to do as a film—if you could, although you would have to wait until the era of being politically correct about it has passed. The comparison to *Huck Finn* made my imagination go.

Harper also told me that [the character of] Deal was based on Truman Capote, and that was very helpful to me. The contribution Alan made was to say, "Now look, just stop worrying about the time frame of the novel and try to bring it into focus in one year of seasons: fall, winter, spring, summer." Architecturally, that was a big help. Then I felt I could compress and take away and add from that point of view.

Of Mice and Men, again I resisted. But I had great respect for [the actor-director] Gary Sinise. My great resistance there was it had been done so much—what in the world could anybody ever say that was different? I had spent my young manhood pretending I was Lenny. (*Foote does an imitation.*) Everybody was doing Lenny in those days. But then I reread the novella, and I was struck by how fresh it seemed, particularly how it related to today, with the rootlessness and the hopelessness and the migratory conditions. I felt quite taken with it. Then—I know I'll get into trouble for saying this, because it's considered a classic—I happened to run off the [Lewis] Milestone film [*Of Mice and Men,* 1940], which I decided was terrible. I thought it was full of clichés and everything I didn't want to do. Gary agreed with me. He said, "Don't pay any attention to that silly thing." He had a great passion about the male-bonding idea. He sent me a film, which I'd never seen, called *Scarecrow,* with Al Pacino, who I think is a remarkable actor, and Gene Hackman, also a wonderful actor. It is a tale of two guys on the road—very different from Steinbeck—but suddenly, I found myself interested in doing *Of Mice and Men* and exploring it.

Were you on the set of all of your big four films?

No, just the middle two [*Tender Mercies* and *The Trip to Bountiful*]. For *Mockingbird,* I was there for all of the casting. I did some of the screen tests. I played Gregory [Peck's] part in some of the screen tests with the kids. With [Gary] Sinise, I was there for the first week, and I went back the last week.

On 1918, On Valentine's Day, *and* Courtship, *you functioned almost as a codirector.*

Gary Sinise (left) and John Malkovich in the 1993 film *Of Mice and Men.*

I was.

You directed the actors?

I did.

Is that the best of both worlds? A writer who gets to deal with the performances but doesn't have to deal with the technical stuff?

That's the only way I could do it. I would never want to direct a film completely. Too much time is consumed.

How do you work with actors? What do you say to them?

First of all, I try to pick actors that speak the same language as I do. I'm not didactic about that. There are certain actors who don't know anything about the Method yet are wonderful actors. They have instincts. I try to create an atmosphere of trust, so actors don't feel they are being judged, and so they can experiment and try things. I kind of edit for them and talk over problems that they may be having, see if I can find solutions that are helpful to them. That's really how I do it. I know too well ever to insist on someone doing it only one way. I welcome what the actor can bring. Five different actors are going to do the same scene differently. That I welcome.

Do actors recognize that you are writing in the 'beat'?

I don't talk about it. But I think that's why actors like my work. Mostly, too, because they love the subtext of it.

You've worked with Robert Duvall several times. What does he mean to you as an actor?

Oh, my lord. He's kind of my talisman. I just depend on Robert. So many times I've turned to him, and I just know whatever he does is going to be wonderful. He brings total commitment to the character he is playing and great integrity to his work.

Can you tell me a little about your history with him?

He was doing a play of mine called *The Midnight Caller* [in Sanford Meisner's acting class], and Sandy Meisner called me up and said, "Get on down here and see this young man in your play, because I think you'll be very pleased." Robert Mulligan was in town, and his then wife, Kim Stanley, was also around. My wife and I went down with them to see this production and were just taken with this young man playing a young alcoholic who totally disintegrated during the play and finally killed himself, though you never saw that—you just heard the character had done that.

When we were casting *Mockingbird* and thinking about who could play Boo Radley, my wife said, "What about that young man we saw?" Fortunately, Bob [Mulligan] had seen him also and said, "Yeah, you're perfectly right. Let's use him." That was the beginning. Then Robert was in *The Chase,* though I had little to do with it. Then we did this wonderful project called *Tomorrow.*

For my money, that's Duvall's best performance.

He's inclined to agree with you.

Robert Duvall (at left) and Gregory Peck (center) in *To Kill a Mockingbird.*

Even with The Godfather *and* Apocalypse, Now *in the running.*
Have you ever seen my film *Convicts*?
No.
You should see it. Because he's extraordinary in *Convicts*. Anyway, Robert and I did *Tomorrow* first as a play, then as an independent film. Then came *Tender Mercies* and then *Convicts.*

You don't talk very much about your other sixties screen credits: The Chase, Baby, the Rain Must Fall, *and* Hurry, Sundown . . .
The Chase is simply based on my novel.*
I thought you did a little consultation on the film.
Just before they went into production. But the film is so far away from my original work that I never thought it had much to do with me.
Did you talk about the script with Lillian Hellman?
No, Sam Spiegel. Lillian was, by that time, away.
Did they incorporate any of your ideas?

---

* *The Chase* was based on Foote's 1956 novel of the same name (New York: Rinehart), which, in turn, is an adaptation of his 1952 play.

I don't really know. I hope so. I only saw it once. I'm not fond of it at all.

How about Baby, the Rain Must Fall*?*

Baby, the Rain Must Fall I'm very proud of. I worked very closely with Alan Pakula and Bob Mulligan on that, and they shot it here in my home—in Texas. I was very much involved and on the set during the filming. Always with them—they're very inclusive.

What about Hurry, Sundown*?*

Not a word of it is mine. I got along very well with Otto [Prcmingcr], but we just didn't agree on how it should be done. We parted amicably, and he got another writer and had a whole new script written that I've never read or seen. But Otto called me afterwards and asked if, as a favor to him, I would lie and put my name on the script. Since he'd paid me so much money, I felt I couldn't turn him down; so I said yes.

Are you certain not a word of it is yours?

Oh, I know because Otto told me.

Is that the reason why you worked on films only sporadically for a time? Because you had had these unpleasant experiences?

I didn't like working on big films, and so I had to wait until I could find a venue that was more acceptable to me. I liked working on *Mockingbird* and *Baby, the Rain Must Fall* a lot, but they were very personal films, and I just didn't like working on the impersonal, big-budget stuff.

It was *Tomorrow* that really turned me around. That was done for about $400,000, and there again, I felt very necessary and wanted. I was on the set and in the editing room, and that's how I felt it should be with a writer.

Wasn't there a period in the early seventies when you went to the New Hampshire woods and stopped writing?

No, I didn't really stop writing. There was a period in the early seventies when I went to the New Hampshire woods to reevaluate my work, but I wrote a great deal while I was there. I was discouraged because I didn't really have much in common with what I felt was going on in the sixties in the theater. I wasn't terribly interested in taking off my clothes or the kind of profanity that people felt was very liberating. I was interested in it, but I didn't feel a part of it. I felt I had to get away and work, because the other is very distracting: if you're around when everybody is saying, "This is the way to do it . . . this is what's selling . . . blah, blah, blah." I've been through so many different fashions now in theater and writing.

How did you come to write Tender Mercies. *That was a rare, original screenplay for you. Was that written with Robert Duvall in mind?*

No, I don't ever write with people in mind, although very soon after it was finished, I knew it was right for Bob. I was working on my Orphans' Home Cycle, as a matter of fact working on *Night Seasons* and a number of other things. I was living in New Hampshire, and I needed some money. My agent, Lucy Kroll, told me, "They like you out in Hollywood. You're so peculiar—

you won't pitch—but if you would just give me a few lines about something, I could get you some money to write it and to finish these other projects."

I thought about it. I was very interested in my nephew who was part of a group that had been playing around for gigs, as they call them, and the life of musicians reminded me much of what I had gone through as an actor. Most of the group had jobs on the side, and they would sometimes go to play at places where somebody—maybe the manager—had hired two orchestras for the same night, but the first one that showed up got the job. I began to think about a country-western band, paralleling it to my experiences as an actor—that kind of rejection. I told this idea to someone at 20th Century-Fox and she rather liked it and she told me that her boss was coming in from Hollywood. His name was Gareth Wigan, a partner with Alan Ladd, and would I tell it to him?

I thought that was easy enough, so I told it to him. He liked it but said, "There's only one thing. I think somewhere in there there should be an older character." I said, "Okay—I'll think about it." He said, "But I want to make a deal with you. When your agent comes out [to Hollywood], have her come round, and we'll work out a contract."

Out Lucy [Kroll] went. She got off the plane, bought the *Reporter* or *Variety,* and the first thing she read was that Wigan and Ladd had left Fox.* In the meantime, I had been thinking about the idea, as is my wont. I got intrigued, and because I really don't like to accept money before things are written, I thought I'd just pull in my belt and write it. I did and felt it was a wonderful part for Duvall; so I called him up, and we met in New York at a place I was subletting. I read it to him, and he said he'd do it.

It wasn't all that easy to get it done. It took us almost two years. A man named Philip S. Hobel and his wife, Mary-Ann Hobel, were very helpful as producers; then of course [the director] Bruce Beresford was a great gift to us. I had seen *Breaker Morant*—which I loved and still love as a film—but I didn't think he would be interested in this at all. In the meantime, we'd been turned down by many directors. Bruce was sent the script in Australia. He told me he usually waits a month before reading a script, but something told him to go to this one right away, so he read it. Halfway through it, he called up and said he'd do it. He said, "I just have to know one thing—if I can get along with the writer." And we got along very well.

Did he change it much?

Not much. The essence of it was always there. I think maybe there was some narration that he felt was unnecessary—things like that. He edited more than changed.

---

* Twentieth Century-Fox President Alan Ladd, Senior Vice President Jay Kanter, and Vice President Gareth Wigan announced in June 1980 that they would resign from the studio as of December 1980.

Robert Duvall and Allan Hubbard in *Tender Mercies,* directed by Bruce Beresford.

What about Duvall? Did he do any writing on the set?
When he was working out scenes, there were things he did that I incorporated into the film.
The title Tender Mercies *comes from the Seventy-ninth Psalm.*[*]
It's from a lot of psalms, actually, but it's also from the Seventy-ninth.
How did you settle on that title?
I don't know. I just love the phrase.

It's often said that a writer has about three stories in him, and that he spends a lot of time rewriting or revising them in various guises. It may or may not be true. What do you think about that?
Thematically, if you're talking about themes, I think themes do reappear constantly in one's work. I thought what Ben Brantley said about *Night Seasons* was very perceptive,[†] and I'm going to write him a little note and thank

---

[*]   Psalms 79:8: "Let thy tender mercies speedily . . ."
[†]   Horton Foote also directed *Night Seasons,* which starred his daughter, the actress Hallie Foote, as Laura Lee Weems, "a small-town, family-smothered spinster." Ben Brantley wrote in the *New York Times* (November 7, 1994) that "father and daughter conspire to present a lucid anatomy of a subject that has always obsessed the author: the elusiveness of the idea of home. The theme has echoed plaintively throughout Mr. Foote's oeuvre, from his best-known work, *A Trip to Bountiful,* to his nine-play 'Orphans' Home Cycle.' "

him for it. He spoke about the theme of home reappearing in my works, and how it surfaces and was worked out in *Night Seasons,* and that's true. I know it does reappear all the time. It's almost an irony in the sense that [the character of] Josie lives in this apartment and can't even remember names anymore; Laura Lee, all she has are pictures of houses that she pastes into a scrapbook; and Thurman and Delia, who get a house, it's hell for them—because they fight all the time—home has no meaning for them at all. In that sense, it's a very ironical use of the desire for home.

You're often said to have an affinity with Faulkner—perhaps because of York County and Harrison, Texas—and people also compare you to Chekhov. But in our conversations, you have mentioned Flannery O'Connor, Katherine Anne Porter, Reynolds Price, Eudora Welty.

Peter Taylor is another. I haven't mentioned him yet. Now I will, because he's been an influence on me, and another important influence is Elizabeth Bishop.

Really?

Oh, yeah. I read her all the time. Marianne Moore, T. S. Eliot, Ezra Pound—they also had an enormous influence on me. Faulkner? I admire him greatly, and I've adapted him; as a matter of fact, there's another Faulkner project that may come about, an adaptation of *The Old Man* which I first did forty years ago for *Playhouse 90.*

That's also where Tomorrow *started.*

That's right. There's talk now of reviving *The Old Man* as a film, which I would love to do. I have a great affinity for Faulkner. I know stylewise I have learned much more from Katherine Anne [Porter] or Elizabeth Bishop, however. In other words, I'm a taker-outer rather than a putter-inner.

How so?

I'm not a minimalist—I don't mean that. But I like to eliminate. Faulkner, I think, is a grand master of the rolling phrase and the long sentences. I don't know how to do that.

Now, Chekhov? I adore Chekhov's short stories very, very much, and I love his plays—no question about it—but in some ways, I feel closer to his short stories. He was a great short story writer. Of course, he is a great playwright.

How does a play occur to you?

Boy, if I knew that—if I could patent that—I'd be a rich man. All kinds of devious ways.

Do you still take long walks to stimulate the writing?

Yes, I also keep notebooks, and sometimes just a phrase in a notebook will start me off. I never know. I've also learned that you can't really predict the time for the consolidation of the idea. You can use your will, and you can say, "I know this is wonderful—I'm going to make it work," and it just won't do it. Something is larger there, and you have to say, "Okay, you win." Katherine

Anne Porter has that theory about the drawer: you put something in a drawer, and when you go back to it, something has happened to it. Sometimes something bad happens to it.

Could you write a play that is set in New York City?

I could try. I don't guarantee what would happen. I don't hear it. Lord knows I've spent a lot of my life here, and I keep thinking to myself, "I really would like to write a play about the theater." Maybe I will. I just don't, instinctively. Other themes are somewhere in there (*points*), and they keep resurfacing—knocking, knocking—saying, "Let's go."

You can't push it or force it, call or bend it to your will.

No, you can't.

But the fact of the matter is, you've written a score of television plays—by now, thirty or so—you've written screenplays—

Yes, I work all the time. All I'm saying is—

Do you have all these different projects going at different times in different drawers?

Sometimes I do. One might run out of fuel; then you just take up something else. It's a very mysterious thing—writing. It's like acting: You can study techniques until you drop over on your face. Then there's the *x* factor. It's not fair, because I know the most wonderful, the hardest-working people in the world that are actors. They know all the technical things, but nothing much happens. The same with many writers that I know. But with certain writers, their talent is the essence of the person. It's something that's uniquely theirs. It's—

Grace?

Grace, maybe. It's like the palm of your hand. It's your *voice*. You can pick up certain stories and know immediately who wrote that story after three or four paragraphs. I don't think that can be taught, and I don't know where that comes from. It's one of the great mysteries, as far as I'm concerned.

Did you always have the same voice? Can you discern periods in your work?

I can, but I can tell you that the root is always there. The preoccupations are always there. The search is always there. Sometimes it's done better than other times, and I hope and trust I've learned something through the years, although there are certain of my early things that I'm very impressed with. Some of it I don't think I could do today.

Do you, after all these years, think of yourself principally as a playwright?

I am first and foremost a playwright. I don't mean that to be quite as dismissive as the way it sounds. I really would hate to give up screenwriting. There was a time when I would just tell you right off: I'm a playwright—and that's it. But I've learned from being a screenwriter. I think I've learned, although I'm discouraged right now. Because the way I like to do films is to do independent films. I'm not a big studio man; I just don't operate well with them. Therefore, I'm not aggressive about films. I have three films in different stages of progress right now. But they're all very hard to sell and hard to do.

One of them Duvall wants to do, if he can get it off the ground, and I hope he will, called "Alone." Then I was commissioned by Eddie Murphy's company to write a film about blacks, which I'm very proud of. And Bruce Beresford is dying to direct that one. It's called "The Man of the House." They're trying to find a studio to finance it right now, because Murphy himself won't be in it.

The third project is called "The Parson's Son." It's an original, but I was paid to write it by a company called Wind Dancer. It would be their first feature film. Mostly they've done television—*Home Improvement* and *The Cosby Show,* for years. Again, it's a very unorthodox story. The other two are Harrison; this one is outside Harrison. They had sent me a short story to dramatize; I liked the story, but I didn't feel it could be a film. When I met with the author, I learned he is a third-generation Lutheran minister—and I got very interested in him. That's literally what the film is about—his history and his personal story, and what it meant to grow up as the son of a Lutheran minister.

Whatever happened to your Bessie Smith project?

Someone could do my Bessie Smith script right now, if they felt they could do it for $12 million, but Bruce [Beresford] feels it has to have at least $18 million, and nobody can get that much money for it.

This is a script you wrote—

Many years ago. It was written for Columbia Pictures. [The choreographer-director] Joe Layton wanted to do it; then Columbia backed away because musicals—particularly black musicals—weren't considered commercial. So I didn't own the rights for a long time, but I have a copy here, and one of my sons, who wants to be a producer, was rooting around, looking for material, and he pulled out "Bessie" and loved it. I said, "You picked the wrong thing—because I don't own it." But he was very aggressive about it and found the money to buy the script back.

Didn't the producers of Driving Miss Daisy *want to do it at one time?*

Yes. Very badly. But their budget was $28 million.

Is your work on all of these unproduced screenplays finished?

My work is done. When it gets closer to production, maybe there will be things to do, but my work is done.

Walon Green:
Fate Will Get You

Interview by Nat Segaloff

The documentary producer David L. Wolper once remarked that Walon Green "could go into a steamy jungle with the barest of essentials and work with the delight of one holidaying on the Riviera." Wolper suggested that Green has a fondness for desolate places (perhaps that's why he sent him there so often to produce and direct shows), but Green does not. For him, locations such as deserts, islands, high-tech arenas, and both urban and tropical jungles are where his characters are forced to live. They are often villains and outcasts— sometimes society's dregs—but frequently honorable men struggling in a dis- honorable world, captive in events larger than themselves. They are almost always male, but they are macho only in order to survive; in Walon Green's world, guns and fists are last resorts. Mettle is something you carry within.

Nowhere is this clearer than in *The Wild Bunch* (1969), the film that not only brought world attention to the director Sam Peckinpah but also cast its shadow on all westerns made since. An unquiet mixture of blood and nostal- gia, it tells of Pike (William Holden), who in 1913 leads a gang of train rob- bers on one last job while he is pursued by his former friend, Thornton (Robert Ryan), now a turncoat. Although Hollywood westerns had not died out completely when it was made, *The Wild Bunch* nevertheless became the seminal "end of an era" picture that began a new one in screen violence. It was Green's first script but not his first film experience.

Green was raised around the Hollywood studio system: his mother divorced his father, who was in the air force, when Walon was a year old; and she moved from Baltimore to Beverly Hills to marry the Fox-based songwriter James V. Monaco ("You Made Me Love You," etc.) in 1937.

After such varied schooling as the El Rodeo Grammar School, University of Mexico, and Göttingen University in Germany, Green returned home to take odd jobs (construction, pool cleaning) while devising a way to enter the film industry.

"At the end of 1962, I decided that I was somehow going to get into the film business. In those days you had to find somebody whose father or brother would give you a job. I suppose I already had a way in, but it didn't occur to me to use it. Of course, at that time when people said I ought to be a writer, I wanted to make *Nanook of the North* [1922], and go off somewhere and make a documentary. This was also, by the way, when you could have fired a cannon through Warner Brothers or 20th Century-Fox in the middle of the day and not hit anyone."

The reason you could fire cannons into empty movie studios was television, which also became Green's entrée to show business. He called on an old grammar school chum, Jack Haley Jr., who was then making television shows for David L. Wolper. At that time, Wolper, a former salesman, was reshaping the American television documentary. His technique of assembling stock footage into well-written, commercially savvy shows (*Biography, Hollywood and the Stars,* etc.) left the networks' ponderous news specials in the ratings dust. When *The Making of the President: 1960* (1964) won Wolper an Emmy— then rare for an independently produced program—the industry took notice, and Wolper Productions expanded its staff.

"What David did is very underrecognized," Green averred. "Now he's a big shot because of the Olympics, but he really did bring documentaries into the entertainment hours of television. *National Geographic* and *Cousteau,* which were on PBS and network for years—all came from him."

Green was hired to research story ideas, often on the slimmest of notions, which Wolper would then try to sell to sponsors. "Somebody would come in and say, '*A Day in the Life of the World*—do a presentation on it,'" Green remembered. "That was about all you got. You had to write punchy, flashy stuff. That was when I figured out that writing was really a craft."

Later, when Wolper's activities slowed, Green was laid off. His multilingual skills from student years spent abroad won him work as a dialogue coach and unofficial script doctor on such international productions as *The Outrage* (1964), *Rio Conchos* (1964), and *Saboteur: Code Name Morituri* (1965). Yet, despite working with stars such as Paul Newman and Marlon Brando, Green quickly realized he was headed for a dead end.

"It was a chance to write and hear stuff that you wrote said by good actors," he recalled, "[but] I didn't see any way to progress there." Swallowing a 50 percent pay cut, he returned to Wolper. Green convinced Wolper and house producer Mel Stuart that a troubled television *March of Time* segment titled "Search for Vengeance," about the Nuremberg trials, could be saved by actually going to South America and asking around about the fugitive Nazi doctor Josef Mengele, whom several German publications insisted was hiding in Paraguay.

"I passed myself off as a German-American from some German family in Pennsylvania, because I could speak German but couldn't pass for German," he said. He returned with footage establishing that "Mengele was a real presence there. People came right out and talked about how Roosevelt was a Jew and all sorts of stuff that made a good show. We had the first interview with Simon Wiesenthal, who at the time was living in a [small flat] in Vienna.

"The fact that I'd shot it and it all cut together—because now I knew that movies weren't made on one strip of film—[had a result:] They said, 'You're a director.' " After Green produced, directed, and wrote several nature shows for *National Geographic* ("Reptiles and Amphibians," "The Amazon"), his next step was to produce *The Hellstrom Chronicle.*

Hellstrom was an alarmist documentary warning that insects would outlast mankind, for which Green won the Oscar for Best Documentary in 1971. Green, however, had continued to pursue dramatic writing, and while he was still working on *Hellstrom,* his first script—*The Wild Bunch*—reached the screen. Released in 1969, it catapulted the then thirty-three-year-old writer into the front ranks of Hollywood screenwriters and has kept him there.

Like many working Hollywood screenwriters, Green lives far enough away from the studios (near Malibu) for privacy yet close enough to attend meetings. He has been married four times.

Walon Green in his office at Universal Pictures, 1992. (Photo by Nat Segaloff.)

A gentle, well-read man with a soft voice and laconic sense of humor, Green connects the subjects of his diverse scripts with one word: apocalyptic. "I used to deny it, but I don't anymore," Green said. "I used to be obsessed with apocalyptic thinking. Then I look at the films I've liked the most, not in terms of shtick but in terms of story and the whole film, and they are apocalyptic films. *Hellstrom* is an apocalyptic film; *Wild Bunch* is an apocalyptic film. *Sorcerer* is *definitely* apocalyptic. Fate will get you no matter what you do to undo it. It always creeps into what I'm doing."

WALON GREEN (1936–   )

1964   *The Outrage* (Martin Ritt). Dialogue director.
        Rio Conchos (Gordon Douglas). Dialogue director.

1965   *Saboteur: Code Name Morituri* (Bernhard Wicki). Dialogue director.

1969   *The Wild Bunch* (Sam Peckinpah). Co-script.

1971   *The Hellstrom Chronicle* (Walon Green). Producer, director.

1977   *Sorcerer* (William Friedkin). Script.

1978   *The Secret Life of Plants* (Walon Green). Co-script, director.

1979   *The Brink's Job* (William Friedkin). Script.

1982   *The Border* (Tony Richardson). Co-script.

1983   *WarGames* (John Badham). Uncredited contribution.

1986   *Solarbabies* (Alan Johnson). Co-script.

1989   *Crusoe* (Caleb Deschanel). Script.

1990   *RoboCop 2* (Irvin Kershner). Co-script.

1993   *Sniper* (Lucho Llosa). Coexecutive producer.

1996   *Eraser* (Charles Russell). Co-script, co-story.

Television credits include numerous David L. Wolper documentaries; *The Search for Vengeance* (1966, codirector); *Spree* (1967, codirector); "Winged World," *National Geographic* (1967, co-script); "Reptiles and Amphibians," *National Geographic* (1968, co-script, producer, director); "The Amazon," *National Geographic* (1968, co-script, producer, director); *Plimpton! Adventures In Africa* (1972, co-script, director); *Strange New World* (1975, co-script); *Mysteries of the Sea* (1979, script); *Robert Kennedy and His Times* (1984, miniseries, script); *Hill Street Blues,* numerous episodes (1985–86, writer-coproducer); *Three of a Kind* (1989, TV pilot, script); *Law and Order,* numerous episodes (1992–1999, writer-coexecutive producer); *N.Y.P.D. Blue,* numerous eposides (1994–1995, writer-coexecutive producer); and the telefilm *Without Warning* (1994, co-story).

Academy Award honors include an Oscar nomination for Best Original Screenplay for *The Wild Bunch* (co-story with Roy N. Sickner; co-script with Sam Peckinpah); and a Best Documentary Oscar for producing *The Hellstrom Chronicle*.

There was a discernible Wolper style—somewhat portentous, like Theodore H. White. Did you pick that up when you were working there?

Well, Teddy White, who wrote the *Making of the President* specials, was our paragon. There were other guys who wrote really well. Marshall Flaum was a terrific writer and filmmaker. I got a crash course from Bill Edgar and other guys like Tom Fuchs. It was a place where we helped each other. If a guy was desperately seeking something and I knew where it was, I'd say, "Do this or that." When I'd have trouble with something, somebody would come and say, "Oh, I know how to fix that. Do this." But the nice thing about it was that it didn't have the backbiting and insidious climbing that a lot of these places have. It was almost scholarly.

Did you always conceive The Hellstrom Chronicle *as having a human host, actor Lawrence Pressman playing entomologist Nils Hellstrom, as opposed to the traditional voice-over narrator?*

No. It was to be a big documentary epic about how insects would survive man and inherit the earth. When we cut it together with all the insect and natural history footage, it was one of the great disasters. It was myopic—all close-ups—you were totally disoriented by about thirty minutes into the film. The optical problems were so overwhelming to the senses that the narration no longer meant anything. Wolper went completely crazy at that first screening. In fact, to this day he tells me that it's the most hysterical he's ever been. He did a *pageant* in the screening room! He, [the producer] Mel [Stuart], and I had meeting after meeting, and the truth was that none of us really knew how to fix it. We tried to recut it, we tried different things. There was some feeling that I had linked it too much to ecology, which was a new word, but I hung in there. I said, "That's got to be what it's about."

Finally, we got David Seltzer,* who had worked for Wolper before and was talented and smart—and he sat through one of these screaming sessions and watched us all yell at each other. Wolper said at one point, "You two [Green and Seltzer] are so smart, you ought to get on the screen and tell the people what this movie's about." I said, "We ought to get a scientist." Wolper said, "I

---

* David Seltzer later wrote *The Omen* (1976) and made his directing debut with *Lucas* (1986).

don't want some stupid scientist. I hate scientists." And Seltzer said, "Why don't we make up a guy who tells people what the movie is about?" It was like *boing!* and that was it; that was the solution. It's funny, because the movie's caught a lot of flack for that, but boy, it solved the problem.

The Walt Disney nature films never used an on-screen presence.

But if you look at them, the only one where the Disney people tried insects was a film called *Nature's Strangest Creatures* [1959], and it doesn't really work. They had the same problem we did, so they tried intercutting it with [time-lapse] plants opening and scenic stuff like that, but the film just sort of frittered away.

Hellstrom had to evolve beyond just showing an insect and giving quasi-real facts about natural history and cutting its movements to music. The idea was not just to look at insects and say how interesting they are but to relate it to a bigger, overall theme, which is that there are really two important life forms on the planet, man and insects. Man succeeds through intellect; the insect, through adaptability. Now, take away all the favoritism and the fact that man may be God-created and all that, which is actually better? And we made the case for the insect, for adaptability.

And you went from insects at Wolper to The Wild Bunch?

The Wild Bunch I'd written while I was dialogue coach [on *Saboteur: Code Name Morituri*]. When I was working on the "Reptiles and Amphibians" documentary, a producer at Wolper showed me a *Variety* blurb that my script was being made. What had happened was that I was broke, of course, and had sold it for $5,000. I was to get $10,000 more if it was ever made. Roy N. Sickner was cowriter of the original story. He was a stuntman on *Morituri,* and he had a kind of a western story with a train robbery and a shoot-out at the end and a lot of good ideas in terms of action. It was sort of based on Butch Cassidy, but I'd never heard of Cassidy when I wrote the movie and called it *The Wild Bunch.* I didn't know there was a real Wild Bunch or a Hole-in-the-Wall Gang. I hadn't researched that aspect of it. We had written a treatment, and then Roy had found a backer to put up $5,000 [for us] to write the screenplay, which I wrote on my own. Then Roy took the screenplay and found Peckinpah. Peckinpah rewrote the first draft; then I did a little more work on it.[*] Roy got to be associate producer because I was working full-time at Wolper.

Most of the look of *The Wild Bunch* came out of two documentaries made in Mexico that I asked Sam to look at: a weird mixture of guys in white and

---

[*] According to Marshall Fine, *Bloody Sam* (New York: D. I. Fine, 1991), Peckinpah gave the script to his protégé James Silke for rewrites. The project went to Writers Guild arbitration when Peckinpah demanded first script position and co-story credit. His request was refused, and the credits now read: "Screenplay by Walon Green and Sam Peckinpah. Story by Walon Green and Roy N. Sickner."

guys in frilly European uniforms, a whole bizarre mixture of cultures—Indians in sombreros standing next to a guy in a white Panama suit.

How much did Peckinpah change your script?

I can tell you with some degree of accuracy, because it was changed specifically rather than generally. In the opening robbery and shoot-out, he added the character of the dim-witted L.C. [Bo Hopkins], who is ordered to stay by Pike's [William Holden] group and is killed by the sheriff's people. Later we learn that he was the grandson of Sykes [Edmond O'Brien]. Rather than disgrace the boy, Holden lies to Sykes that L.C. died heroically.

Peckinpah added something else kind of funny. I had written Angel's [Jaime Sanchez] visit to his former Mexican village, where he sees that his girl has become involved with the local dictator, General Mapache [Emilio Fernandez]. I'd written that he goes there on his own; it was about seven pages long and completely in Spanish. Sam had the good sense to bring the other characters into it and have it play in English.

Then he gave the movie the ending I really like: I had ended it with the Wild Bunch getting killed in Mexico and Thornton [Robert Ryan] telling his bounty hunters to load up the bodies and take them back, while he chose to go

"A revelation kind of film": from left, Ben Johnson, Warren Oates, William Holden, and Ernest Borgnine in Sam Peckinpah's *The Wild Bunch.*

off on his own. Sam added Thornton staying in Mexico, while his men, heading back, get killed. Sykes returns to find Thornton and asks if he wants to join him to fight a war in Mexico: "It isn't like it used to be, but it'll do," and they ride off together. That was completely his.

The Wild Bunch *has been restored on home video to include a long-missing flashback that explains how Holden was wounded, not in a battle but shot by a jealous lover.*

Sam wrote that, too. And there was the sequence where Pike blows up a bridge, so Thornton's men can't follow them, which originally was a cable across rapids, but they couldn't find a location, so he wrote a bridge sequence.

There's a funny story about the location, which was Parras de Madero, Mexico. They went looking all over, town to town, for locations in Durango and northern Mexico, and Peckinpah was unhappy with all of it. Finally, they were driving back and saw a sign that said Parras. They said, "Hey, there's a town named that in the script. Let's go look at it." So they did and said, "This is it!—exactly as in the script. There's a town and a hacienda outside, and here's the main street, and here's where the bank could be." They called me and said, "Why didn't you tell us that you wrote it to a specific town; you could have saved us all this riding around." I said, "I didn't. I've never been in that town in my life. I just picked the town that [the revolutionary] Francisco Torreón was born in."

I went down to Parras for about two weeks, and that was the first time I ever met Sam. I liked what I heard he was about—a guy who gave everybody a lot of shit and stood his ground.

Was he condescending to you, the kid?

He was kind of surly, actually. I got into an argument with him right off the bat. I was trying to talk him out of that great bridge sequence—an admission of stupidity here!—I originally had a cable crossing where the guys hooked onto a cable to get across the river, and halfway across, instead of blowing up the bridge, the cable is cut, and they get swept into the rapids. Peckinpah said, "There aren't any rapids here like in Sacramento," and he named about ten rivers in northern California that I'd never heard of. He said, "I know what a river looks like, and you don't. But go out and take a look at them." Sickner or somebody said, "Don't bring up the river anymore to him. He's really pissed off and doesn't want to hear about it."

The next day, I got a Mexican pilot and flew out in a Cessna tail-dragger. We landed beside the river and banged the shit out of the plane. I thought Sam would *really* be mad. Oddly enough, the fact that we'd nearly crashed while landing in a bad spot impressed him. He said, "Well, you nearly killed yourself, but you know what I'm talking about, right?"

He thought I was kind of an oddball. One thing I had in my favor was that every time I saw him I was just arriving from Africa or Borneo or some place like that, so I wasn't just some guy who wanted to be a Hollywood screenwriter. I think, indirectly, this baited his curiosity, as though he thought, "If I tell this guy to fuck off, he's just gonna be on a plane to Panama. He doesn't give a shit."

I remember that once I went to have a meeting on the script with him—it was after the *Geographic* show on reptiles that I'd done had aired. He said, "I saw your show last night. It was really terrific—I really liked it."

They say he could be difficult.

I heard all these stories about him, but frankly, I never saw him behave badly. It's such a wussy thing to say, but the times when I was involved with him he was totally professional and really excited about the film. Who can tell when a guy's in the middle of shooting a picture? He seemed unpleasant, but most directors seem unpleasant when they're shooting a picture. Subsequent to that, I tried working on a picture with him called "The Diamond Story," which Warner Brothers hired me to rewrite for him. I found him difficult to communicate with, and the whole thing turned to steam. [It was never filmed.] But I sure liked what he did with my *Wild Bunch* script.

Of all things, what led you to write a western as your very first dramatic script?

It was really a decision that was made for me. I liked action, and somebody had approached me to write a movie about skiing, which I knew nothing about. It was a chance to make two thousand dollars, but I just sat around ski resorts—it was supposed to be about the swinging crowd—and I realized I didn't give a shit about it. But I always liked westerns, and I never felt that I'd seen the western I wanted to see.

I always felt they were too heroic and too glamorous. I'd read enough to know that Billy the Kid shot people in the back of the head while they were drinking coffee; it had to be a lot meaner than that. Plus I knew a lot of ranchers and cowboys, and they were *mean*. I wrote it, thinking that I would like to see a western that was as mean and ugly and brutal as the times, and the only nobility in men was their dedication to each other. There must've been a time when that world was dying out, and the men who had survived it were just looking for a way to go in the style in which they lived. I figured that's the way it was; so when I wrote it, it was kind of a revelation kind of film—not one that would show you what the *real* West was but one that was not like any other western.

The film is notable for, among other things, photographing violence in slow motion. Was that Peckinpah's touch, or had you written it into the script?

The violence in slow motion is very expressly in the script. I put the slow motion in because when I wrote it, I had just seen *The Seven Samurai* [1954], which had the first use of slow motion in an action scene that I'd ever seen. [The director Akira Kurosawa] uses it two or three times in that film. And I thought, "Wow, that's great! How would it be to see a whole action sequence in slow motion?" So I wrote all the slow motion into the sequence, and they shot it and cut it like that. Luckily, they had covered it both ways; when they shot it and cut it together, it was a disaster because the sequence was fifteen minutes long in slow motion. They were gonna ditch it and go with normal speed. It was Lou Lombardo [the film's editor] who came up with the idea of just cutting to that moment of action in slow motion, and he reshaped the sequence.

There were several disastrous previews of the film. They took it to Nassau to the Warner Brothers convention with all the exhibitors, and it was a disaster; so they were afraid of the film. They showed it at USC [University of Southern California], and the students there hated it—it was peace and love time, you know. The film was deliberately mean-spirited, and Sam executed it that way. I mean, when friends of mine saw the film, they thought that I had betrayed them. I said, "You people don't get it. You're looking at the nature of man. He's excited by violence. The film is about what's wrong inherently with the beast, with the creature itself."

William Friedkin, who was also at Wolper while you were there in the mid-1960s, chose you to write Sorcerer *as his first film after* The Exorcist *[1973]. How did that happen?*

I hadn't seen him in about three or four years. I was at Warners, writing and producing a TV pilot called *Strange New World* [1975], a two-hour movie from an original story by Gene Roddenberry. Bud Smith [Friedkin's frequent film editor and a Wolper alumnus] ran into me there and said, "Billy's been trying to find you." I'd worked for the BBC in England for a year, and I'd been hard to find. He said, "He wants you to write a movie for him that takes place in South America." I said, "It takes place in South America? It's got to be either [a remake of] *The Wages of Fear* [1952] or [a film of Peter Matthieson's novel] *At Play in the Fields of the Lord.*" Bud said, "Yep, it's *Wages of Fear.*"

I don't know why he picked me; I'd never worked with him before. But I came in and wasn't even interviewed. He said, "You know the story?" and I said, "Yeah," and he said, "Let's do it." I sort of got freaked out because he had become so big; I had to reacquaint myself with him. It has been my experience that with other people you knew when you started out, if they make a movie like *The Exorcist,* you didn't come back to them at the same level. Fortunately, with Billy this was not true.

What had you been doing for the BBC?

I never really got anything done. I got to work for them because the *National Geographic* shows I did were being re-released as the *Nature* series in Bristol. I wanted to do a show on a man called Eugene Marais, who was sort of the van Gogh of natural history. I wanted to go beyond the purely nature film into the dramatic film.

Marais was a poet in turn-of-the-century South Africa. He was a strange guy who dabbled in opium and got the idea that he could actually live among animals as one of them. He thought he could be the dominant male in a troop

A scene from *Sorcerer,* director William Friedkin's 1977 remake of *The Wages of Fear.*

of baboons. He lived among the baboons and wrote a book called *The Soul of the Baboon,* which is really an analysis of this society, about how tyranny was the natural state of mankind.

After that, he dug into one of those monstrous termite mounds and would spend days and days inside, and he wrote *The Soul of the White Ant.* The idea was that these termites are social insects—not individuals—and that the mound was like a body with different parts that were like different organs. It's quite a remarkable book. He sent his books to Maurice Maeterlinck, who spoke Flemish, and since Marais spoke Afrikaans, Maeterlinck could read them. Maeterlinck just took Marais's name off, presented them, and won the Nobel Prize. He became famous, and Marais then went completely to the other side: he moved into the mountains and lived with a beautiful African woman named Laila and was the outcast of society before he died. What a character!

The film you and Friedkin made from The Wages of Fear *was* Sorcerer. *How did it develop?*

I went in some wrong directions. I wrote a bunch of shit that he hated, sixty pages of a different movie that he would have never made. I was panicked by the enormity of it until we started talking on a more personal level, and then I keyed in. I would write maybe fifteen pages at a time; we'd talk about it; then, I'd move onto the next fifteen, sometimes only four or five, sometimes twenty. We went through five scripts like that. We wanted a cynical movie where Fate turns the corners for the people before they turn them themselves.

Sorcerer *was originally written for Steve McQueen, but he dropped out for a variety of reasons; and you went with Roy Scheider. Did you have the time to rewrite for him?*

I guess we actually had the time, but we just didn't do it. That character was very underwritten, and I think Scheider could've used some more dialogue.

There are some powerful sequences in Sorcerer. *Which came first, the set pieces or the story as a whole?*

When I first started working on it, there was a question as to whether the rights could be had for the film; so the story had to be taken directly from the book [by Georges Arnaud], which is just a French pulp novel. A lawyer from Universal [which cofinanced *Sorcerer* with Paramount] warned me there were certain [film] sequences we could not use, such as the boulder on the road and the backing onto the bridge and one or two others.

When you write a sequence such as the bridge crossing, do you write out shots or just put down "They cross a bridge"?

I write stuff out—in that case, in lugubrious detail. I really poured on the coals. It's funny how when you write a script, you worry about things that you don't need to worry about. I was worried that when they'd come to the bridge, everybody would say, "Why don't they just turn around and go back—they obviously took the wrong road." But it never bothered anyone who saw the movie.

Critics had it in for Sorcerer. *They were offended that anybody would try to remake* The Wages of Fear.

I think it's a better film than *Wages of Fear*. *Wages of Fear* is more famous, but, you know, when most people talk about *Wages of Fear* and you listen to them, they're not really talking about the movie. I remember seeing it at the time and thinking, "This is fantastic!" but when you see it now, it's sort of a typical European left-wing movie of the time.[*]

You and Friedkin next made The Brink's Job. *Dino De Laurentiis was saying that he wanted it to be like* Big Deal on Madonna Street, *[1956] where these incredible screwups manage to pull off a crime. Did you ever see the script that was prepared for John Frankenheimer to direct before he dropped out and was replaced by Friedkin?*

---

[*]   The American version of *The Wages of Fear* was restored for limited theatrical release in 1991. The deletions had included some of the violence and most of the politics.

I didn't see it before I wrote my script; I saw it when I was in arbitration. The thing is, Billy [Friedkin] had been interested in *The Brink's Job* earlier and heard that Dino had the script and [John] Frankenheimer was directing it, and he said to me, "God, I'd love to do it, because Tony Pino [the leader of the Brink's Robbery gang] would've been the perfect guy for Lou Costello [of Abbott and Costello] to play. It's a potentially funny story."

Then, when Frankenheimer fell out, Billy called me and said, "You've got to come back to Boston; we're going to do *The Brink's Job*. There's a script but I'm not going to use it. Read Noel Behn's book [*Big Stick-Up at Brink's!* (New York: Putnam, 1977)], come to Boston, and tell me what you think the movie should be like." So I read it, went to Boston, and said it should be sort of theatrical, an immoral comedy like *Threepenny Opera*. Boston's a *Threepenny*-type town.

You said you were attracted to the gentlemanly code that Boston's criminals had, unlike those in New York or Los Angeles, where they'd all like to kill each other.

They were all neighborhood guys, they knew each other, they had odd respect for each other. We decided to play the film from their point of view, not take an editorial position on whether the crime was right or wrong—just play it as they saw it. I really like that film; I think it does what we wanted it to do.

The trick was to drive the plot and establish a large number of characters, all at the same time.

We cut the actual number of characters way down—I think there were sixteen guys in the original robbery, and we cut them down to about seven. The robbery itself was long-term—a kind of a career event where people were going in and out of the Brink's place for years. They actually stole $150,000 from the trucks over a three-year period, but Brink's never admitted it. It was a hard script to write from a plot point of view, but we decided to not go with the standard caper where the robbery is the big tense moment. Instead, we played the film off the characters and the relationships between them, because that's what we liked. I had to figure out what I needed—which were the major characters.

Specky [Specs O'Keefe, played by Warren Oates] was the character that ratted on them, the one who blew the whole thing at the end. Then there was Joe McGinness [Peter Boyle], the guy who screwed it up and was the catalyst for the thing falling apart and, in fact, stole the money. And Tony Pino [Peter Falk], whose idea it was. They were locked in. Jazz Maffie [Paul Sorvino] was a real character because he was a dilettante. He did *seventeen years* in prison for doing something that he thought would be amusing. At the time I met him, in the late 1970s, he was still telling his wife that he had never been inside the Brink's garage or associated with it. The character of Sandy Richardson [Gerald Murphy] was originally a longshoreman who went out on thefts and still showed up every day on the docks.

*   *   *

You wrote a draft of At Play in the Fields of the Lord *for Bob Rafelson that was never made,* as well as other scripts that went unproduced. Is it painful for you to talk about the projects that fell apart?*

Are you kidding? You couldn't be a writer if it was painful. Another one I worked on for almost a year was *WarGames.* Lawrence Lasker and Walter Parkes did whatever their final draft was, and then I worked on it with [the director] Marty Brest for about nine months after that. Then, after Marty was fired and John Badham came on, Lasker and Parkes came back on. With all due respect to Lasker and Parkes, I'm perfectly happy to tell you my contribution to that movie. If that movie had been an adaptation rather than an original screenplay, I would have had a credit on it. I arbitrated and lost, and I think I lost fairly. I don't say they screwed me out of my credit. It's a very hard call when it's an original story, because so much has to be given to the fact that someone has to conceive of it; and they did conceive of it, and I really came in as a hired gun. I think I improved it a lot, but the essence of *WarGames* is definitely theirs. Had it been an adaptation with 33 percent,[†] I would've made it.

This story is an interesting one that I don't mind mentioning names on. I was working on *Robert Kennedy and His Times,* I guess. I called Marty Brest about two weeks before *WarGames* was coming out and said, "God, we've got to go see it." He said, "Naw, I don't know if I can do that." He was so down. Then he called me back and said, "It's playing right across the street from where you work. Let's just walk up the street and see it." So we went across the street and saw it. It was a more emotional thing for him, clearly, than it was for me. He really had the rug pulled out from under him. There was no professional reason in the world to fire that guy. He was a good and adept and really talented filmmaker. But there was an animosity toward him. Marty is a guy who is not good at meetings. He's not a great bullshit artist. And Freddie Fields [then production head of MGM] is like some kind of pheromone—something that attracts horseshit. And it was impossible to get any of that from Marty. The guy was fired not for his performance in the set, which was brilliant. Everything he shot that I remember seeing is in the movie. There were sequences in the movie that were, not only the way he shot them, but the way he *cut* them.

You wrote The Border *for Jack Nicholson, and you're writing* Crusades *for Arnold Schwarzenegger. When you write a script without a star in mind, what sort of changes must you make when an above-the-title person signs aboard?*

---

*   The project was filmed in 1991 by the director Hector Babenco.

†   Under Writers Guild rules, "Any writer whose work represents a contribution of more than 33 percent of a screenplay shall be entitled to screenplay credit, except where the screenplay is an original screenplay," in which case the amount of new material must be 50 percent. *WarGames* was an original screenplay.

Basically, whatever they want. It's all within reason with those people you mentioned. Sometimes, some people have a very particular take on a character they play. Then you have an obligation to think how this person will work in this role. An example of that: you would not have written a film heavy on dialogue for Steve McQueen. You certainly wouldn't hesitate to be heavy on dialogue with Jack Nicholson.

In the cases where I have written for or even with a star, I usually try to know him, try to figure out what he does well, what works with him. I don't know if I have the best ear for that. I have read scripts that people have written where you can read the script and hear Jack Nicholson talking. I didn't write *The Border*—Derek Washburn wrote the script, and I did a lot of work on it. I tried to write it with what I thought would work best for Nicholson; he also inputted pretty well. He's real good with his stuff.

What was your involvement with the science fiction film Solarbabies*?*

I cowrote the script with a first-time writer named Doug Metro. Mel Brooks [Brooksfilms produced the movie] called me, and I saw the finished film with Maurice Jarre, who had decided to score it on the basis of the script.

"Jack inputted well": Harvey Keitel (left) and Jack Nicholson in *The Border.*

We were both somewhat shocked and disappointed with what we saw. I worked on the film a bit in the editing—we did some voice-over to try to fix it—but we never really fixed it. Everybody said I should take my name off it, but if you've gone all the way through a movie and approved this actor or that director, you can't then say, "Oh, I don't like it."

Solarbabies came out in *1986, and the next credit for you is* Crusoe *in 1989. What happened for three years?*

1986 to 1989 was [Don] Simpson and [Jerry] Bruckheimer ["Due Process"], and a movie for Marty Brest called "The Heist." [Neither has been produced at this writing.]

Crusoe *was a favorite project of yours that took nearly twenty years to reach the screen.*

I didn't actually work on it for twenty years! I wrote it intending to direct it myself in '73 or '74, and couldn't get a deal together. Then I didn't work on it again until I was at Fox and the producer, Andy Braunsberg, was back in town and said that he could revive interest in the project. So I picked it up and read it again. I like the film actually, but it's a subject that I didn't really master in the screenplay, and it's not mastered in the film. It's *so* hard to do. But it was fun to try it. I think it was an intelligent stab.

Weren't you almost forced off your own project?

This is a rather sleazy story. I was writing on the film and Braunsberg was producing it when I happened to get a copy of the [Writers Guild] strike list, and his name jumped out at me. I called him and said, "Andy, you're on the strike list." He asked, "What does that mean?" I said, "It may mean a lot of things, but I *am* loyal to the Guild; and you've got to straighten this out, or I can't work on the film."[*] So he went to England and hired another writer [Christopher Logue] to polish the script. A version of the script came to me where the scenes were exactly the same, but every single word had been rewritten—and Island [the film company] was saying, "Well, we can buy the other person's script 'cause it's basically the same story after all. It *is* a classic." I had my lawyer advise them that they could do that, but I would go to the wall.

It was transposed to the slave trading days of 1808 and introduced a second Man Friday. Was that yours?

All of it. All of it. The only thing that was his was the boat that came at the end of the film: in his, it was a scientific expedition; and in mine—I have two versions, actually—in one, it was slavers; in the other, it was a boat where their attitude was similar to that of traders, and they wanted to take Crusoe away but not the black. He [Logue] added the scientific expedition, which was

---

[*]   Under Writers Guild rules, a Guild member may not write for a producer who has refused to sign a union signatory agreement or who appears on a "strike" or "unfair" list.

interesting. It was a good idea, but that was it. They [Island] were within two or three days of shooting the film, and they still hadn't agreed to buy the property from me. They finally caved in. I can imagine they thought, "Well, we better buy it from him, or he's gonna sue us." I think I got paid for it the day they started shooting.

I thought Aidan Quinn [Robinson Crusoe] was good. There are a couple of scenes I really like in the film: the dog's death and his [Crusoe's] first meeting with the warrior, where he gets caught in the warrior's snare and is hanging upside down. The warrior arrives and taunts him—their roles are reversed.

I worked on that a long time—what's an interesting way to have these guys meet? There were some things they shortcut, like the fight between him and the warrior in the quicksand. The quicksand thing wasn't in my script; they added it because they cut other stuff. They were running out of money.

Is the screenwriter's job diminished if you have an essentially visual story such as Crusoe?

You're definitely more susceptible. No question about it. Dialogue's a funny thing. It can be a crutch to a not-so-great story. If the characters and dialogue are funny, it sparks. But when you don't have it, then the structure really weighs heavily. The problem in *Crusoe* was one of predictability. In the first draft, I didn't have the false Friday, and I would read the draft and get to that point and say, "God, this is where people think they've seen this movie. What can I do?" I came up with the idea of the false Friday. Crusoe captures the guy, and then he finds out there's another guy he really doesn't want to have on the island with him. I've always thought that having to really face the natural world is the best comeuppance for man, being an ape like he is. There's probably nothing that puts him in his place as well. It's so hard to write movies and say what you want to say. Oliver Stone does it, but the things he wants to say are fairly contemporary and fairly headliney. It's much harder when your sense of theme is more literary.

You are one of the industry's most respected but least-publicized script doctors. Having had Crusoe *wrenched away from you, how do you feel when you're asked to doctor someone else's script?*[*]

It's a job. A lot depends on the problems involved. In the case of *RoboCop 2,* I got a call from the producer, Jon Davison, who said that he had a first draft [by Frank Miller] that he had to turn in to Orion [Pictures] that he had problems with, and wanted me to read. I read it and said, "Well, yeah, if I were you, I wouldn't turn it in." They were up against a real time crunch. I was working on something else and told them to hire another writer right away, but

---

[*] According to Writers Guild rules, an additional writer must inform the original writer that his or her work is being rewritten.

that Frank Miller was familiar with the characters and his action writing was pretty good. I said to keep Frank and let another guy structure the script, lay off a lot of stuff on Frank and you might get it done. They had to have it in five weeks. He said, "Can't *you* do it?" and I said, "No, I'm doing something else." Mike Medavoy [then production chief at Orion] called the company I was working for and got them to release me. Frank and I locked ourselves away and in four weeks had the script.

The film has a lot of different endings.

The film was very different from the script. We wrote—I wouldn't say an *entirely* different story—but a *considerably* different story than was in the [original] script. Tim Hunter had been the director, and he was on his way out. They hired Irvin Kershner. I did a rewrite on it for Kershner, and then Frank did a polish. Then they went to Texas, and while they were shooting, Frank was rewriting some more. Kershner changed it a lot—I did not feel for the better. The human story—you know, RoboCop's family and kid—did not appeal to him so much, and he didn't like the character that Nancy Allen played. There was a real trap in cutting that character, because, unlike Superman or Batman, you don't have a Clark Kent or Bruce Wayne with RoboCop; and if you don't have a real human for RoboCop to interact with, the humanity just goes in the toilet. So the film is very cold. But it wasn't intended that way.

We tried to write the humor of the second film in the dark, twisted level of the first film. I liked the first one and thought it was terrific; I didn't think we could improve on it. I think it's a trap to approach a sequel, thinking, "Let's try and do something different." But I guess this happens a lot with the directors of sequels. The director of the second film looks at the first film and thinks, "Well, Paul Verhoeven did it that way; I don't want to do it that way. I don't want a reality-based humor." That's what Kershner did. If you actually took the lines of my draft, you would see that the tone and style are very close to the first film; but if you look at the final draft, you'll see that it's gone in the direction of comic book.

It sounds as though there are times when a director simply doesn't understand the script but plows ahead anyway.

I don't know if "doesn't understand the script" is the right way to put it, but I have had the experience where a director's concept of a film appears to be completely different than my own, and what I see is just about unrecognizable. Directors rarely tend to give very much in preproduction meetings about what they intend to do with a film. But it's not as discouraging in a meeting as it is to see it in a screening!

Since you have been hired to see the errors in other people's work, has this made your own craft better?

I suppose it does, but it doesn't as much as I wish it did. *Seeing* them isn't the problem; *fixing* them is the problem. Often you read a script, and you say,

"Oh, here's the problem," or "Pull this scene up, and it'll change the whole middle act"; and you go into the meeting, and everybody thinks you're fantastic. Then you go back and read your own pages, and you agonize over them, twisting and writhing, trying to draw something out that will fix your material with the same deftness that you've applied to the other.

You went back to television in the 1980s, notably with Hill Street Blues. *Were you becoming disenchanted with movies? What was television offering that movies did not?*

I was frustrated after "Night Sail",* and I just wanted to do something and sit there and see it. Plus they offered me a lot of money. I didn't go to [*Hill Street Blues's* executive producer] David Milch, who was my friend, and say, "I'm frustrated, I want to do something." I was wearing that around when he said, "Would you ever, in a million years, ever even think about . . ."—this is how David talks—"would you ever anticipate, maybe even consider working in television and making, say, $500,000 a year?" Well, that was it!

What you're doing is writing chapters for another guy's book. The characters are all set, which is both a blessing and a curse. It's a blessing for the ones you like, and it's a curse for the ones you don't like. That show was written in an interesting way. There was an interior jargon on the show. We knew that they needed five to seven separate stories every week.

Unlike with features, were you conscious about having to have a commercial every seven or eight pages?

You welcome it. It gives you a chance to conclude an act very clearly and begin the next one very clearly. That show had two traditions: a joke at the beginning in the squad room and a roll call. We stuck with those traditions. The other tradition we adhered to was that nothing was ever shown that the cops couldn't see. It was constraining but an interesting challenge.

You also wrote the miniseries Robert Kennedy and His Times *and managed to preserve tension over six hours even though the ending was already known.*

It was an interesting reflection of the times and the period in which it was released. It was supposed to come out in 1984, and the Republican Party protested its release in an election year, so it came out in 1985. A lot of critics attacked it politically as a paean to liberal politics in America, but it got some very good reviews. In fact, the one I'm the most proud of was an editorial review in the *Washington Post* that said it was a film to show that this was not

---

* A high seas adventure about a young couple menaced by a maniacal charter-boat captain, "Night Sail" was based on Frank DeFellita's novel *Sea Trial.* The actors Barbara Hershey and Michael Nouri were cast in the leads before the director William Friedkin brought Green aboard to rewrite it. Green said sarcastically, "That's the story of how Billy, with my help, turned a 'go' project into a development deal."

a period to back away [from] or be ashamed of, but rather a period to examine when the nation attempted to be what it was meant to be.

As we speak, you are in preproduction for "Crusades," in which Arnold Schwarzenegger has agreed to star, and which Paul Verhoeven wants to direct. It sounds like a big project that also involves controversy—religious fanaticism, Christianity, and so forth.

I worked on it for a year and a half. Right now, it's at the stage where Arnold likes it, and Paul and I like it but feel it has a problem. So I have let a couple people I know, who are really good on structure, read it. I didn't tell them what was wrong with it. Sometimes you can dedicate yourself to something so strongly that it makes you crazy, yet maybe there isn't a real problem there.

So I gave it to [my writer friend] Jeff Lewis. The problem starts on page 66. He read it, and called me the next week and said, "You've got a problem, and it starts on page 66." I was really relieved!

"Got any ideas?" I said. "Well, I got a simple idea," he said and gave me a one-line idea that really helped the script. It was so easy. The movie is about a character who's a thief. To escape being hanged, he cons his way into being part of a Crusade. Then it goes into the Crusade, which involves fake religious relics that are nevertheless used to legitimize early Christianity, but we lose his goal. He escaped from prison, but what is he going to do in the Crusade? For some reason, we had missed it. We wrote these terrific adventures, but when you got to page 66, you were at the end of the basic plot. All my friend did was to say, "Go back to the beginning. Remember, this man's a thief. If he's going to Jerusalem, he's got to be thinking about stealing something. The logical thing for him to steal would be the true cross, because he could hold everybody up and ransom it for a kingdom."

Action has to be towards something, not away.

Exactly! As much as I think I know, I spent six months looking in the wrong direction. I can't *tell* you the dancing and footwork and shtick I performed to cover it and make it happen, and there it was.

Some of your writing has taken place on the set. Do you ever throw an actor's comments to you back at them as dialogue?

I have done that, sure. In *The Border,* Jack Nicholson came up with better lines than there were in the script. In *Brink's* rehearsals, a couple of guys had better lines. Warren Oates was a guy who put little curves on things and made every line I wrote sound better than it was—changed a word and made it better. Often the actor has a better grasp on a character than the writer does. When an actor gets into it and gets it right, in most cases it's beyond what a writer can do. I hear about writers who won't allow a word to be changed; I'm not that way. I have a fix on the character in my mind, and it's usually not the actor who plays it—it's the character. Then I see the actor do it, and if it works for me, I say, "Yeah, that's the guy. In fact, it's better than the guy." And if it's not, I say, "Uh-oh."

Do you write much "on spec"?*

Not as much as I should. I think every writer should make more of an effort to write on spec, because it is the sort of essential power writing that a writer can do. But it's hard to go back to it when you've worked with directors. If you've started a project with Paul Verhoeven, you read his reaction; he's excited and you're excited and he likes that and he doesn't like this; but you get a better idea how to fix it, and you get into the process. When you write on spec, it's the torture of writing something and then having to step away and really hammer it with your own criticisms. It's hard.

What are the hardest kinds of scenes for you to write?

Exposition. I hate them; I really hate exposition. I hate scenes that serve as plot. However I've written it, I always think there's a better way and I didn't find it.

How do you bring characters into a room?

I hate introductions. I never write phone calls; I *hate* phone calls. I never believe there's anybody on the other end.

There aren't a whole lot of love scenes in your work.

I know it! Actually, I like writing love scenes, and I will have you know that I won an award for my sensitive portrayal of women and women's dilemmas in a *Hill Street* episode.

You're a literate, soft-spoken, very gentle-seeming man, yet you've been involved in some of the most violent movies in film history. How do you account for this dichotomy?

Well, I've always liked action. To me, the excitement of seeing good action is something that I enjoy. I'm not personally violent, but I'm excited by it. Most people who have any mythology at all, it goes from one act of incredible violence and horror to another—even the Greeks and the Balinese. The fantasy of action—the chase can be much more exciting than the kill. The kill is dull; the chase is thrilling. The extremes of violence that you see now—puppets being eviscerated—has become workaday stuff and doesn't have the punch, to me, of a girl walking through an apartment complex with the camera behind her and you don't know what's going to jump out from offscreen. A well-shot scene by [Roman] Polanski is violent when there's no violence taking place. It's knowing just the right amount to give—to excite the violence in ourselves and our capacity to imagine it. I took a shot at adapting Thomas Harris's *Red Dragon* [released as *Manhunter,* Michael Mann 1986] and know how hard it is

---

*   Spec scripts, which are written "on speculation" with no assurance of sale, offer a screenwriter creative freedom but are also a gamble. In the early 1990s, such spec scripts as *The Last Boy Scout, Basic Instinct,* and *The Ticking Man* fetched immense fees ($1.75 to $3 million) as studios bid against each other for ready-to-shoot work. When the buyers invariably discovered that the scripts required much rewriting, the feeding frenzy abated.

to get it on screen. What he left unstated was what was really horrible. When we talk about Conrad, you read *Typhoon,* and it's this wonderfully described action that takes place in your mind. I mean, I also like Henry James. I liked that even as a child. I like confrontations where Nature itself is a player. *The Treasure of Sierra Madre* [1948] was my favorite film because it wasn't just men against men; it was where they were, and the environment itself was also a character in the film. For example, I don't like car chases and shoot-outs and typical action movies. I don't like kung fu movies. I have often come under criticism for that when I'm writing—"The story or the environment undercuts the character, and it should be the character driving the story." I don't find that life is like that; if life were like that, Michael Milken would have his problems solved.

Studio executives seem to like what they call character-driven movies because they're easier to fit a star into.

I've had actors say, "Why does this happen? I could have done something there." And I say to them, "You didn't. It happened, and that's your problem."

Charles B. Griffith:
Not of This Earth

Interview by Dennis Fischer

> Some of his early scripts were unique
> and unusual, even brilliant.
> —Mark Thomas McGee, *Fast and Furious:*
> *The Story of American International Pictures*

Of all the writers who worked for Roger Corman, the most unjustly neglected is Charles B. Griffith. When films such as *Not of This Earth* or *The Little Shop of Horrors* are discussed, his contributions are often ignored; but it is Griffith's screenplays that have made a number of these fondly remembered, offbeat films as enjoyable as they are.

In getting these films made, Griffith has had a number of bitter experiences, not the least of which was having his story and characters from *The Little Shop of Horrors* made into a musical without his consent.

Howard Asherman, who wrote and produced the musical remake, dealt only with Roger Corman, who claimed to own all the rights. Since then, there has been a settlement that will give Griffith credit on future productions of the play and the film. Today, after years of fashioning scripts for films with low budgets and encountering endless hassles, Griffith has trouble finding work. He has been classified as a writer and director of nonsense. "They think of me as a crazed, far-out writer," said Griffith, "so I'm not taken seriously."

This is highly unfortunate. It is not Corman's direction that draws people to *The Little Shop of Horrors;* it is the blackly humorous plot and outrageous comedy. Griffith's film *Gunslinger* was the first western to have a female marshal. *Not of This Earth* is an intelligent science fiction revamping of *Dracula. Rock All Night* helped introduce the fabulous Platters. *The Wild Angels* led to a series of biker movies and helped launch the careers of Peter Fonda and Bruce

Dern. *Eat My Dust,* both written and directed by Griffith, was a top-grossing low budgeter. Mostly, Griffith will be remembered for the wild comedy of *Little Shop, Bucket of Blood,* and *Death Race 2000,* which made B movie viewing an unexpected delight.

While Griffith's films are well documented, little is known about the man himself . . .

Charles B. Griffith (1930–   )

1956   *Gunslinger* (Roger Corman). Co-story, co-script.
        It Conquered the World (Roger Corman). Actor, uncredited contribution.

1957   *Flesh and the Spur* (Edward L. Cahn). Co-story, co-script.
        The Undead (Roger Corman). Co-story, co-script.
        Naked Paradise (Roger Corman). Co-story, co-script.
        Not of This Earth (Roger Corman). Co-story, co-script, actor.
        Attack of the Crab Monsters (Roger Corman). Producer, story, script, actor.
        Rock All Night (Roger Corman). Script.

1958   *Teenage Doll* (Roger Corman). Story, script.
        Ghost of the China Sea (Fred F. Sears). Producer, story, script.
        Forbidden Island (Charles B. Griffith). Producer, director, story, script.

1960   *Bucket of Blood* (Roger Corman). Story, script.
        Beast from the Haunted Cave (Monte Hellman). Story, script.

1961   *The Little Shop of Horrors* (Roger Corman). Story, script, actor.
        Ski Troop Attack (Roger Corman). Story, script.
        Atlas (Roger Corman). Story, script.

1962   *Creature from the Haunted Sea* (Roger Corman). Story, script.

1963   *The Young Racers* (Roger Corman). Uncredited contribution.

1965   *The She-Beast* (Michael Reeves). Uncredited contribution.

1966   *The Wild Angels* (Roger Corman). Story, script.

1967   *Devil's Angels* (Daniel Haller). Story, script.

1968   *Barbarella* (Roger Vadim). Uncredited contribution.

1975   *Death Race 2000* (Paul Bartel). Co-script.

1976   *Eat My Dust!* (Charles B. Griffith). Director, script.

1979   *Up from the Depths* (Charles B. Griffith). Director.

1980   *Dr. Heckyl and Mr. Hype* (Charles B. Griffith). Director, script.

1981   *Smokey Bites the Dust* (Charles B. Griffith). Director, script.

1986   *Little Shop of Horrors* (Frank Oz). Musical remake of *The Little Shop of Horrors.*

1990   *Wizards of the Lost Kingdom II* (Charles B. Griffith). Director, script.

Plays include the story and script basis for the musical stage version of *The Little Shop of Horrors.*

No one ever asks me about my background ... my roots were in show business, since my mother was an actor; my father, when a young man, was in vaudeville; and my grandfather was a tightrope walker in the circus. It was automatic that I would go into the business. I went to military school, but nothing else really interesting ever happened to me. I got into the picture business as a result of some scripts I did for the 1951 soap opera *Myrt and Marge.* My grandmother played Myrt, and my mother played Marge.

How did you begin your association with Roger Corman?

I was out here with my grandmother, writing TV scripts, which were never made, and trying to break in as a screenwriter. I had written about seven

Roger Corman and writer-director Charles Griffith (right) on the set of *Eat My Dust!*

screenplays and a friend of mine, [the actor] Jonathan Haze, took them all over to Roger. Haze was already working with [the actor] Dick Miller and [the writer] Bobby Campbell and a lot of other people*—they were all crazy *schlubs* in the early fifties. Anyway, Roger called me and hired me to write a western, which I did, and which was never made. Then I wrote another western, and it wasn't made either. Then Corman taught me about budget. My third try was *Gunslinger,* and that one was made in 1955.[†]

It was supposed to be a six-day picture, but it got rained out, so it took seven. It was shot in the rain around an old ghost town, and it came out gorgeous. No one had shot in that light. They always thought you had to have hard light and hard reflectors and everything. You had that English countryside look right out in Topanga Canyon.

Your first science fiction script was It Conquered the World, *but it was credited to Lou Rusoff.*

Lou Rusoff had a brother dying in Canada, and he needed the money. The script Lou wrote was very confusing, so Roger gave it to me. I had three days to rewrite it, so I started from scratch.

Didn't you also play a scientist in that film?

That's right. I was also the sailor that died at the beginning of *Attack of the Crab Monsters.* Beach Dickerson was steering the boat, and when he swerved, I fell out. The boat went over me, and I was hit by the propeller. The sound man ran to rescue me, which got Roger mad because he ran into the shot.

Despite their low budgets, many of the science fiction films you wrote in the fifties had some interesting ideas. For example, Not of This Earth *used teleportation long before* The Fly. *How did that film come about?*

After I wrote *Gunslinger* and had patched up *It Conquered the World,* I went over to Roger's office, which was the size of a dinette, and said, "Don't you think it's time to do another science fiction film?" He said, "Okay, go ahead," and that was that. So I wrote *Not of This Earth,* and that started all this X-ray eye business. Most of Roger's themes got established right in the beginning. Whatever worked, he'd come and take again, and a lot of things got used over and over . . .

During the production of *Not of This Earth,* I was married to a nurse, and she helped me do a lot of medical research. I remember how we cured cancer in that script. Somehow the film was a mess when it was finished. About the time we saw *Gunslinger,* my wife was so shocked at the difference between the script and the picture that she never went to see another movie of mine.

How did Attack of the Crab Monsters *come about?*

---

* Robert Wright Campbell was nominated for an Oscar for his co-script for *Man of a Thousand Faces.* An early Roger Corman stalwart, he wrote or cowrote *Teenage Cave Man, The Young Racers, Masque of the Red Death,* and *Hell's Angels on Wheels,* as well as other low-budget classics.

† Charles Griffith's writing partner on *Gunslinger, Not of This Earth, Flesh and the Spur, Naked Paradise,* and *The Undead* was Mark Hanna—who is not mentioned in this interview.

"Made of Styrofoam and fiberglass": a scene from *Attack of the Crab Monsters.*

Roger came to me and said, "I want to make a picture called 'Attack of the Giant Crabs,' " and I asked, "Does it have to be atomic radiation?" He responded, "Yes." He said it was an experiment. "I want suspense or action in every scene. No kind of scene without suspense or action." His trick was saying it was an experiment, which it wasn't. He just didn't want to bother cutting out the other scenes, which he would do.

We didn't cut much in those days because pictures always came in short. So that's what happened. There was always something going on in that picture, but it was dumb. I mean, in the script, [the actor] Mel Welles says, "Strange, there's no sign of life on the island," and Roger cuts to seagulls taking off from the cliff. Caw, caw. (*Chuckles.*)

Why did he do that?

Oh, atmosphere. He wasn't really listening to the dialogue.

You didn't like the idea of radiation making things big?

It was called "gobbledygook" and was meant to sound rational. Did you know that Ed Nelson was under the crab prop? He later ended up starring in *Peyton Place.* Jack Nicholson may have been under it part of the time. Yeah, he was around the set, schlepping in those days, too.

The crab was made of Styrofoam and fiberglass around an aluminum frame, was fifteen feet long, cost four hundred dollars, and it wouldn't sink. I had to shoot it underwater, but there was no way to *get* it under water. [Griffith was second unit director.] We tried tying iron and rocks and things on it, but that didn't work. It flew up out of the water whenever we tried to get it to sink. But, despite our problems, *Not of This Earth* and *Attack of the Crab Monsters* were released on a double bill that made a 400 percent profit the first week.

The monster from *It Conquered the World* was not much of a monster either. When [the female lead] Beverly Garland first saw it, she said, "This SOB couldn't conquer anything," gave it a good kick, and knocked it over. In *Not or This Earth,* [the actor] Paul Birch was supposed to wear wraparound glasses, so you couldn't see the sides of his eyes. They stuck gaffer's tape on the sides of his glasses. You can see it if you look. In that film, I was in the scene at the newsstand at Las Palmas.

I had the worst time with titles. I hated some of those titles they put on the films. I did one called *Teenage Doll,* where every page of the script was rejected by the censors, and I had to write it over again during the weekend. I once wrote a script in twenty-four hours called *Rock All Night.* Lord Buckley was supposed to play Sir Bop in that film. He was a friend of mine, and I used to write material for him. He was a great character.

After that came The Undead.

One day Roger said, "I want you to do a *Bridey Murphy* picture." *Bridey Murphy* [i.e., *The Search for Bridey Murphy,* 1956] was being done at that time as a big-budget picture, and the book was still relatively popular. [The book and the film were about a woman who, when hypnotized, remembered her past lives.] I thought it would be dead by the time we could get anything out, but I wrote this story which I initially called "The Trance of Diana Love." Curiously, I separated all the different things with sequences with the devil, which were really elaborate, and the dialogue in the past was all in iambic pentameter. Roger got very excited by that. He handed the script around for everybody to read, but nobody understood the dialogue, so he told me to translate it into English. The script was ruined, but *The Undead* [the final title] was a fun picture to shoot, because it was done in ten days at the Sunset Stage, which was a supermarket on Sunset Boulevard. We filled it with palm trees and fog, and it was the first time Roger had used any of that stuff. He didn't like to rent anything. You could see the zipper on the witch's dress and all the gimmicks were very obvious and phony—Roger deliberately played to skid row, a degenerate audience.

I was surprised to discover that you directed your first film in 1957.

I started out as a director on *Forbidden Island.* I was trying to raise money to make independent low-budget pictures and wound up at Columbia with a five-picture writer-producer-director contract. I made two pictures under it, wrote and produced both of them, and directed one. [The other film Griffith produced was *Ghost of the China Sea,* with David Brian and Jonathan Haze, which was directed by Fred F. Sears.] They were really terrible. It stopped me for twenty years from ever directing again. They were really rank. You see, I got chicken and started to write very safely within a formula to please the major studios, and of course, you can't do that.

How did the idea of combining a monster movie and a gangster melodrama come about? That's a rather bizarre combination.

You see, we had set movies that we would do. One of them was *Naked Paradise,* which was made in 1956 about a robbery in a pineapple plantation in Hawaii where the hero is operating a small sailboat and is hired by the crooks to take them to safety. When there's a robbery in Hawaii, the government shuts down the seaports and airports, and nobody can get out. So that was the thing. The crooks hung around in this house waiting to be picked up while all the action happened, and they all kill each other off.

That was successful, so we did it again in South Dakota. Roger says, "I want *Naked Paradise* using a gold mine instead of a pineapple plantation. Put it in South Dakota and add a monster." I didn't know how to add a monster to that script, so I had it all wrapped up in a cocoon in a cave just threatening to break loose all the time. That became *Beast from the Haunted Cave.*

Creature from the Haunted Sea was the same picture again, only this time instead of a plantation, it's the Cuban National Treasury, and the same gang of crooks taking off, but with an added zaniness, because Roger wanted another comedy. He still didn't know that the comedies were going to flop. The monster was made by Beach Dickerson for fifty dollars with a fur coat, two Ping-Pong balls, and garden trowels for claws.

Creature from the Haunted Sea was the simplest of the comedies. Roger called me about three o'clock one morning. At the time, he was shooting *The Last Woman on Earth* [1961], which Robert Towne wrote, down in Puerto Rico. He got me to write the script for *Haunted Sea* in three days, and I sent it down to him in pieces. I didn't get to read the first scenes to see what the hell had gone on in them. It was definitely off the wall. He'd shot about half of it, maybe two-thirds, and then Roger decided he wanted to play a character. So I wrote the character of Happy Jack Monahan for him to play—who commits suicide, falls in love with a whore, cries, and who has to do every possible emotion. Roger had to hire an actor to do it. He was enraged! (*Chuckles.*)

The pictures didn't make any money because he was releasing them through his own Filmgroup Company, and he knew right away that comedy was not automatically an exploitation market. But he tried it again with *The Raven* [1963].

How much time did you have to write the screenplays for Bucket of Blood *and* Little Shop of Horrors?

Five days each. We did *Bucket of Blood* first, which was not meant to be a comedy, according to Roger. It became one because of me. It was the same situation where these sets were going to stand for another week.

The ones from Diary of a High School Bride?

Right, you know the story. *Bucket of Blood* had to be rushed through, and it had to be a comedy. Roger asked me, "How do you shoot comedy?" and I told him to shoot it just like anything else. That was that, and it worked. We got applause on the set during the reading of the beatnik poetry, and that got Roger very excited. It was the first time anybody had ever liked anything. So we had to do it again right away. We sat down during shooting, and he insisted that it had to be the exact same picture, scene for scene, with just some of the names changed and so on. And I figured, "Oh, well, I'll just go from satire to farce, and he'll never know the difference."

Bucket of Blood *is one of the few films that chronicles something of the beatnik era.*

The beatniks in the coffeehouse scenes were all my friends. I didn't know too many of the poets, but everybody went to coffeehouses in those days. And the thing is, those were the sets that were there to shoot, the ones from *High School Bride.* Roger said, "Write a horror picture for those sets." There was a beatnik coffeehouse, a jail, a funky pad with nothing in it, and the lumberyard was the studio lumber department. So there really wasn't much of a choice. That's what dictated it being a comedy.

And Little Shop of Horrors *was actually shot in two days and three nights?*

Roger shot the interiors in two days on the stage—fifty pages a day—and I did the exteriors all around town, which took four days and nights. Mel

Jack Nicholson's dental appointment, a famous scene from *The Little Shop of Horrors.*

Welles, who produced second unit on *Little Shop,* helped out, but that was about the entire crew. Everybody else we got from skid row. We gave them ten cents a shot to act in the picture and got all kinds of good stuff. We got fifteen minutes of picture for $1,100, which was not too bad. The whole picture cost $27,000.

Didn't you also play a holdup man in the film?

Actually, I played four parts—the guy who runs out of the office with his ear bitten; the gangster that sticks up the flower shop and gets eaten by the plant; a shadow on the wall; and the voice of the plant, which was supposed to have been dubbed, but I did it on the stage, so Jonathan Haze would have something to react to. We just left it in because to dub over would have been a little too much money and trouble.

All my relatives were in that picture too. My father was the guy in the dentist's chair who got the mirror broken in his mouth. My kid brothers and sisters were in the crowd scenes. At that point, Roger and I were getting along very well, and I got away with a lot. I got away with rehearsing the cast ahead of time. Roger wouldn't let you do that later. It would take too much time.

Now you can't change anything unless he orders it changed. You can't try anything. The director of *Deathsport* [Henry Suso] came up to me and said he had a fabulous idea of shooting at night. I said, "You'd better tell that to Roger." He had worked out how he could use filters to get "day-for-night." Roger told him no night and no day-for-night. That was it. Anything you'd suggest to him, he'd say no. Anything. Ask anybody who works for him now. He'll gather people together and tell them nobody in his company knows how to make a picture.

The talents that worked for Roger got their chance because they were willing to work for nothing. These days everything is stolen. The ideas are stolen, the money is stolen from the people doing the work, the medical benefits are stolen, the residuals are stolen—there's no pension or welfare—and then the final picture is stolen from the audience because it's a piece of crap. That's low-budget exploitation picture-making.

Getting back to *Little Shop of Horrors* . . . I didn't even know it had been released. I had moved to Israel and then to Rome after making *Atlas.* When I was in Rome, Michael Reeves phoned from Montreal, but he said he had to get off the phone because *Little Shop of Horrors* was on television and everybody in town was watching it. That was the first news I'd heard that *Little Shop* was going to be a cult picture.

I'm curious about Atlas. *I don't think I've ever seen it.*

You're lucky. I've got a print of *Atlas,* and it's probably blood red by now. *Atlas* was a mess. It was a doomed project. I was involved in an Israeli war picture about helicopters, which never got finished, when Roger decided to make *Atlas.* This was after *Little Shop,* and I wanted to make it as *Atlas, the Guided Muscle,* but Roger wanted to make a Hercules, Italian-type thing.

Roger had a deal to shoot it in Puerto Rico, so it was going to be a jungle picture about Atlas and Zeus. Ancient Greece could have jungles, so why not?

But I was on my way to Israel because of the helicopter picture that collapsed in the desert. So Roger and I flew to New York together, and we worked on the details of *Atlas*. Then I boarded a ship going to Israel. I made it to Naples and received a cable saying the company had gone bankrupt and good luck. I was stranded in Israel for two years, and Roger wouldn't send me the fare to get out. I wound up doing some pictures in Israel [*Hatsankanim* and *Frontier Ahead*].

Then Roger called me up from Athens and said he was going to do *Atlas* there instead of Puerto Rico after all, but I had to rewrite the script completely. So I went to Athens, and he paid me $200 to rewrite it and $50 a week to be associate producer, production manager, action director, do first-aid duty and everything else. He picked up a girl [Barbara Comeau] who did all the other work. She was wardrobe, script girl, and makeup, and she had no experience at all. "Women know how to do makeup," Roger says, "and anybody can do scriptwriting."

We used local talent from around the town near Athens, and the picture was written in just a few days. It was terrible. Frank Wolff and a couple of other actors came over, but they were very rebellious. Roger was in a towering rage throughout. There was a Greek cameraman and a Greek crew. Nobody knew left from right. The army couldn't march. They tore the noseguards off their papier-mâché helmets, so that their relatives could recognize them in the picture, and there was paper hanging down from their helmets. The tips of their spears were hanging down because they were made out of rubber, which I had to have done at a tire shop around the corner of the set. It was a lot of fun.

We were shooting in public buildings, and of course, they threw us out of all of them. The permits said we could shoot there, but not with actors. So I'd go to all the archaeological sites and use the excuse that there were a lot of wars around here lately [in the script]. We bribed the guards at the gate to let us shoot. Roger broke his sunglasses in half and had a temper tantrum. He went a little mad during that picture. We went off afterwards and got shipwrecked.

One night we were in Athens just before *Atlas* started, and we went out and met some pimps in blue shirts who were passing out leaflets for free beer in one of those whorehouse nightclubs. I tried to tell Roger what it meant. He said, "Free beer. It says right here 'One free beer,' so let's get a free beer." We got a free beer and were immediately hustled by these chicks with a glaring bouncer behind them. We went out and had another free beer until we came to this place that said it had a floor show at ten o'clock and 2 A.M.

Roger said, "Let's go back and see the floor show at 2 A.M." We returned, and there were these two hookers who came and sat with us. "Aren't you going to buy us a drink, honey?" So Roger started buying them champagne, and he had this girl sitting on his lap, necking with her, and I just sat and watched the whole thing. There was still no floor show, however, and Roger got mad. The bill finally came, and it was for sixty dollars. "I'm not paying sixty dollars for this," Roger said. "And there's no floor show!" The band started walking across [the floor], and we ran out. We escaped from the place and we didn't pay the bill.

But the Greeks froze the money we brought in, so we couldn't use the cash to shoot the picture. We all had to share hotel rooms, but nobody did any sleeping. They got me cheap at fifty dollars a week.

Weren't you supposed to write The Gold Bug *for Corman's Poe series?*

Yes, I was supposed to write *The Gold Bug* for Vincent Price, Peter Lorre, and Basil Rathbone. I thought, "Oh, boy, what a cast!" I got very excited. When they were doing *Masque of the Red Death* in London, I met Vincent on the set; and Roger told him what I was doing, and he said, "Yes, yes, tell me about it." I said, "Well, you're taking Basil Rathbone down a burned-out corridor of your southern mansion with no roof on it and the walls are charred and you're using it for a hock shop for all the family heirlooms and you're showing him all the family portraits in the hall . . . "

Bruce Dern (second from left) and Peter Fonda (in leather jacket) in *The Wild Angels.*

"Oh no," Price said, "Not again! I can't stand that cliché one more time!" I explained that the portraits are all the famous cliché paintings that everybody knows. You look at the last one and say, "This is my mother—doesn't she have an enigmatic smile?" So he caught on right away and told me we had to have "the Laughing Cavalier" as his uncle, Oliver Goldbug.

It was going to be *Little Shop of Horrors* again, where Peter Lorre worked for Vincent Price as his sort of slave around the place in this huge hockshop; and at night they would hear this haunted music, and it would be the gold bug dancing on the strings of the harpsichord doing the Gold Bug Rag. Peter Lorre kept the bug in a snuff box and stayed friends with it by giving it drops of Yugoslavian booze. The bug would sting or bite people and turn them into gold, which is a variation of *Little Shop of Horrors* and *Bucket of Blood*. And there were all these famous poses, too. There was a one-armed bandit and a little girl by the pool in the White Rock ad, and they offered the statues for sale. Then when the buyers tried to melt them down, they'd turn into flesh.

But the script was very long, over three hundred pages, and [Corman's partner and producer] Sam Arkoff was enraged. It never got made.

What did you do on Revenge of the Blood Beast, *aka* She-Beast?

I wrote that picture in three days to get an airline ticket for my girlfriend. [Griffith worked as screenwriter and second unit director.] That was originally a comedy about communistic Transylvania with Barbara Steele, Mel Welles, and Paul Maslansky, who played a cop and produced. That was shot in a couple of weeks, but there isn't much I can tell you about it. It's a cult film in Europe.

How did you end up working as a screenwriter on Barbarella?

[The actor] John Phillip Law was a friend of mine, and [the director] Roger Vadim was looking for another writer for *Barbarella*. John recommended me and [the producer Dino De Laurentiis] hired me. I stayed with Vadim and Jane Fonda in their house outside of Paris and worked on the script. They'd already shot some of the picture when I was called to work on it and had even temporarily scored it with Beatles music. It was really bad.

Why did Terry Southern get the screen credit?

He took the material from the French comic strip, but that's all he did. Then they hired fourteen other writers before they finally got to me. I didn't get credit because I was the last one. I guess I rewrote about a quarter of the film that was shot, then reshot, and I added the concept that there had been thousands of years since violence existed, so that Barbarella was very clumsy all through the picture. She shoots herself in the foot and everything. It was pretty ludicrous.

The stuff with [the actor] Claude Dauphin and the suicide room were also part of my contribution to the film. But the most fun was staying at their house and talking all night with Vadim about politics—it was during the *Pueblo* incident[*]—and talking with Jane all day about movies. At that time, she wasn't known for her politics or for being a good actress. The military invited her to entertain the troops in Vietnam, but she was planning to defect and entertain the Viet Cong. Everyone was looking at her and imagining her plowing through the jungle with the Viet Cong and what would have happened to her.

How did you get involved with Death Race 2000?

I came back from Europe and I called Roger [Corman] and he said, "I've got something for you." I looked at the script, which was by Robert Thom, and it was completely bizarre, unshootable, and crazy, but it did have a lot of interesting things in it. "You're asking *me* to change this?" I asked Roger. He and I were always having trouble over the bizarre things in my screenplays. He told me that since the script had been written by a bizarre person, he figured it took another one to fix it.

So we started from scratch.[†] There were some original things we kept out of our version: Frankenstein, I know, and those cars—another idea of Roger's—were added later. I met Paul Bartel, who was already set to direct it, and we reached a mutual conclusion that the film had to be a satire, somehow a political satire, because there was nothing else we could do with those cars.

Roger, however, wanted a straight, hard-hitting drama, so it was a conspiracy with Paul and everyone in the office at times to keep Roger from knowing. I worked on a long-lost and forgotten version that was very funny and extremely bizarre, but Roger found out about it and canceled the entire script. He was really enraged. So we started again on a much more modified, but similar, straight version, which Paul shot. He left out all the blood, so Roger hired me to be a second-unit director and put in all those blood bits. I told Paul that the way I would do them would be so absurd and so overstated that the film would still stay funny. It didn't happen in the case of *Heckle and Hype*. I fought with the producers over blood and gore versus comedy, and lost as usual.

I've heard that at one time Roger wanted to rev up the engine noises in Death Race *and drown out most of the dialogue.*

He does that a lot. He'd play up the sound effects or turn the music way down, so that it would sound very distant, and he'd play with the dialogue, too. He was very big on sound effects. Yeah, he played with *Death Race* and tried to get rid of as much comedy as possible.

Would you describe some of your second-unit work?

The picture was in the can, so I took the stuff and had to add a lot of action. I looked through the material and added to it in different places. For example,

---

[*] The *Pueblo* was a US intelligence ship captured allegedly within North Korean territorial waters in January 1968. The crew were held for eleven months, then released.

[†] Ib Melchior's story provided the basis for *Death Race 2000*'s script.

the scene where Sylvester Stallone drives down to the end of the pier was changed. Originally, there was a man sitting in the outhouse with the top door open and the machine-gun car pulls up and there's a conversation with Stallone while this guy is still in the outhouse. A dumb conversation. Stallone backs up and knocks the outhouse with this guy in it into the river and drives on. There wasn't enough action in that for Roger, and you could see when the outhouse fell into the river that there was nobody in it.

I went back, got rid of the outhouse, cut around the outhouse, and had a fisherman sitting there and Stallone chase the fisherman up the river. There were bits and pieces of both scenes, but all of Stallone's dialogue was from the other scene.

Was it a successful film for Roger?

It did about two and a half million dollars, so it must have been.

How would you describe Roger Corman? At times, he is referred to as an idiot savant—*part genius, part deranged person.*

Deranged, yes. Genius, no. The genius that he might have had is gone. He used to be full of ideas and Freudian concepts, and he'd throw these things out to the writers and get them all hot. They would work like crazy, but he would have forgotten what he wanted to do. He was only interested in saving money, so his intellect ground down to almost nothing. When you see some of his crap, there are a few moments of interest. That wasn't true of some of the other shockers that were being made at the time. Those producers knew what they wanted, and that was pure garbage and no great loss. Roger's stuff was 99 percent garbage and 1 percent is of interest.

He did, however, show some technical skill as a director and his films are usually well paced.

He took everything out that wasn't fast and ruined every picture that way. In recent years, he has ruined all of his pictures, and they're losing money. They are incomprehensible. Did you see *Smokey Bites the Dust?* It went right through town without being seen.

Wasn't that film built around stock footage?

That's true. Roger hired me a few years before that, in 1977 or '78. It all started with a news broadcast. The police were complaining that *Eat My Dust!,* and other pictures like it, inspired kids to chase down the freeways and challenge the cops and run other cars off the road. There were lots of people blamed for this, and Sheriff Pritches called this Car Wars. As soon as the newscast was over, the phone rang, and it was Roger. "I want you to do a picture called 'Car Wars,' " he said, "using the stunts from five old New World pictures."

I wrote a script which wound up being called "Wham Bam, Merci, Madame." It was insane and used all the stunts in different ways. But Roger hated the script and never did the picture.

In 1983, however, he called again and offered me a lot more money than he ever had before. I guess I got flattered, and I went ahead and did it. He had Max

Ron Howard in *Eat My Dust!* written and directed by Charles Griffith.

Apple in Texas go ahead and write a script around all the wrecks and chases. But Max wasn't allowed to see the footage. It was too expensive to rent a Movieola and send Max prints or anything else, so he had only vague descriptions written down on what the stunts were—and nothing worked. So I made a lot of changes in it, and that made Roger angry. He tried to cut it just to the action of the old pictures, but he couldn't, because he needed all the distribution rights. Then he cut all the motivations and all the character development. It was a mess, a jumbled mess! The same thing occurred in *Up from the Depths.*

Wasn't Up from the Depths *Corman's attempt to do a Jaws film?*

Of course it was. He stole it from *Jaws* [1975], *Jaws 2* [1978], and *The Deep* [1977]. It was written by a secretary at the office with the intention that I would polish it up.* I was hired to direct, but Roger wouldn't pay Writers Guild prices—he thinks the Writers Guild is in a conspiracy against him personally—so the idea was that I would use my director's perogative to polish up an impossible script.

---

* The credited scenarist of *Up from the Depths* is Alfred Sweeney. Griffith is listed as director only.

So I wrote a zany version called "Something Fishy" and the Filipinos [the producers and investors] were crazy about it. They made a funny-looking fish for it, and we were all set to go; but they sent the script to Roger, figuring he would love it, and of course, he hit his desk and told them to fire me and everybody else. They wouldn't fire me, so I still had to do the polish, but I did it just for action.

There was a lot of excitement to just go ahead and shoot it, but then the action didn't work because the Filipinos didn't work. The fish never worked once. It was supposed to attack people, to chew them up, and thrash all sorts of things, but it didn't do anything. I had a right-to-left fish and a left-to-right fish, and a fin and a head which would come across the ocean on huge bamboo rafts towed by outrigger canoes. It would take them two hours to cross the bay with this stuff. It never worked.

The speedboats never worked because the propellers were beaten up by the coral reefs. The underwater shots didn't work, because there were no lead weights to get people down. They were bobbing to the surface. And nobody would show up. You would get ballroom extras on the beach and beach extras at the ballroom. There weren't any American cars available because all American cars belonged to rich people who wouldn't rent them. It was great being there for six months.

I had a 106-minute rough cut that I sent back. When I arrive in LA, the next day, it [*Up from the Depths*] was 75 minutes long. That was some of Roger's creative editing. I've never seen the picture. I just saw the black-and-white work print that I was working on. *Smokey* and *Up from the Depths* were the last two pictures that I did for Roger, and they were both so butchered that it has made it impossible for me to get work. Those pictures are so bad no one can sit through them.

What about Dr. Heckyl and Mr. Hype*?*

That's my old friend Menahem Golan from Israel. I stayed at his house about ten years ago and worked on a couple of pictures that were never made. He told me to call him up if I wanted to make a picture, so I did. He wanted to make "Happy Hooker Goes to Hollywood," but it took my agent too long to negotiate, so it was already in the works with other people.

So Golan asked me what I wanted to do. I told him that I specialize in black comedies, and I had a list of things I wanted to show [the writer-director] Francis Coppola. There were a lot of things on that list that were jokes and were not intended to be pictures. But one of the films on the list was "Dr. Feelgood and Mr. Hype," in which a hippie invents a new drug that turns everybody into advertising executives.

He said, "You want to make a funny *Jekyll and Hyde*?" I responded, "Sure." He gave me the go-ahead, but I had only three weeks to write it and to prepare the picture, one week of which was in [the actor] Oliver Reed's hands, four weeks to shoot, and two weeks to edit. It was terribly, terribly rushed for a modern picture in color with lots of elaborate art direction and stuff. This cost $750,000 and Cannon couldn't release it. [The film was quickly sold to cable.]

Heckyl and Hype could have been a very good picture. Dr. Heckyl is a monster podiatrist. He is very humble and meek and helpful and nice to everybody. His attitude is that good-looking guys can get away with murder. Oliver was great as Heckyl. Wonderful. He played the part with a kind of New York accent and everything, but when he was Hype, he didn't know how to do it. . . . Reed played Hype as Oliver Reed, slow and ponderous. He didn't understand my interpretation, so the picture jars, and half the people get up and walk out.

What do you think of the violence in today's horror movies?

Hate it! I was one who did it in the years when we couldn't show violence. In *The Undead,* for example, I had a scene where we back somebody against a wall and the headman swings an ax cutting off the head and the body slides down the wall with blood spurting from the neck. The head stays on the ax blade against the wall. In the fifties, filmmakers couldn't do anything like that, so we were all frustrated in those years. But, boy, as soon as it started to appear on the screen, it made me sick. I don't want to do it or see it.

What are your future projects?

I'm writing one called "Out of This World," which is a very large-scale science fiction film. I can't tell you about it because the idea is the best part so far. New World wanted me to come back and write a sword-and-sorcery picture, but they didn't want to pay me, and I wasn't going to do it for nothing. Let's see, there's "The Real McCoy" and "Oy Vey, My Son Is Gay," which will be the Jewish *La Cage aux Folles* for Cannon. But that's all I can tell you about now.

John Michael Hayes:
Qué Sera, Sera

Interview by Susan Green

François Truffaut: "To my mind, *Rear Window* is
probably your very best screenplay in all respects.
The construction, the unity of inspiration, the wealth
of details."

Alfred Hitchcock: "I was feeling very creative at
the time, the batteries were well-charged. John
Michael Hayes is a radio writer and he wrote the
dialogue."

—François Truffaut, *Hitchcock*

In a quintessentially quaint house with a white picket fence in rural West Leb-
anon, New Hampshire, seventy-five-year-old John Michael Hayes recounted
the many vicissitudes of his personal and professional life, both in and out of
Hollywood.

Fortune has alternately smiled and scowled upon him. When it came to his
career, Hayes experienced the heaven and hell of Alfred Hitchcock. The four
films they made together in a remarkably short period of time during the mid-
1950s—*Rear Window, To Catch a Thief, The Trouble with Harry,* and *The Man
Who Knew Too Much* (1956 version)—would seem to provide the defining
moments of Hayes's résumé. But an initially harmonious working relationship
turned sour. According to Hayes, Hitchock nurtured the fledgling screenwriter
only to betray him ultimately.

Throughout a hardscrabble working-class childhood, during which he
endured temporary disability, Hayes worked his way through the system on
the strength of his writing skills. The first in his family to enter college, he
spent summers as a newspaperman, at one point covering a police beat. A

promising entry into radio broadcasting was forestalled by the army, which drafted him during World War II. Later, calamity struck again in the form of a crippling illness.

After fully recovering, Hayes went west in the late 1940s. A job writing radio mysteries led to an offer to try his hand at screenplays for the motion picture industry. It also led to an association with Alfred Hitchcock, who had heard his radio whodunits and recognized a kindred talent.

In 1954, the first Hayes-Hitchcock collaboration was the elegant and witty *Rear Window,* replete with sexual double entendres that were bold for their time. It ranks as Hayes's masterpiece and one of Hitchcock's finest.

The Trouble with Harry, while sweetly improbable, is also full of funny, frenetic wordplay. The even more suggestive *To Catch a Thief* has that je ne sais quoi. (Remember the repartee from the picnic sequence that begins, "Do you want a leg or a breast?"). And although Doris Day lacks the blithe charm of Grace Kelly, the clever writing of *The Man Who Knew Too Much,* a remake of Hitchcock's 1934 film and the last picture that Hayes did with the director, manages to draw the viewer into a suffocating web of intrigue.

By the time the last of the Hitchcock-Hayes films was released in 1956, the partnership had crumbled. Apparently, Hitchcock had no desire to be known as a co-master of suspense. While the great director did not exactly stumble on alone—his carefully picked screenwriters were always crucial to his success—some critics think he never succeeded as sublimely as when Hayes was by his side. "In the quartet of films scripted by John Michael Hayes," Donald Spoto writes in *The Dark Side of Genius: The Life of Alfred Hitchcock,* "There is a credibility and emotional wholeness, a heart and humor to the characters that other Hitchcock films—like *Strangers on a Train* and *I Confess* before, and others after—conspicuously lack."

Qué sera, sera. Hayes went on to adapt Grace Metalious's small-town soap opera *Peyton Place* (New York: Messner, 1956). It was a prestigious and daring film in its day, with Hayes earning his second Oscar nomination for Best Adapted Screenplay. (The first was for *Rear Window.*) And the film holds up fairly well, although it does not have the cachet of a Hitchcock production.

Hayes had a productive decade in the 1960s. Among the top directors he worked with, not always happily, were Henry Hathaway and William Wyler. *Butterfield Eight, The Children's Hour, The Carpetbaggers, Harlow,* and *Nevada Smith* were all distinctly high-profile adaptations. Hayes seemed to specialize in films about people with delusions of grandeur. At their best, some of those 1960s credits maximized his strengths, showing off resourceful characters, offbeat dialogue, superb plotting.

Then fate frowned on him once again. After a series of near misses—scripts commissioned but not produced—Hayes unwittingly secured a financial stability that would keep him from writing and limit his creative output in the latter half of the 1970s. And then, genuine tragedy—his wife's terminal cancer and Hayes's own partial blindness from macular degeneration of the retina—transformed his life in the late 1980s.

Even so, in 1994, a new John Michael Hayes film—only his second original screenplay—emerged. *Iron Will,* a Disney adventure about a determined boy in a dogsled race, was a victim of rewrite mania. Yet perhaps its iron-willed hero could be seen as an alter ego for the writer who had battled his way back from an almost twenty-eight-year dry spell between screen credits.

While he, too, copes with cancer, Hayes has been teaching screenwriting at Dartmouth College. He worries that he has turned his frequent lectures on Hitch into a cottage industry. Thanks to *Iron Will,* he is once again fielding offers from Hollywood. Strange as it seems, one of them is for a sequel to *Rear Window.* One thing is sure: if this film is ever made, at least Alfred Hitchcock won't be around to claim credit for the screenplay.

John Michael Hayes at Dartmouth, 1994. (Photo by Joseph Mehling, Dartmouth College.)

John Michael Hayes (1919–   )

1952   *Red Ball Express* (Budd Boetticher). Script.

1953   *Thunder Bay* (Anthony Mann). Co-script.

1953   *Torch Song* (Charles Walters). Co-script.

1954   *War Arrow* (George Sherman). Story, script.

1954   *Rear Window* (Alfred Hitchcock). Script.

1955   *The Bar Sinister* (Herman Hoffman). Script.

1955   *The Trouble with Harry* (Alfred Hitchcock). Script.

1955   *To Catch a Thief* (Alfred Hitchcock). Script.

1956   *The Man Who Knew Too Much* (Alfred Hitchcock). Co-script.

1957   *Peyton Place* (Mark Robson). Script.

1958   *The Matchmaker* (Joseph Anthony). Script.

1959   *But Not for Me* (Walter Lang). Script.

1960   *Butterfield Eight* (Daniel Mann). Co-script.

1962   *The Children's Hour* (William Wyler). Script.

1964   *The Chalk Garden* (Ronald Neame). Script.

1964   *The Carpetbaggers* (Edward Dmytryk). Script.

1964   *Where Love Has Gone* (Edward Dmytryk). Script.

1965   *Harlow* (Gordon Douglas). Script.

1965   *Judith* (Daniel Mann). Script.

1966   *Nevada Smith* (Henry Hathaway). Script.

1994   *Iron Will* (Charles Haid). Story, co-script.

Television script credits include the telefilms *Winter Kill* (1974), *Nevada Smith* (also coproduced, 1975), and *Pancho Barnes* (1988).

Academy Award honors include Oscar Nominations for Best Adapted Screenplay for *Rear Window* and *Peyton Place*.

Tell me how you got into journalism.

I was eight when I started writing. At fourteen, I started writing for money. I was born cross-eyed and had many operations. I lost two and a half years of school, between second and fifth grades. I had ear infections that came as a result of my eye problems, so I had nothing to do but read. I went door-to-door, asking neighbors for books. I read Shakespeare, religious philosophy, history. I became word conscious, which led to a fascination with the process of writing. I knew this was the world that I wanted to be in.

I later worked on school newspapers and began sending items to local newspapers when I was twelve, thirteen, fourteen. I turned the money over to my father. Anything I could bring in helped. My father was a song-and-dance man in vaudeville, who went to work in a factory as a tool-and-die maker but lost his job during the depression. He ended up on the WPA [Works Progress Administration]. My grandfather had the oral tradition of Irish storytellers.

We lived in State Line, New Hampshire—population fifty-two. When we moved to Massachusetts, I was editor of a Boy Scout newspaper. Then, during high school, I wrote for the local paper, the *Worcester Telegram,* for ten cents a column inch. But I wrote so much I was making more than the regular reporters, so they put me on salary. At sixteen, I was hired by the head of the Associated Press and went to Washington, D.C. My column was "A Young Man Looks at His Government." I got ten dollars a day. Then the *Boston Globe* called . . .

I was able to fulfill my dream of going to college. No one in my family ever had. I had scholarships and I worked. I attended the University of Massachusetts, then called Massachusetts State College. In the summer, I would go back to the newspaper business. I had a police beat and saw the arrest process, went out on ambulance calls, covered homicides and suicides. Later, that gave my writing a frame of reference, because I'd seen a lot of the criminal side of life. I was on firm ground. It wasn't an alien world.

How and why did you make the transition to film?

After college, I could have gone on with academic work at Duke University, gone back to the *Worcester Telegram* or to the AP. I chose a scholarship from the Crosley Corporation in Cincinnati to learn broadcasting at a radio station. That led to writing daytime serials for Proctor and Gamble. Then I was drafted into the army for four years during World War II. I never went overseas or into battle, because I only had one good eye. They assigned me to special services, putting on entertainment for the troops at camps in California, Oregon, Missouri. Then, I ended up as a medic in the infantry.

After being discharged, I developed rheumatoid arthritis and was in bed for a year. It took me ten months to walk again. I had to use two canes.

I had little money, but I hitched to California in 1948 and found a job at CBS Radio the day I arrived. I wrote for Lucille Ball's *My Favorite Husband* and some suspense shows. Then, in 1951, I started writing B pictures for Universal.

The first of those was Red Ball Express. *Didn't the director, Budd Boetticher, become a matador or something?*

(*Laughs.*) He was a roommate of John Kennedy at Choate. He came, I gather, from a social, rich family. He went to Spain and became a bullfighter. On the set, he used to bring his bullfighting cape and do veronicas and other things that bullfighters do. He was a very pleasant, easygoing guy. He was a lot of fun.

At this time, when you were starting out in the early 1950s, were there people who showed you the ropes?

There was a writer named Borden Chase, who did *Red River* [1948] and other action pictures.* He helped me out a bit, but the rest of it, really becoming cinematic, I had to learn myself. I just learned as I went along. I used to haunt sets at the studios and watch everything I could. I took notes. And I made a lot of mistakes. Also Charles Schnee—actually, he and Chase wrote *Red River* together—gave me a lot of tips. He was at Metro [MGM]. He had a B-unit there.

Were you inspired or influenced by other writers?

Definitely. Preston Sturges and Dudley Nichols. I used to study their work. And I liked Philip Barry's plays, the swing of his style.

About two years into your B-movie career, you met Hitchcock?

Yes. I had worked on a radio show called *Suspense,* which was a half-hour drama. Then I worked on *The Adventures of Sam Spade* and a number of other radio detective shows. He used to listen to them. He heard my name all the time. That's really what got him interested in me, because I doubt if he had gone to see *War Arrow* or *Red Ball Express* or anything else. So he inquired about me. It turned out we had the same agency, MCA, but we were in different departments. He gave me a tryout, and it stuck. He needed a writer for *Rear Window,* so I went from B movies to A movies overnight.

How did that all come about, the decision to make Rear Window?

Paramount found *Rear Window.* Hitch had left Warner Brothers and was looking for a home. And Paramount said if he could get a screenplay out of a Cornell Woolrich story, they would make a deal with him. They gave him a collection called *After-Dinner Story,* by William Irish [Philadelphia and New York: J. B. Lippincott, 1936], a pen name of Cornell Woolrich. Out of about five or six stories, he liked "Rear Window" and brought me in on it.

I understand the Grace Kelly character was your own idea.

---

* Borden Chase, born Frank Fowler in Brooklyn in 1900, was a novelist and scriptwriter best known for rugged adventure and western stories for directors such as Raoul Walsh, William Wellman, Anthony Mann, and Howard Hawks. His credits include *Winchester '73, The Far Country,* and *Man without a Star.* Chase's novel *The Blazing Guns on the Chisholm Trail* provided the story basis for *Red River*; he cowrote the screenplay with Charles Schnee. His television work included pilot episodes for the *Daniel Boone* and *Laredo* series. See Jim Kitses's interview with Borden Chase in *The Hollywood Screenwriters,* ed. Richard Corliss (New York: Avon, 1972).

"From B to A movies overnight": Alfred Hitchcock conferring with John Michael Hayes.

There was no girl in the original. I created the part. Hitch had done *Dial M for Murder* [1954] with Grace Kelly, and she was beautiful in that film; but there was no life, no sparkle there. He asked me what we should do with her for *Rear Window,* so I spent time with her for about a week. My wife, Mel, was a successful fashion model, so I gave Grace my wife's occupation in the film. The way the character posed, the dialogue—it reflected actual incidents in our life.

Were there tricks or techniques that Hitchcock taught you? Things you weren't doing in radio or in B movies?

I like to write dialogue. It's one of my skills, character and dialogue. Hitchcock, of course, grew up in silent films, and all those directors who did silent films have a tendency to rely on the camera as much as they can. And I caught some of that spirit. Hitchcock taught me about how to tell a story with the camera and tell it silently.

We used a long camera movement to open *Rear Window.* In *The Man Who Knew Too Much,* in the scene at Albert Hall with Doris Day and Jimmy Stewart, we had written some dialogue in case we needed it, but we didn't intend to use it if we didn't have to. Hitch, with his mastery, felt that without dialogue this whole final sequence where the assassination is about to take place—of a central figure from some nameless country—would be stronger. We discovered we didn't need the dialogue at all. But we wrote it protectively.

You incorporated so much clever, risqué banter in your scripts for Hitchcock, particularly Rear Window *and* To Catch a Thief. *Was there a method to your madness?*

Oh, sure. We had censorship in those days. So, if I could do it and make it amusing enough, I could get away with it. I used to do that on radio, on shows like *The Adventures of Sam Spade.* By the time they figured out what I was really saying, it was too late to censor it. I think suggestion is better. I'd rather say things through a literary device that's interesting than just say it out flat. So much of my dialogue is indirect, with layers of meaning, sub-rosa meanings. It's more challenging to write that way, and people remember the lines. Frequently, people came up to me for autographs, and they quote some of those lines from my Hitchcock movies.

Did you often write with specific actors and actresses in mind?

Certainly. I knew Grace Kelly was going to be in *Rear Window* and that Jimmy Stewart, if he liked the treatment, was going to play in it too, so I was able to write for them specifically. I wrote a part specially for Thelma Ritter if they could get her, and they did.

Later on, I knew Cary Grant was going to be in *To Catch a Thief.* He used to bring in material all the time, and the idea there was to delay him until it was too late to do it. But he did it in an amiable, enthusiastic way. He was full of ideas, always wanted to improve things; it wasn't because he didn't like what was there. Of course, sometimes the studios made their own [casting] deals for their own reasons. But they would ask my opinion.

You really seemed to specialize in adaptations. Over the years, only two of your screenplays were originals. What were some of the other sources for your Hitchcock films?

After *Rear Window,* the next one was a book by David Dodge about adventures on the Riviera [*To Catch a Thief* (New York: Random 1952)]. We did *To Catch a Thief* out of that. After that, it was a remake of *The Man Who Knew*

Too Much that Hitchcock did in the early thirties in England. And *The Trouble with Harry* was a book by an English writer, Jack Trevor, whom he admired. Generally, studios bought properties and looked for a writer.

Was Rear Window *a good first experience with Hitchcock?*

That was my first A picture with a big director, and I was so keyed up. I didn't enjoy it as much as I should have, because I was worried about everything. Yet it turned out well. We worked beautifully together.

Your next film was The Trouble with Harry. *Tell me a little about shooting that on location in Vermont.*

We had a lot of trouble with *The Trouble with Harry.* We wanted autumn foliage, so we did background shots. Then a big storm hit, and the next day, no leaves were left on the trees. We took thousands of Vermont leaves back to Hollywood and plastered them on California trees in the studio. Many exteriors were shot in California and interiors shot in Vermont.

Shirley MacLaine had just gotten married the night before she showed up on the set. I remember Hitch saying, "There goes the picture." He felt that this was going to be her honeymoon, so her mind would not be on the work. It was her first movie and her first marriage.

"Everything fit into place like a jigsaw puzzle": Wendell Corey (back to camera), Grace Kelly, and James Stewart in *Rear Window,* directed by Alfred Hitchcock.

Rear Window *was shot in the studio, but after that, you and Hitchcock seemed to be all over the map.*

To Catch a Thief was on the Riviera. I took Grace Kelly to the casino to learn how to play roulette. She ended up not only winning money at the table—no great amount—but she won Monaco! She wanted to see the palace grounds, so I asked for permission; and she went and met Prince Rainier. I told her that I'd heard he was a stuffy fellow.

The Man Who Knew Too Much was made in Morocco and London. Hitch and I talked about doing other screenplays set in South Africa and Brazil. He had ideas of places he wanted to go to. We never made any, of course. He'd consider exotic locations whenever he could. Not only would he make a good film, but he'd also have an adventure.

What was Hitchcock like on a day-to-day basis?

His whole life was motion pictures; there didn't seem to be much else in it. He just loved what he was doing, and he transmitted that feeling to you, rather than hovering over you like a giant genius. He was encouraging. He used to say, "It's only a movie. Don't worry about it, just do your best, and let the public decide." Hitch was humorous and relaxed on the set. We'd go to dinner or lunch, but in no sense was I his personal confidant. He used to go over his early pictures and tell me how he had solved problems.

But then friction began to develop between you and Hitchcock. Did it start while you were in the south of France shooting To Catch a Thief?

I don't recall any real problems then. I think the worst fight we ever had was over the ending of *To Catch a Thief.* We had different ideas. I wrote twenty-seven different endings and still don't like the one that was used. We had a couple of slam-bang script fights. Still, we got along fine until I got too much press.

When we went to Paris for the premiere of *To Catch a Thief,* I was getting mentioned everywhere—they value writers in Paris—so I was promptly banned from all public relations events. If I was mentioned in the fourth paragraph of a story, that was okay but not in the first or second. I was becoming known for my dialogue and characterizations. They even talked about "the Hitchcock-Hayes fall schedule" in either *Variety* or the *Hollywood Reporter.*

When you show up in the same sentence—Alfred Hitchcock and John Michael Hayes—that was more than he could bear. He wanted to be the total creator: Alfred Hitchcock Presents. Hitch was so unkind about giving credit.

In an interview he did with François Truffaut years later for example, Hitch tried to make it seem as if he had written the screenplay for *Rear Window.* I heard about that too late; I tried to contact Truffaut, but he had died. I did a sixty-five-page treatment of *Rear Window* that Jimmy Stewart committed to, that Paramount committed to. I had met with Hitch once or twice. He had *nothing* to do with the writing.

I was nominated for an Oscar. When I won the Edgar Allen Poe Award [for *Rear Window*], the first time it was ever given for a movie, I showed Hitch the ceramic statuette, and he said, "You know, they make toilet bowls out of the same material." Then he almost pushed it off the end of a table.

People believe he did everything. They just don't pay attention to the credits. Hitchcock had some big writers on his films, but you would never know it: Robert Sherwood [*Rebecca,* 1940], Samson Raphaelson [*Suspicion,* 1947], Thornton Wilder [*Shadow of a Doubt,* 1943]—Pulitzer Prize–winning playwrights—Maxwell Anderson [*The Wrong Man,* 1956]. Starting with *Rear Window,* I began to get a great deal of attention. Critics focused on it, and pretty soon, I was being linked with him. That was my undoing. Four in a row, and then we parted because I was being too identified with him.

It was during *The Man Who Knew Too Much* that Hitch turned on me. He insisted we put the name of a friend of his on the picture—Angus MacPhail— who had done none of the writing.* Hitchcock was paying me too little to begin with. On top of that, he wanted me to do the next script for free, something he owed Warner Brothers called *The Wrong Man.* He said, "If you don't do this, I'll never speak to you again." When I refused, he said, in essence, Let's see how far you go without me, kid.

But you did go far.

Yes. On my next project, *Peyton Place,* I got twice as much money as for all four Hitchcock pictures together.

Did you realize all along that you were being underpaid by Hitchcock?

My agents told me to be quiet and do the work, that it would be worth money in the future. But they were, of course, in Alfred Hitchcock's corner, more than in mine. So they didn't encourage him to raise my salary. When I left, the offers came in, and the money was big. So what I did get was a diploma from Alfred Hitchcock University, which was valuable.

Hitchcock's advisers asked him when his pictures got into trouble—on *The Birds* [1963] and *Marnie* [1964] and *Torn Curtain* [1966] and *Topaz* [1969]—to bring me back. But he never would, because it was an admission that he needed me, and he'd never do that. Those pictures didn't have the characterizations, the believability. They didn't have the fun. The films we made together, people call it his golden period. It was a tragedy. We were a great team.

---

* Angus MacPhall received co-credit for the 1956 version of *The Man Who Knew Too Much.* A British writer who started as a titlist in the silent era, he functioned as a story editor at Gaumont and Ealing studios, and collaborated on scripts including *Whisky Galore* (aka, *Tight Little Island*). Among his other screen credits are two other Alfred Hitchcock films—*Spellbound* and *The Wrong Man.*

Apart from making more money, what was life like for you after Hitchcock? You were nominated a second time for an Academy Award with Peyton Place, *which got nine nominations altogether.*

Fortunately, I had a successful picture in *Peyton Place,* which showed that I could get along on my own, that it wasn't just Alfred Hitchcock that made me a good writer. I could do other things.

Peyton Place and *Rear Window* are my favorite films. *Rear Window* came out so well: everything fit into place like a jigsaw puzzle. Technically, it was more polished. But *Peyton Place* was emotionally satisfying. The relationship between Mark Robson and myself was marvelous. He was very creative and helpful. I had a small-town New England background of my own, and I understood the setting and the people and the patois and the feelings.

What did that mean in the evolution of the screenplay?

I just felt comfortable with the material. I tried to tell the story of the difficulty adolescents have passing through that invisible pane of glass as they become adults. I examined the turmoil they go through, especially in the town of Peyton Place. I was sympathetic to these young people. The first draft was nearly three hundred pages, and it took eight drafts to finally boil it down. I had little bits of my own philosophy woven in—I always do that. I drew on my

Diane Varsi (left) and Lana Turner in *Peyton Place,* directed by Mark Robson.

own experience of living in two small New Hampshire towns. It was not an alien land to me. I could see the town in my mind. I could feel it.

The hard part, of course, was to get over the censorship hurdles; we had to imply things. Everybody had read the book, so we couldn't disappoint them—without offending the censors and without offending the other countries in which it would be seen. Getting the Catholic Church's Legion of Decency seal was probably the most difficult thing. People felt it was a book that couldn't be made into a picture. We had to make it acceptable but entertaining and good. And the Legion didn't change a line. The man in charge, Monsignor Biddle, told me, "John Michael, you've done it!" He was a jolly fellow, reminded me of Barry Fitzgerald.

Weren't there also some funny location problems on Peyton Place?

Yes. We thought Vermont would be easy to film in. We knew a lot of officials in the Vermont Development Commission. However, the book was very scandalous. It shocked the whole world. It had been banned in Boston and every Catholic country. Despite that, it sold ten million copies—at that time, more than *Gone with the Wind.* A Vermont legislator stood up and pledged to pass a law against having *Peyton Place* filmed in his state. It was also kept out of Massachusetts, Rhode Island, and Connecticut. For a while, we thought we'd have to do it in Oregon or Washington. But we contacted Senator Margaret Chase Smith in Maine. She got word to Governor Edmund Muskie, and he loved the idea. He told us, "Maine is yours!" But when we needed some autumn foliage, 20th Century-Fox borrowed Paramount's Vermont outtakes from *The Trouble with Harry*!

After Hitchcock, what was it like to work with other legendary directors? I'm thinking of William Wyler and Henry Hathaway.

All famous producers and directors have enormous egos. And it was difficult to work with some of them. Wyler was the most difficult of all.

More so than Hitchcock?

Hitchcock and Mark Robson were the easiest directors. They were amiable and easy to get along with. Wyler and Hathaway were not. They wanted *their* viewpoint told instead of *yours.* I don't know why they hired me and paid me all that money and then insisted I do it their way. We had many script fights.

Wyler was the most difficult director *ever.* He would not let you sit down and really write. Every ten pages, you had to turn them in, discuss, analyze them sentence by sentence, word by word. You could never get into—at least I couldn't—a creative flow. You kept getting interrupted. We did rewriting and rewriting and rewriting, which was ridiculous.

I had a similar problem with Henry Hathaway. He wanted to be part of every page. I prefer to start a screenplay and go through the whole first draft in one fell swoop. To get all the emotion, color, drama, melodrama, purple prose, and everything else that I can put into a story. Because I know that, during subsequent script conferences with the director and the stars, many things get leeched out of it. So I want to put as much as I can into the first draft. I, therefore, have to be given my head, instead of writing a few pages and then having a conference, and writing a few pages and having another conference. It ends up that you don't write the kind of picture you want to write, and the director never gets a chance to see what you can do, because he's imposing his will on you constantly. When I argued with Henry Hathaway about *Nevada Smith,* I inevitably lost. But at least you've got to put up a good fight.

In the case of Mark Robson, I did *Peyton Place* completely before he read it. And, therefore, our conferences were concerned with cutting it down and trimming it and making it workable, rather than have him participate in the creative aspect of writing it.

As for Hitchcock, he let me write on my own, and then we conferred afterwards. We had some conferences, but he didn't go over pages. We'd sit and discuss the thing in general. I'd do a first draft and a second draft; then, we would do a shooting script, and that's when he would break up the story into shots, specific camera angles. He'd draw sketches. If I had a film with two hundred shots in it on my first or second draft, we'd end up with six hundred, because he broke it down into every single camera angle. Hitch did not like to make changes. When we finished setting up the shots before the picture was started, he'd say. "The picture is made now. All we have to do is sit on the set and make sure they follow what we've worked out here."

Hitch would never change the script unless the writer agreed to it. Too many directors think just because they're a director they know how to write, and they don't. On *The Carpetbaggers* and *Where Love Has Gone,* Edward Dmytryk was tempted to come in with dialogue and write long speeches. Those directors who write on location and change things are the bane of writers, because you don't see what mistakes they're making until it's too late. You just can't improve off the cuff on the set, because you upset the whole build of the emotions and the texture of the picture. On location, things happen weatherwise or otherwise. But you work hard to get the script tight and right. Tampering with it is very dangerous, especially in a suspense story.

With an important director who has a long track record of hits and awards, it's hard to stand up for your viewpoint. Directors have a tendency to fall back on things that they're used to which are safe. If they hire a talented writer, they should let him write it and then discuss the directorial changes. That's the difficulty of working with extremely successful, older, talented, even brilliant directors.

I remember once telling Willie Wyler that he was wrong about something, and he took me around his office and he showed me every award he'd won— and he had many—and he read all the inscriptions. It must have taken him thirty minutes. Then he said, "Now tell me I'm wrong. What does all this mean?" And I said, "Well, those were things you've done in the past. I think you're wrong now."

Did you sometimes feel, in a strange way, justified to see bad reviews?

Yes. I once had a debate with a producer over a Gable picture, *But Not for Me* [1959]. After the preview, the producer said, "I wish I'd listened to you. You were right."

I've seen bits of some of my pictures when I wanted to run down the aisle and say, "No, no. That's not the way it's supposed to be." But other things that directors did surprised me and delighted me and made things more interesting. So you lose a little, you win a little.

I still remember a line from the review in the *Los Angeles Times* of *War Arrow* with Jeff Chandler and Maureen O'Hara, which came out in 1954: "The director struggled valiantly with the material given to him." That was an original story of mine—a true story—about Seminole Indians being moved from Florida to Arizona because they were rebellious. So they used them as scouts to subdue the Kiowa, and you had Indians against Indians. The review was so unfair. The director, George Sherman, took out four action scenes and replaced them with four talk scenes, which talked about the action but didn't show it. The studio heads at Universal later said, "We know what happened: It's not your fault."

Were you pleased with how The Children's Hour *and* Nevada Smith *turned out?*

Not at all pleased with *The Children's Hour* and somewhat disappointed with things that happened in *Nevada Smith*. Hathaway went on location and made changes in the script himself; then, he called me because he got into trouble. I had to fly down to Biloxi and try to straighten it out. Those pictures weren't as enjoyable as the others were, where at least I got to state my case in my first draft.

Was Lillian Hellman involved behind the scenes in The Children's Hour?

Willie Wyler was in constant contact with Lillian Hellman. Don't forget they had made another version earlier, in the thirties, and Lillian Hellman did the screenplay for that.* Wyler was very nervous about pleasing her, and she was a hovering influence over the whole thing. I never talked with her, but she wrote long letters to Wyler. He had another writer working on the film, who left before I came on. I myself would have been happy to leave. I wasn't happy at all with the atmosphere or the final result. At the end, I became ill. There were two scenes left. Hellman did them.

Tell me about Judith. *That was a Lawrence Durrell piece . . .*

Yes. Durrell was a brilliant English writer. He wrote an original story based on the time when Israel was trying to become a state. They had another writer on the project to begin with, and they were on location for months trying to

---

* The earlier film version of *The Children's Hour* was titled *These Three* (1938). William Wyler also directed this film from Lillian Hellman's adaptation of her play. The cast included Merle Oberon, Miriam Hopkins, and Joel McCrea.

Shirley MacLaine (center), Audrey Hepburn, and James Garner in a tableau from director William Wyler's 1962 remake of Lillian Hellman's *The Children's Hour.*

shoot scenes. Danny Mann, for whom I'd done *Butterfield Eight,* persuaded me to come over and do a rewrite, which I did in eighteen days. They started shooting when I was on page 21, hoping it would come out all right. There was a lot of conflict over the film. It went way over budget. Sophia Loren was getting a million dollars to play the part—which was then remarkable.

A number of pictures I did were emergency rewrites. The pressure is always so great. Cast and crew sitting around, waiting to shoot. The studio has an enormous investment. They start shooting the first few pages. The same thing happened to me on *Harlow.* They started shooting in sequence and then cut each reel, doing sound and the music behind me. Once a sequence was done, it was set in concrete. We couldn't change anything. Later on, you couldn't balance the picture. The same thing was true on *The Man Who Knew Too Much.* We went on location when they only had a few pages of the script.

On these emergency rewrites, not only do you have only two to three weeks to do a script that they've worked on for months and months without solving the problems, but they're actually shooting what you're writing. I was able to write rapidly and considering the problems, it's remarkable how well some of these films came out.

Why would Hitchcock, who was always so prepared, begin shooting The Man Who Knew Too Much *without a finished script?*

Time moved faster than he realized. The things we'd finished, he shot first. Then I had to cable him, send pages to him every day. We did have an outline, and of course, we had the original picture, so he knew what he was going to do.

Did the people you worked with become friends?

Most of the relationships with stars were professional. I did socialize a little with Clark Gable. I visited Grace Kelly in the palace, my wife and I. Very interesting. It was only a year after she married Prince Rainier III, and she hadn't changed much; but the prince was the kind of person I didn't fully appreciate.

There were only a few writers who really entered the social whirl of Hollywood. You're leapfrogging from one picture to another. You don't maintain these friendships. I had a very exciting career, but there was always a lot of pressure, a lot of things had to be done in a hurry. The only exception was Hitchcock where, except for *The Man Who Knew Too Much,* we took all the time we wanted.

In the 1960s, there was such rapid social change in America. Did that affect your work for Hollywood?

Hollywood really didn't change much until the seventies. The sixties got a little more liberal. I didn't feel any disruption. I must say that I later wished I could have gotten away with things that would have made my films more real and adult. I was a dramatic innocent. I wasn't concerned with shocking people. I wasn't getting any message to do anything wilder in the sixties. Most of those breakthroughs came from independent productions, and later the studios followed along. Nobody said, "Let's get down and dirty." If we redid *Butterfield Eight* now, it would be a sexier picture. The book wasn't in front of the public's mind at the time the way that *Peyton Place* had been, so we didn't have any censorship troubles. We had a rape in *Peyton Place,* and we approached it carefully. I always worked from my own standards and tastes.

You did something like eleven pictures after breaking with Hitchcock but then, starting in the mid-1960s, nothing. Why?

I was very fortunate. Careers don't always last a long time. After 1965 and *Nevada Smith,* I did eight screenplays that, for different reasons, were never made. Two producers died. Two left the studios. One screenplay I did with Mark Robson fell apart for legal reasons. Another script I worked on for a long time with Irwin Allen got dropped because we couldn't get Air Force cooperation. There was another one that Paramount was going to do, but then they decided it was too expensive. I got paid for all of them, but for reasons that had nothing to do with quality of the writing, the projects were all dropped. With all the good luck I had before, I was having bad luck now.

From 1959 through 1969, we lived in Maine. It was a dangerous thing to do, because out of sight, out of mind. Perhaps it was an unwise move. I wanted more of a rural, outdoor life. Eventually, we moved back, but I never enjoyed California.

Then, I signed a contract with Embassy Pictures, Joseph E. Levine's company, which he up and sold to Avco. Avco went out of the picture-making business and just stayed with distribution. But they had an ironclad contract with me, so I spent six or seven years as a vice president there, although I know nothing about distribution. I actually had a ten-year contract, which we condensed from 1975 until 1981.

They kept saying, "We're going back into making pictures," but they never did. I couldn't work for anybody else because there was so much money involved, and I had a family to support. I wasn't about to throw the job away in times when a whole series of pictures I'd written were being canceled.

When my wife, Mel, became ill with ovarian cancer, I retired because I had to take care of her. We moved to New Hampshire. We knew they had a fine hospital here. Dartmouth offered me a professorship.

I did some television things from New Hampshire. While Mel was in treatment in 1986 and 1987, I wrote a CBS-Orion picture called *Pancho Barnes.* I also did a four-hour version of the life of Indira Gandhi, but the company I wrote it for went bankrupt, and the political fortunes of India prevented it from ever getting made. I began a life story of Wild Bill Donovan, who worked for the OSS which later became the CIA. I stopped working on that in 1988 when my wife died. She was my muse, my catalyst. I wrote before I met her, but I wrote better when she was here. In 1987, I also began losing my sight. I'm legally blind now. My wife's gone, and my children and grandchildren are scattered all over the country. So there's a long black period in my life.

But suddenly, in 1994, there was another John Michael Hayes credit on the big screen, Iron Will.

I rewrote a story I'd done in 1986 or 1987, before I lost most of my vision. Friends believed in it and submitted it to Disney. It's about a dogsled race from Winnipeg to St. Paul. A boy who wants to go to medical school trains an oddball bunch of house pets and enters the race. McKenzie Astin stars as the young man who uses mutts instead of professional racing dogs, and he doesn't have a sled made by a master cabinetmaker. It's an adventure. Man against the elements, against impossible odds. Truly true grit and determination. Kevin Spacey is a reporter who sees beyond the race itself into the human drama. The idea came from a news clipping. It's an historical piece set in 1917.

With *Iron Will,* I finally sat down one day to write something for myself again, something that came from my heart. Most of my other films didn't express what I felt. I wrote the story *and* the screenplay. This one was supposed to be all mine. But then they brought in other writers to Disneyize it.

Are new offers coming your way as a result of the publicity on Iron Will?

Well, Disney inquired about doing another story with me, but we couldn't agree on the premise of it or on the way it was to be told. Warner Brothers also submitted a story to me that I didn't want to do because it was too depressing. In the past year, with my cancer and chemotherapy, I've had a very low energy level. I've been ill a great deal, and I don't see very well anymore. But if a story came along or I thought of a story I liked. I would work on it.

And there's someone who wants you to do a sequel to Rear Window*?*

I was offered an absolutely monumental sum of money, half a million dollars, by the man who owns the rights, Sheldon Abenal of the American Play Company in New York. That money would help me in my old age. Hitch only paid me fifteen thousand dollars for the original *Rear Window.* You would either have to cast new people or set it in modern times, pick it up with their children or something. Tentatively, I was going to keep it in the same time period.

I don't know. Some pictures have a magic that's almost indefinable. Grace is gone. Hitch is gone. Jimmy's too frail. Wendell Corey's gone. Raymond Burr is dead. We couldn't recapture that kind of innocence. What could it possibly be?

But I've done a story, just in case.

Ring Lardner Jr.:
American Skeptic

Interview by Barry Strugatz and Pat McGilligan

At the age of twenty-six, Ring Lardner Jr. shared the 1942 Academy Award for Best Original Screenplay for *Woman of the Year.* Five years later, he was cited for contempt of Congress for refusing to state whether he was a member of the Communist Party. He was then blacklisted and sent to prison for a year.

Lardner's screenwriting career spans more than five decades. The son of one of the country's leading sportswriters and humorists, he grew up around some of the greatest writers of the century. Lardner dropped out of Princeton, became a newspaper reporter, and then, at the request of David Selznick, went to Hollywood as a publicist but gravitated to screenwriting.

Passionately committed to left-wing politics, Lardner became active in the Communist Party. After World War II, he was called to Congress with nine other screenwriters, producers, and directors, and refused, on constitutional grounds, to reveal his political affiliations. Known as the Hollywood Ten, they appeared before the HUAC, signaling the beginning of the blacklist, when anyone with even vaguely leftist leanings was prevented from working in the entertainment industry. When the committee demanded an answer to the question "Are you now or have you been a member of the Communist Party?" Lardner gave the now famous reply: "I could answer it, but if I did, I would hate myself in the morning."

After serving a one-year sentence in federal prison for the offense of contempt of Congress, Lardner finished a novel he had begun there. The book, *The Ecstasy of Owen Muir,* was published in England first, then America (New York: Cameron and Kahn, 1954). After that, he survived the blacklist by writing television films that were shot in England and sold to American networks with pseudonymous credits. It would have been much easier for him to work in England, but the US State Department denied him a passport until a

Ring Lardner Jr. in New York City, 1994. (Photo by William B. Winburn.)

Supreme Court decision in 1958.* In 1962, thanks to the efforts of Otto Preminger, Lardner was once again employable in the motion picture business, and in 1970, he won his second Academy Award, for *M*A*S*H*.

Lardner remains active, having recently completed a screen adaptation of Roger Kahn's book about the Brooklyn Dodgers, *The Boys of Summer*. Sur-

---

* The US Supreme Court ruled in favor of the artist Rockwell Kent, in the case of *Kent v. Dulles*, in 1958, breaking the State Department's stranglehold on passport rules by deciding "the right to travel can be removed only with due process under the Fifth Amendment." For many, international travel resumed. For others, "even after the Kent decision, the right to travel remained restricted" (David Caute, *The Great Fear: The Anti-Communist Purge under Truman and Eisenhower* [New York: Simon and Schuster, 1978]).

prisingly, he is not bitter. Despite having chronicled and suffered from the foolishness of the human race, Lardner has maintained a sense of dignity and equanimity.

Ring Lardner Jr. (1915–   )

1937   *A Star is Born* (William Wellman). Uncredited contribution.
        Nothing Sacred (William Wellman). Uncredited contribution.

1939   *Meet Dr. Christian* (Bernard Vorhaus). Co-script.

1940   *The Courageous Dr. Christian* (Bernard Vorhaus). Co-story,
        co-script.

1941   *Arkansas Judge* (Frank McDonald). Coadaptation.

1942   *Woman of the Year* (George Stevens). Co-story, co-script.

1943   *The Cross of Lorraine* (Tay Garnett). Co-script.

1944   *Marriage Is a Private Affair* (Robert Z. Leonard). Uncredited
        contribution.
        Laura (Otto Preminger). Uncredited contribution.
        Tomorrow the World (Leslie Fenton). Co-script.

1946   *Cloak and Dagger* (Fritz Lang). Co-script.

1947   *Forever Amber* (Otto Preminger). Co-script.

1949   *Britannia Mews / The Forbidden Street* (Jean Negulesco). Script.

1950   *Swiss Tour / Four Days Leave* (Leopold Lindtberg). Dialogue.

1951   *The Big Night* (Joseph Losey). Uncredited contribution.

1959   *Virgin Island* (Pat Jackson). Co-script (under pseudonym).

1960   *A Breath of Scandal* (Michael Curtiz). Uncredited contribution.

1963   *The Cardinal* (Otto Preminger). Uncredited contribution.

1965   *The Cincinnati Kid* (Norman Jewison). Co-script.

1970   *M*A*S*H* (Robert Altman). Script.

1971   *La Maison sous les Arbres / The Deadly Trap* (René Clément).
        Uncredited contribution.
        La Mortadella / Lady Liberty (Mario Monicelli). Co-script
        (1972 English-language version only).

1977   *The Greatest* (Tom Gries). Script.

Television credits include episodes of *Sir Lancelot, Adventures of Robin Hood,* and other series, under pseudonyms.

Plays include *Foxy.*

Books include *The Ecstasy of Owen Muir, The Lardners: My Family Remembered,* and *All for Love.*

Academy Award honors include Oscars for Best Screenplay for *Woman of the Year* (original) and *M*A*S*H* (adaptation).

Writers Guild honors include the award for Best-Written Comedy Adapted from Another Medium for *M*A*S*H.* Lardner also received the Laurel Award for Lifetime Achievement in 1989. When the East Coast branch of the Guild instituted the Ian McLellan Hunter Memorial Award for Lifetime Achievement in 1993, Lardner was the first recipient.

When and why did you decide that you wanted to be a writer?
Well, there was always the possibility of writing in our household, particularly newspaper writing . . . my father always thought of himself as a newspaperman, even after he ceased much active newspaper work. The four of us boys published a family newspaper, which we all wrote. We all did various kinds of writing. I was the editor of the literary magazine at Andover.
I wasn't sure that I was going to be a writer even by the time I went to Princeton. I was still thinking about the possibility of either teaching history or studying law, both of which had some appeal to me. But by the end of that sophomore year, I left college, which ruled out anything that required an academic background, and like my two older brothers before me, I got a job on a newspaper in New York.
Those were very hard times for getting a job for most people. It was 1934, the depth of the Depression. It was definitely easier for us to get that kind of job than any other, partly on the basis of my father's name.
Did growing up around writers like Fitzgerald influence you?
Scott Fitzgerald certainly was an influence. I think I went to Princeton because he told me I should. I found both him and his wife quite glamorous figures . . .
We did know a lot of people who worked as writers. Dorothy Parker came at my father's invitation and stayed a week in our guest room because she said she had to be alone to write. And Charles MacArthur and Heywood Broun and Alexander Woolcott and Sinclair Lewis and a number of other writers.
How did you become interested in politics?
While I was at Andover, which was from 1928 to 1932, I became interested—not too heavily—in what was going on in the country. In 1931, I made a speech, impromptu, from the top of a bus en route from Boston to New York that had stopped somewhere for the passengers to go to the bathroom. Some-

thing moved me to get up and talk about Governor Roosevelt as a presidential possibility the following year. And during the convention, the year I graduated [1932], I sat up all night listening to the radio the night they stopped the movement to block Roosevelt.* But that fall, during the campaign, when I was a freshman at Princeton, I no longer supported Roosevelt. I had joined the Princeton Socialist Club and went around with a number of students to northern New Jersey, speaking for Norman Thomas, the Socialist candidate, who was also a distinguished Princeton alumnus, and who came back twice a year and preached in the Princeton chapel and then met in the evening with the Socialist Club members.

How did you go from Roosevelt to Norman Thomas?

I can't really say at this point. I must have read something that summer of '32 that converted me to socialism; I don't really know what it was. After I left Princeton, I spent about eight weeks in the Soviet Union and about a month in Germany, the month Hitler took over, after Hindenburg died. And the contrast was very impressive. I was quite taken with what was going on in Moscow.

When you were in Germany, how did you live?

I stayed with an architect's family outside Munich. A young man in the family there was a member of the Hitler Youth Corps, and we had a lot of discussions about that.

Was he pretty fanatical about the subject?

Yes, he was—on a more intellectual Nazi level: "We really have nothing against the Jews, except that if you look at certain professions, we find there are only two million Jews in Germany, but 60 percent of the lawyers and 41 percent of the doctors, etcetera, are Jews. That deprives Germans of jobs. But we have nothing against them personally. They actually got there because they worked harder than the Germans did."

But they would always make that distinction between Jews and Germans— as if they couldn't be the same.

Did you see any Nazi demonstrations?

Yes. Just before I got there, there had been the purge of the storm troopers when Hitler had flown to Munich and personally seen to the shooting of Ernst Röhm, the head of the brownshirts.

Then, while I was in Munich, he came again after Hindenburg died, and you saw an awful lot of men in uniform. They would be in the street, standing around with people watching this procession go by, which included a limousine with Hitler in the back. And there was this man sitting in the backseat

---

* An opposition coalition led by the followers of House Speaker John Nance Garner of Texas, former Secretary of War Newton D. Baker, and the former presidential candidate Alfred Smith, blocked Franklin Delano Roosevelt from the two-thirds margin necessary for victory on the first three ballots at the 1932 Democratic National Convention. Then Roosevelt offered Garner the vice-presidential spot on the ticket, breaking the opposition and clinching the nomination on the fourth ballot.

with him that nobody else recognized, but I recognized as William Randolph Hearst. A couple of months later, Hearst came out with a front-page interview with Adolf Hitler.

Going Hollywood

You went from being a reporter to going to Hollywood. Tell me about that.

I went to work in January 1935 for the *New York Daily Mirror,* and I worked there until November. During the summer, I visited Sands Point, Long Island, several times, at the home of Herbert Bayard Swope, who had lived next door to us in Great Neck in the twenties and had been the editor of the *New York World,* wrote campaign speeches for Franklin Roosevelt, and was a man known for the parties he gave and the number of celebrities who hung around his place. His son, Herbert Swope Jr., and I had known each other as children and roomed together our second year at Princeton.

One weekend David Selznick was a guest, and I got to talking to him. He asked me if I was interested in working in Hollywood, and I said that I might be. I didn't know. He was starting a new company; he had just left MGM. And then I got a letter from him suggesting that I send him some stuff that I had written, and I sent him some of the material that had appeared in the humor magazine at Princeton, the *Princeton Tiger,* and some other things I don't remember, quite a bunch.

Anyway, in the fall came this offer to sign a seven-year contract, which was then standard in Hollywood. The only thing that wasn't standard about it was that it started at forty dollars a week, with options every six months.

I was making twenty-five dollars a week on the *Mirror,* so that was a distinct raise. It didn't say specifically what I was supposed to do; they could use me almost any way. But he had mentioned the publicity department or something like that, which was tied in. So I decided to sign the contract and flew out to Hollywood.

I went to work in the publicity department for his first publicity director in this new company, Selznick International, who was replaced pretty soon. Selznick had told him that he didn't want any publicity about himself personally; he just wanted publicity about the company. And this fellow, Joe Shea, took him literally. So Selznick fired him and hired a man named Russell Birdwell, to whom he told the same thing. But Birdwell didn't pay any attention and just put out as many stories as he could talking about this young genius, David Selznick.

What were your specific duties?

First I was on the set of the picture they were making, *Little Lord Fauntleroy* [1936], starring Freddie Bartholomew and Dolores Costello Barrymore. And I would just do interviews with actors and people around and whatever Birdwell assigned me to . . .

Then, after I had been there about a year, Selznick was preparing *A Star is Born* and had asked Budd Schulberg, who was a reader in the story department, and me to do some work on the script.* Dorothy Parker and Alan Campbell were rewriting the script by William Wellman and Robert Carson; and Selznick felt we might get some ideas for a few scenes, and he had us tag along as writers . . .

Right around about that time, Selznick also gave me a screen test, which he had the right to do under my contract.

What was the story behind that? He thought you had possibilities?

Yes. George Cukor was assigned to do the screen test, but George passed it off to an assistant of his named Mortimer Offner, who took just a silent test, actually, and it was not very good. The only time Selznick ever commented on it, he said, "I think you are going to be a writer." And it was never seen again except that Budd Schulberg swiped it out of the vaults of Selznick; and one night at a party at his friend Maurice Rapf's house, where they had a projection room—Maurice's father was an MGM producer—they were showing some movies, and they put on this screen test of mine as a short subject. That was the only time it was ever seen.

Anyway, Budd and I started to work on *A Star Is Born,* and as a matter of fact, we came up with the ending used in the picture. It was the scene that took place at Grauman's Chinese Theater. Janet Gaynor was having her footprints placed in cement, and although she was a star under the name of Vicki Lester, she said, "This is Mrs. Norman Maine," in memory of her husband, played by Fredric March. The same ending was later used in the Judy Garland–James Mason version.

We did, as I say, some other scenes. Dorothy Parker said she thought we ought to receive credit on it. According to the Screen Writers Guild rules,[†] we weren't entitled to it, and Selznick wouldn't hear of it anyway. But at least we were, so to speak, graduated into being writers, and he gave us a project to work on with [the producer] Merian Cooper.

Cooper did King Kong *[1933].*

---

*   Budd Schulberg, a novelist, memoirist, and screenwriter, wrote the story and script of *On the Waterfront* and *A Face in the Crowd.* His most famous novel is *What Makes Sammy Run?* a Hollywood roman à clef. Maurice Rapf's screen credits include *The Bad Man of Brimstone, They Gave Him a Gun, Jennie, Call of the Canyon, Song of the South,* and *So Dear to My Heart.* Rapf was blacklisted in the 1950s; Schulberg cooperated with the HUAC investigation. In 1939, Schulberg and Rapf had collaborated on *Winter Carnival,* about their Dartmouth alma mater, with another alumnus, Walter Wanger, acting as producer. Among the uncredited writers on the project was the novelist F. Scott Fitzgerald.

†   The Screen Writers Guild, founded in 1933, was the forerunner of today's Writers Guild. In 1954, when the guild merged with the Radio and Television Writers Guild, the new organization was called Writers Guild of America.

Yes. Then they did a picture called *Nothing Sacred* [1937], with Carole Lombard and Fredric March. Budd was sick at the time, but I was one of the writers assigned by Selznick to think of an ending. I seemed to be becoming an ending specialist. Selznick had had a quarrel with Ben Hecht, who had written the script, and Hecht left with an ending that Selznick didn't like. So, in typical Selznick fashion, he airmailed copies of the script to George S. Kaufman and Sidney Howard and Moss Hart and people all over the country, as well as to some who were in Hollywood, and he also assigned an MGM writer named George Oppenheimer and me. We wrote the ending that was used.

The following year, I or his secretary, Silvia Schulman, revealed to Selznick that she and I were going to get married, and he thought this was a very poor idea. He had just gone through a big struggle with Budd Schulberg about his marriage. His objection in both cases was that these were mixed marriages, that Budd was marrying a Gentile girl, and I was marrying a Jewish girl. He told Budd that he ought to remember that he had producer's blood in him. (*Laughs.*)

About the same time, Selznick wanted to sign Budd and me to new contracts. We would each get a raise from $75 to $100 a week. We went through several sessions with his business manager, Daniel O'Shea, who was arguing about why we should be content with $100 rather than $125, which I think we were asking for. During the course of one of these discussions, the interoffice phone sounded, and it was Selznick's voice saying, "What about Sidney Howard on *Gone with the Wind?*" and O'Shea said, "He won't work for $2,000 a week; he wants $2,500."

And Selznick said, "For Christ's sake, give it to him."

And O'Shea said, "Okay, David." Then he turned to us and said, "Now, boys, you've got to realize—"

Anyway, Silvia advised us to hold out. And we did, and we got the 125 bucks.

A couple of months after we were married, a contract option came up and Selznick let it lapse and I was still there on salary. But whatever projects we were working on seemed pretty ephemeral, and a writer named Jerry Wald, who was working at Warner Brothers, suggested that I go to work there. And I was offered a job in the B department under Bryan Foy, who made thirty pictures a year with budgets under $250,000.

Was that a step down—going from Selznick?

Well, it was a step down in a way, except that at least I thought I could get something made. With Selznick, it wasn't practical for writers at our level: he was only making one or two pictures a year. In any event, I left Selznick in the early part of 1937 and went to Warner Brothers, where I remained for about a year, I guess, without anything really coming out the way I wanted it to.

I worked at Warner Brothers for about a year, and then during the following two years, I worked on a number of projects. I think it was in 1938 that Ian

McLellan Hunter and I worked together for the first time on a series of movies that were made with Jean Hersholt playing a character called Dr. Christian, which he had played on the radio.* We did this with a director named Bernard Vorhaus, who had directed in England and Switzerland, though he was an American by birth. He had come to Hollywood to work for Republic Pictures. I think we worked for him first on a Republic Pictures venture based on a book by Irving Stone called *False Witness* [New York: Book League of America, 1940], on which I think we received some kind of screen credit [on the film, which was titled *Arkansas Judge*].

Then an independent company called Stevens-Lang undertook to produce these Dr. Christian pictures, and we worked on a script they had called *Meet Dr. Christian;* we wrote the next picture entirely, *The Courageous Dr. Christian.* Around this time, I also collaborated with an Austrian writer on an original screen story, which we sold to MGM for a very small sum of money. But we were both interested in getting jobs, so we agreed to sell our story for $5,000, or something like that, provided that we could each work on the picture for $250 a week for a minimum of six weeks or so.

After we made the sale, they paid us off with six weeks' salary—maybe it was only four weeks' salary, I don't know—and gave the story to somebody else to do. I was told by someone at the studio that William Fadiman, who was the story editor at the studio, had said that I would not be allowed to work at MGM; that they never had any intention of letting me work there. This was because by that time I had gotten involved in the reorganization of the Screen Writers Guild, which was fighting the company union called the Screen Playwrights. Also, at Warner Brothers, I had, in collaboration with John Huston, raised money for medical aid to Spain. We would corner people like James Cagney and Bette Davis and Humphrey Bogart at lunch, and get them to contribute to sending ambulances to Spain. John, I must say, was much more persuasive and influential in this endeavor than I was. My job was mainly to goad him to do the spiel.

Fadiman, who was Clifton Fadiman's brother, had apparently gotten wind of these activities and took a position against me. As a matter of fact, that was one of the reasons why, when Michael Kanin and I did the script for *Woman of the Year,* we contrived with Kate Hepburn for her to take it to Metro with no names on the script, so Louis B. Mayer would agree to her terms before anybody at MGM realized who had written it.

---

* Ian McLellan Hunter had a distinguished career. He collaborated with his friend Ring Lardner Jr. In addition to working together on the *Dr. Christian* series for film and *The Adventures of Robin Hood* for television, they also teamed up for the 1964 Broadway musical *Foxy,* a Yukon-set adaptation of Ben Johnson's *Volpone.* Hunter won an Oscar for Best Story for *Roman Holiday* (1953), and shared a nomination for Best Screenplay with John Dighton. His other screenplay credits include *Second Chorus, Mr. District Attorney, A Woman of Distinction,* and, after years of blacklisting and television work under pseudonyms, *A Dream of Kings* (1969).

Katharine Hepburn and Spencer Tracy in George Stevens's film *Woman of the Year.*

Woman of the Year

How did Woman of the Year *start?*

Well, it started with Garson Kanin, really. A friend of mine, Paul Jarrico, had written *Tom, Dick and Harry* [1941], which Garson was shooting. And I visited him on the set one day. Garson said he had this idea for Hepburn, who was still very much in the shadow of the exhibitor's denunciation.* But the play *The Philadelphia Story* was a big hit and brought her back to Metro.

But Garson knew she needed something after the film version of *The Philadelphia Story* [1940]. So he came up with a sort of Dorothy Thompson character. Dorothy Thompson was the only woman columnist at the time. I said I thought it might work, and Garson suggested that I get together with his brother Mike and see if we could work out a story. He had never written anything and was preparing to go into the army because he had been drafted . . .

---

* According to *Me,* by Katharine Hepburn (New York: Random, 1991): "During this period [post *Sylvia Scarlett*], my career had taken a real nosedive. It was then that the 'box-office poison' label began to appear. The independent theatre owners were trying to get rid of Marlene Dietrich, Joan Crawford and me. It seems that they were forced to take our pictures if they got certain ones which they *really* wanted. I felt sorry for them. I had made a string of very dull movies."

How did you work with Kanin or any collaborator?

Generally, by talking out a whole scene or sequence in considerable detail, so that we were substantially agreed on it, and very often two scenes, so that one of us could sit down and write a first version of each. And then we would switch them, and the other one would rewrite the scene. Each would rewrite the other's work, and then we would go at it again together. The process of setting it down for the first time has always required one person being at the typewriter by himself. The collaboration takes place in the plotting and then in the rewriting.

So we started to work out the story, and finally, I wrote it in the form of a kind of novella in the first person and in the past tense. It was told by this newspaperman, a sportswriter, the part [Spencer] Tracy played. I think it was called "The Thing about Women." It was that version that we sent to Kate. Garson probably sent it to her; he was the one who knew her personally. And she responded very well to it. And then we got up this plan of her taking it herself to Louis B. Mayer and talking to him about it.

Was Hepburn involved in developing the story?

Not in the story itself, because we wrote it as a piece of fiction. We wrote it that way, incidentally, after having talked it out as a screenplay, thinking it would work better and be more readable. I had found out that the great obstacle in getting attention paid to a piece of writing in the movies is that people have to read it—and most screenplays don't read very well, and treatments don't either.

Kate had nothing to do with that part of it. But after she read it, she figured out the terms: $211,000: $100,000 for her, $100,000 for us, $10,000 for her agent, and $1,000 for her expenses to come from Hartford. And that $100,000 for us included a screenplay and all the revisions that would have to be done on it, although no scene had been written yet.

Once MGM went for the deal and we started to work on the script, we had a number of consultations with Kate, including a few sessions that took place in Michael Kanin's house, where she stayed around for hours, late at night, while we were talking and sometimes actually writing some of the stuff, and she took quite an active part in the sessions.

Then what?

Well, after we finished the first draft of the screenplay, we got more actively involved with the people who were going to do it—with [the producer] Joe Mankiewicz and George Stevens, the director—and we had many consultations with them, resulting in revisions. Once the picture started shooting, there was relatively little to be done. We were free to be on the set whenever we wanted to. We both had signed contracts with MGM and were working on another script, so it was convenient to drop in on the set almost every day, and sometimes that would result in a conference with George Stevens about something.

Did you get along well with him?

Yes, through the shooting of the picture. But then, when we thought it was all through—it had been cut and was getting ready for a preview when Mike and I and our wives went to New York on vacation, [and] when we got back— we found out that the studio executives had decided they didn't like the ending and decided to shoot a new ending and had assigned a writer, John Lee Mahin, who had been president of this company union of screenplay writers that we had fought against—but who was a pretty good writer*—to write this revision, and they had a version of it by the time we came back.

Well, we objected strenuously. We didn't like the ending. The whole theory behind it seemed to be that there had to be some comeuppance for the female character.

Why did they think she needed a comeuppance?

The executives at MGM, including Joe Mankiewicz, supported by George Stevens, felt that the woman character, having been so strong throughout, should be somehow subjugated and tamed, in effect. They felt it was too feminist, and they devised this ending that involved Hepburn trying to fix break-fast in an apartment that Tracy had taken by himself. It was based on some comedy routines that George Stevens had done back in his silent picture days when he used to do Harry Langdon comedies. Even on paper, it was conceived of quite broadly.

And so we objected to it in theory and then objected specifically to a number of lines, etcetera. And George and Joe did agree that some of our points were well taken, and we were allowed to revise Mahin's work within the context of the scene as planned, not to try to go back to our old ending, which they didn't like, or to devise something different.

So we did modify it somewhat before it was shot. But then Stevens went the other way in the shooting, and the action was quite broad, and we were disappointed in the result.

What kind of business did the film do when it was released?

It did very good business. I believe it was the first picture to run three weeks at the Radio City Music Hall.

And it won the Academy Award in what areas? Do you remember?

I think the only Academy Award was for us: for the Best Original Screenplay.

How old were you?

Twenty-six.

Were you at the ceremony?

---

*   John Lee Mahin, a favorite writer of both Clark Gable and Victor Fleming at MGM, where he spent most of his career, is profiled in the first *Backstory*.

No, by that time I'd gone to work for the Army as a civilian employee writing training films. So I just heard about it. I was working at the cooks and bakers school at Camp Lee, Virginia, writing a picture called *Rations in the Combat Zone.*

What did the success of Woman of the Year *mean to you—to your career?*

Oh, it meant a great deal. It meant, in the first place, that MGM, after we had finished the script, offered us—and we signed—a contract at a lot more money than either of us had been making. Really, from then until 1947, I never had any trouble getting work.

The Communist Party

When did you join the party?

In 1936.

You knew Budd Schulberg in Russia?

I met him first there. He and Maurice Rapf were students there; they were both students at this Institute at the University of Moscow. We didn't know each other very well there, but we spoke.

He was very political back then.

Very. As a matter of fact, Budd really recruited me into the Communist Party. We were working together on *A Star Is Born* or had started on that thing for Merian Cooper; I know we were collaborating on something. I had written a letter on Selznick International stationery to *Time* magazine, which they published in connection with something they had said about the Stalin-Trotsky rivalry, and I was correcting a point of fact. Somebody apparently in the Communist unit to which Budd belonged said, "Hey, isn't this the guy you are working with? And if he is writing this kind of pro-Stalinist letter, why haven't you recruited him?" So Budd went to work on me.

How did he do that?

It wasn't very hard.

The people who were in the Communist Party, were they a social group?

Yes. Over the next couple of years, not only were most of my friends writers but they were mostly Communists. Both tendencies were, I think, unfortunate: it's not good always to be with like-minded people.

Schulberg and his wife were romantic figures in a way, weren't they?

Yes, she was a very glamorous, very beautiful woman, and Budd, who was not at all prepossessing in appearance or speech—he stuttered; it was more pronounced then than it is now—was nevertheless regarded by everyone as an extremely devoted and idealistic fellow, as well as a very talented individual. So they were definitely a sort of role model.

What was the general political climate in Hollywood?

People were becoming quite political about the Spanish Civil War, which broke out in the middle of that year, and about what was going on in Germany.

The most popular political organization in Hollywood at that time was the Hollywood Anti-Nazi League, which Donald Ogden Stewart was chairman of, but most of the work was done by Herbert Biberman and Beatrice Buchman, Sidney Buchman's wife.*

Also, toward the end of 1936, the Screen Writers Guild, which had been effectively smashed a couple of years before, began to reorganize because of the Wagner Labor Relations Act, and we were working toward a Labor Board election, which took place in the spring of 1937. There was also a strike going on, in '36 through '37, of the various crafts—the non-IATSE-AFL crafts,† carpenters and painters—supported by the office workers and readers; and the Screen Actors Guild [SAG] was heading toward its first contract and, as an AFL union, was in a position where they had to decide whether to support the IATSE or this other AFL group. It was a very close battle, and there was a big political fight in SAG. At one point, they actually passed a straw vote to support the strikers and respect picket lines, but when it came to an actual vote, they didn't.

What did it mean to be an active member of the Party? What do you think you accomplished by being a member? What do you think the Party accomplished?

What it meant to be an active member was mostly spending a lot of time at meetings of various sorts. The year after I joined the Party, I was preempted by the board of the Screen Writers Guild to become a member of the board representing the young writers, and then in an election, I was elected to the board. I had meetings of the guild board once a week and usually a committee meeting another evening of the week, and there was a regular Party branch meeting about once a week. And very often a writers' faction—these were writers who were members of the Party, as well as a few who, for various reasons, were not but were very close to the Party—would meet and would discuss policy in the guild. With one thing and another, I found I was going to meetings five or six nights a week. And Silvia, who joined some months after we were married, was going to a good many of those, too. And there were other types of meetings as well.

We did play a part, I think, in most everything that was going on in the Hollywood scene. Organizations such as the Motion Picture Committee to Aid Spanish Democracy, the Hollywood Anti-Nazi League, and the League of

---

*   Herbert Biberman was also one of the Hollywood Ten. Besides Ring Lardner Jr., the others, several of whom are mentioned in this interview, were Alvah Bessie, Lester Cole, Edward Dmytryk, John Howard Lawson, Albert Maltz, Samuel Ornitz, Adrian Scott, and Dalton Trumbo.

†   The International Alliance of Theatrical Stage Employees (and Moving Picture Machine Operators), or IATSE, is the union representing every branch of motion picture production in the United States and Canada, and is affiliated with the American Federation of Labor-Congress of Industrial Organization (AFL-CIO).

American Writers would not really have functioned anywhere near to the extent that they did without the very active participation of Communists in their forefront. Nor, I think, would the unions that were being formed or reformed at that time—the guilds of actors, writers, and directors, etcetera, and the emerging office workers union, etcetera—have gotten as strong as fast as they did without the extra work that the Communists put into organizing and recruiting people for them.

The nature of the work we did changed twice during that period: Once in the fall of 1939, with the outbreak of the war in Europe and the Nazi-Soviet Pact, the Russian war against Finland, etcetera, when there was a very sharp division for a while between Communists and liberals—most of the latter being supporters of the British and French in the war and most of us remaining pretty skeptical about what the Allies were up to in the war. And then, of course, when Hitler invaded the Soviet Union and when Pearl Harbor was attacked, there was another big shift and with much more unity on the liberal and left side of things.

Why were you skeptical of the Allies in the beginning?

The basic skepticism was what I still think is a well-founded fear: That the people who were in charge of those governments—Neville Chamberlain in England and [Edouard] Daladier in France—were likely to, if they got a chance, make some kind of deal with Hitler to turn the war against the Soviet Union, which was a very popular idea in British and French circles.

What did you think of the nonaggression pact?

We thought it was just that: a nonaggression pact. And we justified it on the ground that Stalin and the Soviet Union generally had kept advocating collective security in Czechoslovakia and Poland, etcetera; that they had finally despaired of ever getting an agreement to oppose fascism collectively; and [that it was done] in self-defense because they feared German aggression backed by the Western powers: they had signed the pact to give them time.

But gradually, it emerged that there was more to it than that: there was the active splitting up of Poland; there were certain economic exchanges going on that were distasteful. But still, as we saw it—as I saw it, anyway, and as I think most of my comrades did, too—this was understandable and could be justified.

How did you see your politics as they related to your writing?

It was pretty difficult to find much relationship between them, except to the extent that when I was able—after *Woman of the Year*—to make some selection in what I was doing, I tried to get assignments that had some potential for progressive content.

We had what was called a clinic within the Communist Party, where writers used to meet and discuss each other's problems with scripts and sometimes with other kinds of writing: books, etcetera. That was, I think, helpful to many individuals in just working out certain technical story problems and things in conjunction with their colleagues. But I can't say that it had much of a broad effect on the content of what was done in the movies.

Did the studios or the Party try to influence the political content of scripts?

When they finally came before the House Un-American Activities Committee in 1947, the heads of the studios maintained that there was never any real question about the content of pictures because they retained control of content. And largely, this was true; they did. What things a few writers might have been able to sell them or slip into a script were of minor consequence. Basically, it was the studio heads who had charge of the content of the films, and there was nothing we could do about it.

Wasn't there a story about a script you had written for [the producer Sam] Goldwyn called "Earth and High Heaven"?

Yes. That was toward the end of the war, in 1945, I think. He hired me to work on what was to be the first picture on anti-Semitism. It was an adaptation of a novel about anti-Semitism in Montreal by a writer named Gwethalyn Graham [*Earth and High Heaven* (New York: J. B. Lippincott, 1944)]. Goldwyn's wife, Frances, a former showgirl who was non-Jewish, had persuaded him that he should make the picture. He was extremely nervous about it.

I had a few conferences with him, and we more or less discussed what was to be done with this script. And then he went away on some wartime mission—he went to Russia, actually—that had to do with the picture *North Star* [1943], which Lillian Hellman had written. When he came back, I had written the first draft of the screenplay. After he read it, he called me in and started a conference by saying, "Lardner, you've defrauded and betrayed me."

I said, "Well, I can see that you don't like the script. What do you mean about this 'defrauding and betraying'?"

He said, "Well, I said 'defrauded,' because we agreed on a treatment, and you wrote a treatment before I left; but this script is not that at all."

I said, "There were some changes. Naturally, you make changes as you write the screenplay." So finally I said, "How did I betray you?"

He said, "One of the reasons I hired you for this particular script was that you are a Gentile. But you betrayed me by writing like a Jew."

And I couldn't answer that.

I did relate this conversation that night to my friend Gordon Kahn,* who

---

* Born in Hungary, Gordon Kahn was one of the original Hollywood Nineteen, unfriendly witnesses summoned to Washington, D.C., in October 1947 to testify as to their political activities in Hollywood. When he was blacklisted, Kahn wrote one of the first accounts of the blacklist, *Hollywood on Trial*, and throughout the 1950s, he wrote numerous newspaper and magazine articles under pseudonyms. Kahn had many script credits in Hollywood including *The Sheik Steps Out, Navy Blues, I Stand Accused, Tenth Avenue Kid, The Road Back, Ex-Champ, A Yank on the Burma Road, Tarzan's New York Adventure, Northwest Rangers, Song of Nevada, Two o'Clock Courage, Her Kind of Man, Whiplash, Ruthless,* and *Streets of San Francisco.*

said, "What did you do—write it from the right-hand side to the left-hand side of the page?"

But Goldwyn then hired six or seven other writers in succession over the next three years to rewrite this script, and he was dissatisfied with it each time. Finally, Darryl Zanuck came out with *Gentleman's Agreement* [1947], and Goldwyn said, "He stole my idea." But he never made "Earth and High Heaven."

Fritz Lang and *Cloak and Dagger*

Tell me a little bit about Cloak and Dagger *and working with Fritz Lang.*

I came on the project after there was already a script written by Boris Ingster and John Larkin. Fritz didn't like the script they had at all, so my job was to do a complete rewrite as fast as possible. Then, just on the verge of shooting, Albert Maltz was brought in to rewrite behind me. They were behind schedule, to put it mildly. Albert and I were working at the same time, usually not on the same scenes.

What was it like working with Lang? Was he personable? Did he involve himself very much in the development of the script?

Of course, I knew his reputation and his films, so I welcomed the opportunity to work with him. I remember we worked mostly at his house. He took the story very seriously. He did not do any actual writing—he just contributed ideas—but he was very helpful. He was very respectful of writers.

The name of John Wexley [who collaborated with Bertolt Brecht and Lang on Lang's film *Hangmen Also Die*] came up once somehow. Fritz said, "He is a dishonest man." I, who knew John and wasn't too fond of him, nevertheless felt this was going too far. I said, "What do you mean he's a dishonest man?" Fritz said, "He's thoroughly dishonest. When we worked on the script for *Hangmen Also Die,* I told him the script had to be shortened by about twenty pages, and he came back with a script that was twenty pages shorter; but I found that only ten pages in actual length had been cut out, and the rest was by his instructing his secretary to put more lines on a page!" This was a fairly common writer's offense and not exactly a crime. But Fritz was very moral about it.

The monocle which Fritz wore was very distinctive. The only other person I knew in Hollywood who wore a monocle was Gordon Kahn. Gordon was small in stature, and he liked to say that without the monocle, he was just "that little Jew writer," but with it he was "that little Jew writer with a monocle," and that made him more memorable. The monocle probably was a real thing that Fritz needed, but I imagine that he wore it intentionally. After all, many people who have that one-eye problem wear glasses with plain glass in the other eye, because it's not as conspicuous as a monocle. But like Gordon, in his way Fritz liked the impression that the monocle gave.

I liked Fritz. He was a hell of a good talker. He said funny things, mostly of a dry wit and mostly detrimental about other people. I think we had a good and productive time together, so much so that I remember I had discussions with him about at least one other project which did not—or at least my involvement did not—come to fruition.

Did he talk about politics at all?

I think he was generally of the left and sort of against the establishment anywhere and everywhere. I don't know if he talked very much about American politics.

The film I think turned out not only far-fetched but bland in many respects.

Though I haven't seen the picture in nearly fifty years, my recollection is that it was a moderately satisfactory movie. I remember when I came to work on the script, I met [Gary] Cooper. He said, "Look I want you to understand one thing. I'm supposed to be playing an atomic physicist in this picture, and the only way I can get away with playing an atomic physicist is if you keep the lines very simple . . . "

I don't know how it affected things, but I remember also that Fritz didn't get along with [the producer] Milton Sperling.* At a few conferences, they behaved quite nastily to each other. There seemed to be an almost personal dislike between them. I remember shooting started on a Monday. We had a final conference on the Saturday before, at the end of which Milton, trying to make peace with everybody, said, "Now, we're going to start shooting on Monday. We've had a lot of disagreements. There's been a lot of harsh words going back and forth, but all that's behind us now, and let's forget it. And Fritz," Milton added, very conciliatory, "I will see you on the set Monday morning." And Fritz said, "*That* will not be necessary."

The Hollywood Ten

When the war ended, did you detect a change in the political atmosphere— the beginning of the cold war, etcetera?

Yes, quite rapidly. I think it probably came quicker in Hollywood than in most other places, because during the last six months of that war, most of the same group that had been involved in that strike back in the late thirties, under the leadership of a man named Herbert Sorrell, started a strike against the studios. And it was the position of the Communist Party during the war that there

---

* Milton Sperling had a fifty-year career as a screenwriter and producer, highlighted by an Oscar nomination for his script for *The Court Martial of Billy Mitchell* (1955). He was also Harry Warner's son-in-law. His life story is sketched in the book *Hollywood Be Thy Name* (Roeklin, Calif.: Prima, 1994), written by his daughter Cass Warner Spelling and Cork Millner, with Jack Warner Jr.

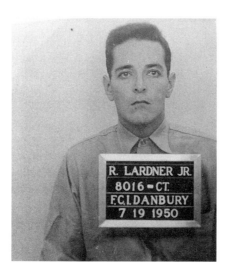

Ring Lardner Jr. jailed as one of the Hollywood Ten in 1950. (Prison photograph.)

should be no strikes and no support for strikes until the war was over. So we did not actively help. There was some money raised, because we were basically sympathetic with what was going on, but we thought they had called the strike prematurely.

And when the war ended in the summer of 1945, the strike was still going on, and that condition persisted for six months after that. As I recall, it was a long, drawn-out, and quite violent struggle, with a lot of violence taking place on picket lines. Many of us marched on those picket lines in '45 and '46. That strike divided Hollywood very much into a sort of liberal-left camp that supported the strike in varying degrees and the conservative element in the Screen Actors Guild which, by the time it was over, I think included a new president, Ronald Reagan.

At the same time, there was an organization called the Hollywood Independent Citizens Committee of the Arts, Sciences and Professions, or HICCASP. The New York office was called NICCASP; in Hollywood, it was HICCASP. The members were very enthusiastic supporters of Roosevelt during his fourth election campaign, and many supported what Henry Wallace stood for subsequently. But there did arise a split between those who were more inclined toward Harry Truman's policies and those of us who thought Henry Wallace was the man who should run in 1948.

In the 1946 congressional elections, there were some very keenly contested races in California with quite a clear choice between liberals and conservatives, including Richard Nixon, who was running for his first term in Congress.

On the national scene, we knew that there were big industrial conflicts going on. The United Electrical Workers Union and other unions that had a somewhat left orientation were trying to carry on strikes, and they were being opposed by the hierarchy in the AFL. I guess the AFL and the CIO were still separate at that time. This was the time when the so-called Truman Doctrine in regard to Greece and Turkey was promulgated, and when Winston Churchill made his Iron Curtain speech in Fulton, Missouri, with President Truman seated alongside him. This was the time when we all seemed to be going in the wrong direction.

When were you served with a subpoena? Do you remember that moment?

It was in September, I think, of 1947. I remember it particularly because we had just bought a new house. I had been divorced and remarried to [the actress] Frances [Chaney], my present wife, who was the widow of my brother David, who was killed as a correspondent for the *New Yorker* in World War II. We were married in 1946, and in the summer of 1947, we bought a house in Santa Monica with a tennis court—generally quite a nice place—and we were in escrow with it when subpoenas arrived. We had been aware of the possibility of this threat; even a year before, there had been talk of HUAC visiting Hollywood. From our honeymoon up in northern California, we had talked to somebody on the phone—I think it was my friend Hugo Butler—who had said it was best to stay out of town for a couple more weeks, because there were supposed to be subpoenas coming around. Well, it didn't happen then. But it had been very much in the air for a whole year.

Dalton Trumbo and I had a couple of times discussed what we would do if it came up. We decided that it was not a good idea to deny membership in the Communist Party, although some of our colleagues had done that before the California State Un-American Activities Committee. We just felt that there were too many stool pigeons and various other ways to find out, and you could get yourself in a much worse situation for perjury; it would be very hard to organize any sympathy around that. On the other hand, we thought it would be a bad idea to answer yes to the question, because the studios would probably use it against us, and also because it made it less feasible to refuse to answer further questions about other people.

You anticipated that they would proceed along those lines?

Yes. We therefore felt the most sensible policy was just not to answer questions and to challenge the right of the committee to ask any questions at all. The two of us had agreed that was the position we thought best to take.

It was only after it became known that there were nineteen of us who had received subpoenas [and were] known as unfriendly witnesses—as opposed to people who had received subpoenas who, we believed, were going to be cooperative witnesses—that we got together at meetings in Hollywood, all nineteen of us, with the exception of Bertolt Brecht, who was then in a considerably different position. He was an enemy alien all during the war; the rest of us were citizens.

We met with some lawyers, and Trumbo and I brought up this idea of not answering any questions. There were problems with that position. There were several people who wanted to say yes, they were Communists; they felt it was time to raise the face of the Party. But we raised the point—and the lawyers agreed with us—that it would then be very difficult to take a position against naming practically everybody they knew.

We discussed the Fifth Amendment, and there was some dispute as to whether that would really work. The Smith Act, under which the Communist Party leaders were later convicted, had not been invoked against them at that time; it wasn't until the next year that they were arrested. So we would be saying, "It's a crime to be a Communist and therefore I plead self-incrimination." And the committee members could say, "What do you mean, a crime? It's a perfectly legal Party." But beyond that, we thought that that position would not do anything to challenge the right of the committee to function.

In other words, it was a freedom of speech issue?

Yes. We were saying: "Under the First Amendment, there is freedom of speech and freedom of the press—and that includes the movie business. Therefore, Congress cannot legislate in this field—and Congress has no right to investigate where it cannot legislate."

What about the issue of political affiliation? Did that come under the First Amendment also?

Yes, that it was our business what political party we belonged to or believed in. And Alvah Bessie at that time pointed out to the committee that Dwight Eisenhower was then refusing to say whether he was a Democrat or a Republican—and we should have the same rights as he did.

So gradually the policy of not answering questions and of challenging the committee was agreed upon. More or less, we all agreed that we were going to do that, although we didn't want to seem to be doing it by agreement. Our lawyers additionally advised us that it was a good idea to say we were answering the question, but in our own way, while never actually answering it.

And we went along with this last tactic, which actually turned out to be a bad idea and just made us seem to be more evasive than we were, and it didn't accomplish anything in the end.

Could you describe what it was like testifying? What was going through your head?

I was somewhat frightened, I guess, of the idea of appearing before this committee. Incidentally, I didn't know definitely that I was going to appear. They had given ten people out of the nineteen definite dates on which to appear; the other nine of us were told we didn't even have to come to Washington; we were told that we could wait until we were given a definite date.

But we decided as a matter of policy that we should all go together when the hearing began. After a week of friendly witnesses' testimony, they went on to some of the unfriendly witnesses, and I still had no idea whether I would be called or not.

My wife and I had been going to the hearings every day. Finally, one day, I think it was on a Thursday during the second week of the hearings, we decided we didn't have to be there that morning. We were listening to the proceedings over the radio in our hotel room when suddenly [HUAC Chairman J. Parnell] Thomas or [Robert] Stripling, the counsel for the committee, called out my name to come to the stand, and Robert Kenny, who was one of the lawyers representing us, said, "He is not here." And Thomas said, "What do you mean he is not here? He has been sitting right down there day after day."

It seems that this was really occasioned by the fact that a picture of Frances and me sitting there had appeared on the front page of the newspaper *PM* the day before, and it had also appeared in a Washington paper. It was the fact that we were getting newspaper attention that sort of called the committee's attention to us, and I was therefore called out of turn. As a matter of fact, one of the people who was given a definite date—Waldo Salt, I think it was*—was not called, because they called off the hearing that day after I appeared, followed by Lester Cole and Bertoit Brecht, who was the last witness.

As I say, it was on a Thursday morning that we heard about it on the radio at the hotel. So I hastily got dressed and went down to the Senate Caucus Room where the hearings were being held, and met with our lawyers. We had a practice then, just before anybody was about to testify, for the prospective witness and the lawyers to take a walk in the outside gardens surrounding the hotel where we were staying, on the theory that there were not apt to be microphones there, and there would then be a discussion as to what might come up on the witness stand. I had such a discussion, but that afternoon they didn't call me. It was the next morning, Friday, that I was called.

I had no great confidence in my ability to be articulate before this committee or to make any great points at such a hearing. The experience of my colleagues who had preceded me—the way they were jumped on and shut up—made me less confident.

I just couldn't see any real good coming out of it and determined that I would try to make a couple of points about why I wasn't answering these questions; that was about the maximum good you could accomplish—namely, to get in a phrase or two. And that's what I tried to do.

---

* Waldo Salt, another one of the original Hollywood Nineteen was subsequently blacklisted, but he charged back, after the 1950s, to write such memorable and Oscar-winning films as *Midnight Cowboy* and *Coming Home.*

Prison and the Blacklist

Jumping ahead to after your sentence. What was your prison experience like? Were you scared?

Yes, that was really a considerable unknown, both as to what it would actually be like in prison and what it would be like with our particular offense. I faced that with a good deal of uncertainty and pessimism, because I didn't think it was going to go well.

It turned out, on the whole, not to be nearly as bad as I anticipated. The first three weeks we spent in the local—which is also the federal—jail in Washington in fairly confined circumstances. We were each put in with a prisoner there on another charge. Because we were just there temporarily, we were not given jobs or anything. So we just got out once a day into a very restricted yard, where you couldn't do anything but walk around in a circle. So that was quite confining. We then were sent to various institutions in different parts of the country.

Lester Cole and I were both sent to Danbury, where my mother, who was only about thirteen miles away, was able to visit once a week.

Were you put in the same cell?

No. In Danbury, every new inmate went through an orientation course, which involved living in a segregated part of the prison in a kind of dormitory and spending a few days learning about prison life and discipline and so on. Then we were released into the general population and assigned jobs according to whether we were classified as maximum security or moderate security or light security. Those who were light security were allowed to have jobs working outside the prison walls.

There was a farm in Danbury where they grew vegetables and things, and raised chickens. For some reason, I never figured out why, Lester Cole was granted this light or minimum security job, and I was classified as moderate security and could only have a job inside the walls. I was assigned to the Office of Classification and Parole to work on a typewriter from Dictaphone records that had been dictated by the officers at classification and parole. They were histories of each inmate as he came in and recommendations to the parole board.

When did you first realize you were blacklisted?

We returned from the hearings in Washington not sure of what was going to happen. We thought we had a pretty good chance to win the case, based on the court decisions so far, and we thought if we won the case, the studios would not take any action, would not get enough support to take any blacklisting action.

However, there was a meeting called the very next month in New York: The heads of companies in New York met and passed a resolution that ten of us would not work—and anyone else who took the same position couldn't work—until we had been cleared by the committee, and that they would not knowingly hire a Communist or anyone who refused to answer questions of a congressional committee. So that was then put into effect in varying degrees. Only five of the ten of us were actually working at studios then.

Where were you?

I was under contract at 20th Century-Fox. I was in kind of a special situation because after I came back from the hearing, Otto Preminger asked if I would work on an adaptation of a book he had bought, and we started working on it. So they were giving me a new assignment after the hearing.

This later became an issue in a civil case when a jury decided that they had waived their right to fire me by giving me a new assignment. But a judge threw that out, and at a second trial, we settled out of court for a relatively minor amount of money. Anyway, Darryl Zanuck made a public statement that he wasn't going to fire anybody unless he was specifically urged to do so by his board of directors. But the 20th Century-Fox board got together and obliged him. I was the only person at the studio . . .

How did they let you know?

I was in Otto's office—we were talking about the story—when a message came that Zanuck wanted to see me. And Otto said, "Not both of us?" (*laughs*), and the message was "No, just Lardner."

And then, when I went to Zanuck's office, I was shunted off and did not get to Zanuck himself but to his assistant, Lew Schreiber, who told me that my contract was terminated and I was supposed to leave the premises.

I told this to Otto. He was very distressed but couldn't think of anything to do about it. I met with a couple of people—Philip Dunne and George Seaton, a writer-director—both of whom said they were going to walk out with me. But I told them I didn't think that would be a very good gesture; if they could get a substantial number of writers to do it, it would be better. They tried, but they couldn't get anybody else, and they then agreed that it wouldn't amount to much. So I left 20th Century-Fox.

When you learned that people like Schulberg were cooperating with the blacklisters, were you hurt, disappointed, or did you see it coming?

There was some surprise and some disappointment. I heard about that when I was still in Danbury. It was a couple of weeks before we were to be released, and I had achieved a single cell, where I could do some writing. And a fellow inmate came to the door and said, "Hey, they're talking about you on the radio."

I went into the common room, and the radio said there were these new hearings going on, and that a writer named Richard Collins had named me. He was one of the group of young people in the Communist Party that I had run into when I had been recruited, and I heard that he had been disaffected; so I wasn't too surprised by that.

But then during the rest of that year, 1951, there were more hearings in Washington, and later in the fall, in Los Angeles, a number of people had testified. Some of them I was quite surprised by. But, in particular, I knew that Budd had had nothing to do with the Party since 1940–41; and I had once talked to him, and he felt very strongly about some Russian writers that he had met when we were both in Moscow in 1934, who had since been purged. But, still, that Budd volunteered, really, to appear before the committee because someone had named him—he wasn't subpoenaed and he wasn't working in Hollywood at the time and there was no particular reason why he had to clear himself—surprised me.

But others were more understandable. Some of them did it under quite strong pressure and didn't—like Budd, [the director Elia] Kazan, and some others—have some other kinds of work that they could do. Some of them were extremely dependent on Hollywood to support themselves.

What was the impact of the blacklist?

Well, the impact was to create intimidation in the motion picture business and in the emerging television business. It affected the content of pictures to some extent, because people avoided subjects they thought were controversial. The studios started making anti-communist pictures, which the committee more or less specifically asked for, and although they didn't do very well, there was a tendency to stay away from material that might be controversial. There was, I think, an increased kind of escapism in pictures. Certainly, the impact was strongest on the three hundred or more who were blacklisted. But it also threatened people who sort of got nervous about being revealed as entertaining dangerous thoughts.

Do you think this was an attack on freedom of speech?

Yes. I think it certainly had a limiting effect on freedom of expression in Hollywood.

In the end, of course, it didn't last, and it didn't achieve very much. It really basically died of ridicule, partly because of the number of issues that came up in relation to Academy Awards and partly as a result of a campaign largely led by Dalton Trumbo to make fun of the whole process and its contradictions. So by the time it began to break up in the sixties, most people looked back on it as a bad idea or as a kind of laughable one. By the seventies, it even became more or less a kind of honor to have been blacklisted.

People have characterized your actions with the Hollywood Ten during the blacklist as heroic.

I would say that we did the only thing that we could do under the circumstances, except behave like complete shits, and that doesn't amount to heroism. I think there has been some difference of opinion about this. But, as I recall it—my version of it, anyway—we figured out the most sensible thing to do, we thought we had a good chance of winning, and we played it that way.

Uncredited Work

Let me ask you about a couple of directors you worked with—in each case, without screen credit. What were they like? Were they very literate? Starting with William Wellman . . .

Wellman was reasonably literate, but you could never class him as an intellectual. He knew his craft very well and resisted Selznick's attempts to control him. He could be funny and entertaining, but it was a mistake to cross him as I did in the following instance:

A conference in Selznick's office on *A Star is Born*. Present: D.O.S. [David O. Selznick], Wellman, Budd Schulberg, and me. I said there was no reason why the character played by Lionel Stander should be as abusive as he was to Fredric March in a racetrack scene; there was no prior explanation for his nastiness. Wellman replied, "He's drunk." I said that didn't do it for me; I thought anyone who was nasty when he was drunk was nasty when he was sober. "I'm nasty when I'm drunk," Wellman said. "That proves my point," I made the mistake of saying. Our relations after that were noticeably cooler.

How about a couple of directors whose films bookend the 1950s for you— Joseph Losey and Michael Curtiz? I'm assuming The Big Night, *directed by Losey, was relatively impersonal for both of you, and that Curtiz was pretty far gone by the time you did work on* A Breath of Scandal.

You are right in your assumption that *The Big Night* was a quickie and not of any great importance to Joe. He needed the salary in order to get to exile in England before he was subpoenaed, and I think he finally did have to leave before editing was completed. Hugo Butler had been working on the script for Joe, but he was even more hard pressed and took off for Mexico with the job unfinished.* My wife, Frances, was working with Joe on the set, and I had recently returned to Hollywood after my prison stint in Connecticut. Joe asked me to finish Hugo's job and paid me, as I remember, a thousand dollars, which may have been his own money.

Both before and after that, I had discussions with Joe about more serious projects we were contemplating, and I looked forward to working with him; but none of them worked out.

---

* The credited scenarists for *The Big Night* are Stanley Ellin (on whose novel, *Dreadful Summit,* the film is based) and Joseph Losey.

Hugo Butler, one of the blacklisted generation, earned an Oscar nomination in 1940 for his screenplay for *Edison, the Man.* His other Hollywood credits include *The Southerner* (for Jean Renoir), MGM's 1938 version of *A Christmas Carol, The Adventures of Huckleberry Finn, Lassie Come Home, Miss Susie Siagle's, From This Day Forward, A Woman of Distinction, He Ran All the Way, The Prowler,* and *The First Time.* In Mexico during the 1950s, he wrote *The Adventures of Robinson Crusoe* for Luis Buñuel. He cowrote *Cowboy* in 1958 but was denied screen credit. After the blacklist, he was credited, notably, with his wife, Jean Rouverol, for the script of Robert Aldrich's *Legend of Lylah Clare.* His father was Frank Butler, the screenwriter who won an Oscar for his *Going My Way* co-script in 1945.

As for Michael Curtiz, the man did have a feeling for film, but he never mastered the English language. I can't really judge what it was like to work with him, because by the time I did, he was definitely in decline, and the picture, *A Breath of Scandal,* never a great idea to begin with, suffered as a result. Some of the scenes he shot were so bad that Paramount had to hire Vittorio De Sica anonymously to reshoot them. I was still anonymous, and Walter Bernstein, who had been cleared, accepted the dubious credit for the screenplay.[*]

So much of your career is uncredited—apart from and including the blacklist. Were you always that amenable to doctoring work? Were you diffident about credits for long periods? Did it sometimes give you a freedom, working without the baggage of your name?

I don't think my uncredited work is particularly unusual for a writer who was on the scene as long as I was. Perhaps mine has been revealed to a greater extent than most, because researchers have found studio records or old preliminary scripts for movies I never would have mentioned myself. The early ones—*A Star Is Born* and *Nothing Sacred*—were Selznick scripts for which he encouraged us, among others, to propose improvements. The ones with Otto Preminger were on pictures he was shooting while he and I were preparing a future one. Others are projects I worked on for a while, and then someone else took over.

Perhaps a more remarkable aspect of my record, for a writer who was generally considered successful, was the number of scripts I wrote that were never produced, far exceeding the number that were.

Did you do any still uncredited and usually uncited motion picture work during the 1950s, during the height of the blacklist? Or was it all television shows and your novel? Can you cite any instances?

The only other picture of mine that was made during the blacklist was a British project called *Virgin Island,* a joint venture with Ian McLellan Hunter. We chose a pseudonym out of the blue—Philip Rush—and when the picture opened in London, a historian of that name wrote an indignant letter to the *Times,* repudiating the credit. Before that, the director, Pat Jackson, had arbitrarily, without even letting us know, done a rewrite, which consisted mainly of adding unnecessary dialogue and detail. Both Sidney Poitier and John Cassavettes, who had signed to star in it on the basis of our script, expressed disappointment when they were given Jackson's script on arriving at the West Indian location.

Hunter and I also did a script for a movie Hannah Weinstein, our producer of television films, wanted to make, but she couldn't get a deal on it.

---

[*] Walter Bernstein, the finishing writer, also goes uncredited. See the interview "Walter Bernstein: A Moral Center" elsewhere in this book. *A Breath of Scandal* was officially credited to Sidney Howard, based on the play *Olympia,* by Ferenc Molnár.

Can you quantify how many television shows you wrote during the period of the 1950s? Where did you get your—not your fronts—your pseudonyms?

From 1954 to 1959, Hunter and I did five pilot films, all of which sold as TV series. In each case, we would do a number of scripts in the series and then move on to the next one, assembling a corps of writers, mostly American and blacklisted, to provide new scripts for the series that were airing. The closest I can come to the number of half-hour film scripts we did overall, the two of us, is more than 100, less than 150.

We used the same pseudonyms all the way through for correspondence and payments—we had to open bank accounts under those names—but we let Hannah Weinstein's office in England choose names to put on the scripts. They had to keep changing these because if the network people in America who bought the series noted the same name on a number of scripts, they might ask for personal contact with the writer.

Otto-Intoxication

You worked quite often with Otto Preminger. What was the basis of your rapport with him? How did you first get together with him, and why did you continue to work together over such a long period of time?

Otto was a very bright man with a lot of humor and curiosity about almost everything. He was very good company, and we spent a lot of time talking about people and the world in general rather than about the work at hand. He had the minor defect of possessing a fair amount of ego and the major one of a really bad temper. The temper could be confusing because sometimes it was real and sometimes deliberately put on to achieve his purpose. It was directed almost exclusively against actors in the course of their work on his set, but certain actors like Burgess Meredith, John Huston, and Clifton Webb were never subject to it. The most abused victim in my experience was Tom Tryon, and I think it is fair to say that Otto was responsible for turning a limited actor into a successful novelist.

It would always start comparatively mildly after a rehearsal or a take, with something like "No, that wasn't right," and build to "What are you trying to do to me?" to "You're deliberately sabotaging the whole picture!" I described the process as Otto-intoxication—a phrase he first took offense at and then found amusing.

Although he frequently criticized scenes I had written, it was completely without temper, and as far as I know, he never did treat any writer that way.

What were the pluses and minuses, for a scenarist, of writing a film script for Preminger?

His approach to a draft of a scene was to go after it word by word, detail by detail, questioning everything, and often being satisfied with the answer. His instincts often turned out to be right, but sometimes he stuck stubbornly to a bad idea and insisted on the scene being rewritten his way. Occasionally, he would admit later that he had been wrong, sometimes after the picture was released.

Which of the Preminger films has the most of Ring Lardner in it? Why in that instance?

The two scripts on which I worked with Otto most exhaustively were never made: The first, based on *Ambassador Dodd's Diary* [by William E. Dodd Jr. and Martha Dodd (New York: Harcourt, Brace, 1941)] and *Through Embassy Eyes,* by Martha Dodd [New York: Harcourt, Brace, 1939], was about the rise of Hitler and the Reichstag Fire trial in particular. Darryl Zanuck had gone off to war after making *Wilson* [1944] and the statement that if that didn't earn a profit, he would never permit a historical picture again. When he returned to the studio, he circulated my script among his producers and executives, and was so impressed by their praise, he offered me a contract at more money. But the figures on *Wilson* led him to cancel our project.

The second was my first open job after fifteen years of blacklist, and Otto, who had already used Dalton Trumbo's name on *Exodus* [1960], made a point of announcing he was hiring me to adapt the book *Genius,* by Patrick Dennis [New York: Harcourt, Brace and World, 1962], about an eccentric director making a movie in Mexico. Otto liked the way the script worked out but maintained that he had to have either Rex Harrison or Laurence Olivier or Alec Guinness in the role for the picture to work right. Unable to get any of them, he put it on the shelf.

So, as it turned out, I had effective influence, in each of these instances [working on a script for Preminger], only on the movie Otto happened to be shooting at the time. While I was working on the Nazi script, for example, it was *Laura* for which I rewrote all the Clifton Webb dialogue and contributed to a few other scenes. Jay Dratler wrote me a note of gratitude for not challenging his sole screenplay credit.

The other picture, which Otto prepared and shot while I was supposed to be on salary for *Genius,* was *The Cardinal,* starring poor Tom Tryon. Otto, who was making a largely sympathetic portrayal of a Catholic prelate, knew I was an agnostic, and he had read my satirical novel *The Ecstasy of Owen Muir* about Roman Catholicism in America. But he also knew I was very well informed about Catholic rituals and practices. I rewrote many scenes to achieve what he wanted, and wrote them in a way I would never have done under my own name. Interestingly enough, after I had worked on the script in New York, Boston, and Vienna, and before I went to Rome for more of it and consultations about *Genius,* Otto hired another skeptic, Gore Vidal, to make some changes. One night at dinner, Gore and I taunted Otto with our joint conclusion: that he had unfailingly over the years bought the rights to some of the worst novels ever written and, in most instances, had made superior movies from them.

Hollywood in the Sixties

Did you and Terry Southern ever work together in the same room on The
Cincinnati Kid? *I'm trying to imagine the hybrid sense of humor. Did you
start the project with Peckinpah? How did it all unravel?*

I have never met Terry Southern. That was one time I thought a script of
mine was going to be done as I wrote it, because I sat with Peckinpah and the
cast for a week of readings, during which I changed lines to fit the actors'
needs or for other reasons. Then I went happily off to New York on vacation as
Sam started to shoot. The next I heard was that Martin Ransahoff, the producer, had fired Sam, ostensibly for shooting a nude scene with Sharon Tate,
and hired Norman Jewison to replace him. Jewison decided to change the
location of the story from St. Louis to New Orleans, and hired Southern, with
whom Ransahoff had just done *The Loved One* [1965], to do that and other
changes.*

Peckinpah's reputation, incidentally, somewhat similar to Bill Wellman's
thirty years earlier, marked him as unstable and unpredictable. In my experience with him, however, he was consistently a reasonable and helpful collaborator.

*You had a unique, perhaps not to be wished for, vantage point of returning
to Hollywood and screen assignments after a long, Rip van Winkle–like sleep.
How had the situation changed for screenwriters in the 1960s? Was there anyone left in the executive suits that you had known? Was it a frantic, behind-
the-times Hollywood?*

The old moguls were beginning to die off, and there was an increasing
number of more or less independent projects as opposed to ones originating at
the big studios. The personnel in the front offices included some unfamiliar
faces, but that trend was not as marked as it became later when, each time I
traveled to California, it seemed all the executives had been replaced by much
younger people. The only basic change on the business side was the fact that
each script was a separate deal between a producing company and a writer,
instead of an assignment under a studio contract.

But there was another change affecting style and content. The 1950s were
notable for a decline in controversial themes, mostly as a reaction to
McCarthyism. But it was also the period when Hollywood craftsmen became
fully aware of the new wave of postwar movies in Italy, France, and elsewhere.
By the time of my return in the 1960s, American filmmakers had adopted
much of this European technique. At the same time, they observed or shared
the new political awareness of the Vietnam [War] generation and began,

---

*   See the interview "Terry Southern: Ultrahip" elsewhere in this volume for Southern's
side of the story.

directing their appeal as always to the young, to experiment with more provocative themes.

These developments made it all the easier for me to find my way back into the business. Fortunately, my name had been solidly enough established before the blacklist for me to be easily employable after a gap of fifteen years when that institution began to dissolve. This was decidedly not true of a large percentage of writers and other film workers who were barred during the fifties, and many of them were never able to work in the business again.

For me there was the added consideration that I was personally sympathetic with the New Left and its concerns about war, nuclear weapons, and the environment. Although I never found much satisfaction for myself in marijuana, I did grow a crop of it in an isolated section behind our barn in Connecticut. When the success of *M*A*S*H* gave me a choice among subsequent assignments, my choice of controversial ones was certainly one of the reasons so many screenplays of mine remained unproduced. Perhaps the best of these, from a book *Farragan's Retreat,* by Tom McHale [New York: Viking, 1971], concerned a reactionary family in Philadelphia with a son who went off to Canada to escape the draft.

*M*A*S*H*

Tell me about the origins of M*A*S*H.

I had written a blurb for my friend Roger Kahn's book about Jews in America, *The Passionate People* [New York: Morrow, 1968], which the publishers, William Morrow, apparently liked so much they asked me to do one for a new book they were publishing called *MASH* [by Richard Hooker (New York: Morrow, 1968)]. Incidentally, the book, the screenplay, and the movie throughout its shooting were always referred to that way, without the asterisks, which were introduced by someone in the advertising department as they prepared their campaign after the movie had been shot. Anyway, I saw a way to put together what were really separate short stories about the same people in the same location and make a movie of it, and I gave the book to my friend [the agent-producer] Ingo Preminger [Otto Preminger's brother], who shared my enthusiasm. We gave it and a pitch to Richard Zanuck and David Brown, and they made a deal with Ingo's company to buy the rights and produce a movie.

What were the main points of evolution and change from the book to the film script?

The book was uneven in style and credibility, with some incidents that were just too wild and improbable to be acceptable in a movie. I took some of the main incidents, invented a couple more, and organized them into a continuity that I thought would work, even though it violated the cardinal rule that a story involves a change of character in one or more of the principals. In my

Donald Sutherland and Elliott Gould in *M*A*S*H,* directed by Robert Altman.

adaptation, the main characters were the same all the way through, and the illusion of a story had to be sustained by the action and the comedy.

I'm told that you considered setting the picture in Vietnam originally. True?

For about two minutes, Ingo and I discussed making it Vietnam instead of Korea and quickly realized the war that was still going on was just too close to many people for us to be funny or properly irreverent about it. By keeping it the Korean War, we could satirize the whole idea of American involvement in Asia, which consisted to a large extent of bringing American institutions like football over there instead of learning what Asia and its institutions were all about.

Did you have anything to do with the casting?

No. I remained in New York after Preminger and Altman came there for conferences with me that led to my doing the shooting script. Only when I went to the [West] Coast to begin work on another picture for another company did I even visit the set.

How did Altman get involved? What were your first impressions of him?

Your book on Altman [*Robert Altman: Jumping off the Cliff* (New York: St. Martin's, 1989)] is accurate about how he got involved after so many other directors turned down the second draft of the script. He and Ingo and I had a couple of long conferences in Bob's hotel room in New York, and I was very favorably impressed by him, his enthusiasm for the script, and most of his suggestions for improving it. I felt that the rewrite I then did was what all three of us had agreed upon.

Altman was widely quoted as saying the script was "awfully hawkish" when he first got his hands on it, and that he turned it into an anti-war film. True or false? How did it develop into an anti-war film?

This is the weirdest and most outlandish of all the quotes attributed to Bob on the subject. Whatever other changes, mostly improvements, he made during the shooting, the anti-war and anti-military spirit was equally present in the screenplay and in the finished picture. That was what I was mainly referring to when I said, on a number of occasions, that Bob and I had the same attitude toward the material. Incidentally, he was also quoted more than once as saying he would never have considered *M*A*S*H* as a movie if he had read only the book.

What input did Altman have in the final form of the script?

Altman made many changes in the script, and most of them were, in my opinion, beneficial. If I had known at the time I was presented the Oscar that Bob was not going to get the one for Best Direction, I would have made a point of acknowledging his collaboration. He added the business of the stolen jeep at the beginning and the subplot of an affair between the nurse Leslie and Colonel Blake. He greatly expanded the use of the public address system; he kept the character of Hot Lips in the latter part of the story; he cut the death of Ho Jon after shooting it; he revised the ending; and he added several significant pieces of dialogue, including what is probably the biggest laugh: Dago Red's "He was drafted." I should add, in my own defense, that part of the reason it gets such a good laugh, and this applies to another joke Bob added, which I can't remember now without seeing the movie again, is that he stopped all extraneous noise for the clear, unmistakable delivery of the line. A number of what I thought were pretty funny lines when I wrote them are not differentiated on the soundtrack from the incidental chatter going on at the same time, and the audience doesn't really hear them.

The only changes I objected to were some out-of-place slapstick in the opening scene; having practically the entire company join Hawkeye and Duke in singing "Onward, Christian Soldiers"; and expanding the football game beyond its proper proportion in the story.

Altman has said there was a lot of improvisation on the set. Were you on the set at all? How much improvisation was there? How much deviation from the script? How much improvement? How would you characterize the extent of Altman's touches?

I visited the set only once, leading Altman to call out, "Hey, somebody find the script! Here comes the writer!" Despite the joke, he kept pretty close to the scenes as written, encouraging improvisation mainly in a couple of scenes between [Donald] Sutherland and [Elliott] Gould. And there it was a matter of letting them rephrase the lines in their own words, sticking to the main content of each speech and the purpose, construction, and resolution of the scene. As I said before, I think the reason most of his touches worked was that we had the same attitude toward the material. For instance, when they had to get rid of the ringer on the opposing football team, I had the anesthetist go into the scrimmage and give him a knockout shot. Bob added the touch of swabbing the injection site first.

What were your feelings, winning the Oscar the second time around? Did you feel it was a kind of political as well as professional vindication?

As I said, I was in an Army camp in Virginia when the Oscar was awarded for *Woman of the Year,* and I didn't hear about it till the next morning. The second time, I was there and hoping, though I really felt Altman had a better chance than I did. Waldo Salt, with *Midnight Cowboy* [1969] the year before, had been the first blacklisted writer to get an award under his own name; I was the second and the only one of the Hollywood Ten to get one. By that time, it was becoming almost an honor to have been proscribed, and as it had been for Waldo, the applause when I went up [to receive the award] was greater than writing awards usually get. I found it a pleasant and satisfying experience.

Muhammad Ali, The Greatest

Is it purely circumstantial that the son of one of America's greatest sportswriters—and more than that, much more than that—became the screenwriter of the life story of one of America's greatest boxers? Or did you . . . go after the job? Were you always a sports enthusiast? Did Ali have any input or involvement in the script?

The producer of *The Greatest,* an Englishman, may or may not have been familiar with my father's name. In any case, he approached me through my then agent. I also talked to the director, Tom Gries, before agreeing to take the job. Ali was very closely involved, and a good part of my script derived from his account of how things had happened. [*The Greatest: My Own Story,* by Muhammad Ali, with Richard Durham (New York: Random, 1975)]. The fact is that I was mildly interested in prizefighting but much more so in his particular character and place in American life.

What kept the film from fulfillment?

One factor that ended up as a great weakness in the picture was the decision to cast a young actor as Ali in his early years and then switch to Ali playing himself. The transition didn't work: it clearly wasn't the same man, and we should have anticipated the problem, though it would have been a very difficult decision to make to do it otherwise.

Another reason the movie turned out badly was Tom Gries's sudden death before he had a chance to edit it. He had a lot of ideas in his head about how

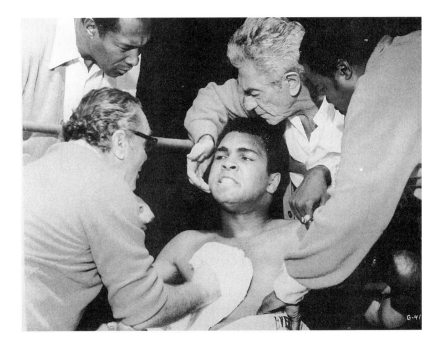

Ernest Borgnine (back to camera) and Muhammad Ali in *The Greatest.*

he was going to put it together, but the Columbia studio people specifically declined to consult with either of the two people who had the clearest idea of his conceptions: the assistant director and me. Instead, it was edited by committee, with predictable results.

Summing Up

How have your politics changed over the years?

Like a great many other people on the Left, I came to realize belatedly in the postwar period how wrong our image was of Stalin and what was called Communism. The collapse of the Soviet Union dashed my last hope that there was any possibility of regeneration from within. The lack of freedom, the inefficiency, and the corruption make me at least consider the possibility that these defects may be inherent products of bureaucracy.

Still, my basic answer is that Communism, like Christianity, is a beautiful theory that has yet to be tested, because it has never been put into practice.

It is also true that my politics have changed because of two considerations that didn't exist when I became a Communist in the 1930s, and that seem more important to me now than any economic or political system. I refer to the threat of nuclear war and the threat of ecological damage.

Do you see any themes running through all your various works?

If we include my two novels and my unproduced screenplays, it could be said that a recurrent theme is the struggle of individuals with unconventional values to find expression for them in a society that prizes conformity. Just a few years ago, I was attracted to a true story of two innocent men who spent eight years in death row largely because of their associations with marijuana and motorcycle gangs. The screenplay I wrote was widely praised, but no one wanted to sponsor it, largely, it seemed, because it questioned that popular institution, the death penalty.

*One thing I see in some of your works—*The Ecstasy of Owen Muir *and* M*A*S*H—*you deal with men who try to be moral, but who are stuck in intrinsically immoral situations.*

Well, you might say that's a variation of the theme stated above and of the frequent contradictions between theory and practice. It also goes back to what I said earlier about Communism and Christianity: the fatal difference between fine principles and the way they become distorted in real life.

You virtually left yourself out of The Lardners *[New York: Harper and Row, 1976]. Let's put it this way: you were discreet about your presence in the family saga. Can we ever expect an autobiography from you? Why or why not? I think people are hungry for candor and revelation, politically and otherwise, about that era. Is there still a residual fear of the government and police?*

Responding to the last question first, fear of repression is certainly not a consideration in my eightieth year. As a matter of fact, I have been setting down some autobiographical material recently, but I haven't yet hit on a form for putting it together. I may just abandon it in favor of a play or a novel dealing with Hollywood in the forties and fifties.

Richard Matheson:
Storyteller

Interview by Pat McGilligan

Richard Matheson's fan club is a big one, and his name is familiar to horror, science fiction, and fantasy fans around the world.

In Hollywood permanently since the late 1950s, Matheson is responsible for classic science fantasy films (*The Incredible Shrinking Man,* based on his own first novel), vintage television episodes (fourteen of the best, early *Twilight Zone* segments; plus noteworthy contributions to *Alfred Hitchcock Presents, Star Trek,* and *Night Gallery*); a slew of stylish Edgar Allan Poe adaptations for the producer-director Roger Corman in the 1960s (including *House of Usher, The Pit and the Pendulum, Tales of Terror,* and *The Raven*); and landmark telefilms (Steven Spielberg's breakthrough made-for-TV feature *Duel; The Night Stalker* about a vampire in Las Vegas, which won the Writers Guild Award for Best Television Script; and *The Morning After* with Dick Van Dyke as an alcoholic corporate executive).

Scriptwriting has fueled and financed his fiction writing and vice versa. While maintaining his Hollywood footing, Matheson has continued to write an impressive number of short stories and novels. Many have been adapted for the big or the small screen, sometimes by Matheson himself, sometimes not. Horror was a longtime specialty, and two of Matheson's scariest books have had a long life in print. *I Am Legend* (New York: Walker, 1970), about the sole survivor of a global plague, has been filmed twice, as *The Last Man on Earth* and *The Omega Man.* His haunted-house novel, *Hell House* (New York: Viking, 1971), is one of the all-time spookiest. Somewhat watered-down but still terrifying, it became the 1973 film *The Legend of Hell House.*

Since the early 1970s, Matheson has eschewed sheer horror and ranged far and wide. He has adapted one of his own novels, the time-travel romance *Bid Time Return* (New York: Viking, 1975), into the film *Somewhere in Time.* He developed Ray Bradbury's *Martian Chronicles* into a television miniseries. He and Steven Spielberg have maintained a long-standing association, which began by chance and has continued out of mutual admiration. In 1983, they worked together again on *Twilight Zone—The Movie.* Matheson was involved in three of the four segments of the anthology film, including one that recycled his own original episode from the 1960s, "Nightmare at 20,000 Feet"; later, Matheson consulted and wrote for *Amazing Stories,* also for the 1985–87 revival of the *Twilight Zone* series on television. In addition, Matheson contributed the script for *Jaws 3-D,* the third in the Spielberg-originated shark-amok film series.

Matheson has made a career sidelight out of mining the material of other fantasists, and has faithfully, if sometimes loosely, scripted not only literary works by Edgar Allan Poe and Ray Bradbury but also the speculative fiction of Fritz Lieber, Jack Finney, and August Derleth. A 1990 Matheson-scripted telefilm, *The Dreamer of Oz,* offered the writer's sincere, warm-hearted paean to the famous author of children's books, L. Frank Baum (portrayed by John Ritter). The *New York Times* television critic John J. O'Connor declared the telefilm "shamelessly on target."

Recently, Matheson has returned to his boyhood enthusiasm for westerns. His 1991 novel *Journal of the Gun Years* (New York: Berkley, 1991), about a legendary marshal who reveals the harsh truth about himself in his journal, was hailed by Stephen King, one of Matheson's many admirers, as the best book he had read that year. It won the coveted Golden Spur Award for western writers, and was followed by *The Gunfight* (New York: Berkley, 1993).

Matheson is a tall man with a trimmed beard and thinning blond hair. He is soft spoken, mild mannered, equable. An interview with him quickly turns searching and philosophical. Raised as a Christian Scientist, nowadays the writer remains preoccupied by metaphysical questions. Indeed, in 1993, Matheson published his first nonfiction book, an exploration of the writings of Harold W. Percival, about the quest for spiritual enlightenment, called *The Path* (Santa Barbara: Capra Press).

Paying the bills has always been an important motivation for a productive career. The struggle to eke out one's existence, the terror of the mundane, the ordinary man caught up in macabre circumstances—to some extent, these recurrent Matheson motifs, imagined into unforgettable extremes, have found their inspiration in his own life of hard work and the uphill climb that he discusses in this interview.

A lover of classical music, Matheson finds time to compose music and, with his wife, helped found a small theater organization in the community where he lives. For many years, he acted regularly in local stage productions. Community and family remain important to him. His elder son, Richard Christian Matheson, already has a solid reputation as a motion picture, television, and fiction writer, and was his father's cowriter on the 1990 screen comedy *Loose Cannons.* His younger son, Chris, cowrote the two highly successful films *Bill and Ted's Excellent Adventure* (1989) and *Bill and Ted's Bogus Journey* (1991), as well as *Mom and Dad Save the World* (1992). Daughter Ali is also a writer, story editor, and producer. His older daughter, Tina, somehow managed to escape writing; she is a social worker.

We had a good chuckle on the day I arrived to interview Matheson at his home in Hidden Hills, California, a planned community an hour's drive north of Los Angeles. I happened to be wearing a jumpsuit, and had just come from spending time with the director Martin Ritt, who was notorious for always wearing jumpsuits. Matheson confessed that he too was invariablely a jump-suit man, although he wasn't wearing one that day.

After the interview, Matheson took me outside and rummaged around in his garage, generously proffering copies of several of his books that I hadn't

Richard Matheson in Calabasas, California, 1993. (Photo by William B. Winburn.)

caught up with. When I went away, my arms were full, and I was shivering with the anticipation of pleasure.

Richard Matheson (1926–   )

1957   *The Incredible Shrinking Man* (Jack Arnold). Script, based on Matheson's novel *The Shrinking Man.*

1959   *The Beat Generation* (Charles Haas). Co-story, co-script.

1960   *House of Usher* (Roger Corman). Script.

1961   *Master of the World* (William Witney). Script.
        The Pit and the Pendulum (Roger Corman). Script.

1962   *Tales of Terror* (Roger Corman). Script.
        Burn, Witch, Burn! (Sidney Hayers). Co-script.

1963   *The Raven* (Roger Corman). Script.

1964   *The Comedy of Terrors* (Jacques Tourneur). Story, script.
        The Last Man on Earth (Sidney Salkow). Co-script, under the pseudonym Logan Swanson, based on Matheson's novel *I Am Legend.*

1965   *Die! Die! My Darling* (Silvio Narizzano). Script.

1967   *The Young Warriors* (John Peyser). Script, based on Matheson's novel *The Beardless Warriors.*

1968   *The Devil's Bride* (Terence Fisher). Script.

1969   *De Sade* (Cy Endfield). Story and script.

1971   *The Omega Man* (Boris Sagal). Based on Matheson's novel *I Am Legend.*

1973   *The Legend of Hell House* (John Hough). Script, based on Matheson's novel *Hell House.*

1975   *Les Seins de Glace / Icy Breasts* (Georges Lautner). Based on Matheson's novel *Someone Is Bleeding.*

1980   *Somewhere in Time* (Jeannot Szwarc). Script, based on Matheson's novel *Bid Time Return.*

1981   *The Incredible Shrinking Woman* (Joel Schumacher). Based on Matheson's novel *The Shrinking Man* and his 1957 script.

1983   *Twilight Zone—The Movie* (John Landis, Steven Spielberg, Joe Dante, George Miller). Segment 2: "Kick the Can" (Steven Spielberg), co-script; segment 3: "It's a Good Life" (Joe Dante), script; and segment 4: "Nightmare at 20,000 Feet" (George Miller), story and script.

1983   *Jaws 3-D* (Joe Alves). Co-script.

1990   *Loose Cannons* (Bob Clark). Co-script.

Selected television credits include the following episodes for *The Twilight Zone* series: "And When the Sky Was Opened" (1959, based on his short story "Disappearing Act"; "Third from the Sun" (1960, based on his short story); "The Last Flight" (1960, script); "A World of Difference" (1960, script); "A World of His Own" (1960, script); "Nick of Time" (1960, script); "The Invaders" (1961, script); "Once upon a Time" (1961, script); "Little Girl Lost" (1962, script based on his short story); "Young Man's Fancy" (1962, script); "Mute" (1962, script based on his short story); "Death Ship" (1962, script based on his short story); "Steel" (1962, script based on his short story); "Nightmare at 20,000 Feet" (1963, script based on his short story); "Night Call" (1963, script based on his story "Long Distance Call"); and "Spur of the Moment" (1964, script).

Other television episode credits include "The Return of Andrew Bentley," *Thriller* (1962); "Time Flight," *Bob Hope's Chrysler Theater* (1966); "The Enemy Within," *Star Trek* (1966); "The Big Surprise," *Night Gallery* (1970); "The Funeral," *Night Gallery* (1972), based on his short story; "The New House," *Ghost Story* (1972) and *Amazing Stories* (creative consultant, 1985–1987).

Telefilms include *Duel, ABC Movie of the Week* (1971); *The Night Stalker, ABC Movie of the Week* (1972); *The Night Strangler, ABC Movie of the Week* (1973); *The Morning After* (1973); *Dying Room Only, ABC Movie of the Week* (1974), based on his novelette of the same title; *Scream of the Wolf, ABC Movie of the Week* (1974); *Dracula* (1974); *The Stranger Within* (1974, based on his short story "Mother by Protest"); "Amelia," part of the *Trilogy of Terror* (1975, based on his short story "Prey"; the other two parts were based on his short stories "The Likeness of Julia" and "Millicent and Therese"); *Dead of Night* (1977, three segments, including one based on his short story "No Such Thing as a Vampire"); *The Strange Possession of Mrs. Oliver* (1977, story, script); *The Martian Chronicles* (1980, script); and *The Dreamer of Oz: The L. Frank Baum Story* (1990, co-story, script).

Published novels and short story collections include *Fury on Sunday, Someone is Bleeding, I Am Legend, Born of Man and Woman, The Shrinking Man, The Shores of Space, A Stir of Echoes, Ride the Nightmare, The Beardless Warriors, Shock!, Shock II, Shock III, Shock Waves, Hell House, Bid Time Return, What Dreams May Come, Journal of the Gun Years, The Gunfight, By the Gun, Shadow on the Sun, Earthbound, 7 Steps to Midnight, Now You See It,* and *The Memoirs of Wild Bill Hickock.*

Nonfiction works include *The Path.*

You started out in journalism, right?

Sort of. I had always wanted to be a writer, but I was very good in mathematics—I would say "unfortunately" now. A group of students from the grade school I was going to, about twenty-one of us, took a mathematics test, and five of us got into Brooklyn Technical High School. By an error in judgment, I went there for four years and majored in structural engineering, taking all of those incredibly arcane, technical courses.

When I got out of the Army, I went to a vocational advisory service. I could have gotten into any technical college, because I had so many credits—and this Brooklyn technical school, at the time, was very highly regarded. When the vocational adviser, bless his heart, realized what I really wanted to do—when he found out I wanted to be a writer—he combined my engineering background with journalism, and wrote to colleges saying I wanted to be a technical writer. He got me into the University of Missouri journalism school on the GI Bill—only it was a better deal, Public Law 16, because I had had frostbitten feet.

How did you make the leap from technical journalism into writing fiction and fantasy?

I never was in technical journalism. That was just a ruse to get me into that school. But I was in journalism, and as soon as I could, I became the music reviewer [of the college paper]. I used to review all the concerts and stuff. I wrote little plays there. A friend of mine and I wrote a musical they performed for the J show back in '47, or something like that. One of their early shows had Jane Froman in it.*

I always knew I was going to be a writer. But I came from a background where you didn't consider being a creative writer as a logical means of making a living.

What was your background?

An immigrant family. The idea of writing for a living was not really a feasible one to them, I think. The other people I knew during that time didn't think it feasible either. After I got out of college and was trying to write for a living, they'd say, "How long are you going to give it? When are you going to get a job?" A friend's mother, who was Irish, would ask me, "When are going to go to *woik?*"

At first I tried to get a job in magazines or newspapers when I got out of J school. I went back to New York, still trying to play the role of earning a living like a sensible human being. There was an editor of *Esquire* magazine whose name was Donald Berwick. He said to me, "Why don't you get a night job doing anything, and write in the daytime?" So that's what I did.

---

* The singer Jane Froman survived an airplane crash and became a popular figure during World War II. The story of her life was turned into the 1948 movie *With a Song in My Heart.* She briefly attended the University of Missouri School of Journalism.

Was there any kind of cultural background or impetus from your family?

I learned classical music from my family, from my sister and my mother. I read a lot; my sister read a lot. I was taken to the library when I was very young, and I became an omnivorous reader. My sister, again, was a great moviegoer who took us to the movies a lot, living in Flatbush, where there were, like, ten theaters within walking distance. I went to the movies constantly. I always went to the Saturday matinees, and you'd go whenever else you could. If you were staying home, sick from school, and you could get away with it, you'd sneak over to the movies.

What were you reading when you were growing up—science fiction and fantasy?

I read a lot of fantasy when I was a kid. Science fiction, I never read until I sold a story which they told me was science fiction.

Fantasy, like H. P. Lovecraft?

No. I never read H. P. Lovecraft. Actually, my reading was very unguided. When I was a real young kid, I read these huge volumes of fairy tales—*The Red Fairy Book, The Green Fairy Book, The Orange Fairy Book.* I read all of them. It's a joke by now, but I keep telling people I read a book called *Pinocchio in Africa.* That was one of the first books I took out of the library. People swear it doesn't exist. I don't know if Collodi—the guy who wrote the original—wrote it, but I swear I read it.* I read all of Kenneth Roberts's historical novels. Arthur Machen's *The Great God Pan.* Anything I could get my hands on.

Did you dream of writing movies?

Well, I always liked movies. Whether, in my teen years, I ever gave credence to the idea that I could actually write them, I don't know. But I corresponded with people like [the producer] Val Lewton when I was a teenager.† I remember writing to him and telling him that I had figured out two of his secrets for scaring people: one was that you lead the viewer's eye to one side of the screen and then have something jump out from the other side; the other was an extended period of silence, suddenly broken by anything—like a horse nickering in the stable—that would make you jump out of your skin. He wrote back to me that he and his editors, Robert Wise and Mark Robson, were delighted I had been able to figure this out. (*Laughs.*)

When you were watching movies, growing up, were you particularly affected by the movies that were fantasies?

Oh, sure. Nothing horrific, because my mother wouldn't let me listen to [the radio program] *Witch's Tales* and things like that. She wanted to protect

---

*   Eugenio Cherubini, *Pinocchio in Africa* (Boston and New York: Ginn and Co., 1911).

†   The producer Val Lewton was in charge of a special production unit at RKO in the 1940s, noted for turning out atmospheric, low-budget horror films, some of which—including *Cat People, The Leopard Man, The Seventh Victim, The Ghost Ship, Curse of the Cat People, The Body Snatcher,* and *Isle of the Dead*—have come to be regarded as minor classics.

me. She used to let me listen to *Let's Pretend,* which was on the radio, and which, in the early days, was almost as horrific as *Witch's Tales.* But she wouldn't let me go to the movies to see anything like that. I remember once she took me—I must have talked her into it—to *The Werewolf of London* [1935], with Henry Hull. When he started changing into a werewolf, I fell down and crawled up the aisle and stayed in the lobby. I couldn't handle it.

I liked fantasies—but they were the ones about benevolent ghosts. *Topper* [1937], *Heaven Can Wait* [1943], *Here Comes Mr. Jordan* [1941].

Did you have gods or paragons among the fantasy authors you were reading?

Not when I was young. Later on, William Golding, who's sort of a fantasy writer, stood out for me.* Oddly enough, years later, I was going to a gym in Reseda, swimming in the pool there, and a guy said to me, "I see you made the cover of *Saturday Review.*" I said, "I did?" He showed me the magazine. I swear to God, it was me, but it was William Golding! We were like twins. Amazing. It was like a doppelgänger effect.

Gods among directors? Obviously, Lewton.

You mean [the director Jacques] Tourneur†—but I don't think I was that aware of directors; I was just aware of movies in their entirety. The overall effect. If I had an idol when I was thirteen, it was Errol Flynn because I loved swashbucklers. I've always wanted to write one. I still haven't had a chance—to this day. Maybe I'll write one on my own.

I'm drawn toward fantasy—I always have been. But I love westerns, detective stories, mystery, suspense, swashbucklers, love stories, anything.

What was the night job you got?

My brother managed a place in New York where you typed up these metal address plates for magazines—I'd get a penny, penny and a half a plate. My mother and I would go together; we both did it. Then I'd write during the day.

What prompted you to move to California?

I really was drawn toward films. After I got out of college, even more so. I told you I had had frostbitten feet—a romanticized description of what they call trench foot, where your feet get wet and cold—that's how I got discharged from the Army. And my feet got very cold in Brooklyn, where I lived, especially during the winter when it was extremely cold.

Partly it was the attraction of the climate?

I probably used the climate as an excuse to myself. I lived on East Seventh Street in Brooklyn with my mother and I remember walking down the street one day and the wind was so cold and so loud I was screaming into it and I

---

* William Golding's first published novel is also his best-known, *Lord of the Flies.* He was awarded the Nobel Prize in literature in 1983.

† Jacques Tourneur was the director of many of the producer Val Lewton's best-known horror and suspense films.

couldn't hear my own voice. That was the day I decided I was going to go to California. It seems remarkable to me now, that I would have the chutzpah just to leave.

My agent had a writer out here, William Campbell Gault, who met me at the bus station and let me stay at his house for a few days. And he introduced me to other writers, including a group called the Fictioneers.

Who were the Fictioneers?

Mostly western, detective, and pulp writers. There was William R. Cox, Les Savage, Bill Gault—a whole pile of them. Hank Kuttner was the only one in the group writing science fiction and fantasy.* I don't think [Ray] Bradbury ever went to that particular group. It was a social club. We would meet for dinner and talk.

Was it an exchange of ideas?

I don't think so. They were hardboiled old pros. I don't think they sat around talking about creativity. They were more likely to talk about the prizefight the night before or the ballgame.

Were you the junior echelon?

I was the kid of the group. They were all in their late thirties or early forties.

When you say a lot of the Fictioneers were pulp people, do you mean "pulp" affectionately?

Sure. When I went to college and took writing courses, they would always talk about the distinctions between the pulp writer and the slick writer and the art writer. I came to realize that was ridiculous. There are only interesting stories and dull stories, no matter where they're printed.

The author Donald Westlake, speaking apropos of Jim Thompson, told me that what happens when you're writing pulp is: You're writing fast for the money, so you write along and get halfway through the story and suddenly realize you're in a knot. What you really should do is go back and untangle it properly, so that the story is clear from beginning to end. But because you're writing fast, you don't—you keep the knot and throw in a line, "Oh, yes, and he had divorced her three months before she was killed," to keep the story going. So that pulp has all the energy and style and the lure of literature, but frequently it's all knotted up illogically.

By that token [Robert] Ludlum would be a pulp writer still, because that's how he does it. Apparently, he doesn't really plot; he just starts out his stories

---

* William Campbell Gault is the author of many hardboiled and mystery novels including *Blood on the Boards; The Bloody Bokhara; Dead Hero; Death out of Focus; Don't Cry for Me; The Hundred-Dollar Girl; Run, Killer, Run;* and *Vein of Violence*. William R. Cox's many mysteries and westerns include *Bigger Than Texas, Death on Location, The Duke, Firecreek,* and *Hot Times*. Les Savage's novels include *Hangtown, The Hide Rustlers, Last of the Breed, The Royal City, The Silver Street,* and *Teresa*. Henry Kuttner's science fiction is anthologized as *The Best of Henry Kuttner,* with an introduction by Ray Bradbury. His novels include *Beyond Earth's Gates, Big Planet, Return to Otherness, The Time Axis,* and *The Well of the Worlds*.

and lets them roll all over the place. Somebody told me—and this person swore it was true—that Ludlum wrote one book and got to the middle of the story, killed off the main character, and then thought, "Oh, my God, what do I do now? I still have half a book to write . . ." So he had the guy's twin come back to finish the story. He had been out driving around, trying to figure out what to do when he saw a Gemini laundry truck. So the book became *The Gemini Factor.* That must be why they almost never make films out of his books, because you cannot make head nor tails of his stories. They sent me *The Osterman Weekend* before they made it [into a film], but I turned it down because I couldn't figure it out. They finally made a picture out of it, and I didn't know what the hell was going on. It was incomprehensible.

And the director [Sam Peckinpah] was going downhill, which didn't help matters. Under the condition of writing for the least amount of money per word imaginable, can a pulp writer maintain a high standard?

Of course it's better to be a little more careful. I never wrote *like* a pulp writer. Once in a while, you get inspired, like I did when I wrote a story called "Madhouse"—ten thousand words—and I rattled it all off in one sitting. But that's a rarity. It's much better to be a professional and a craftsman, and to rework things.

To this day, I've never written to the market. I've always written just what interested me and pleased me. As the perfect proof of that, just at the time when the horror novel was really starting to go crazy, I gave it up after I wrote *Hell House.* I had lost interest in it. I still have no interest in it. Now, it's like an industry, for Chrisakes.

When you were out here in the early fifties, was there much interaction with the film industry? Did you go to parties with Hollywood people?

No, no. I had nothing to do with Hollywood at all. Our hero was William R. Cox, who worked for Universal as a contract writer making $350 a week, which at that time was just a staggering amount of money to us. He was writing what he referred to as "tits-and-sand movies" for people like Yvonne DeCarlo and Jeff Chandler. We were in awe that he was making that much money.

You published your first short story in 1950?

Right.

And came out here in 1951?

Right.

Was it hard to make a living at first?

Oh, sure. I remember there was a point—'53, I think—when we had only $300 left; then I sold *I Am Legend,* and they paid $3,000 down. [It was published by Fawcett in 1956.] That saved my life. I think I borrowed that $300 from Bill Gault, too.

Why did six or seven years go by before you started writing movies? Was it that hard to break in?

Actually, I never even tried. Every once in a while, my agent would get interest, a call from *The Dick Powell Theater* once, but nothing ever came of it. I never in my heart of hearts thought anything would. Then, in 1954, we went back east because we were running out of money—my wife and I and our daughter and son—and I went to work for my brother again. He had his own business by then.

That was when I wrote *The Shrinking Man.* My agent, Al Manuel, sold it to Universal. They just wanted to buy the book. I recognized that this was my chance—now or never—to write the screenplay. They probably figured, "Let him have his ten weeks; then, we'll have it rewritten . . ." At the time, I was still living on Long Island.

That motivated your return to the West Coast?
Right.

When you adapted your novel into a screenplay, what kind of accommodations did you have to make in your thinking?
I took to it like a duck to water. I've always written visually when I write novels or short stories. I can see it as I write it; therefore, the reader can see it, and therefore, my prose transposes pretty easily to films. If you write that way,

Grant Williams under attack from a spider in *The Incredible Shrinking Man.*

to me, it's just a question of learning the technique of film writing, which isn't that complicated. It will take you about maybe a week to learn it. I *over-learned* it. I wrote intricate camera descriptions, which was perhaps ridiculous. But I've always written detailed shooting scripts. To a lot of writers, it's a mistake. They always say, "Why bother? The director will change it." I do it anyway. It works out—sometimes.

In *Duel,* Spielberg shot my script. He embellished it, obviously, and made it marvelously interesting, but it was my script, my through-line, and many of my shots.

What was the reaction of Universal to your Shrinking Man *script?*

They had it rewritten. Richard Alan Simmons, who became one of the producers of *Star Trek,* rewrote it. I sent in a long rebuttal of why I should have solo credit. At the time, I thought I had coped with the whole thing masterfully, but I think he just backed off and let me have the credit because it was my first picture.

He was nice about it.

I think so.

But parts of the script are still his.

Sequences. It was still fundamentally my story, of course, but there were things . . . the paint-can sequence, for example.

There is really not another movie like The Incredible Shrinking Man—*the story is so philosophical about life.*

I know. I didn't really appreciate it for a long time. Actually, it wasn't until my son Richard became a professional writer that he pointed out how unusual it was for its time. The ending alone was unusual for its time.

In writing the script, I wanted to follow the structure of the book—which was sort of like *Last Year at Marienbad* [1962]—where you plunge right into the story and then have flashbacks. I had actually written the book manuscript the other way around, starting from when the main character was big. But by the time he got to be small, maybe one hundred pages had gone by, and I thought, "Geez, this is real boring." So I restructured it. I did the same thing with *I Am Legend.* I restructured that book too, so that you were just plunged into the story, and the flashbacks brought you up to date.

In *The Shrinking Man,* the first moment is the spider chasing him through the cellar, instead of telling the whole continuity of how it happened; then, I could pick specific points along the way to fill in the story.

Universal wouldn't go along with your structure.

No, they didn't do it that way. It's a straight continuity, as you know.

How about the unusual ending? They kept that.

[Albert] Zugsmith, the producer, kind of liked it.

You wrote more than one script for Zugsmith.

Quite a few, but none [of the others] ever got made.

What kind of a person was he?

The prototypical big-cigar, flushed, heavyset producer. Every time I saw him, he would say, "I'm going to give you a writing lesson, kiddie . . ." But he was nice to me.

Did the jobs come in rapidly after the film of Shrinking Man?

No. Not at all.

Television?

No. I came out here again in '55. I didn't start working in television until four years later.

You went through another dry period?

Very dry. I wrote a sequel to *Shrinking Man* for Zugsmith: "The Fantastic Little Girl," about his *wife* shrinking. Not made. I wrote two entire versions of *Gulliver's Travels*—one in which he's a boy. Then, at that time, *Around the World in 80 Days* [1956] was coming out, so Zugsmith had me write another version. He visualized David Niven as Gulliver, a sort of English wastrel, drunk, falling off a boat. And Cantinflas as a Lilliputian soldier.

Wasn't The Beat Generation *a Zugsmith project too?*

Yeah, that was after he left Universal and went over to Metro. Actually, that film was based on a true case history which he had all this material on—about a guy who would meet salesmen and talk to them on the road, learn all about their houses, where they were during the day, what they did; then he would go and attack the wives while the salesmen were still on the road. I wrote it as a police procedure film. It ended up . . . well, you know how. I remember a copy of the script, many drafts in, where Zugsmith had meticulously crossed off *police* everywhere and had written in *fuzz*. It turned into absolute nonsense. Lewis Meltzer also worked on the script . . .

You started writing for television in? . . .

Nineteen fifty-nine—when Chuck Beaumont and I went in to see *The Twilight Zone* people.* I had an agent for years and years who didn't do anything for me, and then I switched to Preminger/Stuart, so did Chuck, and suddenly we got phone calls for appointments. We both started working on *The Twilight Zone*. I started working on *Lawman*. He and I wrote a bunch of stuff for different shows.

What kind of hands-on involvement did Rod Serling have on The Twilight Zone?

Whenever I see one of my scripts for that show, it's always my dialogue— word for word. Respecting writers as he did, Rod let you do your own thing. It was really a nice experience. That was the first time I worked in television. I

---

* The television and motion picture writer Charles Beaumont, who died at the age of thirty-eight, has become a cult figure among science fiction and fantasy fans. His screen credits include *Wonderful World of Brothers Grimm, Seven Faces of Dr. Lao,* and *The Intruder* (from his novel). But the bulk of his work was in television, where he wrote a number of memorable originals for *The Twilight Zone, Alfred Hitchcock Presents,* and *Thriller* series.

didn't know how nice it was. We would have three-day *rehearsals,* for God's sake, where we sat around tables with actors and directors, and discussed the show. That's still pretty unheard of in television.

Yet, I have to say, I have really gotten more satisfaction out of other things on television. I've had more things on television that I felt good about than I ever had with films.

Would you have story conferences with Serling?

Yes, of course. You wouldn't just write a script that they thought was perfect. You'd go in to see him and [the producer] Buck Houghton, and sit and discuss changes.

Serling was always pushing the show in cerebral directions, with scripts that were thoughtful or thought provoking or somehow meaningful. Was that explicit in story conferences?

People always ask me why *The Twilight Zone* is still alive, and I always say, "Because the stories are so interesting." That's what I do. I tell an interesting story. I think that's why I'm still around.

I had never done a television script. Ordinarily, they would ask for an outline, or so I was told. But the first show I did, the idea I presented to them was so vivid that they just said, "Yes, do it."

You presented it orally?

Yes, to Rod Serling and Buck Houghton. I just said, "A World War I airplane pilot goes through a fog, lands, and he's in a modern SAC base." They said, "Yeah, do it," because the image was so vivid. Then I had to figure out the story.

Did you do the same sort of oral pitch with other people—with, say, Alfred Hitchcock?

No. I met Alfred Hitchcock once when there was a chance I was going to write *The Birds.* I never saw him otherwise. I guess I would meet with Joan Harrison and Norman Lloyd, the producers of the show. I only did one one-hour show anyway—based on a novel of mine—*Ride the Nightmare.* I never worked on the half-hour show.

Was any other TV experience as good as The Twilight Zone*?*

Oh, *Lawman* was just as good—it was wonderful because of the producer Jules Schermer. If the scripts were the way he liked them, he never let anybody change a word. The lead, John Russell, was not the greatest actor in the world, but there was this director who used to work with John Ford who directed a few of them. I wrote a couple of outlines, and Jules said yes. He had total control. The scripts and the shows turned out very nicely. I got a Writers Guild Award for one of them.[*]

---

[*] Matheson earned a Writers Guild Award for Best One-Half Hour Episodic Drama for his "Yawkey" segment of *Lawman* in 1959. He also collected a Writers Guild Award for Best Adaptation from Material Not Originally Written for Television for *The Night Stalker* in 1972.

At the same time you were still writing short stories—which many writers consider the perfect, elegant form. Did you at all consider TV to be lesser work or job work?

No. I never considered that about anything. I just tried to do what interested me the most. That's why I've suffered such terrible disappointment when things turn out badly, because I put myself into everything—to this day. I just finished a script for Universal based on Conan Doyle's *The Lost World,* and it turned out great. Everybody was delighted with it. Then, what happens? Universal bought [the novel] *Jurassic Park.* That's going to be their dinosaur picture, so mine is out the window. That's crushing to me.

You mentioned that Joan Harrison bought a novel of yours and turned it into a television episode. Was that happening a lot with you—that people were buying your short stories and novels, as well as original stuff?

Yes. But mostly original stuff. I did one *Combat.* I remember Bob Blees, the producer, introducing me around, "Here is the very talented Mr. Matheson . . ." I wrote the script. When I got the script [back] in the mail, I thought they had sent me the wrong script. At that time, I was not as aware of multicolored pages as I am now. Somebody had rewritten it totally. That was the birth of Logan Swanson, my pen name, which has appeared on some pretty punk stuff.

Mostly TV stuff?

No. Even fiction. On one occasion, it was because I had two short stories in the same anthology, and the editor didn't want to use my name twice; so he used Logan Swanson. I also had Logan on a novel called *Earthbound.* For the first time in my career, these women editors were fiddling around with my style. I got so ticked off that I was going to cancel the whole book. But they were already setting it into type, so I said, "All right, put Logan to work again."

Does his name appear on some motion pictures?

Oh yeah—*The Last Man on Earth,* the first [film] version of *I Am Legend.*

Where did the name come from?

My wife's mother's maiden name is Logan, and my mother's maiden name was Swanson, actually, in Norwegian, Svenningsen. But in this country it was changed to Swanson.

How did you get involved with American International, Roger Corman, and the low-budget horror cycle of films?

I guess my agent was approached, and I went in to talk to them. They were going to do "Fall of the House of Usher." I met with Roger—he was the first one I met with. It took a while before I met [the American International executives] Jim Nicholson and Sam Arkoff. I was under the impression, at first, that I was working strictly for Roger. I guess he got a producer's credit on all those pictures, but I don't know how much producing he actually did.

He gets a director's credit . . .

Oh, well, he always directed.

How did Corman strike you?

You can't dislike Roger. You like him from the moment you meet him. I like him to this day. (*Laughs.*) He's just an extraordinarily decent, pleasant guy.

You say that as a kind of backhanded compliment. As if he didn't give you much else in the way of input.

One thing that sticks in my mind is that I always was cutting the script. Roger was always telling me that it was too long. Then, when I would cut it, it always turned out to be too short. I would have to come in at the last minute and add something.

Were you on the set doing much work?

I don't think I ever actually worked on a set. After I wrote these scripts, there was very little further writing. Sometimes I would do no rewriting at all. I was on the set quite often but just as a spectator.

What did you think of Roger's directing?

Oh, he's very, very concise. Very rapid. He's a camera director, not an actor's director. I don't think he would ever say he was an actor's director. He just gets the people and assumes they are going to know their job. The one thing I heard him say the most, as I've said before, is "We're on the wrong set . . ." He'd finish a shot and say, "We're on the wrong set," and walk very rapidly to the next setup. They shot those pictures in, like, two weeks.

The thing with Corman is, he couldn't slow down. He really stopped working or directing prolifically after his success, when he could afford to slow down. He was like a pulp writer who couldn't make the transition to success.

Exactly.

Did you have much of a feeling for Poe's work?

Not much. I read some Poe when I was in college and when I was younger. It's just that I poured myself into "Fall of the House of Usher," the first one. I read the story. I really tried to get the whole essence of it. The outline I wrote was like a work of art. I took it really seriously.

I'm sure they only wanted to do one picture, and that was it. They had no idea it was going to turn out so well. Not only the script but [also] Roger's direction, and [the actor Vincent] Price did a nice job. It just kept running and running and running all summer. They were running it on double bills with *Psycho* [1960].

How do you rate those Poe pictures? Which turned out the best?

Of the ones I wrote, the first one. Although the later ones—*Masque of the Red Death, Tomb of Ligea*—may have gotten closer to Poe. All of them, I think, were more like Lovecraft stories presented as Poe pictures.

Probably the best of mine was the *House of Usher*. Pure Poe-try, should I say? The second one, *Pit and the Pendulum,* that's just a little short story which I had to make a whole picture out of. I had this idea for a mystery-suspense film, something I had never used before, and I just thrust it into that mold.

The Comedy of Terrors, which isn't Poe, [Jacques] Tourneur directed, and I think it's very funny. I am proud of that picture and of the fact that I got AIP [American International Pictures] to hire Tourneur.

Earlier on, I had asked for Tourneur on one of my *Twilight Zone*s. I think I've told this story before. They said, "Well, he's a movie director. I don't think he can handle this time schedule . . ." As I recall, he did the shortest shooting schedule of anyone—twenty-eight hours. He had this book with every shot in it and detailed notes. He knew exactly what he was doing every inch of the way. He was so organized.

After a while, I couldn't take the AIP things seriously anymore. That oh-my-God-she-isn't-dead-she's-been-buried-alive sort of thing. How long can you be serious about that? *The Raven* was just an out-and-out comedy.

Your bent is more realistic. Just a touch of the supernatural.

That's my idea of the best fantasy and/or scary stories. Everything totally realistic, except for one little element that you just drop in. Like *Rosemary's Baby* [1968].

By this time, the mid-1960s, with all these wonderful credits, you must have been besieged by work.

I don't think I was ever besieged by work because I don't have a specific image. Usually, they want you to do the same thing [over and over]. Because I always wanted to do something different, I never really got into any kind of roll in any one direction. But I couldn't have done the same thing over and over again, anyway. If I had tried, the scripts would have gotten worse and worse as I got less and less interested.

Apart from AIP, you have always done a lot of work at Universal . . .

It seems I can't get away from Universal. I started with *The Shrinking Man. Duel* and *Somewhere in Time* were at Universal. And I worked on *Amazing Stories* as a creative consultant, at Universal, for a year.

Let's talk about Duel *and Steven Spielberg. When you first met him, did you have any idea that this was going to be a great figure in the history of movies?*

Nope. *Duel* was his first film. I remember the producer, George Eckstein, saying, "Well, they stuck me with some hotshot director . . ." I was told that when they saw what he had been filming out in the desert, they wanted to cancel the film, but he was too far into it.

You wrote it for Universal. They assigned it to Spielberg?

Yeah. George Eckstein was the one who approached me. He became the producer, and I worked on the script for him. He had a terrible time getting it made. Apparently, at one point, they were going to try to make a movie out of it with Gregory Peck. Only they couldn't get Gregory Peck. They tried for other directors, and they couldn't get one. They tried for other actors. Finally, they had to shut down *McCloud,* so they could use Dennis Weaver. I remember him, Eckstein, one day on the phone saying, "Well, I got a truck . . ." That's all he had at that point—a truck. (*Laughs.*)

"Like a kid with a toy": Dennis Weaver in *Duel,* directed by Steven Spielberg.

There was never much dialogue, per se?

No. Although I had more voice-overs, which were taken out. I had more of the character talking to himself. I'm glad it was taken out.

Did you have meetings with Spielberg?

No. I met him when they were shooting. I went out to that café where they were shooting a scene—after the main character is run off the road, he goes into this café and orders a cheese sandwich. I thought at the time that the café was open for business, and they were just letting Spielberg shoot there. Those people looked so real to me. It never crossed my mind that these were actors and actresses playing parts. I saw Spielberg setting up a shot—he was like a kid with a toy. But we didn't see that much of each other.

He's the type of person who might have read your stories or novels.

The only thing of mine I know he read is *What Dreams May Come.* My recollection is he called me one Christmas day—he and Amy Irving—after he had finished reading it. He thought it was wonderful. I asked, "Do you want to make a movie out of it?" We played around with the idea through the years. But he's always so busy.

He came back to you for help on Amazing Stories.

Yeah. That was after the *Twilight Zone* movie and "the gig of the season," as my agent called it. It was a lot of fun. In the beginning, a bunch of us met in a huge conference room at [Spielberg's production company] Amblin. There was food on the bar counter, and after working about three hours, we had a delicious meal on the patio. And the meetings themselves were a ball. Steven was usually there; [the Amblin executives] Frank Marshall, Kathleen Kennedy; [the supervising producers, Joshua] Brand and [John] Falsey; David Vogel, the producer; [the consulting writers] Bob Zemeckis and Bob Gale; [the story editor] Mick Garris. We'd sit and discuss ideas. I guess I did well, because I became the creative consultant for the show's second season.

I remember an idea I came up with in one meeting. The premise was that, in the future, a spacecraft would come down and the aliens would examine this strange environment. Then, when they took off, the down angle would reveal gradually that it had been Disneyland. I came up with the notion that in the space craft, the aliens would remove their helmets and big ears would pop up, and we'd see that they were giant mice; they were turned on because they had found the source of their god. I remember Steven slowly laying his face down on the table—he was so amused by the notion. Unfortunately, it was never made.

There was a period of time in the seventies when you went back to writing fiction. I read somewhere that in the long run, you feel television and movies detracted from your more serious writing.

Well, I have always put out probably the same amount of work. But a lot of it I didn't get paid for. I was doing some on speculation, which didn't sell. Or I was writing a script for somebody and getting paid, but it was never made. I've got so many scripts that were never made—which I thought were good. If I had written them as novels, they probably would have sold. I would have done better to write a novel.

But as my wife always points out, we had four children to raise. It takes a lot to raise a family of four, and we needed it. I don't regret it. I don't recall ever taking a job out here that I literally felt that I had to hold my nose to do. That's probably one reason why I haven't been flooded with work. I've turned down more than I've done, because I have to be fired up.

I didn't always have the choice. And they weren't paying big money for my kind of book back then. As I said, I got $3,000 for *I Am Legend*. If I wrote *I Am Legend* today, I'd probably get quite a bit of money.

You probably got more money for the Twilight Zone *movie than for all of your* Twilight Zone *episodes collected together.*

Oh, absolutely. When I started out in television, I remember, I had to hold out and play tough in order to get $1,500 for a half-hour script at that time. Now, what do they pay? Twelve thousand dollars is the minimum, I think, for a half-hour script . . . or more.

Do you feel some of your television and film writing is as good as your best novels? Or do you make any distinctions in your mind?

No, not if it's well done. The only difference is, if it's brilliant and well done, like *Duel,* you can't take all the credit for it. A novel and a short story—you might have had a helpful editor, but it's all you. If a movie that you wrote is brilliant, you have to credit the director, the cameraman, the composer, the actors . . . it's different. Novels are more personally satisfying.

Yet, when it's your own source material . . . I don't think anyone in the world would have written Duel *except for you. Whereas* Star Wars *seems to me to be more generic—in the best sense of the word perhaps—although that may be a little too easy to say now, with hindsight, than before it was made.*

I guess.

Whereas Duel *is highly original and has a personality that is distinctly Matheson.*

I don't know. I spent years writing a book that was going to be two thousand pages long, about a spiritualist family. I wrote about two hundred pages, and my editor read it and said, "Only Matheson could—or *would*—write such a book." (*Laughs.*) That was true.

But I had the story for *Duel* for a long time. I tried to peddle it. I distinctly remember trying to sell it to the series with Ben Gazzara about the guy who was dying, called *Run for Your Life.* Nobody wanted it. People always said, "It's too thin." I never would have sold it to TV or movies. I had to write it first as an novelette for *Playboy.* After it was published, then suddenly people thought it was wonderful.

Because they could see it—

In black and white, word for word, all the description. Otherwise, they didn't have the imagination to envision it.

I'm surprised you did leave horror novels behind. You have written a couple of cult classics. And there have been some pretty good horror movies based on some of your books—like Legend of Hell House.

That could have been more frightening, actually. Actually, they were very discreet about it. My book is much more terrifying. I wrote the script, but there were certain parts of it—anything that was actually visual—which they took out. Like the scene where Pamela Franklin is raped by the ghost—in the book, and probably in my original script, I described what it looked like as the ghost was lowering itself down on her. It was ghastly. Perhaps wisely, they decided not to show anything. You never really saw anything in that picture. It was all suggestion.

Your inclination would be to show the terror?

Well, I did in the book. The book was just totally overt, not subtle at all. A very overt horror story—graphic and blatant in every way. I got it all out of my system.

"My book is much more terrifying": Pamela Franklin and Clive Revill in the film version of *Legend of Hell House,* directed by John Hough.

*   *   *

Bid Time Return *was certainly a change-of-pace novel, a sweetly romantic love story that was also a suspenseful mystery. Was the film version faithful to your script? I know that the film [*Somewhere in Time*] has a huge cult following.*

Yes, it followed my script, and I'm delighted with the way it turned out. The filming of it was such a lovely experience for everyone. I remember attending the first meeting of all the crew members, and they actually applauded me when [the producer] Steve Deutsch [now Steve Simon] introduced me. And people kept coming up to me during the filming on Mackinac Island to tell me how much the story meant to them.

When the film did badly at the box office, it was a great disappointment to everyone. Though I think it made a profit eventually. The videocassettes have rented and sold well, and there have been many showings on cable; so the film lives on. It's amazing how many people I meet who say they love that film. There is something in it that struck a romantic nerve.

I know that you have continued to work in television as often as films. How did you feel about the way The Martian Chronicles *turned out?*

"A film that struck a romantic nerve": Christopher Reeve and Jane Seymour in *Somewhere in Time*, directed by Jeannot Szwarc.

I tried to be as faithful to the book as I possibly could. I think they did an inferior job. In Part 2, there were some good moments. There was one particular scene with Fritz Weaver in a church, where he thought he was experiencing the coming of Christ. It was a marvelous scene. It had the feeling the whole thing should have had.

What about this thing you just finished, about L. Frank Baum?

It's called *The Dreamer of Oz,* and I've just seen it. It's a wonderful piece of work, a biography of Baum and the story of how he came to write *The Wizard of Oz.* John Ritter plays Baum. David Kirschner, who produced *Child's Play,* is the producer.

I was at Kirschner's house, and he was talking to me about making a film out of a play I have written—a suspense horror play—when I saw all this stuff lying around, all these drawings and plans for the Oz film. I said, "Why didn't you ask me to do this?" He always thought of me as a horror writer. That's the way they categorize out here. But once I mentioned it, he thought it was a good idea. It was a labor of love for all of us.

Is it fair to say that your work in the eighties has become more soft edged—still fantasy or cerebral, but going away from things like The Shrinking Man, *the horror films, and* Duel—*towards more romantic or comic sto-*

ries like Somewhere in Time *and* Loose Cannons *the script you wrote with your son?*

Actually, we wrote two. Oh, they were not soft edged. One, which was called "Face Off," was totally rewritten by the director Bob Clark. He rewrote almost every word.

Why?

Because they let him. They bought this picture for a lot of money, everybody was wildly enthusiastic about it, and then they got a director who they let rewrite the whole thing! It would have made a wonderful picture the way we wrote it. They made a horrible, horrible picture.

What was the original concept?

It was a police-action picture but a comedy. About this older detective who has been on this serial killer case and is partnered with a guy who's had a breakdown in the past, but he's a wonderful criminologist. The criminologist has a multiple-personality disorder. So throughout, at any key moment, the criminologist splits off and becomes someone entirely different, much to the confusion and anger of his partner. It turns out the murderer is a Wayne Gretzky type—that's why we called it "Face Off"—who uses an antique ice skate that he has had sharpened for killing.

The film [of "Face Off"], *Loose Cannons,* is about a porno group vying with some neo-Nazi group to get a porno film of Adolf Hitler . . . it was so ludicrous. It dropped like a stone in the market and deservedly so. It was pitiful.

You said there were two that you wrote together . . .

We sold another picture that Richard Donner was going to direct. We met with him and his wife for some time. We revised it. Everybody loved our script, except of course the producer. Now it's being rewritten by someone else. Who knows if we'll recognize it when we see it.

What's it called?

"Shifter" was our title—about a shape shifter.

In general, do you find it harder to get stories all the way through to filming? Is the Hollywood of today that much different from the Hollywood you first got to know in the late 1950s?

My recollection is that the people I met back then were all older than me. They had been in the business for quite a while. They had experience. They had credentials. Nowadays, you meet the young executives, young producers, young agents, and their credential is that they went to Yale Law School. I don't know how good they are, or how much they really care.

Actually, I don't feel the same way about films that I used to. No, I don't mean films; I mean the film business. I still love films. It's a wonderful medium of expression; nothing like it. But the business . . . I just haven't been able to beat it. I should have gone into production, directing, some inside job. I had an agent once who said that if I went into film production only to protect my scripts, I'd be making a bad mistake. I can't think of any other reason to go into film production, at least for me.

But I didn't do that—my own failing—I'm a loner who likes to sit in a quiet, isolated room and write. The hurly-burly of the business would have been too much for me. When I first started in it, I was only twenty-nine years old, and I was popping Valiums like candy then. *Now* . . .

Anyway, it was my own fault. I can't blame the business for being what it is. And there's always something new and hopeful that you're working on. Even as I say this, a script I just finished—on Nikola Tesla—shows great promise of turning out well because of the director, Walter Murch, and the people involved in the production.

A lot of your signature film ideas lend themselves very well to a "wienie" synopsis.

They always say you should be able to tell any good story in two or three lines—or even one sentence. You couldn't categorize my work that way completely. And you can't say, "This is a story about Lawrence of Arabia . . ."; that's such an expansive character. But give me virtually any film or story, and I can probably reduce it to two or three lines. And I hope my films fit into that category.

Does the inspiration for you usually begin with the story idea?

Yeah. Through the years, I have been able to get more and more into character, but I never went into stories based on characters. I went into stories based on a story idea. Then I put characters in the story that I hoped would be believable and realistic in real life and maybe move you. But I'm a storyteller. The story is the thing. They can put that on my tombstone: Storyteller.

Where do your ideas for stories come from?

When I was writing short stories, some of my ideas would come from other books because I read omnivorously. Someone would mention something in a short story, totally overlooking what they had said, and I would pounce on it like a tiger. For example, there's a section in *Wild Talents,* one of Charles Fort's books, [New York: Garland, 1975], where, in several paragraphs, he describes, literally, a sequence that I made a whole short story out of. I couldn't believe when I wrote it that nobody ever latched on to the connection. He said in future times, psychic girls would fight wars; they will visualize terrible things happening to soldiers. And I got a great story out of that.

Most of my ideas have come from films. When I lived in Brooklyn, I went to see a *Dracula* film and the idea came to me: If one vampire was scary, what if the whole world was full of vampires? That became *I Am Legend.*

Another time, I went to see a comedy with Ray Milland and Aldo Ray [*Let's Do It Again,* 1953]; and Ray Milland was leaving an apartment and he put on Aldo Ray's hat and it came down way over his ears. At that second, I thought, "What if a guy put his own hat on and that happened?" That's where I got the idea for *Shrinking Man.*

It's not an exaggeration to say most of your ideas come from other movies—

And most of the ideas come from *bad* movies. Because if they're good movies, you're absorbed and not distracted. If it's a bad movie, if you're a movie buff, you stay and watch anyway. But as you're sitting there, you drift off. Something will happen [on the screen] . . . and it will spin off [in your mind] into something else.

When you're reading a story, I think, if the story is really boring you, you will stop reading it. You have to concentrate or stop. In a movie, you don't have to concentrate. You can just sit there. Things will come into your eyes but not really into your brain. And you drift off in a different direction . . .

Do you have any idea what it is about yourself that draws you to fantasy or speculative scenarios?

It's just what I am. It's what I was born as. It's what I'm composed of. I'm pretty much a believer in astrology, and I think what I am inclines me in that direction.

I don't think it comes down to genes necessarily, but it was there when I was born. Because when I started to read, I was drawn to that immediately. I wasn't drawn to anything else. I didn't want to be a fireman, I didn't want to be a policeman. And when I was seven, eight years old, I was writing little poems and stories and giving them to the *Brooklyn Eagle.* They published my poem about Columbus and a short story about an eagle who saved a little boy.

I wrote little fantasy stories throughout high school and college. And when I got out of college, science fiction was in its ascendancy. So I started writing science fiction, although I had never read it and didn't know anything about it. All my life, I've read fantasy, and I like fantasy. I don't mind being categorized as either a fantasy writer or an offbeat writer. I am that. But it's just that I am interested in doing other stuff too.

You don't feel that being inclined towards fantasy had anything to do with your environment.

No. My environment had nothing to do with it. We were from an immigrant family—

There was no grim reality you had to escape from into your imagination?

Just the horrible reality of the Depression and wondering—not where the next meal was coming from, I never felt endangered in that sense—but I was always aware that things were difficult. As a result of which, that insecurity is part of my nature too. Whether it's built in or whether that came from my environment, I don't know, but I have this dread of financial insecurity.

It sounds like you have good reason—there have been ups and downs.

Oh yeah. When we bought this house, for more money than we'd dreamed of spending for a house, that year I earned almost *nothing.* It was staggering to me. Terrifying.

Did you have a particularly religious upbringing?

I was raised as a Christian Scientist. When I was in the Army, I utilized my religious beliefs in order to feel safe in combat, protected, which was a little ironic because my blood pressure went up to about 170. What your conscious mind feels and what's really going on inside of you are two very different things, of course.

In college I started going to all the different churches. I kept a diary of my reactions to each of the churches and my "superior" observations of each religion. (*Laughs.*)

I left the church. We never took our kids to church. Yet I regard myself as being very religious and as having very extreme and specific metaphysical beliefs. I find them very valuable and comforting. But I don't go to a church. I don't subscribe to any one religion.

The metaphysical beliefs are reflected in your work to some extent.

Actually, Christian Science wasn't that bad of a religion to be raised in, because there's no sense of fear involved in it. Over the pulpit in the church, it says: God Is Love. They raise you with that idea. You can walk away from that because it doesn't frighten you.

Yet in your work you're fascinated by fear.

Yeah. What is *Duel* but the ultimate paranoiac's nightmare? I have an introduction that I wrote for my collected short stories that deals with the whole idea, which I maintain is true, that you can discern the mental state of the writer in his stories. I ran through my stories chronologically over a twenty-year period to show what my state of mind was—towards parenthood, marriage, and other things. The underlying theme of almost all my stories then was paranoia. Something out there is trying to get you.

During the [Writers Guild] strike recently, I sold a couple of short stories—the first time I had written any short stories in a decade. It was interesting for me to note that in both of them the premise was, not that there's something out there that's trying to get you, but that there's something *inside* your head that's trying to get you. (*Laughs.*) Which is much more to the point.

Did you at any point study or read philosophy?

Oh, sure. I read a lot of philosophy books.

Were you affected by any one book or philosopher in particular?

The one book that has affected me the most, which I subscribe to totally, is called *Thinking and Destiny,* by Harold Percival. I've read hundreds and hundreds of books on metaphysics; I have my own modest library. I used maybe eighty books to research *What Dreams May Come,* my novel about afterlife. But this one book [*Thinking and Destiny*] incorporates everything that I believe. You can buy it through The Word Foundation in Dallas.

Would it be fair to describe your work as existentialist?

I think the theme of almost all my work has been one man up against some terrible situation and trying to survive it, from *The Shrinking Man* to *I Am Leg-*

end, even to my war novel, *The Beardless Warriors* [Boston: Little, Brown, 1960]. It's a positive premise ultimately—the protagonist comes to some kind of understanding or triumphs at the end. *The Shrinking Man*—he still exists in another dimension. *I Am Legend*—the character comes to realize that he has to die because *he* has become the terror in the world, instead of all these vampires that were terrorizing him before. *The Beardless Warriors*—the main character matures by the end of the story.

You come from a fairly complacent upbringing . . .

My mother came over to this country from Norway at a very early age, and immigrants clustered together for safety. They were fearful about this whole new environment. They chose to come, but they were surrounded by strangeness, and it frightened them. My mother was thirteen when she came, and she was always fearful of what was out there. Be careful. Don't misbehave. Oh, you mustn't do that or say that. You mustn't *think* that.

To an extent, then, that psychology of paranoia was inherited.

I was certainly exposed to it. My mother had this immigrant psychology—which generated fear of the unknown—and she turned to religion, which is a protection.

One of the things that distinguishes Shrinking Man *and* Duel *is that the protagonists are utterly ordinary. They're not supermen or Victor Mature.*

Well, I grew up in that kind of background, and I always chose to apply the horrors, the terrors, or the mystical elements in a very banal neighborhood environment.

On the other hand, two later novels I wrote were very different, *Bid Time Return*—which they made into [the film] *Somewhere in Time*—a time-travel love story, and *What Dreams May Come,* [New York: Berkley, 1978] a love story about life after death.

I wrote a screenplay based on *What Dreams May Come,* that at one time was going to be directed by Wolfgang Peterson, who did *Das Boot* [1981], but nothing came of it.* It's clear to me that Hollywood does not want to make a serious picture about afterlife. Pictures like *Ghost* [1990] make a brief, momentary excursion into the afterlife—just a couple of feet beyond this earth—and then they immediately pop back and tell the story. My story goes entirely there and stays there. I don't think they'll do that. Pictures like *Ghost* are popular. And they squeeze a few metaphysical values out of the yocks and mysteries. But how much can you play for yocks if you're actually going into afterlife—I don't know.

Anyway, I don't do the old-fashioned sort of horror story anymore. I don't want to do that anymore. I have probably lost readers because of that. They

---

* At this writing, *What Dreams May Come* has been revived as a project and is scheduled to go before the cameras with Robin Williams as its star and New Zealander Vincent Ward as director. Matheson did not write the script.

liked my hard-edged, scary stuff from the early days. They probably think my brain has turned to Jell-O.

Could the idea that you were influenced by this paranoia in your youth be connected to the fact that you're just now beginning to experience more range and variety in your work?

That's an interesting idea. You mean, I've finally broken loose and am trying new things? But I've always tried . . . I have written all kinds of stuff that nobody was interested in. So many times people have said to me, "You're ahead of your time." I got so fed up with that line that I didn't want to hear it anymore. To me, that meant only that I wasn't making any money. That I was out of step. Maybe I was ahead, but what's the difference? I might as well be behind.

In a sense you feel overly categorized.

I think I'm getting out of it. It took a hell of a long time. They are not comfortable with you unless you are categorized. It's so much easier to say, "Oh yeah, Matheson. There he is on the horror shelf. Hire him to do this."

Right now, I'm adapting what is considered to be a horror novel. I'm also doing a live-action musical for TV. I may be doing a film eventually, about the Mafia. And there's an old western novel of mine, which Mark Harmon is interested in doing. Originally, it was an outline for a film that I wanted to sell—I must have written it twenty years ago—and it's only now that someone is interested.* And it is only now that it is going to be published.

Sounds like you're peaking now.

If you hang around long enough and don't die off, they figure you're here to stay. (*Laughs.*)

Which of your own pictures are you most satisfied with?

Duel. The Morning After, which I think is a wonderful piece of work. Both *The Night Stalker* and *The Night Strangler. Somewhere in Time. The Dreamer of Oz.* Of the ones I did for AIP, probably I liked *The Comedy of Terrors* the best, and it wasn't even Poe. A handful of TV half-hours, mostly *Twilight Zone* and *Lawman.* And maybe next year I'll have something else to add to the list . . . who knows?

---

* Matheson reports that as of this writing nothing has come of the Nikola Tesla script, the horror novel adaptation, the live-action musical, the Mafia film, or the Mark Harmon western. "As is Hollywood's wont," Matheson explained.

Wendell Mayes:
The Jobs Poured over Me

Interview by Rui Nogueira

Wendell Mayes was born on July 21, 1918. He came from Carruthersville, Missouri. He went to several colleges—Vanderbilt, Johns Hopkins, Central College of Missouri—without graduating. He became interested in the standard writers—Hemingway, Steinbeck, Dos Passos, Fitzgerald—and began writing in their styles until he discovered his own. He took up writing as a serious career after World War II, though never as a journalist. He first tasted real success in the days of live television and sold original teleplays in substantial numbers during the early fifties.*

Wendell Mayes (1919–1992)

1957   *The Spirit of St. Louis* (Billy Wilder). Co-script.
        The Way to the Gold (Robert D. Webb). Script.
        The Enemy Below (Dick Powell). Script.

1958   *From Hell to Texas* (Henry Hathaway). Co-script.
        The Hunters (Dick Powell). Script.

1959   *The Hanging Tree* (Delmer Daves). Co-script.
        Anatomy of a Murder (Otto Preminger). Script.

1960   *North to Alaska* (Henry Hathaway). Uncredited contribution.

1962   *Advise and Consent* (Otto Preminger). Script.

---

*   This interview was transcribed by Gillian Hartnoll.

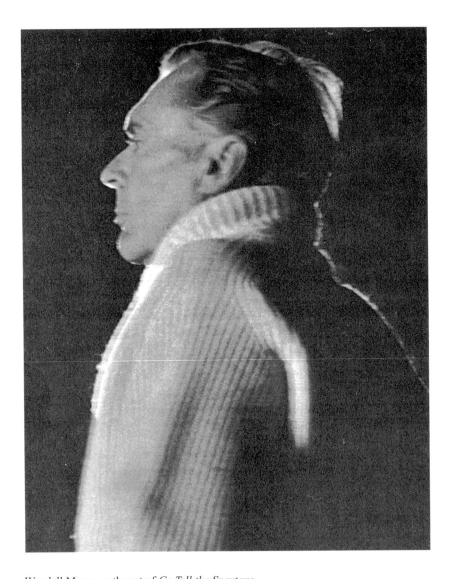

Wendell Mayes on the set of *Go Tell the Spartans*.

1965   *In Harm's Way* (Otto Preminger). Script.
        Von Ryan's Express (Mark Robson). Co-script.

1967   *Hotel* (Richard Quine). Producer, script.

1969   *The Stalking Moon* (Robert Mulligan). Producer, script.

1972   *The Poseidon Adventure* (Ronald Neame). Co-script.
         The Revengers (Daniel Mann). Script.

1974   *The Bank Shot* (Gower Champion). Script.
         Death Wish (Michael Winner). Script.

1978   *Go Tell the Spartans* (Ted Post). Script.

1979   *Love and Bullets* (Stuart Rosenberg). Story, script.

1982   *Monsignor* (Frank Perry). Co-script.

Television credits include the telefilms *Savage in the Orient* (1983) and *Criminal Behavior* (1992).

Academy Award honors include an Oscar nomination for Best Screenplay Based on Material from Another Medium for *Anatomy of a Murder.*

Writers Guild honors include a nomination for Best Script for *Anatomy of a Murder.*

My first screenplay was with Billy Wilder, who brought me from New York to Hollywood for *The Spirit of St. Louis* in 1955. The great problem with the film was we had a man sitting in an airplane by himself, and the problem was how to sustain the interest in the story. I think it was a picture that was made thirty years too late, and I think it should have been called "The Lindbergh Story" or something like that, because when they put it out as *The Spirit of St. Louis,* everyone seemed to think it was an old musical, and they didn't know what the Spirit of St. Louis was.

There was something unusual about the way I was employed by Billy Wilder. He's a great bridge player, and he read a man called Goring on bridge at the time. He had had one writer working on *The Spirit of St. Louis,* and they had either disagreed or the writer got sick or something, and he was looking for a writer. And he was reading Colin Goring on bridge, and right next to the column was John Crosby's review of one of my television plays. He read that, and he called up New York and said, "Let's hire this fellow Wendell Mayes." So if he hadn't been a bridge player, I would never have been employed.

Billy Wilder's a writer, and we simply wrote a screenplay together, in a room together, walking around, talking it out. We would write a scene just as you would imagine a scene would be written. I would say, "Suppose he says *this* . . . ," and Billy would say, "Yeah, let him say that, and *then* he says . . ." It isn't the best way in the world to write, and it doesn't work for everybody, but it does work for Billy Wilder. We would scribble it down on a piece of paper, then call in a secretary, and she takes it out and types it, and then we look at it. That's the only collaboration that I've ever had. Everything else I've done by myself.

I wrote a picture that was before its time, which slipped by quite unnoticed. It was called *The Way to the Gold,* with Sheree North and Jeffrey Hunter, directed by Robert Webb. It was an interesting picture, but the studio and the people who publicize pictures didn't understand that it was a comedy. They thought that it was a big melodrama, so it slipped by.

Then I had a western, that I think was a superb western, called *From Hell to Texas.* It was done by Henry Hathaway, with Don Murray and a darling actress called Diane Varsi, who very shortly thereafter quit films because she started a breakdown. Henry Hathaway is very easy for a writer to work with. He's absolutely dreadful for actors to work with: he's probably the toughest son of a bitch in Hollywood. He is tough for a reason: Hathaway is not the most articulate man in the world, and he maintains control of his set and of his crew and his actors by being cantankerous and rather cruel sometimes. He knows what he's doing; he isn't doing it out of hand. He's doing it deliberately because this is the way he's discovered he can work. It isn't true with a writer. He's a very gentle man when you sit down with him in a room to write. He doesn't feel that he has to browbeat you. I haven't come across a director who didn't make it as easy as possible for me to write. They actually try to conform to the way the writer works, rather than make the writer conform to some way they want him to work.

My first film that received notice was *The Enemy Below,* directed by Dick Powell with Bob Mitchum. It was not a financial success for some reason, although on television it has become one of the big pictures—but it got good critical notices. Its original ending was better. You remember where the German captain is on the submarine surrounded by fire, and the character played by Mitchum brings him across on a rope? All the men were off the ship but these two men. Now these two men were burnt-out cases, both of them. They are not there for any reason except that they have to be there. The moment Mitchum gets hold of him [the German], and starts pulling him aboard, the ship blows up, and at that point, you pull back to watch this tremendous explosion, and you keep pulling back until there's nothing left for the audience to see but the great, vast, empty sea with a little group of boats floating on it. The point was Dick and I both felt that these two characters were men who had no reason to live. There's much more feeling if they should die, one finally trying to help the other after killing him. But the studio said, "No, you like both of them. You can't kill them. It'll disappoint the audience." Nothing. So we had the ending with them standing smoking a cigarette on the back end of the destroyer, something like that. One of those things one must do.

Then I did a picture that wasn't so good, except it had an interesting idea that we were not allowed to follow through on—again with Mitchum and Dick Powell—called *The Hunters.* It was about a man who loved war, but we had a problem trying to sell a hero who loved war. I know *The Hunters* was supposed to be an adaptation, and the novel was an interesting novel. I was

"A woman's film rather than a man's": Gary Cooper and Maria Schell in
Delmer Daves's film *The Hanging Tree*.

called in on it, actually, in desperation, because they had a starting date, and
they really didn't have a script to shoot; and while we used the title, what I
wrote was from start to finish an original screenplay. There wasn't anything
else to do, because the novel could not be adapted. It was too internal. They
do make mistakes in Hollywood in buying material. They will buy a novel that
is terribly internal, and the only way you can really do it is if you have a voice-
over explaining what the character is thinking. In doing a film, your characters
can't think; they can only speak or move, and you've got to tell the story with
their voice or their movements. What they're thinking, nobody knows.

Then I had a western—I think it was Gary Cooper's last western—called
The Hanging Tree, directed by Delmer Daves. Daves is a writer himself. He's
very easy to work with, a very sweet man. Cooper wasn't very well, and I
know that he had great trouble riding a horse at the time, because he had
something wrong with the hip; so they kept him off the horse as much as they
could. It was the only western that I think that *I've* ever seen that was a
woman's film rather than a man's film—Maria Schell playing the blind heroine was marvelous.

Gary Cooper was a very interesting, a very complex man. He was not a
simple person at all. I think he was one of the best actors film has ever had. I

don't think anybody recognized it, even though he won—I think—two Academy Awards.* Henry Hathaway was the first to point out things to me about Cooper, before I even worked with Cooper. He said, "Everything Cooper does is original. He thinks about it. You have to watch it to realize what makes Gary Cooper on film. You don't just stand him up there; it's things that he does." He said he had Cooper in a film, and there was a gunbelt hanging on the wall; and Cooper's direction was to go over and take the gunbelt off the wall. In the rehearsals, Cooper kept fooling around with it, and Hathaway said, "Coop, what are you doing? Just take it off the wall." And Cooper said, "I want to take it off *my* way." So Hathaway said, "All right, do it your way," and Cooper fooled around with the belt for a few minutes and said, "Okay"; and they rolled the cameras, and he walked over and instead of grabbing it off the wall, he took two fingers and he placed them under the belt and he lifted it off the wall. Hathaway said no one in the world but Gary Cooper would have done that. That was why he was so original. Those who say that Gary Cooper hesitates over his lines because he doesn't know them are lying. He was a professional, like John Wayne. Cooper and James Stewart—both have a great sense of timing in dialogue. It's more recognized, and I think it's easier to recognize, in Stewart than it was in Cooper, but Cooper was highly original at the delivery of lines. He knew what he was doing.

Then I did *Anatomy of a Murder* for Otto Preminger. It was a good movie. I think it was one of my best screenplays. And I did two other pictures for Otto—*Advise and Consent* and *In Harm's Way*. I wrote another script for him, but it never did get off the ground, not because of the script, but actually because the rights to the material were confused—that was Steinbeck's *Cannery Row*.† So it sits on the shelf, but maybe some day it will be made.

No one was cast when I started working on *Anatomy of a Murder*. Stewart was cast after it was written. Lana Turner was cast and then stepped out, and Lee Remick came in. It was written without any actors in mind.

I didn't know Otto when he called me from New York. I don't really know how he got on to *me* or why he employed me. But he called me from New York and asked me if I'd read a novel called *Anatomy of a Murder* [by Robert Traver†† (New York: St. Martin's, 1958)], and I said, "No, but I will read it." And I read it and called him back, and I said, "I think it's a filmable motion picture." So he called my agent and made a deal, and I went to New York and met Otto there and started to work on it.

---

  * Gary Cooper won Oscars for Best Actor for *Sergeant York* and for *High Noon*. In addition, he received a special Academy Award in the 1960 ceremony shortly before his death.

  † *Cannery Row* was made into a film in 1982, the directorial debut of screenwriter David S. Ward (*The Sting*).

  †† Robert Traver is the pseudonym of John Donaldson Voelker.

From left, Lee Remick, James Stewart, and Ben Gazzara in *Anatomy of a Murder.*

When I work with Otto, we discuss over a period of time, say, the first fourth of a screenplay, where we want to go with it; and then I will go off and sit down, and I will write the first fourth. Then I come in and Otto reads it and we discuss it again and we get the construction and the arrangement of scenes to please both of us. Then we move on to the next fourth of the story. I've never gone through a whole screenplay with Otto and then gone off to write, because Otto doesn't like to plan that far ahead—and actually, I don't either because sometimes good things come without planning step-by-step straight through a screenplay. With other directors, I have gone off and written a screenplay and handed it to them. They've asked for certain changes, and that was it. Otto's very good from a writer's point of view. Unlike many directors and producers, Otto does not make up lines when the writer isn't there. He will call the writer and say, "Look, I need a line of dialogue here." One of the things that drives a screenwriter absolutely crazy with many producers and directors is that they won't call the writer; they will simply toss in ad lib lines of dialogue that are almost invariably absolutely dreadful, that the characters wouldn't say. It isn't really done quite so much anymore. They used to hate the writer, and the moment they got the screenplay, they used to say, "Get off the lot; we don't want you around bothering us." Nowadays, a writer out here has a good deal more respect and a great deal more money.

I've never worked as a contract writer. That was before my time. I've always worked on one specific film for a flat fee. But I've never been driven to write fast just to get the money. I suppose there are writers, particularly in television today, who crash the stuff out as fast as they can and then rush onto something else; but the flat deals paid writers now are very substantial, and they're usually paid enough to work a year very comfortably.

Advise and Consent was actually a rather close adaptation for a very good reason. It was [based on] a very big best seller [by Allen Drury (Garden City, N.Y.: Doubleday, 1959)]; and when you sit down to adapt a best-selling novel, you do feel that since ten million people have read the novel, they must like it, and they want to see what they've read. So we made a great effort to try to translate that book to film. The introduction of most of the characters by the phone is not in the book, but we had to introduce a great many people very fast in order to start the thing. What was on film was very close to what was in that novel, and I don't mean dialogue necessarily, because very few novelists write dialogue that actors can speak. It was the same *thought* that was in the novel but not in the same words. We put in the scene with the ambassador's wife visiting the Senate chamber, which was not in the novel, very obviously for the European audiences, because if you talk about a Left and Right in Europe it means something entirely different from Left and Right in the Senate.

I don't believe that the scene was in the book where [Henry] Fonda confesses to Franchot Tone as the president that he was a member of a Communist group, and Tone tells him that he must not tell the truth about this, because it is more important that he should continue his political career and follow him as president. I don't think that Fonda did go to the president, but I think that the president knew. I've forgotten what device they used in the book, but we did that largely because we felt that the character of Fonda, as we were presenting him, was a very sympathetic man, and that he was an honorable man, and that he would have done this. In the novel, he did not. The author of the novel, Allen Drury, hated the picture. He's very conservative—as a matter of fact, he's an archconservative—and Otto and I are liberals, so we didn't do justice to his conservative point of view. His character of Leffingwell, the part Fonda played, was not a sympathetic man; he was a crook. I believe that Drury was immensely more sympathetic to the Charles Laughton character. Don Murray's [character's] problem of homosexuality was in the novel, but the scene where he goes to the gay bar was mine, that was original. I did that, rather than use dialogue exposition of what the situation was, because we could show it. In the novel, someone told it. I don't think he ever encountered the man who had been his lover at all. But, still and all, it told the same story.

I was least fond of *In Harm's Way* out of the three pictures I've done for Otto, and this was probably because it seemed to me to be a twice-told tale. It was a war picture that had been *done* before, the kind of thing that had been done *many* times before. There were things in it I liked very much. I thought that the love story between an old admiral and an old broad came off awfully well, and because John Wayne and Pat Neal were marvelous in the roles. John Wayne's a great pro. John Wayne never blows a line. He'll come in letter perfect. The other actors will blow lines, but he will stand there patiently, wait for them to get their lines, say his in his own way.

It inhibits me to know who is going to play a part, because in a scene in which I know, for example, John Wayne is going to play a role, I will say to myself, "Well, John Wayne can't *say* that line of dialogue," so I won't write it. Now in *In Harm's Way,* John Wayne was hired after the screenplay was written. It was not written for John Wayne, and if I'd been writing it for Wayne, there are certain speeches that I would not have written, because I felt he could not read the lines. As it turned out, John Wayne *was* able to read the lines and read them very well indeed—so I think it was a better film because I didn't know he was going to play the role.

I wanted Wayne to die and the son to live, and Otto wanted the son to die and Wayne to live. His argument was—you can't kill John Wayne. So he won, and perhaps he's right. You can cut a leg off or an arm or an ear or something—you can maim him for life—but you can't kill him.

I wasn't crazy about Brandon de Wilde as the son. There was a good scene where Wayne first meets his son after all these years, out on a little boat where he and his son have this—actually—a conflict that they don't really talk about; you just *feel* that it's there. This is a good scene. Some of it I actually didn't really believe. I always find it difficult to believe anything, because it always seems so convenient to me that characters turn up in the proper place at the right time. I know audiences don't think about it, but as a writer, *I* think about it. I don't like things to be convenient. Maybe this is another reason why I was not terribly fond of *In Harm's Way.* I think some of Otto's best direction was in *In Harm's Way*—unquestionably, it was. Dana Andrews's admiral was really a bit, but Dana Andrews was remarkably good in it. It was not a caricature; it was a very believable officer.

I didn't much care for the Kirk Douglas character. I thought he was sort of dragged in. He had a few things that were rather good, but actually that gung ho, derring-do, flying the plane after raping the girl, somehow doesn't seem part of the story to me; it seems like something else. I could have written a picture *about* the character that Douglas played. If we could have done more with the character, it would have been more interesting to me.

Otto can be very stern with actors, he can actually be very cruel, he can be very loud. You see, Otto is an actor, and he has *great* discipline as an actor, as a director. He himself is a disciplined man, and he expects other people to be disciplined. I think probably the thing that Otto detests most of all is an actor who is not a professional, who does not behave as a professional. A man, or a woman, is being paid a lot of money to come on the set, read some lines, do a job, and instead they want to exhibit their egos, and this Otto will not contend with. Many directors have another way of working . . . I think Richard Quine is inclined to want to charm the actors.

I had a great deal of freedom in *In Harm's Way.* I wrote the first screenplay, when Otto was in Europe, without him at all; and then I went to London and started to do a rewrite, and Otto shelved the project. And then I believe it was about maybe two years later that the picture began and [I] had a fresher point of view and did many things that were not in the book at all. And I think we improved it for that reason, since we had quite forgotten the novel.

I also wrote *Von Ryan's Express* for Mark Robson and *Hotel* for Richard Quine. *Hotel* was a big best seller and Warner Brothers employed me to write a screenplay and to produce the picture. The studio felt that Richard Quine and I would get along well together, which we did, so he came in as director. We had a terrible time casting it. It was one of those situations where the studio wants to make a picture because they need something to take care of their overhead. They had nothing shooting, so we had to move very quickly in the casting. We all recognized that it was an old-fashioned formula picture, and perhaps if we had had bigger stars, it would have gone at the box office as well as *Airport* [1970].

I am very fond of *Hotel,* but afterwards, I swore I'd never produce anything again. I took the producing job because Jack Warner was a friend of mine. When he called me and asked me to do the book, he said, "Listen, could I ask you to produce it and save me some money?" I said okay. But I found producing to be the most boring occupation I'd ever encountered. The detail that you have to be burdened with is just not worth the effort—like whether one of the actors should have pockets in the rear of his britches. And you have to be on the set all the time. Shooting motion pictures is a very tiresome job.

If you ask me what kind of person Jack Warner was, my answer will be a cliché: he was a showman. Zanuck was a showman. Harry Cohn was a showman. All these people were showmen, and that's the only way to describe them. They were in the business from the time they were sixteen years old; they grew up in it, and they had the feel and scent of show business about them, which doesn't exist now. Jack Warner would make a decision about a piece of material, not because it would make a lot of money, but because he liked it as a story. If you look at the studio's record of motion pictures, it's a fascinating record. And Jack Warner was the person that said yes to all of them.

He was also involved in the scripts. Now, that isn't true anymore. If a writer is working on a script for 20th, Paramount, or any of the studios, he never meets the man running the studio anymore. As far as I know, the man running the studio doesn't even read the scripts anymore; he's too involved with the corpora-

Wendell Mayes with Rod Taylor on the set of *Hotel.*

tion. But when you wrote a script at Warner Brothers, you dealt with Jack Warner. You went and sat in his office. He had read the script, and he had notes in the margin of his copy for you. He told you what he liked and he didn't like. Look, Jack was a very astute, hard-nosed businessman when it came to dealing with the people who worked for him. A lot of people didn't like Jack Warner. But I've discovered that the people who didn't like Jack Warner were the people who didn't get what they wanted from Jack Warner. And I was very fond of Jack Warner because he was kind to me when I was young.

I've had a lot of disappointments. In Hollywood, everybody does. But I'll tell you about my greatest disappointment. There was a producer, David Weisbart, who was a close friend of mine, who had made many pictures, all of them quite small, none of them exceptional except *Rebel without a Cause* [1955]—as a matter of fact, he produced *The Way to the Gold,* one of the first things I did. And he had this dream of making the definitive great picture about General Custer. So he said, "Would you be interested?" and I said, "How much time would you give me?" and he said, "All you want. We'll pay you for as long as you sit and write it." So I began my research, and it took me a year to get it down on paper. It was a fascinating theme—it was a Greek tragedy in a western. The forces that produced the battle, I won't even try to tell you, but how it came about is one of the most fascinating things that you can imagine. It had never been researched properly. We sent it to [the director Fred] Zinnemann, and he called from London and said, "I'm mad about it. Will they hire me?" And they hired him, and he came over, and we began to cast and look for locations. In the meantime, they were budgeting the film. They asked for absolutely no rewrite because Zinnemann said, "This is it; we shoot"—which is very pleasing to a writer, of course. They hired Toshiro Mifune to play Crazy Horse, a great piece of casting, and they were not reaching for any big stars at all . . . he would probably have been the most prominent name in the thing. Very early on, when I started to write it, there was discussion with Charlton Heston. I had lunch with him one day, but Zinnemann didn't want him as Custer. Before Zinnemann, there was some talk of Kurosawa doing it, but it was decided that the language barriers would be just too much for this kind of massive undertaking.

One of the things that was going to be marvelous in it was: the battle occurred on June 25th, 1876 . . . the first part of the film would be fairly standard-size film, but on that day, in the middle of the film, the screen would begin to open until you're in Cinemascope for the rest of the picture.

Well, the budget came in at eighteen million, and the studio said, "Well, we'll have to shoot it in Mexico; we can't afford that much money." And this infuriated Zinnemann because he said, "How can you make a picture about Custer with Sioux Indians in Mexico. We've got to go where it happened. We've got to go to Montana." But they tried to find some locations in Mexico, and they got the budget down to fifteen million, even though Zinneman was very unhappy about it. But even that was too much, so the studio decided to shelve it because it cost too much, and they had to pay Fred off, and we went miserably back to London.

Later, there was a Custer picture in Spain, a cheap movie starring Robert Shaw. Interestingly enough, Robert Shaw was going to be our Custer. I guess he'd fallen in love with it, so that he still wanted to play Custer, regardless of whether it was a good or bad movie. Anyway, that script still sits at Fox. Maybe some day they'll make it.

I'll tell you what was attractive about *The Poseidon Adventure:* the money I was offered. I knew that it was going to be a big, bad, popular motion picture. I was the first writer on it. After I did a couple of rewrites, I asked the producer, Irwin Allen, to please relieve me of the job. I had done all I could. Then he brought in Stirling Silliphant. Stirling worked on it and changed it quite a bit, enough so that I think he got first credit.[*]

---

[*]   Stirling Silliphant does receive first credit, followed by Wendell Mayes's name. See the interview "Stirling Silliphant: The Fingers of God" elsewhere in this volume for an additional perspective on *The Poseidon Adventure.*

The reason *The Bank Shot* [based on the book by Donald E. Westlake (New York: Simon and Schuster, 1972)] turned out to be such a strange movie is because the director was Gower Champion, who had never directed a movie. I loved [Donald] Westlake's novels, and I felt that Hollywood had never truly done justice to his peculiar brand of humor in motion pictures. I was trying to do that brand of humor, something that is just slightly tilted, which at first you don't realize is slightly tilted. It was a charming idea, this Westlake book, the idea of not simply robbing a bank but stealing the whole building. What happened is that Gower tried to turn it into a farce, and it didn't work. The people weren't equipped to play farce. Gower was a nice guy and a marvelous stage director; but the film simply wasn't deft, and it should have been. He held pretty much to the script but ruined what I thought was a good piece. He was the only bad experience I've ever had in my career with a director. I was bitterly disappointed.

Around the same time I was also working on *Death Wish*. I think the first studio involved was United Artists. Because I'd worked for Otto Preminger at UA [United Artists], Arthur Krim was a friend of mine, and through Krim, Hal Landon, the producer, sent the book [*Death Wish,* by Brian Garfield (New York: McKay, 1972)] to me. I was immensely intrigued with the book. I must tell you, from the moment I read it, I knew it was going to be a blockbuster because it was coming at just the right time. The outrage at crime in the streets was a big item. It didn't surprise me when I read in the papers later on—I was in London at the time of the opening—that audiences were stamping their feet and screaming in the theaters.

I had a great deal to do with how the film turned out; I could see it in my mind before I put a word on paper. I didn't stick to the book very much. I had to do an awful lot of inventing, which I must say [the author] Brian Garfield was not very happy with. But sometimes novelists are not happy, and there's not much you can do about that. I think when novelists sell to the motion pictures, they should do what Hemingway did, and just walk away and forget about what might happen to their work.

Go Tell the Spartans took about eight years to get produced. I really didn't have much hope of anyone ever buying it. But I was fascinated with Vietnam and why nobody had made a picture about Vietnam. *The Green Berets* [1968] was a gung ho picture; it could have been World War II. Vietnam was an absolutely fascinating war, however. The political ramifications are quite fascinating because it [military involvement in Vietnam] tore this country asunder the way it tore France apart. The same thing happened here that happened there, and to an extent, this is what my story was about. It took place in 1964, shortly before escalation when all the soldiers were professional, and they were fighting the war the same way the French had fought the war, with these little outposts everywhere. A group of American advisers with a company of Vietnamese are sent to regarrison an old French garrison that was deserted in

Burt Lancaster (at left) and the troops in *Go Tell the Spartans,* directed by Ted Post.

1953. There is a French graveyard there of three hundred graves. Nailed on the tree is a sign in French that says: Stranger, Go Tell the Spartans That We Lie Here in Obedience to Their Laws. Now you know that exactly the same thing that happened to the French is going to happen to them. My script wasn't gung ho; it wasn't anti-American; it was, I hope, the truth and an interesting tale.

When I first submitted the book [*Incident at Muc Wa,* by Daniel Ford (Garden City, N.Y.: Doubleday, 1967)] around town, they ran screaming. Fox ran from it. Paramount ran from it. They all ran from it. They would not make a picture about Vietnam. So I took an option on the book myself and wrote the script and started, slowly, pushing it, peddling it. I carried the option all those years. I had optioned several other things over the course of time, which I had written screenplays for, but this was the first thing that I optioned that finally did go. It was also one that I was in love with. I could see how the relationships of the people who were in the novel could be turned into a story, a war picture that could really get hold of you.

The script isn't faithful to the book at all, incidentally; but the novelist loved the movie. I sent him the script, and he wrote me a little note, saying he wished his novel was as good as my screenplay. That was very sweet of him. For one thing, in the novel there was a newswoman wandering through the story, and I eliminated her completely. I invented some characters that were not in the novel. I made the story much more of a tragedy; the wipeout at the end [of the film] was not in the novel. And the part [Burt] Lancaster played was much stronger than in the novel. He was not a man who had been a major, for the curious reasons I gave him, all of his life. All this and more was invented.

Finally, one day, Teddy Post called me. Ted hasn't done a lot of features, he got stuck in TV; but he's a good director who has never been recognized for his real talent. He had read the script and remembered it. He was working for the American Film Company and called to ask, "Whatever happened to that script of yours about Vietnam that I read a few years ago?" I said, "I've still got it." He asked me to send it over to him, and within three days, he called back and said they're going to go for it. Just like that. The American Film Company was prepared to go with anyone they could get. Burt Lancaster was the first one they submitted it to, and he said, "Yes, I'll do it. Let's go." He didn't ask for a thing, not a single line change.

The filming was done right out here near Magic Mountain, down near a little river, and if you panned up too high, you could see Magic Mountain. They had to do extra work on the sound, because when they were shooting at night, you could hear the roar of the freeway. Some of the cast were Vietnamese refugees; some had been officers. I thought Lancaster was wonderful in it. He put up some of the completion bond himself. The picture was made for a million bucks, and I think it's better than *Platoon* [1986].

I had gotten into the habit of adapting already established material. Not by choice. If I had the courage just to sit down and write originals and get them on the market and try to sell them I would have, but I'm afraid I was a coward and decided the money was awfully big for these things I was being offered. And it was a period, when I first came out here, where very few original scripts were being made. The studios wanted preconceived material. There were a few occasions when the reason I did something was quite simply money, but what generally attracted me was not action, not plot, but the human relations that occur during the story. Generally speaking, I did choose material that I liked; so if some of the pictures were not very good, it's my fault.

The world changed out here in the late 1970s, and that's one reason I started to write originals. I had one original made, at the beginning of the change. I called it "Love and Bullets, Charlie." They shortened it to *Love and Bullets,* totally destroying the whole idea of the title. That was a [Charles] Bronson picture. I wrote a very tricky script in flashback: A man was hired to bring a gangster's moll from Switzerland back to the States, where she would confess to certain things, implicating certain gangsters. She was killed en route. The man hired to bring her back realizes, through some clue, that maybe the gangsters didn't kill her. Somebody else might have done it. So he sets out to retrace his steps. Now, in retracing his steps, someone is trying to kill him, while in flashback, what has already happened takes place in continuous action; so what you had was a continuous action, past and present. A very interesting concept.

They sent the script to John Huston, and he went for it. They flew me down to Mexico. I was down there with John for a week in his jungle compound. He loved to be the *patrón,* you know, and had built this strange compound that had no telephones, its own generator, with houses made of canvas that opened in the daytime. He had a whole tribe of Indians serving him. I had met him before, but I never had the opportunity to work for him. He was very enthused with the script. Then I came back to the States to work on it, incorporating his suggestions. In the middle of this time, he had an aneurysm and had to have a quick operation. Then he was off the film. They brought in another director. The changes he wanted to make would destroy what I had written. I told the producer that I would prefer to walk away. So it was rewritten, and the idea of the flashback and the double action was gone; and what audiences saw, although my name is on it for story and as screenwriter, is half of what it was.

I must tell you, I didn't come out here with any rosy ideas of being an artist. I was an actor in the theater. I didn't really know much about motion pictures. I had always known I could write. When television began to rule in the early days, I realized, when I was at liberty, that I could probably write something that could sell, and I sold the first thing I wrote. Then I sold four or five others. Then Billy Wilder picked me up and brought me out. If you collaborate with Billy Wilder, you have a career.

I was by this time well into my late thirties. I wasn't doing well as an actor. I knew if I was going to have any money, I'd better grab the chance. The jobs came fast. They were pouring over me, and they poured over me for twenty years. I could pick and choose, and there were a couple of years that I didn't even bother to work. But I never got over my love of the theater. I had great respect for motion pictures, but it was not something I had chosen to begin with. I fell into it. I'm not mocking motion pictures, understand, because I've done awfully well out here.

I haven't really done that much in the 1980s. My career was winding down anyway. The young people were coming on. The town was full of young writers fresh out of school. They could be gotten cheaply. Some of them turned out to be pretty good. Most of the writers of my generation were allowed to go to grass. There's no question that there's a lot of heartbreak among some of the older writers and directors. Happily, I was one of those that it didn't really bother, because I was quite ready to stop being hired.

The people who run the studios nowadays all seem to me to be stamped out of the same cloth. They're film-school people, and what they know is what they have been taught in film schools. I don't sense any original minds at all. I'm not saying there aren't any original minds, but in my few encounters—I'm pretty well retired, except for the things I'm writing myself; at least I'm no longer for hire—that's the sense I have. There may be some very talented people in the studios. I haven't met them if there are.

Hollywood studios are conglomerates now. When I came out here, I got in on the tail end of old Hollywood. It was quite wonderful. What has changed in the studios now is that they simply are not happy places. The fear is tangible. There is no continuity of employment for people. The managements of the studios are icy. They don't *know* the people down the line like they used to. All that has changed, and I don't think for the best.

When I interviewed Wendell Mayes in October 1991, he had just gotten out of the hospital after undergoing tests and treatment. He had read the first two Backstorys, *and was eager to cooperate for a session that would update his 1972* Focus on Film *interview, with Rui Nogueira. Mayes told me he was in some pain and asked if I would mind if he stood for most of the interview. Yet he looked fine—handsome and radiant, with an ascot around his neck, like an actor in the winter of his years—his humor seemed good, and he was patient with my questions. When I told him that later on I would be sending a photographer around to take a portrait of him for the book, he said, "Send him around soon. At my age I might be ill. Who the hell knows, I might be dead." I thought he was kidding.*

The photographer did not get to him in time. Mayes died of cancer on March 28, 1992, at age seventy-two. In later years, he had been working on some pet projects, both original ideas and adapted scripts, one of which came to fruition after his death. The ABC television movie Criminal Behavior, *starring Farrah Fawcett, from Mayes's teleplay, was broadcast in May 1992. An adaptation of Ross MacDonald's The* Ferguson Affair *(New York: Warner, 1960), with MacDonald's male lawyer transformed into a female protagonist, it was vintage Mayes—boasting an intricate plot, raucous characters and clever situations, bristling dialogue—a terrific sign-off for a long and impressive career.—P. M.*

Irving Ravetch and Harriet Frank Jr.: Tapestry of Life

Interview by Pat McGilligan

No matter their résumé of accomplishment, the American (one is tempted to say "distinctly" American) scriptwriters Harriet Frank Jr. and Irving Ravetch have maintained a stubborn privacy. Throughout their careers, they have refused interviews and dodged publicity. The press kit for their most recent motion picture did not contain a photograph of them, and the studio was hard put to supply one. They make clear their preference to let the work speak for itself—and indeed, it is a formidible body of work.

At first, they worked, not as a team, but as lower echelon writers at MGM, beginning in the mid-1940s; then came salad days of studio assignments, westerns, and melodrama, up through the mid-1950s.

A team since 1955, they have consistently tackled difficult and unusual material. They have written provocative adaptations of William Faulkner's novels and dipped into the worlds of William Inge, Larry McMurtry, and Elmore Leonard. In their diverse screenplays, they have excoriated poverty, racism, poor labor conditions, and social neglect. Closely collaborating with the director Martin Ritt, they wrote an impressive run of eight quality features over thirty years.

Once a year, the Hollywood branch of the Writers Guild names a recipient of its highest accolade, the Laurel Award. Typically, only one Laurel Award is given annually. In 1990, Frank and Ravetch (together often referred to as the Ravetches) received that tribute of their peer group, joining the company of such previous eminences as Dudley Nichols, Robert Riskin, Billy Wilder, Nunnally Johnson, John Lee Mahin, Joseph L. Mankiewicz, Preston Sturges, Richard Brooks, Samson Raphaelson, Paddy Chayefsky, and others—including Horton Foote and Ring Lardner Jr. in this volume.

Ravetch and Frank are the rare example of a Hollywood screenwriting team who met and married on the job, and not only have they stayed married, but in time they have become successful, as well as "very amiable," collaborators.

After a year of letters, phone calls, evasions and delay, in 1990 Ravetch and Frank agreed to talk about their careers. The interview took place at their hilltop home above Laurel Canyon in Los Angeles, filled with art, sculpture, fabrics, books, prints, and paintings. According to an admiring profile of their residence, "Irving Ravetch and Harriet Frank, Jr.," by Michael Frank, in *Architectural Digest* (April 1990), the equal collaborators "part company when it comes to their house, which is filled with a varied collection of eighteenth- and nineteenth-century European antiques, and is exclusively—

Irving Ravetch and Harriet Frank Jr. in Los Angeles, 1993.
(Photo by William B. Winburn.)

and passionately—Frank's domain. Collecting has been her lifelong hobby. It began, like her love of movies, in Portland, Oregon, where her Aunt Beck ran an antiques shop. As a small girl, she fell in love with a Dresden rose jar, which her aunt let her pay off at ten cents a week."

Doubtless, the interview was like one of their writing sessions—the team disagreed vehemently at points, leavened disagreement with humor, finished off each other's sentences, topped each other's jokes.

This interview took place when their longtime friend Martin Ritt, director of their last release to date, *Stanley and Iris,* was still alive. "Since *Stanley and Iris,*" Irving Ravetch reported, "we've written an original screenplay on the life of Katherine Mansfield, but the world is apparently not eager to witness the story of a major short story writer who died an agonizing death from TB. For the moment, it joins some other unproduced work of ours on a shelf, but I do feel that one day its day will come.

The Difficult Family of Minnie Valdez, our first—and last—venture into the land of TV pilots, we shall not, at this moment, speak of."

Harriet Frank Jr. is always working on a novel, one of her "human comedies," and has published two to date. As for her husband, he has no interest in trying to write one. "I've never written any prose at all," Irving Ravetch said. "I have no sense of the rhythm or tone."

A collection of three of their best scripts was published in 1988, *Hud, Norma Rae, and The Long, Hot Summer: Three Screenplays by Irving Ravetch and Harriet Frank, Jr.,* with an introduction by Michael Frank (New York: Plume).

Irving Ravetch (1915–   ) and Harriet Frank Jr. (1917–   )

1947   *Living in a Big Way* (Gregory La Cava). Story and co-script by Ravetch.

1948   *Silver River* (Raoul Walsh). Co-script by Frank.
Whiplash (Lewis Seiler). Co-script by Frank.

1950   *The Outriders* (Roy Rowland). Story and script by Ravetch.

1951   *Vengeance Valley* (Richard Thorpe). Script by Ravetch.

1953   *Lone Hand* (George Sherman). Story by Ravetch.

1955   *Ten Wanted Men* (H. Bruce Humberstone). Co-story.
Run for Cover (Nicholas Ray). Co-story.

1958   *The Long, Hot Summer* (Martin Ritt). Script.

1959   *The Sound and the Fury* (Martin Ritt). Script.

1960   *Home from the Hill* (Vincente Minnelli). Script.
The Dark at the Top of the Stairs (Delbert Mann). Script.

1963   *Hud* (Martin Ritt). Coproducers, script.

1967   *Hombre* (Martin Ritt). Coproducers, script.

1969   *The Reivers* (Mark Rydell). Producers, script.
         House of Cards (John Guillermin). Script under the pseudonym
             James P. Bonner.

1972   *The Cowboys* (Mark Rydell). Co-script.

1974   *Conrack* (Martin Ritt). Coproducer (Frank), script.
         The Spikes Gang (Richard Fleischer). Script.

1979   *Norma Rae* (Martin Ritt). Script.

1985   *Murphy's Romance* (Martin Ritt). Script.

1990   *Stanley and Iris* (Martin Ritt). Script.

Novels by Frank include *Single* and *Special Effects.*

Published screenplays include *Hud, Norma Rae, and The Long, Hot Summer: Three Screenplays by Irving Ravetch and Harriet Frank, Jr.*

Academy Award honors include Oscar nominations for Best Screenplay for *Hud* (adaptation) and *Norma Rae* (adaptation).

Writers Guild honors include nominations for Best Script for *The Long, Hot Summer* and *The Reivers,* and the award for Best-Written American Drama for *Hud.* The Ravetches received the Writers Guild Laurel Award for Lifetime Achievement in 1988.

Harriet, you got your start through your mother, who worked at MGM in the 1930s and 1940s. Her name was also Harriet Frank? . . .

Frank: She was a story editor. That's why I'm Jr. She functioned as an editor on a lot of scripts, and she was consulted by a lot of directors.

Ravetch: She was a Scheherazade. Obviously, [the studio executives] Louis B. Mayer or Eddie Mannix were very rough types who did not sit down over the weekend to read *Crime and Punishment.* Her job was to read these immense novels and find the movie story in them, roughly, and then tell an hour version to the whole [production] board, so they could decide whether to buy the book and make the picture. She was brilliant at it. I know for a fact that six months later a producer would call her, having gotten stuck on the third act of some script, and say, "Could you come back . . . do you have your notes on the original story you told us?" She would review her notes, come down, and tell the story again, and they would straighten the script out.

What was her background?

Frank: She did some short-story writing. She had a radio program in Portland, Oregon, during the Depression. She was a lecturer. Very bright. And a very good editor. When the Depression struck, she came to California and got involved with Metro-Goldwyn-Mayer as a story editor.

And brought you along?

Frank: Nepotism.

What about your father?

Frank: He was a shoe business tycoon.

Tell me a little about your parents, Irving.

Ravetch: My mother was born in Safed, in Palestine. My father was born in Berdichev, a town which is famous for its Jewish mystics, in Russia, in the Ukraine. I was born in New Jersey.

Frank: And your father was a rabbi?

Ravetch: I was a rabbi's son. I learned how to write, because a poor rabbi mobilizes his entire family to help. My job was to write bar mitzvah confirmation speeches for the young men when they reached thirteen. Each speech began the same way, I'm afraid: "Today, I am a man . . ."

How did you get to the West Coast?

Ravetch: Because I was dying of asthma. I had double pneumonia every single winter in the East, and the doctors told my family to get me out here, either to Arizona or California. They chose Los Angeles.

You both attended UCLA?

Ravetch: We went to UCLA at different times. Hank and I—Harriet—actually met at MGM. MGM was so fabulously wealthy that they could afford to run what they called a Junior Writing Program, in which they literally trained junior writers. There were thirty or forty of us.

How long did that program last?

Ravetch: It lasted for years. Hank was a junior writer; I was a short subject writer, which was quite a good training. Please make that distinction [between us]. For example, there was a short subject series I worked on called *Crime Does Not Pay* . . .

Frank: Talk about a checkered past . . .

Ravetch: Out of which came people like [the actor] Robert Taylor. After our training period, we graduated to being senior writers, almost imperceptibly. It was [the producer] Pandro Berman who gave me my first chance one day, harnessing me with an older writer on a project called *Before the Sun Goes Down*. This was the MGM prize novel of the year [by Elizabeth Metzger Howard (Garden City, N.Y.: Doubleday, 1946)]. So fabulously wealthy was MGM that the studio would select what they considered the best novel of the year and award it a prize: their version of the English Booker prize. This year—I think it was '45—it was *Before the Sun Goes Down*. That was my first major screenplay and my first job as a senior writer, in collaboration with an older man, Marvin Borowsky—a fine fellow, a good writer.*

Did Borowsky actually teach you things, or was it more a case of learning by doing?

Ravetch: Learning by doing. He treated me as an equal.

What had you been studying at UCLA?

Ravetch: English lit.

MGM officials would roam through UCLA and pick out interesting people?

Ravetch: They had some method of scouring the universities to find likely young people, but as Hank says, she got her job through nepotism, pure and simple; she makes no bones about it. I got my job because I was already a pretty proficient radio writer. After I went to college, my asthma got me out of the army, and I got my first job at KNX radio station, around 1942-ish. I wrote patter for western singers—for between numbers.

Frank: What a sordid past you—we—have . . .

Where did you meet? At an MGM story conference?

Frank: Aw, it's very romantic . . .

Ravetch: You want the story? I saw this lovely creature, and she was up the hall, about fifty yards. I knew a chap in the office next to her, so I went to him and said, "A deal: I give you fifty dollars, you give me your office." He said, "Done and done." So I paid for the office next to her and courted her on L. B. Mayer's time.

Some writers I've spoken to say that the writer's table at MGM was bunk; others say it was glorious hobnobbing. Which was it?

Frank: It wasn't the Round Table, I can tell you.

Ravetch: Neither of us were at the writer's table very much. We were talking marriage, so we went off the lot practically every day.

Frank: I remember some common agonizing about how we were overlooked and [how] our vast talents were underexploited.

Ravetch: We bitched a lot.

Frank: And we played word games a lot. There was a *sort* of camaraderie.

What kinds of things did you work on as a junior writer? Did you often work in tandem with senior writers?

Frank: No. The studio would just hand you scripts and say, "Do something about the dialogue," or "We're not satisfied with the storyline." Since we were

---

* Among Marvin Borowsky's screen credits are *Pride of the Marines* and *Big Jack,* Wallace Beery's last film. According to *Variety,* before coming to Hollywood in 1940, Borowsky worked for the Group Theatre as stage manager for Elmer Rice, and for the Theatre Guild as playreader.

all underpaid and eager, we took whatever was handed to us. We worked on many scripts—sometimes with credit, sometimes without. Finally, when we got slightly long in the tooth and beyond the status of juniors, then we announced, "We're no longer junior writers. We think we are senior writers and should be paid the minimum."

MGM said, "That's fine . . ."?

Frank: No. The studio fired both of us. When we came back from our honeymoon, we were out of jobs. I went in and asked them why. Well, they said it was "economics," and so on. I said they hadn't read any of my scripts and it was reprehensible, and I walked out. They were deep-sixing the whole program.

Ravetch: They were retrenching.

Frank: They do that periodically while they are building an extra swimming pool for themselves. It wasn't until I went to Warners that I was really considered a senior writer. After being fired, I got a job as a full-fledged adult writer at Warner Brothers, and Irving . . .

Ravetch: For a period, I just stayed at home and wrote original western stories.

When you were in college, studying English literature, what were you thinking of doing—was it always movies?

Ravetch: Absolutely. I was hooked on movies from the age of seven, from the time I saw *The Cisco Kid* with Warner Baxter. I knew I had to be in that world. It was a siren song.

You weren't going to act or direct—you were always going to write? It was that cut and dried?

Ravetch: There was a long period when I was going to be a terrific actor—and a playwright—but movies were always part of the equation.

For you, Harriet, it was more of a natural progression?

Frank: I think so. I was led to it because of my mother.

Ravetch: Harriet was a very good short story writer, early on—and wrote upwards of one hundred stories for the *Saturday Evening Post, Collier's,* and other magazines. She kept me alive during the early years of our marriage.

What kinds of stories did you write, Harriet?

Frank: Comedies. I don't know how I moved from comedy to stories of social conscience . . .

The short stories were something you did to stay alive professionally after leaving MGM?

Frank: I did a little short story writing on Warner Brothers' time. At Warner Brothers, I had to write tough dialogue for a fight picture with Dane Clark [*Whiplash*], and cowboy talk for Errol Flynn [*Silver River*]. Strange jobs got offered to me at Warner Brothers—but serious and well-paid jobs, too. I pursued them for a while. Then, as I did more screenwriting, I did less short story writing.

How did you get typed or channeled, early on, into westerns?

Ravetch: That may have been my doing, because the western landscape moved me, even as a child. Maybe it was the grim, bitter, eastern winters as opposed to the sight of that glorious sunshine flooding the plains, which I saw in the movies. I wanted to try westerns, and I did. For a long time, I wrote only western originals and had no interest in doing the screenplays. Just sold the original stories. And I was also trying to do a play.

On Broadway?

Ravetch: I did try, two or three times. Bombed, ferociously.

Why did you have that schizophrenia—writing westerns on the one hand and Broadway plays on the other?

Frank: It's called making a living on the one hand and aspiring on the other. (*Laughs.*)

Ravetch: Also called working . . .

Frank: When we formally decided to collaborate, we left westerns behind.

What about Ten Wanted Men, Run for Cover . . .

Ravetch: Vengeance Valley . . .

Those were all westerns, right?

Frank: Let me put it to you this way: we weren't very picky in those days. What was presented was written.

Ravetch: (Laughs.) Right.

How many years had gone by before you started working on every script together?

Ravetch: We didn't collaborate for the first ten years of our marriage.

What led you into collaboration?

Frank: Affection and loneliness.

Sometimes that can lead people away from collaboration.

Frank: He would go down the hall to one room, and I would go to another, to be confronted with two sets of problems. Suddenly, one evening, we said to each other, "This is nonsense. Let's try it together." Happily, we've been doing it ever since.

Ravetch: It was a happy decision.

Frank: It's a very amiable collaboration.

Were you learning gradually how to become storytellers? Was it a developmental process? Was this the point in your careers when you felt you had it?

Frank: (*Laughs.*) Not then, not now. I don't know . . . how does anyone learn their craft? It's like learning to swim: you get thrown into the swimming pool, you paddle around and nearly drown, you reach for the side, and eventually, you learn.

Harriet's primary influence was obviously her mother. How about for you, Irving—something that was imprinted upon your storytelling?

Ravetch: My influences were Noël Coward, George Bernard Shaw, Ferenc Molnár, and [Henrik] Ibsen, because I wanted to write plays. I studied them very, very carefully, took them apart, and put them back together. I read them, studied them, acted them, and *used* them.

Do you still refer to them in your thinking nowadays?

Ravetch: No. That's part of another life.

Frank: That's for pleasure.

Does that list stimulate any comparisons for you, Harriet?

Frank: I was an English major, and I loved to read. I'd like to say Jane Austen was an influence, but heaven forfend that I should do so. It's just the things that pleasure you as you read . . . I don't know that you learn your craft that way. I have a sense that we were thrown into the studio system, and we went by the seat of our pants, by instinct, and by a modicum of luck and happy circumstance. It's all very up for grabs.

Were there veteran Hollywood writers, early on, that you either admired or talked to, who seemed to you to be exemplars?

Ravetch: We liked foreign movies a lot. I preferred French and Italian movies to American movies, because I think our interest lies mainly in character, rather than in driving the story forward.

Frank: Foreign movies seem to take the time to pause and discuss the ambiguities and complexities of life, whereas American producers were always telling us—

Ravetch: "Keep your film moving . . ."

Frank: Always telling us, "Get on with it . . ."

Ravetch: So that so much was lost. It was an impoverished form for us, in many ways, the [American] movies of the 1940s and '50s.

Frank: Whereas we loved [Ettore] Scola, [Vittorio] De Sica, [Marcel] Pagnol, [Ingmar] Bergman.

Ravetch: I think our favorite movies are most like novels. *Oblomov* [a 1980 Russian film, directed by Nikita Mikhalkov] is a good example.

Frank: My Life As a Dog [1985], a recent one, was meandering—it didn't have any immense story thrust—but it had a marvelous sense of worldview from a child's perspective.

Ravetch: The equivocal, the undefined . . .

Frank: It had a tapestry. It would pause. It didn't have to fall all over itself. It just presented itself, the way a novel does.

That's certainly one of the things that is wrong with this generation of Hollywood scriptwriters. Your generation of screenwriters was more literate. They were bookish. They knew books, read books, and loved books.

Ravetch: I must tell you that I personally, have a difficulty with the idea of movies—which I can't call films, incidentally—being an art form at all.

Frank: I don't. C'mon!

Ravetch: When one examines the Russian novels, the Victorian novels— Faulkner—I have a problem.

How about when a film is derived from a wonderful book and is a perfect adaptation?

Ravetch: It lacks the language, the force, and the mystery.

Frank: I don't entirely agree. I have had experiences watching movies that I feel are as artful as a novel.

Ravetch: Harold Pinter wrote an adaptation of Marcel Proust; it would make a good movie, but it can't give you the same sense of the enigma of life.

Frank: No, but what is the French film you adore so—*La Grande Illusion* [1937]? That is as textured as a novel. So was *Wild Strawberries* [1957] and some of Scola's movies—*Bread and Chocolate* [1973]. There are a lot of movies that for me carry the weight of a novel.

*In John Huston's autobiography [*An Open Book *(New York: Knopf, 1980)], he says that a very good script, the actual script itself, if it is well written, can be read as literature. That the script, in and of itself, is a valid form of literature.*

Ravetch: I agree.

Frank: And he made a movie which I admire greatly—which had the richness of a novel—*The Dead* [1987]. A remarkably subtle and layered and textured film.

Once you began to collaborate, there was also a quantum change in what you began to try to do—in the kind of material and the ambitiousness of the projects. Is that partly because the studio system was collapsing, and you had to separate yourselves from the system and find other things to do at that point?

Ravetch: I think it's precisely because we did start working together . . .

Frank: And because we started working with Marty [Ritt] . . .

Ravetch: And whatever faculties we had, we combined into a fresh view.

Would it be fair to say that your talent was also maturing at that time?

Frank: You won't hear me say it!

Ravetch: I know my body was maturing.

When and where did you meet Marty?

Ravetch: When I went to New York on one of my abortive playwrighting forays, a producer optioned a play of mine and gave me the choice of two directors. I picked the one who was not named Marty Ritt, and then the play turned out a terrible failure. Ever since then, I felt, "I have got to make this up"—to myself—not to Marty. So, when I came back to LA and we embarked on our first major feature with Jerry Wald at Fox—*The Long, Hot Summer*—I recommended Marty Ritt.

He had already directed Edge of the City *[1957].*

Ravetch: Right. So there was no question, or any problem, about getting him hired.

Frank: Jerry Wald, bless his heart, took us all on.

"Ten percent of Faulkner": from left, Joanne Woodward, Paul Newman, Anthony Franciosa, Lee Remick, Orson Welles, and Richard Anderson in *The Long, Hot Summer.*

Wasn't Marty still on the blacklist, especially on the West Coast?

Ravetch: That problem almost immediately surfaced. I remember the day
Marty took us aside and said, "Fellas, I'm not going to be able to make the
picture with you. They want me to do something I'm not prepared to do." He
went back east. But somehow it was straightened out very shortly thereafter,
and he returned.

What was the nature, then, of your rapport with Marty?

Ravetch: The same as it was later. The immediate recognition that we were
dealing with a man of principle, a man with a wonderful mind, a man who was
absolutely honest and direct, a man with terrific energies and skills and abili-
ties—to which we responded immediately. We were able quickly to learn how
to speak to him in a kind of shorthand. Very shortly, Marty became like a big
brother to us. He fought a lot of our battles for us. We were a gang of three.

*I gather Marty was unusual to the degree that he protected his scripts—
and scriptwriters.*

Frank: He always protected ours. He always was very stalwart about his writers, very sympathetic to the point of view of writers and their contributions.

Did you know instantly that you were also getting a director who would prove so sensitive to actors, who would be so complementary to scripts like yours that are so attuned to characterization?

Ravetch: Yes.

Why? Was it in the air?

Frank: It was in the man. First place, because he was an actor himself, he was very sympathetic to actors, very attuned to actors, and very patient with actors. Any impatience he felt anywhere else in the world disappeared when he was working with actors. Marty was infinitely patient with actors. He was that way about writers. He was not an attack-and-destroy director where writers are concerned.

Ravetch: We've been very, very lucky. There's a little heresy involved in a screenwriter paying tribute to a producer—there have been some long, bitter fights and strikes against producers—but people like Pandro Berman, Sol Siegel, and Jerry Wald were also men who had high regard for the written word.

Frank: They were all marvelous.

Even Jerry Wald? I have heard a lot of horror stories about Jerry Wald . . .

Frank: Most particularly, Jerry Wald. Jerry Wald took a chance on us, inexperience and all.

Ravetch: More than that, we did not have the harrowing experience with him that many screenwriters did—doing seventeen versions of a script.

Frank: He wasn't in the least difficult. He was supportive.

Ravetch: I had met Jerry when he was head of production at Columbia. This was before I began collaboration with Harriet. He assigned me to do D. H. Lawrence's *Sons and Lovers.* As a result of that abortive experience—because that picture wasn't made until many years later, under a different script and different auspices—he was willing to take another chance.

He treated us very well. He bought the novel of *The Hamlet,* by Faulkner, for us. The script we turned in bore no resemblance to the book whatsoever, and he went along with that.

Did he know the difference?

Ravetch: Oh yes. We're discussing an intelligent man. He read the book and the script and the notes and the revisions—everything.

Frank: We found him very surprising—because we knew the reputation, too. He was steady, he was supportive, he fought the fights that had to be fought, he functioned as a *good* producer.

Ravetch: Absolutely.

Why did he come to you in the first place with a Faulkner book?

Ravetch: We brought the novel to him. Now, mind you, here's a book in which is delineated, possibly, the most evil and vicious character in American literature—Flem Snopes. We turned him around into a romantic hero.

Frank: No, no. Ben Quick was the hero . . .

Ravetch: But Flem Snopes became Quick . . . who became Paul Newman. We made him a romantic hero, so that our story would work. A pretty desperate thing to do to Faulkner. When the picture [*The Long, Hot Summer*] was finished, we asked someone traveling to Jackson, Mississippi, who knew Faulkner, to ask him, with some trepidation, what he thought of it. Faulkner said, "I kind of liked it."

Frank: America's greatest writer of pure fiction.

Ravetch: The novel has fabulous elements. The character of Will Varner—the forerunner of Big Daddy—is very interesting, powerful, and all-encompassing.

Frank: The book is full of vitality.

Ravetch: There's a section in the book, which was later published as a story called "Spotted Horses," which is one of the most hilarious pieces of American literature.

Frank: Faulkner was uniquely gifted. Also, because he had been a screenwriter himself, he was a very tolerant man where other writers were concerned. He knew what laboring in the field was like. He was very realistic about letting go of his work.

Ravetch: And in spite of all the horrors we wreaked on that wonderful book, the film worked.

Did all of your Faulkner adaptations originate with you?

Ravetch: We brought *The Hamlet* to Jerry, *The Sound and the Fury* to Jerry, and *The Reivers* to Gordon [Stulberg]. Yes, they originated with us.

Many of our adaptations made violent departures from the originals. We began with *The Hamlet* and ended with *The Long, Hot Summer.* Possibly ten percent of Faulkner is in that movie. The only really pure adaptation we ever made—except that we invented a second act—is *The Dark at the Top of the Stairs* [from the William Inge play].

How about Hombre *[from an Elmore Leonard story]?*

Ravetch: Fairly faithful.

Frank: Pretty close.

Ravetch: *The Reivers* is pretty faithful, too. But with *Hud,* two key characters were invented: Hud himself is a minor character in the novel and is our major contribution: Alma, too, became an original character. Much of the time, we're doing a hybrid form, it seems to me. They're not adaptations, they're not originals.

Was it serendipity that Marty also happened to be fascinated by the South? And to admire Faulkner?

Frank: When we came to Marty with high enthusiasm for anything, he'd pay attention. Usually, we were on the same wavelength. In the end, we found eight subjects that we liked together. Whenever we were stirred by something, he very quickly responded.

Was serious drama, for some reason, an expression of yourselves that was more basic and truthful?

Frank: All my life, I've seen myself writing comedy. When I wrote by myself, I wrote comedy. Somehow or other, maybe related to Marty in some way, I did go into drama.

Ravetch: The various pieces by Faulkner led us to the South, and the South is the landscape where the greatest evil committed by Americans occured. It's also where there was a terrible, bloody war. So it's full of memories, an indelible, brooding, phantom of a place.

Frank: The issues that interested Marty also interested us—

Ravetch: And vice versa. We have our own social concerns. After all, *Hud* dealt with the greed and materialism that was beginning to take over America, and which has fully done so today. *Conrack* and *Hombre* dealt with racism; *Norma Rae* with the exploitation of the working man, of a great industry that so long resisted being unionized.

Frank: Those stories are just strong stories, and they also make a social comment, which we are not ashamed to make.

Ravetch: We searched out the strongest material we could find.

Frank: We sought the issues that in each instance said something important to us, or that we felt drawn to.

But it stacks up in a certain way. Marty said to me once that he liked projects with interesting characters and a good story, of course—but there had to be that extra edge.

Frank: I think we'd say the same.

Are there pictures of yours—whether directed by Marty or not—that you feel particularly fond of, or that worked out from beginning to end, very much the way they ought to?

Ravetch: Hud, Norma Rae . . . Conrack, I enjoyed . . .

Frank: I was happy with *The Reivers,* too . . .

Ravetch: The Long, Hot Summer—except the ending, which was imposed on us.

Frank: That happens too.

Ravetch: But we deserve the blame. Our name is on it.

What was Marty's usual involvement in the script in the initial stages?

Frank: He waited, unlike most directors. He waited and let each person do his job. He didn't have to wait too long with us. We're not too slow.

Ravetch: We're ten-week writers.

Frank: Fourteen, at the top.

Ravetch: Over the years, ten is our average.

Frank: Marty left us alone. He was a dream director for the screenwriter. That's not common.

If, after the first draft, there were problems, then what?

Frank: If Marty wanted changes, he said so—directly. He was very specific.

From left, Paul Newman, Melvyn Douglas, and Brandon de Wilde in *Hud.*

Ravetch: I must tell you that there's not been a lot of fussing with our scripts. Primarily, there is always cutting. Twenty percent is cut.

You mean you have a tendency to go on too long . . .

Frank: No, we have a tendency to come in at 120 pages, and Marty liked to shoot 100 pages, which made for a two-hour movie. So his rhythm was perhaps slower. But we did not do a lot of rewriting for Marty.

Ravetch: We have been very lucky. We been lucky in the producers I mentioned. We've been lucky in the directors we have worked with—Mark Rydell, Vincente Minnelli, Delbert Mann, Marty Ritt, for sure. And we've been lucky in the actors we've had. Paul Newman—a good citizen. Sally Field and Jane Fonda—decent people. Patricia Neal—a superior woman.

Frank: I don't think we ever ran into an explosion of temperament. (*Pauses.*) Maybe [Steve] McQueen . . . briefly.

Ravetch: It's hard to remember. We've not done a lot of rewriting. There was one occasion—when we turned in a script to Marty—and he said, "It's not dramatic." Failure! Fifteen weeks' work, and it's no good. We knew exactly what he meant, and we knew he was right. We ran out of the room and came back with another script six weeks later. Presumably, it was dramatic, because it was shot.

Frank: We can't tell you a lot of horror stories.

Irving Ravetch and Harriet Frank Jr. at work on the set of *The Reivers.*
(Courtesy of Irving Ravetch and Harriet Frank Jr.)

Which script was that?
Ravetch: I think we'd better not say.
Frank: Nosey! (*Laughs.*)
With Marty, were you always on the set?
Ravetch: With Marty, we were on the set throughout the shooting.

Frank: Always.

Ravetch: We were there before the picture started, and we were there during postproduction. Marty Ritt had such a strong sense of himself—he was unthreatened by the presence of writers at his side.

If the script was being filmed just as you wrote it, what did you do on the set after all?

Ravetch:(*Laughs.*) Not much . . .

Frank: At night, we'd talk together about the work, the performances, how we felt the movie was shaping . . .

Ravetch: Various things come up; changes are dictated by the momentum the picture achieves as it forms.

What is your relationship to the actors vis-à-vis the script?

Frank: If they had questions, they asked Marty.

Is there a wall between you and the actors?

Frank: That's not where writers belong . . .

Ravetch: The director insists that you don't speak to the actors. The chances of causing confusion arise. That's really infringing on his responsibility.

What kinds of things were you discussing at night with Marty? Physical blocking and action? . . .

Frank: No. That was really Marty's balliwick. But he would discuss with us what he hoped to achieve in a scene or its shading and shaping. It was very much like the conversations, I think, that go on in the theater between a writer and a director. It's not adversarial. It's about the work in general, and how it progresses. It's comforting to writers to have a director's ear, and in Marty's case, I think he liked having his writers there just as part of the creative process. But as far as directing is concerned or crossing the line with actors, that's really not appropriate.

I think actors sense that, about writers being present. They know that a director is actually in control of that set, of that picture. In a way, our work is done, unless something comes up that makes the actors extremely uncomfortable, and Marty says, "What can we do to help them?"

Was there a feeling around town, for a time, that you were joined to the hip of Marty Ritt?

Ravetch: No. But when we have taken other jobs and been on other sets, people have said to us, "Did Marty Ritt let you off your leash?"

Frank: We're for hire.

Ravetch: Happily!

Frank: (*Laughs.*) When something's offered.

Ravetch: Norma Rae was one—it came to us from producer Tamara Asseyev.

Frank: There, again, we had producers who were very supportive. We ran into lots of static about using actual factories and the antagonism to the company coming on location [to film] and big mounting costs, but [the 20th-

Actress Sally Field going over a scene with director Martin Ritt for *Norma Rae.*

Century-Fox executives] Alan Ladd [Jr.] and Jay Cantor were stalwart. They stood with us shoulder to shoulder—they were marvelously supportive—men of their word. When Ladd commits to you that he is going to make a picture, he makes it, and he stands by you while you're making it.

Ravetch: Murphy's Romance was another one—Sally Field brought it to us. *Stanley & Iris* was brought to us by [the coproducer] Arlene Sellers. In fact, the last three pictures were assignments . . .

Frank: But it's very hard for us to get married to material. It seems to be much easier if we find something on our own that channels our energies.

What is the reason why the credits stretch out between Norma Rae *and* Murphy's Romance*? . . .*

Ravetch: Perhaps it indicates that we haven't been as enterprising of late as we were early on. We have an original which we sold to Warners, but they couldn't cast it or make it. It was called "Mixed Feelings." We have our share of pictures that aren't made.

Frank: Along with every other writer in town.

Is that an occupational hazard, or is that an occasional source of sadness or tragedy?

Ravetch: An occupational hazard.

You can shrug the failures off?

Ravetch: Oh, absolutely.

Is there any other reason why the credits slow down?

Frank: It's simply getting tougher because our subject matter is not always the kind that will strike management as being highly commercial. You have to find somebody who takes an act of faith in making a movie with you. Then there's a certain degree of just living your life—movies being one part of it— but the pleasures of life being another. As you get on in life, you want to do many other things . . . now, can I get angry and hold forth?

Ravetch: Go ahead.

Frank: I think there is a very nasty undertone in American life, where the appetite for violence is out of control. I think films cater to it shamelessly, and it feeds into irresponsible social behavior. I think that the time has come where, once in a while, whether audiences respond to it greatly or not, it is necessary to propose a different standard. It's become a sort of basic tenet of American entertainment: super violence.

Ravetch: We made a really terrible mistake with a picture called *The Cowboys,* in which John Wayne was killed, and the young boys who were in his charge avenged his death. The picture was never shown in some countries. I think that could happen on a more widespread basis in the Common Market in five—ten years. That will quickly put an end to the making of those kinds of motion pictures.

What do you mean, "a terrible mistake"? A terrible box-office mistake?

Frank: No. We made a terrible moral misstep, because the film shouldn't have ended that way.

Ravetch: The kids could have captured the villains and brought them in for trial. It was not necessary to have the children going out with guns and doing the killing.

Was that in the original source material?

Ravetch: No. That was our contribution. The source material had them round up the villains and bring them all to justice.

That's something you regret?

Both: Absolutely.

Ravetch: That's a major regret.

With all the present-day obstacles, do you have less of a drive to surmount the obstacles and write films?

Frank: No, I'm full of beans and vinegar. I'll take on anybody my weight, any place, any time. But at this point in my life, I don't want to do anything that I don't delight in, one way or another. Either I want to feel passionate about it on a social level or get an immense kick out of it.

Is there a reason that in the last ten to fifteen years—or at least, beginning with Murphy's Romance and continuing through Stanley & Iris—you seem to be moving away from dramatic material and getting into more romantic situations?

Frank: Maybe it's the September time of year, psychologically or emotionally. It's not that you lose your passion for social problems, but there's a deliciousness that you want to experience writing, too. Laughter is certainly part of that—an immensely gratifying part.

What is the history of your most recent film, Stanley & Iris?

Frank: It came from a wonderful book by an immensely talented writer, who is an English schoolteacher [*Union Street,* by Pat Barker (New York: Putnam, *1983*)]. It is a very different book from the film. Her book is a story of poverty and of a group of women who live in really crushing northern England poverty—in which poverty is the enemy and the obstacle for their lives. One of them in the book is married to a man who is illiterate. It's just touched on very lightly in the novel. It is a many-character novel with varying stories—rape, marriage, being elderly and abandoned.

In this book, there is one character, Iris, who is the strong central character. She is a touchstone for the other people. Her husband happens to be illiterate. That, because it is a subject that interests us greatly, seemed to make the project very worthwhile. That was an issue we wanted to fasten on, something we found very important and moving. So we made that the focus of the story.

Who brought the book to your attention?

Frank: Alex Winetsky and Arlene Sellers, who produced it. They had found the book in England.

"An important and moving issue": Robert DeNiro and Jane Fonda in *Stanley & Iris.*

Did they have in mind doing what you eventually did with the story?

Frank: No, this was a small element in a much larger canvas. The book was beautifully written; the author is supremely gifted. It appealed to us on that level.

Why did they decide to come to you?

Ravetch: They knew us, and I suppose they knew we have done pictures of this kind before.

How hard was it to get people around town committed?

Frank: Not hard—because Alan Ladd is courageous. And, as we say, when he says he will do a subject, he does it.

How crucial is it, doing a picture like Stanley & Iris, *to get the cooperation of people of the stature of Robert DeNiro and Jane Fonda?*

Frank: Very. It would be difficult to get the film off the ground otherwise.

At what point did they commit to the project?

Frank: After the script was written.

Therefore, they had no real input into the script.

Ravetch: No actor that we've ever known has had any input into the script, with the exception of Sally Field in *Murphy's Romance.* She was, after all, the producer.

That's remarkable.

Ravetch: When you think of people like Dustin Hoffman and Al Pacino, yes, that's remarkable.

Vincent Canby in the New York Times *was one of several critics who commented negatively on the ending. What happened there?*

Frank: We had what I considered a kind of delicate, offhand ending to the film, which was romantic but didn't tie everything into a neat package. The preview audiences were bewildered if they couldn't see the two characters go off into the sunset together—where, in point of fact, did they go? So we wrote a more specific ending, and I regret it because I think the original one said all that was needed.

Aside from the ending, is what you see up on the screen what you envisioned?

Ravetch: I like the movie.

Frank: My annoyance with the critics is I hate to have what the picture is talking about lost because of their carping. It's an immensely important issue because one out of four Americans can't read.

The things that went awry, went awry. I still think it's a good love story. The two people are very attractive; they're not beating each other up; they have some human concern for each other. I'm not ashamed of the movie. I would do it again.

Ravetch: Amen.

Let's say you're starting a new script. I'm a producer. I've just brought you a great book. You've read it and agreed to adapt it. Now you're going to start. What's the drill? What time of day do you go to work?

Ravetch: We work off the first rush of energy. Nine to one. I sit at the type-writer. Hank paces. We have already made our outline of thirty-five or forty-five major scenes, all on one page.

Who does what? Who starts the ball rolling?

Frank: Who knows? It's really pretty seamless by now.

Early on, was one of you the senior partner; the other, the junior partner?

Both: No.

Does one of you have relative strengths in terms of the characters or the overall arc of the story?

Ravetch: I don't think so, the proof being that when we're finished it's often hard to distinguish who wrote what.

Frank: It's even-steven.

Ravetch: It's really a pure collaboration in the sense that we get together; we talk out problems at great, exhaustive length; we do some kind of an outline together; and every word really is collaborated on. Every word is thrown up in the air for approval—from one to the other. The script is not so much written as it is talked onto the page.

The outline has already been made over the course of a longer period of talking about the story back and forth?

Ravetch: Yes, yes. Everything flows from three to five weeks of really absorbing the material and talking about it. Going for long walks, long car rides, with pads, making notes, writing furiously behind the wheel, having car wrecks.

Do you think about things like—the story is interesting, but it needs an exciting set piece here, a fresh location there? . . .

Ravetch: I'm sure that concerns us early, during outline time, but what really concerns us is that the story is organic, cohesive, that it builds . . .

What are you thinking about principally?

Frank: The people.

Ravetch: Really, of the individuals, all the time.

Frank: Who they are, what their emotional push is, what would bring them into conflict. Their behavior.

Do you write down detailed things about the characters in terms that we never see on the screen?

Ravetch: No. We just try to know them thoroughly.

You're always just putting them into the situation?

Ravetch: We put them into the situation, the event, the conflict. How do they respond? What is their behavior, their complexities, their ambiguities, their paradoxes? Why do they differ, why do they perplex each other?

How they speak differently from each other?

Frank: That comes when we're actually writing. We don't really think about that in the initial stages, because we talk dialogue back and forth to each other [when we are writing], as if we were actors, and that's the method. We're closet actors. I'm terrible, he's good.

Okay, you start on page one. How far do you get in a day? One page, if you're lucky? . . .

Ravetch: If we're lucky, we get two. Two on the average. Three would be a fine day. It's possible that we do the three pages and then redo them again. Often, by the end of the day, we've really done three or four revisions of what amounts to the same three pages. So that by the time the script is finished, it has gone through a number of revisions.

So your first draft is very polished.

Ravetch: It is polished.

Frank: We revise as we work on our first draft—constantly. By the time we've arrived at that final page, we have gone over the script many, many times.

Do you brook any interruptions?

Ravetch: No. It's a sacrosanct period. We are very disciplined. It's an inviolable time. There are no interruptions. Beyond that, it's unthinkable that we should take a workday off. We go at it five days a week.

For the average of ten weeks?

Ravetch: Correct.

Is the phone on?

Ravetch: No, and if it's on, it's not answered.

Are you drinking coffee?

Ravetch: No.

No one is ever here? Marty was never here?

Ravetch: No one is here. We couldn't work with anyone in the house. With us jabbering at one another?

What happens at noon or 1 P.M.?

Ravetch: Whew. A good day's work.

You go off and play tennis?

Ravetch: That's right.

Frank: No. We read it over, we think about it, we talk about it. There's a little pad beside the bed at night. Lots of dinner table conversation relates to it.

Ravetch: It's true; we do go out to dinner at night with a pad and talk over the next day's work. To get a running start.

Do you have any tricks to get started the next day?

Ravetch: We don't do what Hemingway did, which is to stop in the middle of a sentence at a very good point.

Frank: I don't like to leave the day's work in disarray. If there is something that's troubling us, I like to stay with it until it's reasonably in place to be looked at with a cool eye the next morning.

Then . . . the next morning?

Frank: We begin by reading the day's work before.

Ravetch: Just read it to ourselves.

Frank: And if there's something disturbing, we go back, then and there.

When is your best thinking done?

Frank: Bathtub, for me.

Ravetch: At work. Because that energy's precious.

Frank: I'm inclined to brood when the work is done.

Ravetch: We do brood, of course: But the best work is done at the type-writer, as it happens.

How do you know when it is right?

Frank: When does anybody know it's right? C'mon!

Ravetch: It's a click.

Frank: I don't get any clicks.

You're tapping into the unconscious to begin with, so how do you know?

Frank: You make the best and most judicious appraisal of the work that you can; and you're either right, or you're wrong.

Ravetch: That sounds too judicious to me. You know because you're a professional and a craftsman.

Is the work joy or anguish?

Ravetch: The plain truth? Joy.

Frank: We like to work.

Arnold Schulman:
Nothing but Regrets

Interview by Pat McGilligan

Sometimes Arnold Schulman is a hard man to find because he has addresses on both coasts, and because there are long interludes of time when he forays into remote, underdeveloped areas. None of my efforts to locate him were working when Fred Roos, the producer of *Tucker: The Man and His Dream,* helped out, offering a long-standing phone number from his well-thumbed address book. I phoned, Schulman answered. A day or two later, by appointment I rang the doorbell of his Beverly Hills residence.

Wearing something kimonolike, he answered and ushered me into his home, outwardly contemporary in design but inside furnished with tasteful ancient and Oriental touches, right down to a Japanese room with pillows and panels and folding screens, where he does much of his writing. His candor and sense of humor made for instant rapport and for a long, sometimes digressive conversation about an impressive career that began in the 1950s.

He started out as an aspiring playwright, studying form and structure with Robert Anderson, Clifford Odets, and others. He learned to write in workshops while in his spare time dipping into the Method with Lee Strasberg, who directed his first play, *My Fiddle Has Three Strings.* He took on-the-job training as a writer for live television and worked on nearly seventy teleplays. His first play failed; however, Schulman was then beckoned to Hollywood, initially by the director George Cukor and the producer Hal Wallis. He then wrote the screenplay, based on his own Broadway play, for Frank Capra's feature film *A Hole in the Head.*

The sixties were Schulman's Hollywood heyday; the seventies, his nadir (for both hilarious and pathetic reasons); and the eighties, with *A Chorus Line* and *Tucker,* his magnificent comeback. In our conversation in 1991, we did not dwell very much on a current project of his that seemed a comparative long shot—an adaptation of Randy Shilts's nonfiction book *And the Band Played On*

(New York: St. Martin's, 1987), which deals comprehensively with the history, politics, and science of Acquired Immune Deficiency Syndrome (AIDS). In the end, *Band* survived five years of development, twenty-three drafts, three directors, and all kinds of second-guessing. "I lived through every issue we dealt with in the movie—egos, greed politics," Schulman, who also coproduced *Band,* told the *New York Times* at the time of its first airing in September 1993. "It was a nightmare."

Schulman always insisted that he was writing *And the Band Played On* as a motion picture, and that the eventual sponsorship of the cable channel HBO was purely circumstantial. Schulman's credit on-screen and on posters is for the "screenplay," not the teleplay. In many ways, the film is the highpoint to

Arnold Schulman in Los Angeles, 1993. (Photo by William B. Winburn.)

date of a career with more than a few bends, dips, and cartwheels. Schulman's sober, documentary-style, chronological treatment of the AIDS issue places the heterosexual, heroic medical scientist Don Francis (played by Mathew Modine) at the forefront of a multicharacter saga of disease sufferers and scientists (an all-star cast that includes Ian McKellen, Richard Gere, Steve Martin, Lily Tomlin, and Anjelica Huston).

This film is an anguished cry for humanity and a clear, angry denunciation of Reagan era policies that discriminated against the homosexual community. With many excellent reviews, *Band* won a 1994 Humanitas Award for its passionate script, as well as an Emmy for Best Dramatic Movie or Miniseries. It also won the cable programming Ace Award that year for Best Screenplay in its category.

Arnold Schulman (1925–)

1957   *Wild is the Wind* (George Cukor). Story, script.

1959   *A Hole in the Head* (Frank Capra). Script, based on Schulman's play.

1960   *Cimarron* (Anthony Mann). Script.

1963   *Love with the Proper Stranger* (Robert Mulligan). Story, script.

1967   *The Night They Raided Minsky's* (William Friedkin). Co-script.

1969   *Goodbye, Columbus* (Larry Peerce). Script.

1971   *To Find a Man* (Buzz Kulik). Script.

1975   *Funny Lady* (Herbert Ross). Story, co-script.

1976   *Won Ton Ton, the Dog Who Saved Hollywood* (Michael Winner). Coproducer, co-script.

1979   *Players* (Anthony Harvey). Executive producer, script.

1985   *A Chorus Line* (Richard Attenborough). Script.

1988   *Tucker: A Man and His Dream* (Francis Coppola). Co-script.

Television includes numerous script contributions to episodes for *Playwrights '56, Philco Playhouse, Studio One, Omnibus, General Electric Theater, Kraft Television Theater,* and others; and *And the Band Played On* (1993, telefilm, producer and script).

Plays include *A Hole in the Head* and *Jennie.*

Nonfiction books include *Baba.*

Academy Award honors include an Oscar nomination for Best Original Story and Screenplay for *Love with the Proper Stranger;* and an Oscar nomination for Best Adapted Screenplay for *Goodbye, Columbus.*

Writers Guild honors include nominations for Best Script for *Wild is the Wind, A Hole in the Head,* and *Love with the Proper Stranger. Goodbye, Columbus* was named Best Written Comedy Adapted from Another Medium.

Can you tell me a little bit about your background and boyhood?

Let's skip the Holden Caulfield–David Copperfield crap. I really hate that. I hate to read it. I hate to talk about it. My background, my history, where I was born, how I started, etcetera. Let's just concentrate on movies and movie experiences.

You won't tell me anything about where you where born, or how you were raised?

I'd rather not. It's boring. Who cares?

How about, where did you begin as a writer?

I wrote my first piece at the age of ten. In school we were asked to write an essay about something. I wrote my essay, and the next day I got a zero because the teacher insisted I had copied from the encyclopedia. I was stunned, horrified, because I hadn't copied from the encyclopedia; I didn't have an encyclopedia. Later, [while I was] stewing on this, several things occurred to me: One was, if she thought the essay was stolen from an encyclopedia, it must have been pretty good. Also, it was like a light bulb turning on [in my head]: I had never realized that writing was a profession; I knew you could be a doctor, a lawyer, run a store, be a farmer; but I didn't know that when you went to the library and saw all these books that somebody wrote each one of them and got paid for it. It was a job! I thought, "Holy shit," and immediately sat down and wrote a little story and sent it to either *Open Road for Boys* or *Boys Life,* one of those two magazines. They bought it. I thought, "This is it!" and from then on, I've never done anything else or thought of doing anything else.

So you sold your first story at the age of ten. Do you remember what it was about?

It was based on an incident in my life that happened in a little hillbilly town in North Carolina. I don't want to say very much; but we were the only Jewish family in town, and I just didn't fit in. We had just moved there, and I noticed everybody wore overalls. I somehow managed to talk my mother into buying me some overalls, desperately trying to fit in. But I still didn't fit in, because my overalls didn't have patches on them like everybody elses'. That was the basis of the story.

Between the age of ten and your first Broadway play, were you constantly endeavoring to sell your writing?

Yes. At about the age of fifteen, I invented the newspaper syndicate. Of course, it already existed, but it was an invention for me; I was reinventing the wheel. Instead of selling my little human interest stories to one newspaper, as I had been doing, it occurred to me to get a list of every newspaper in North Carolina in those days, and mimeograph my stories and send them to every paper in the state. I didn't know anything about what I was doing. I just wrote at the top: "Usual rates." I'm making up the numbers, because I don't remember; but, say, there were four hundred newspapers and forty used my stories at ten bucks a shot, that would be four hundred dollars a week at a time when this was a monumental sum. So immediately I started making money and got published and never went through that awful period of rejection, struggle, not getting anywhere, that most writers have.

When I was in my early twenties, as I recall, I moved to New York and immediately started writing my first play. I can't remember the precise date. For some reason, which I choose not to acknowledge, I've never adjusted to the concept of time as a system of indelible numbers meticulously recorded by that Great Certified Public Accountant in the sky. Frequently, I'm absolutely certain that something happened to me last week or last year, when in calendar time it could have been ten or fifteen years ago—and the other way around. At any rate, in order to make a living, that's when I started working in live television. Live television was my real training ground.

Why did you move to New York? Did you have family connections?

I'll just say this about my background. I've been on my own literally, since I've been eleven. I never had much schooling—not much high school and only a little college as a special student to learn about writing. After a month of classes at college, though, I thought, "These people are nuts . . . they analyze things to death." I decided to go to New York because that is where writers went.

I hit a lucky streak in New York. I was helped out by a lot of wonderful people. Robert Anderson, who later wrote *Tea and Sympathy,* was teaching evening classes at the American Theatre wing, and I got into his class. Before I started working in television, I wanted to spend all my time learning how to write plays; so I did nothing to earn any money. My rent was eleven dollars a month for a cold water flat on the lower East Side, which I shared with another beginning writer, and my basic diet was gallons of thick black coffee, which I read Balzac drank, and day-old bread a neighborhood bakery sold for pennies. I enjoyed the fantasy of being a starving young writer, but my body didn't.

One night, in the middle of Bob's class, I got so weak and dizzy I had to leave. I had no idea Bob knew it was because I hadn't eaten for days, until about midnight there was a knock on my door, and there was Bob Anderson, having walked up five flights, with two enormous paper bags of groceries. In the morning, I found an envelope he had stuffed into my mailbox. In the envelope were five hundred-dollar bills. There's no way I can describe the impact this act of pure kindness had on me, and no way I can repay it, except to pass it on, which I've tried to do ever since.

Around the same time, the Dramatists Guild formed a group called the New Dramatists, and they selected thirty promising young writers to be part of this group. I was one of them. Among the others were Robert Anderson, Paddy Chayefsky, Bill Inge, Stephen Sondheim—an astonishing group.

Every week we would meet in the conference room at the Dramatists Guild. We'd meet with the great playwrights of the period—[S. N.] Behrman, Sherwood Anderson, Oscar Hammerstein, Maxwell Anderson, [Howard] Lindsay and [Russel] Crouse—and discuss craft. I'll always remember Howard Lindsay talking about comedy. He said, "When you take the play out of town, take your biggest laugh, wherever it may happen to come for the audience, and put it at the end of act 2. Just rearrange the play and put it at the end of act 2. It sounds crazy, but just try it; we've been doing it for thirty years." That kind of thing. We'd sit around a table and ask them questions about "planting" here and "paying off" there, especially about comedy—how the word that gets the laugh has to be the last word in the sentence—really technical craft stuff.

Why did you decide to make the leap from writing fiction to writing for the theater?

I made a lot of idiotic decisions that I regret bitterly now. Originally, I wanted to be a novelist. But it was a matter of expedience. I thought, "A novel is 400 to 500 pages, and a play is 100 to 120 pages." I chose the shorter form to start with. That was the deciding factor, although of course I liked drama and I liked theater.

Did you have any experience or particular love for the theater?

I second-acted a lot—meaning, waiting outside, and when people go back in after the second act, you walk in with them and find a seat or stand up. After I got to New York, I saw everything I could.

How did you go from theater to being involved with live television?

Bob Anderson's wife at that time, Phyllis, was working at the Theatre Guild, which at that time was probably the most prestigious theatrical producing organization in the world. When I wrote my first play in Bob's class, because of Phyllis the Theatre Guild optioned it, with plans to produce it the following year. In order to keep me alive during that time, she got me into television working on *Omnibus, GE Theater*—all the shows now known as the Golden Age of Television. I wrote one every week.

A kinescope of one of mine was shown recently at a festival here—James Dean and Natalie Wood in a half-hour drama on *GE Theater.* Another was shown on PBS—Paul Newman in "Bang the Drum Slowly." When you see one of them now, they don't really hold up. But given the limitations of what we had to do—knowing the character had to be laughing in this scene and, within two seconds for the very next scene, run all the way across the studio and be sitting somewhere else and sobbing—they are amazing.

Live television was the most valuable training a writer could have. We could do anything we wanted. It was an opportunity to learn [by doing] and to see your work performed immediately. You had to learn the technique of writing to allow time for one of four cameras to get from one set to another, to frame the shot and focus, as well as laying out the structure so that the actors, who frequently had to change costumes while running, had enough time to make the transitions. It was like logistics, a military game. Sometimes it was chaos. In almost every show, a camera would conk out, and at the last minute, you'd be feverishly rewriting to rearrange scenes. There wasn't any time for second-guessing. Time pressure gave us the freedom to be bold.

Those early days were marvelous in many ways. Something I miss terribly now is that we were a community of writers then. We were close, we would call each other for help. We were a family. I remember Paddy Chayevsky, who was my closest friend—especially during that period—calling one day and saying, "Boy, I'm in real trouble here. I've got to give [the producer] Fred Coe a script on Thursday, and I don't know what the hell to write . . ." I went over to his place, and we talked about it. He had an idea to do something about some little, short fat guy who can't get a date. We stayed up all night until eight or nine in the morning, working the whole thing out, talking it through. Paddy wanted Marty Ritt to play the part, so in talking the story through, we'd refer to the character as Marty. Paddy wrote it. All I did was act as a sounding board. That sort of thing happened all the time. When I needed help, I would call him or Bob Anderson or whomever. And, of course, we'd go out of town to see each other's plays and make suggestions.

You continued to work in the theater at the same time that you were writing for live television?

Yes. I was also a member of the Actors Studio—the very, very first group—before they moved to the church where they are now, with [Marlon] Brando and Monty Clift. Phyllis Anderson was a close friend of Molly Kazan, who was married to Gadge [Elia] Kazan at the time. She said to Gadge, "Why don't you let him [Schulman] sit in? It will be helpful . . ." I wrote scenes and directed them, and again it was a wonderful experience. I had no idea of becoming an actor, but so that I could understand the process of acting and therefore write better plays, they got me little jobs as an actor. I had two lines in *Come Back, Little Sheba* on Broadway. And I remember Rod Steiger and I were among the extras in Arthur Miller's *Enemy of the People.*

What did studying the Method teach you that was helpful to you as a writer?

My first reaction would be to say it set me back about ten years. But that's facetious, because I did learn a lot about subtext. I learned that very often the best writing is the line that says the opposite of what the person means. Obviously, I learned a lot by osmosis, by doing it, by learning what plays and what doesn't play. It was a really extraordinary piece of good luck, being in the right place at the right time. It was a wonderful time to experiment. Brando,

Clift, Paul Newman, so many others were in the class, and they were in my pieces. They were all available, eager to do any scene you had. We were all working together. Of course, many of them turned out to be the best actors of our generation, but at that time, nobody knew if they'd ever get a job.

Directing actors for the first time, what did that teach you as a beginning writer?

It taught me that actors are dangerous creatures—to beware. (*Laughs.*) Again, I'm being facetious. Actors want to make a contribution, and they should. You cast them because you want a certain quality. But just as I said the best writing is sometimes where you don't say what the person is really feeling or thinking, what actors want to do can be very frustrating to a young playwright. If I wanted the line to be sad, they wanted to play it laughing. As an older writer, I say, "Yes—give me more of that!" I learned a lot from them, working with those incredible people.

Did [Elia] Kazan or Lee Strasberg have much to say about writing?

Absolutely. As I recall, they basically indicated that writing and acting are the same thing. I've later discovered that is true: When I sit down to write, I'm improvising. It's coming, not from my head, but from somewhere else. I learned from that period, I guess, just to *let it happen;* and then to come in afterwards as an editor—distinct from my job as the writer—and do the cutting and editing.

Clifford Odets taught a playwriting class at the Actors Studio, only for writers. His class was fascinating, especially for me. He was one of my gods. And at that time—I don't know why, [but] probably because of the way I was writing—I was called, or considered to be by a number of people, a young Odets, whatever that means.

His class was different in contrast to those once-a-week groups with the great playwrights. They talked about craft. Odets talked about art. Therefore, I can't remember anything he said. It was basically a waste of time for me, an ego trip for him. He was being Clifford Odets, *acting* Clifford Odets. I didn't learn anything specific—like where to put your biggest joke—although I probably learned something by osmosis.

Then my play was ready. We were going to try it out that summer in Westport. I insisted that Lee Strasberg direct it. People said, "You're crazy. You mustn't do this. A wonderful teacher he might be, but he's a rotten director." I was very young and very pretentious—I said no. He too was a god to me. The play was a total disaster because between the lines "Hello?" and "How are you?" each actor did five minutes of "sense memory." The title of it at that time was *My Fiddle Has Three Strings*—I told you it was pretentious. It was a normal-length play that lasted about six hours on opening night. I remember a pivotal moment in my life. In the audience was Noël Coward. At the end of the first act, I sneaked over behind him, wanting to eavesdrop on what he was saying. "Well, actually," he said to his friends, "I think it should have been called 'My Fiddle Has Two Strings—Oy and Vey.' " (*Laughs.*) I thought, "Oh, God, my career is over."

It was a big flop. Meanwhile, I did some rewriting on it. One time I was stuck for a script for Fred Coe, so I took that play and rewrote it into a television play and changed the title from pretentious to even more pretentious: "The Heart's a Forgotten Hotel." Arthur Penn directed it with Sylvia Sidney and Eddie O'Brien. It was a beautiful production, the best it ever was. The next day, I got a call from Gar Kanin, who said, "Would you be interested in turning that show into a play?" I said, "I have already got it as a play." Of course, I had changed it, so it wasn't a play anymore; but I stayed up all night and rewrote it back into a play and gave it to him. Gar didn't like the new title, and by that time, neither did I. Gar came up with *A Hole in the Head,* because we were desperate for a new title. It was a Yiddish expression: You need this like a hole in the head. I had no idea how it applied to the play and still don't.

Then came one of the critical moments that shaped my life, and which I've regretted—one of the big mistakes, I think, in a way, and then again, it isn't. Gar Kanin cast Paul Douglas, David Burns, and other old comics, and we took the play out of town. The audiences went into hysterics at the funny stuff and hated the serious stuff. When the piece was on television, it was very, very simple, not a comedy at all. It ended very unhappily. It was a tiny slice of life, done brilliantly on television. Now we had this gigantic, revolving set, which didn't make any sense for this small play, and the play was all out of whack from where I [had] started.

I was confronted with the problem by Kanin. He was very gentle and wonderful; he would rather have had a flop than disturb a young playwright's life. I realized I had the power to make him do it exactly the way I wanted it to be done and have a flop, and who would care? It would last three days and close on Saturday. Or I knew easily how to fix it and make it into a hit. Just take out the serious stuff, put in more jokes, and give it a happy ending. And that is what I did. Since then, I've felt that is the moment when I sold out. That is the moment when I really sold out.

I've heard writers, especially screenwriters in interviews, asked from time to time: "If you had your life to live over again, would you change anything?" And they say, "No regrets." I have *nothing but regrets.* Everything I've done, every decision I've made in my life, pretty much has been a disaster.

That decision echoed down the line for you?

That's it. From then on, it was not that I was writing down to anybody, but I took the road of "I'll make the movie and follow the conventions," the professional, pragmatic way, rather than the way of the artist.

Was it a case of being corrupted by money?

No, money had nothing to do with it. Later, it got to be money. That decision was not based on money. That was based on being a pragmatic professional, which I had learned in those years of live television. Doing what had to be done at that moment to make it work. We were on the road. I was trained by then that as a professional, my job was to take what I've got and make a hit out of it. You don't sit back when you've got a flop and say, "I'm a wounded artist," and write a letter to the *Times*. Who cares?

Did your decision have anything to do with a possible latent insecurity that you weren't an artist, couldn't be one, didn't have the stuff?

No. None of that occurred to me until years later. I've always regretted not doing what Doc Simon [does]—I'm sorry, Neil Simon; he's not Doc Simon any longer, just like Gadge is no longer Gadge Kazan; he hates that name after everybody's called him that for twenty years. Neil's written a play every year, *and* he's written movies. I could have done that. Unfortunately, I chose other priorities.

Later, money came into it, because money creeps up on you. Your lifestyle gets more expensive. After I started writing movies, we—I was married at the time—moved from a basement apartment, literally subground in Greenwich Village, and bought Joan Crawford's apartment on Sutton Place. It was that leap. Plus, there were two kids and private school . . . now you *better* earn money. And then suddenly you wake up, and you can't pay your taxes; so you've *got* to do another movie.

Did producer Hal Wallis see your play? Is that how you ended up in Hollywood?

Hal Wallis hadn't seen the play when he first contacted me, because it hadn't opened yet. It was cast and announced, but we hadn't gone into rehearsal. I don't recall the precise chronology. But my agent knew Hal and told him about me. Hal had already done *The Rose Tattoo* [1955] with Anna Magnani, and had the option to do another picture with her. She wanted to remake an Italian movie called *Furia* [1948] because she was in love with [Roberto] Rossellini at one time and wanted to be in this particular movie which he was planning to do. When he pushed her aside and fell in love with somebody else—not Ingrid Bergman—she vowed that some day she'd make the movie without him as a kind of vengeance.

It was a dumb story, basically the same story the musical *The Most Happy Fella* is taken from: the mail-order wife. But she wanted to do it, and what she wanted, she got. He asked my agent—Abe Lastfogel of William Morris—if I'd be interested. They screened *Furia* for me and asked if I could figure out any way to do this piece of shit. At first it seemed hopeless; but I figured out a story line and went to Hollywood to meet with Hal, and after listening to me, he said, "Great, go to work."[*]

---

[*] The official credits for *Wild Is the Wind* stipulate that the film is based on *Furia,* a novel by Vittorio Nino Novarse.

That was the only film school I had, and it's all you need. I have since heard this story attributed to many different people, who supposedly said it to other people, but Hal said it to me. He said, "Don't worry about writing for the movies. This is all you need to know: When Sam Behrman came to write a script for me, in the first scene we had to show the husband was losing interest in his wife. Sam wrote a ten-page scene that was brilliant—witty, insightful, marvelous. I said, 'Sam, this is fantastic—as a *play*.' I tore it up and said, 'Here's how we do it in the movies. The man and his wife get into an elevator. He's wearing a hat. He doesn't take it off. The elevator goes down one flight. The doors open; in steps a pretty woman. He takes off his hat. That's all you need to know.' " I realized what he was saying. It's a different language. It is like translating something from French into English, from words into pictures. That really is all you need to know.

Did you have any background as a movie fan?

Of course. I lived in the movies. And I had all this experience of working in television, which was similar to movies, although in some ways, it was more like plays, because we didn't have the luxury of even shooting an outdoor scene. It was always on a single set.

Did you have any attitude towards Hollywood?

No, I never looked down my nose. I liked the process of movies. I thought it was exciting. I was fortunate. My first movie was with George Cukor; my second was with Frank Capra. You hear so much about Hollywood's bad treatment of writers. I guess I slipped in the door in the period between the Golden Age and the Writer as the Hollywood Nigger. With Cukor and Capra, we worked out what we wanted to do, and they never changed a word without asking me. I went to all the sneak previews, was invited into the cutting room, made suggestions all the way through, and was listened to as an equal, a peer. Here I was, a young kid with no experience, and I was listened to; not that they did everything I said, but at least they listened and talked and worked things out.

Were Cukor and Wallis helpful in terms of the script?

Extremely. Very helpful. Unlike now—it astonishes me that it's been allowed to happen—people who have never seen a piece of film or have never written anything, not even a letter, suddenly they are telling you how to rewrite your script. They are in the editing room, telling the editor how to edit the film. It's nuts. In those days, everybody knew what they were doing, and there was mutual respect. You respect my job, I respect your job; and we work together. It was really working together.

Actually, *Wild is the Wind* started out as a project for John Sturges. I worked with Sturges and Wallis on an early draft. But Sturges considered himself an action director, and at the point that it was clear the project was turning into a love story with real people, he either quit or moved on. Cukor was obviously the choice to direct Magnani, the great actress of the day.

Cukor and I met almost every day at Cukor's house. We would begin at some civilized hour, say ten or eleven, break for lunch, and work until three or four. There was never any pressure, never any hysteria, just exploration. We talked and talked and talked. Being a young filmmaker, I was very conscious of visual metaphors and symbols, and he was very receptive. When I got too ambitious, he would gently lead me away from my excess. He was very clear about what he wanted. He and Wallis really knew their craft. "If we are going to do this here, we had better plant it there." "This scene is too long." "You don't need this character; let's combine it with this one." It was all very technical craft stuff.

You're going to have problems if you start making a movie and you don't have a finished script. For some reason, I decided to set this movie on a sheep farm in Nevada. An important scene took place when the lambs were being born; but when the lambs were *actually* being born, the script wasn't finished. We had to go on location and start shooting, because the lambs weren't going to be born again until next year. (*Laughs.*) The birthing of the lambs was going to take place somewhere in the middle of the story—but we didn't quite know where. So I was literally on location, writing the next day's scenes, having no idea what came next [in the script]—nor did anybody else. I took a lot of ideas from the location. I spent an enormous amount of time with Magnani and incorporated little mannerisms of hers into the script. It was a very exciting, stimulating experience.

In his autobiography, Hal Wallis talks a lot about the harsh location and about Anna Magnani proving spoiled and difficult.

She was a pain in the ass. She held up the filming. She asked for a Jeep to be sent to her home in Italy, or she wasn't going to work the next day. She got in bed and played sick, and they had to call in a local doctor from Carson City to the motel where we were staying. He said, "There ain't nothing wrong with this woman. If you want a dark-haired 'eye-talian' woman, we've got hundreds around here. Why don't you get another one?" (*Laughs.*) But Wallis gave her the Jeep. I'll always remember she kept yelling, "With a shovel! Don't forget the shovel!" A Jeep with a shovel? Why, I don't know.

*In his book [*Starmaker: The Autobiography of Hal B. Wallis, *by Hal Wallis and Charles Higham (New York:) Macmillan 1980] Wallis said there was competition between Magnani, Anthony Quinn, and Tony Franciosa for close-ups.*

Yeah, that I remember, everyone bitching and complaining about their close-ups. And Cukor had to explain things to Franciosa—I think this was his first picture. Cukor shot absolutely by the book: the master shot, medium shot, over the shoulder, a two-shot from this angle, a two-shot from that angle, his close-up, her close-up. It was one, two, three, four, five. I remember him explaining to Tony Franciosa, "My dear boy, wait—we're only at *one* now. When we get to *five,* you'll get your close-up . . . we'll do everyone's close-ups in turn." That was the end of that.

Arnold Schulman (gesturing) on the set of George Cukor's film *Wild Is the Wind,* with (from left) Anthony Quinn, Anna Magnani, and Anthony Franciosa. (Photo by Bill Avery.)

Some of the scenes were difficult. We had one scene that Arthur Miller used many, many years later in *The Misfits* [1961], where they were capturing wild horses by tossing rubber tires around them. In this case, the scene had to do metaphorically with this wild creature, Anna Magnani. The horse was *her.* It wasn't an impossible scene by today's standards where you can blow up New York [on the screen], but it was difficult.

Some of those outdoor scenes seem beyond Cukor, especially the horse-capturing scene, which is not filmed as well as it should be.

I think it was second unit.

The situation must not have been very congenial for him—the shooting conditions, the script in progress, Magnani, and the other cast troubles.

It was awful. I remember it very well: the weather, bad food, the motel, Cukor arriving with his own silk pillow to sleep with on location. There was also a lot of—I won't go into the names—midnight crawling from bunk to bunk of the cast. But Cukor had infinite patience. Though in most ways he didn't impose his personality on the film, what he did bring to it was his sensitivity about people and the human condition.

Were you gratified by the result?

There were sections of the film that became really stupid in order to conform to Magnani's revenge: getting even with Rossellini. But there were moments in it that I liked, and I liked the fact that this was the first picture that I can recall where the woman committed adultery and wasn't killed or punished at the end. In this one, the husband begged *her* for forgiveness, which was a revolutionary way of looking at things. That I liked. That was the honest way to do it. I felt the other way was a cliché, and Cukor agreed with me.

Can you compare Cukor with Capra for me in terms of craft, expertise with the script, your experiences of working with them?

They were totally different people, but their working technique was exactly the same. Capra shot exactly the same way as Cukor. That is the way the studios had taught them to shoot. They didn't want to get caught without coverage.

I think of Capra as being more of a frustrated writer than Cukor. Capra shows up in several biographies and sources as grabbing credit as a screenwriter and once in a while being forced into arbitration with the Guild.

In Capra's case, where we had more leisure, we worked on the script line by line and word by word. He and I never had any problem. In fact, he has a little section in his book, *The Name Above the Title* [New York: Macmillan, 1971], about when I first came out to do the screenplay [of *A Hole in the Head*], and he brought up what I thought was a ludicrous idea. I was young, cocky, and I told him it was ludicrous. He laughed and said, "You know, I'm the director. I can do any damn thing I want to." I said, "No, you can't. I'll give you your money back," which has been my attitude throughout my entire career. I have given money back every time someone doesn't do what I want to do. It has screwed my career; my agent thinks I'm crazy; and it hasn't done my bank account any good either. Anyway, Frank and I got along very, very well after that. That established a kind of equality, and when I explained why we couldn't do what he wanted to do—which made sense to him—he understood that I knew what I was talking about.

The preproduction of that film went on for months. It was the most glorious time of my life. Here I was, this young kid, and Frank and I'd have lunch every day at Romanoff's. All the people in the cast came in to see him, one at a time. I got to meet Edward G. Robinson, spend a weekend with Sinatra at his house. Everyone worshipped Capra, and I did too. It was just a beautiful experience.

Again, I was brought into all the decisions, even the technical decisions. In those days, unlike now, Capra would take the sneak previews to many different places. I was always there with him. He had tape recorders set up all over the theater, so he could find out where the laughs were and how long they were, and if they were too long and overcutting another line, we'd leave room for them.

Did you have any sense of him winding down in his career?

I loved the man. I really loved him. He was a sweet, wonderful man. I saw him by accident a few years before his death on the street in San Francisco. We hugged each other and started to cry. We went in somewhere and had coffee and started to reminisce. He still remembered the time and everything that had happened.

But he told me, while we were still in preproduction, that he was thinking of quitting. Because he got on the set one day and could not think of a piece of business in how to stage a scene. He found himself in desperation going back to a piece of business that he had used in a previous film. He decided he had to get out. He felt he couldn't do the job anymore.

How did you feel about the film when it was finished?

The first time I saw the film put together I was mortified. It was so god-damn sentimental that it was nauseating to me. I was embarrassed. I'm still embarrassed. What a metamorphosis! It had started as the Lee Strasberg ver-sion—all art—suffering and pain and heat. It turned out to be Frank Capra's *A Hole in the Head.* Joke, joke, joke, yuk, yuk, yuk. A hell of a metamorphosis. (*Laughs.*)

Even though you were partly to blame? After all, you had been integrally involved in developing the screenplay with Capra.

Yes. But I didn't know how truly sentimental it was until I saw it all put together. When I saw dailies, I might cringe at certain takes; but I thought, "Oh, I'm sure that will be cut out." But Frank didn't cut things out. He just piled it on. Even today, it's running constantly on television, and people will come up to me and tell me how they loved it and cried during it—and I'm thinking, "How is that possible? Are they just being nice? Why bring it up at all?"

Did Capra have the same reaction as you?

No. He thought it was marvelous. In fact, he came to me to write his next movie, about Apple Annie—*Pocketful of Miracles.** I just said no, I couldn't do it. Of course, I couldn't tell him the real reason. I just said it wasn't my kind of thing.

You weren't honest with him?

No.

How about working with Anthony Mann on Cimarron? *Was Mann in a class with Cukor and Capra?*

No. Not at all. He was a nice, sweet man, but I got the feeling he was sort of burned out. The whole film was a disaster. The studio was a mess. The head of the studio was in danger of being fired. There was a lot of tension; the pic-ture was costing too much; and we couldn't get the script right. It was a badly

---

* Hal Kanter and Harry Tugend ended up adapting the script, which was a remake of Capra's 1933 film *Lady for a Day,* based on a Robert Riskin screenplay.

written script. I take my share of the credit. I didn't mean it to be bad, but it was one of those things you get sucked up into.

Was Anthony Mann literate at all?

Oh, he was a nice man. He wasn't literate the way, say, Garson Kanin is literate, but neither was Capra. Cukor was literate.

Was he helpful with script problems?

No. I don't remember talking to him at all about the script.

Why did you even do the film?

It sounded fascinating. I always wanted to do a western, and Anthony Mann was a big-scale western director.

Was Edna Ferber around at all for script discussions?

No, and I destroyed her book [*Cimarron* (Garden City, N.Y.: Doubleday, 1930)]. I regret it. I hope she'll one day forgive me in another life. I didn't mean to. We were just trying to solve the problems of the picture. But once we were given the cast, Glenn Ford and Maria Schell—what the hell was she doing in an Edna Ferber story?—what could we do? We were dead from that moment on.

You had just had some rather dubious writing experiences in Hollywood, yet you ultimately turned your back on Broadway and continued to write motion pictures. Why?

Believe me, I regret that decision now. I regret it bitterly. The movies may not have been great, but the experiences, especially with Cukor and Capra, were wonderful. When I went back to New York and did a Broadway musical [*Jennie*] with Mary Martin, the experience was a nightmare. The play was hideous. There was tension all the time, and nobody was talking to each other. So I said, "Screw this. I don't need this." I wanted to go back to Hollywood, where it was fun. Broadway was traditionally where the playwright was king, but in this situation, Hollywood treated me better.

It was in Hollywood that, at least in the beginning, I was treated like a playwright. So I came back here and had marvelous experiences throughout the sixties, especially with *Love with the Proper Stranger* and *Goodbye, Columbus*.

Your experience was the opposite of most writers—you felt you got more respect from Hollywood than Broadway.

Exactly. Until things changed. Gradually, in the early seventies, there was a change. That's when the writer became the Hollywood nigger. When you look back, that is when the movies started being taken over by conglomerates. Then you got businessmen who didn't know what they were talking about. Up until that time, everybody [in Hollywood] knew the movie business—every inch of it. Everyone knew everything they had to know; and after that, nobody knew anything they had to know but acted like they did, and they demanded you do what you knew was wrong.

Now the writer doesn't get any respect. You are treated like a hired hand, worse, like dirt. It is like: The toilet is clogged up. Unclog it and please get out as fast as you can and try not to track up the rug.

*   *   *

I know from reading David Brown's autobiography, Let Me Entertain You, *that you had at least one* not-*marvelous experience in Hollywood in the* six-ties, *working with Cukor again, this time on the last, never-completed Marilyn Monroe picture,* Something's Got to Give.

I haven't read David's book, but I've been told he said I wore a kimono and sat on the floor when I wrote. Clearly, I was crazy, so he fired me. I still wear a kimono and sit on the floor when I write, and lots of people think I'm crazy—maybe I am—but David and I recall the situation differently.

Actually, I quit. Cukor wanted me because we had such a good experience on the Magnani picture, but when I found out what they were doing to Marilyn, I quit. They were setting her up. A guy from the advertising business named Peter Levathes had come in as head of the studio, having taken over from [Spyros] Skouras, who was kicked out, as I recall, because *Cleopatra* [1963] went so much over budget. Levathes had to prove himself a hero. He had to prove he wouldn't take any shit from any star. He wanted to humiliate Marilyn into quitting and then sue her, I was told.

You were Marilyn's friend?

From way back. I met her when she first left Hollywood and came to join the Actors Studio. I got a call one night from Lee Strasberg, and he said, "I've got two tickets to a poetry reading at the Y. I can't go. Will you take the person I'm supposed to go with?" I said, "Sure." I had no idea it was Marilyn until she opened the door. This was at the peak of her fame. I didn't have a car or anything, so we had to catch a cab. We got mobbed. We finally got to the Y. I'm thinking, "Why does she want to go to the Y? Why didn't Lee tell me who I was going with?" And, of course, the program couldn't go on, because everybody left their seats to catch a glimpse of her. We escaped through a side door and ran up the street with a mob chasing us, and finally wound up on 125th Street in a dinky Chinese restaurant I knew about. That's how I met her, and we became good friends.

What was her condition at the time when you were working on the script? Was she deteriorating, as everybody has written?

I didn't see any of that. When I was with her, she was bright, warm and loving, and in good shape.

She wasn't demanding?

Not at all.

She was on time for everything?

She didn't have to be on time. This wasn't even preproduction. I hadn't written a word. But her agent would call and request things—I remember one thing in particular—and Fox would deliberately say no, doing everything to make her quit. She wanted her regular hairdresser, I remember. No—she couldn't have her regular hairdresser. Whatever she wanted, the rule was, she couldn't have it. Gradually, it became clearer and clearer what was going on—and then I overheard conversations about it between the executives.

As soon as I realized it, I went ape. I think I grabbed David Brown, who is about two feet taller than I am, and shook him against the wall; if not, I wanted to, which is probably closer to the truth. I called Marilyn and told her. She understood what was happening, but there was nothing she could do about it.

You think they succeeded beyond their wildest dreams—driving her to her death?

It's not that cut and dried. But they certainly didn't contribute to her will to live.

Cukor was party to this?

He knew about it.

That's shocking.

The whole thing was shocking to me. She asked me to come back and write the picture and be on her side. I told her I was on her side, and that is why I got out of it. I told her *she* had to get out of it. "If I go back," I told her, "I'm powerless." I have terrible guilt about that experience, still. Terrible guilt. The lingering feeling, however irrational, that if I had gone back, I might have made a difference, and she might still be alive today.

How did Love with the Proper Stranger *evolve?*

It was difficult to sell the idea: In order to escape her family, a young virgin has sex with a stranger and gets pregnant. She looks up the guy afterwards, and during the course of trying to arrange an abortion, they fall in love. People said, "Are you crazy? What kind of love story is that?"

I pitched it around, but nobody would do it. So I said, "Screw everybody. I'm going to write it anyway." At that time, my normal procedure was to do a pitch, not write anything. To me, the idea of a treatment or an outline is ludicrous. You can't write [in an outline], "Here is where there will be a hilarious scene . . ." You have to *write* a hilarious scene. What really drives me nuts is this whole new trend where everything is a cross between this and that. Everything is pitched as a cross between *Stars Wars* and *Wuthering Heights.* That's why I don't go to the movies at all. Occasionally, I'll watch a few minutes of a movie on cable. That's about all I can take. If enough people I respect tell me there is a picture I'll like, I'll go. Otherwise, I don't want most of today's films in my head, because I'll start thinking, "Maybe I should do a cross between this and that," and everything will become derivative.

Anyway, [my agent] Abe Lastfogel believed in the idea. He got Natalie Wood first and sold the script to Paramount. He wanted Warren Beatty because Natalie and Warren were living together, but Warren wouldn't do it. Then he got [Alan J.] Pakula and [Robert] Mulligan, who had just won the Oscar for *To Kill a Mockingbird.* Pakula and Mulligan plus Natalie was fine, so the studio said, "For the other part, let's take a chance on this new kid, [Steve] McQueen."

Why did you think the film turned out so well?

We did it like a play. I was involved like a playwright all the way through. There was mutual respect. Rehearsals on the set, everything. In fact, some of the best scenes in *Love with the Proper Stranger* and *Goodbye, Columbus* were written in rehearsal, just as you would in a play. I would see something and say, "Gee, we need another scene there." I'd write the scene in a corner, give it to the director, and we'd put it in.

McQueen put up with rehearsals?

It may have been his first big picture—I'm not sure—but he certainly wasn't a big star. I didn't pay much attention to him. As I remember, he asked me during the course of filming if I might want to set up a company with him and make other movies. I remember thinking, "Why would I want to set up a company with *him?*" (*Laughs.*) He was very nice and cooperative.

Tell me about The Night They Raided Minsky's. *What happened there?*

I don't know. I got replaced—to my surprise. When I left [after finishing the script], they gave me a party, and I thought the script was all settled. The next thing I knew, another writer was on the film. He added the character of a gangster, I think. I don't know why. I later learned—from a book by the editor Ralph Rosenblum[*]—that they had trouble assembling the film, and that the editor put it together by intersplicing footage from old, silent films. So large sections are things that I wrote, but I had nothing to do with what made the film special—the addition of archival footage—and I wasn't there for the shooting.

Was it just a job for hire? Was it a personality conflict between you and the director, William Friedkin?

I never met Friedkin. I still have never met him.

How did you get involved in Goodbye, Columbus?

Stanley Jaffe and I knew each other casually. Stanley was only twenty-eight years old at the time and had never produced a film. By now I was really flying high, with one Academy [Award] nomination. Stanley came to me and said, "I don't have any money. Will you do this picture for scale, and we'll work out some percentage deal?" I read it and said, "Sure." It was altogether a perfectly wonderful experience from beginning to end.

Why?

Again, because we worked together, like a play—me and [the director] Larry Peerce and the cast and Stanley. In particular, I remember what I think was one of the most affecting scenes in the film—the scene at the wedding where she was feeling guilty about having slept with a guy at her house, and she and her father go off and have a conversation in the corner, and he tells her he loves her and will buy her a mouton coat. I wrote that during rehearsal. I

---

[*]   Ralph Rosenblum and Robert Karen, *When the Shooting Stops . . . the Cutting Begins* (New York: Viking, 1979).

"A nice, little story": Richard Benjamin and Ali MacGraw in *Goodbye, Columbus.*

wrote a lot during rehearsal; we did some rewriting after filming, in fact in postproduction and then reshot some stuff.

Did the novelist Philip Roth have anything to do with the script?

Philip took me to Newark and showed me around—the house where this happened and the tennis court where that happened. He filled me in on stuff that wasn't in the story as he wrote it. That was the sum of his involvement.

As I listen to myself now, I realize that all the films which I was involved with intimately from beginning to end were the satisfying ones. By coincidence, and I say this not to be self-serving, those were the good ones, and the rest of them were not as good. Clearly, that suggests that it should be a law, like marriages: Before you get married, you should live together for a year. Before you do a movie together, all the principals should work together for a few months to see if you are going to get along, whether you respect each other.

Did you have any special identification or empathy with the material? Does that have anything to do with why you might stick with a project longer, or why it might work out better in the long run?

No. As a matter of fact, I thought *Goodbye, Columbus* was just a nice, little story. When I first saw the rough cut of the movie, I thought it didn't work, and that it was merely okay. I remember thinking, "I'm *glad* it's not funny. It's almost better that it's not funny." Of course, it turned out to be a huge comedy. (*Laughs.*) I think I had, like, 7½ percent of the gross, which turned out to be a tremendous amount of money at the time. That's when [Charles] Bluhdorn from Gulf and Western took over Paramount, and everything was in chaos at the studio. So, as a result of that picture, his first picture at age twenty-eight, Stanley Jaffe was made president of Paramount Pictures. Astonishing!

Do you have any particular interest in abortion? To Find a Man *is also about abortion—the second film, after* Love with the Proper Stranger *in your filmography to touch on that subject.*

I got seduced into *To Find a Man*. Ray Stark is the most seductive, irresistible louse in the world. I used to love him, but he is a louse. I loved him, even though he screwed me outrageously time after time. Now I despise him. There were all kinds of carrots that he dangled in front of me to get me to do that script—including directing—things which are too complicated to go into. I won't even go into the disaster aspects of that film, but we parted with me saying, "Go fuck yourself, you prick! I never want to see you again." Afterwards, I was off in India, and I spot a guy running towards me, way off in the distance. He runs and runs and finally reaches me with a cablegram, and it is from Ray: "Are you interested in writing a sequel?" (*Laughs.*) I wrote him a long, long cable, saying, "Go fuck yourself!"

Cut to years later. I had never met Max Shulman. We had lived near each other in Westport, where I would always get his laundry, [and] he got my mail. Then we lived near each other out here—I would get his wine, he would get my groceries. But I had never met him. On a picket line during the big writers' strike, I noticed him, and went over and introduced myself and said, "Even if you have to lie, just say yes to this, Does anyone ever congratulate you for something I did?"—because I was always getting congratulations for something that *he* did. Then he told me this funny story: "When Ray Stark couldn't get you for the sequel [to *To Find a Man*], he called me . . ." The sequel never got made, but he did get paid for working on it. So one Shulman was as good as another to Ray Stark! (*Laughs.*)

Tell me about Funny Lady.

Ray talked me into it. I had sworn never to work with him again. Suddenly, I was at the Beverly Hills Hotel, working on *Funny Lady*. But I blew it. I ran out of steam or something. Jay Presson Allen came in and deserves most of the credit. She rewrote almost all of it, and the funny part about it is that the Guild kept giving me more and more credit. I wasn't doing anything to claim credit; it was an automatic arbitration. We had to write a letter saying what we had done on the script. After the first credits were awarded and I was given credit, Ray was adamant about giving all the credit to Jay Presson Allen and had his lawyer appeal the arbitration; then the Guild came back and gave me *additional* credit. It became a joke. I sent Ray a telegram: "Appeal one more time, and I'll get a 'written-directed-and-produced-by' credit." I'm embarrassed really, because most of it was her screenplay.

You had long stretches of not writing in the 1970s.

I just stopped. I started traveling and went into my own private world. I've always had this unusual pattern: When I'm here working on a script—I know some writers work two or four hours a day, whatever—I work all the time. That's all I do. I don't go out of the house. I don't do anything else. I work day and night, take a nap, and go back to work, until it's done—whether it's three to four months. The minute it's done, I lock the house up and go to another country. Preferably a primitive country—the Amazon, living with the cannibals in New Guinea, lots of time in India. I used to go every year for a month to a Zen monastery in Japan. I don't know why, whether I was searching or what. I only know the superficial reasons: The so-called primitive people are very exciting. It is literal time travel. I can step off a jet and a day or two later be in the Stone Age, literally—with people who use stone axes and spears. They are much more civilized than the people in the movie industry, who use loopholes and lies instead of spears.

Whenever I finished the writing, I used to go on one of these adventures. But the other part of the pattern is that right after one of these adventures, I would head straight to Claridge's in London. I would go from the Stone Age to silk pajamas. I would recoup at Claridge's and then come back and start over again.

Except I realize I did take almost the entire decade of the seventies off. I got disgusted with the way things were going, what was happening, the kinds of movies that were being done, and the way writers were being treated. So I took a trip that led to another trip and another, and suddenly I realized it was the eighties. I came back twice to get enough money to continue traveling.

One was Won Ton Ton, the Dog Who Saved Hollywood*?*

The story of how I got involved with that is too long and stupid to go into. To tell the truth would sound self-serving—the perpetual complaint of writers who get publicly flogged for what the owner of the plantation did. All we're supposed to say is: "Feets don't fail me now!"

At any rate, not only did David Picker, the producer, have every word of the script rewritten, but he hired Michael Winner, the director of all the Charles Bronson *Death Wish* pictures, to "realize" the film, as the post–*Cahiers du Cinéma* directors like to put it. It was written by me as a satire, written by God-knows-who as a slapstick farce, and directed with all the charm and wit of a chain-saw massacre. I had nothing to do with the final picture, and on that one, I was not only listed as cowriter but also as executive producer, and I couldn't get my name off! (*Laughs.*)

Both *Won Ton Ton* and *Players* were totally rewritten from scratch. I had nothing to do with either of them. Nothing. Not a word. They haunt me to this day. Just seeing wonton on a menu in a Chinese restaurant makes me want to throw up.

The other one was Players.

Finally, after all the years, it was a great triumph to me; I got in my contract all of the Dramatist Guild guarantees: I had approval of the director, not a word [of the script] could be changed without my consent, and so forth. Immediately after I finished the screenplay, [the producer] Bob Evans sent me on a wild goose chase to Rome to cast a part he had already cast—I found out months later—with Max Schell. When I got back, I found out that six or seven writers were working on different versions of the script, all at the same time with none of them knowing about the other. Then the company went to Mexico [for the filming], and I couldn't get Evans to show me the dailies. I said, "Bob, you have no right to do this. Look at your contract." He said, "Sue me!" That was the end of that. I had these things in writing, and they meant nothing!

So you sued him?

I did sue him. But I couldn't take my name off the screen. You can't take your name off the screen if you're paid a certain amount of money, unless the studio agrees beforehand—and they're *not* going to agree, because if word gets out the writer took his name off, the picture gets a bad name.

Can't you take a pseudonym?

You can—if you have that clause in your contract in the first place. That's one thing I didn't have in my contract. It never occurred to me that I would be double-crossed.

Is any of Players *your script?*

Not at all. Not a word. But I got the credit, the money, and even the credit of executive producer once again, and from the outside, it looks as though I was totally in charge. I ran a full-page ad in *Daily Variety* and the *Hollywood Reporter* when *Players* came out. On the left side of the ad, I quoted all the major critics, just what they said about the screenplay: "This is the worst script I've ever seen in my life . . ." or "The garbage Arnold Schulman has written . . ." They all mentioned me! The last quote at the bottom of the page was from *L.A. Magazine:* "Bob Evans is particularly proud of his new picture *Players.* It involves the two things he loves best in life, Ali MacGraw and tennis, and as a consequence, he rewrote every word of Arnold Schulman's script." Then in very tiny letters at the bottom of the page: "This ad paid for by the friend"—*friend,* singular!—"of Arnold Schulman and the Society of Battered and Abused Screenwriters." Everybody laughed, and I didn't work for three years.

That must have been really painful.

Not really. I was in my traveling mode . . . until *A Chorus Line.*

I gather that was also a messy situation.

The strange thing about this one is that for years, writer after writer tried to find a way to turn the musical into a movie, and nobody could. Finally, I came up with a surrealistic approach that [the producers] Norman Lear and Jerry

Perenchio must have liked, because they put up twenty-four million dollars of their own money to make it. Richard Attenborough must have liked it, because he agreed to direct it; but for reasons known only to him, Attenborough threw away the script completely and tried to photograph the play.

In addition to this disastrous decision was a set of circumstances nobody could have coped with. After Lear and Perenchio put up the money and the picture was being made, they sold their company to Columbia, and Columbia wanted nothing to do with *A Chorus Line.* So every single element was fighting with every other element, and all the pressure landed on Attenborough. Columbia versus Embassy versus the two producers; everybody disagreeing with each other about the casting, this and that, about everything. How Attenborough survived it, I have no idea, but he is the most decent man in the world, a truly warm, intelligent, beautiful human being.

I'll always remember one meeting we had with the producers over the results of the screen tests; we were going make the final decision as to who would be the leading lady. The meeting was at the Regency Hotel in New York. I offered my opinion, and one of the producers said, "Who asked you? You have nothing to do with this. Go to your room!" "Go to your room"? Like a little kid. I was stunned. I said, "You're right; it's none of my business," and I left. Attenborough had to leave the next morning on the Concorde to go back to London for some reason, and on his way to the plane, early in the morning—he is so sweet and thoughtful—he called me and told me what happened at the meeting after I left and thanked me for my suggestion. In contrast to the asshole producer.

When we had the first preview in San Diego, the list [of invited guests] came back, and my name wasn't on the list. My agent thought it was a mistake and called up one of the executives, another one of the producers. This producer said, "He's the *writer. Writers* don't go to previews." My agent called Attenborough, who got angry and called them on my behalf. "What the hell are they talking about? Of course, he's going to the preview!" What a putdown—*Won Ton,* the *Players,* and now this!

What a horrible litany of experiences.

We're living in a madhouse here. If they take your script, you have to pray the director will understand it, the actors won't fuck it up, they won't throw another writer in, they'll merchandise it okay . . . there are a hundred thousand things that can go wrong, and barely one thing that can go right. The odds are so much against making a movie. Making a good movie is worse odds. Making a great movie is virtually impossible.

Yet you've spent your entire career as a writer for hire.

Yeah, and I hate myself for it. I really do. The sixties were great. From then on, it's been downhill.

You could have made different choices a long time ago.

I know. I regret it bitterly.

*   *   *

I understand that, dating back to the 1960s, you have been doing some script doctoring under the table.

It's interesting work. I never take credit for it.

Isn't doctoring scripts a little bit like selling your soul?

No, it's preserving yourself. You're doing it for the sake of the work, which is pure Zen. There's a purity about it. Either I would like to doctor and stay anonymous, or have complete mutual collaboration. The in-between is where it's awful. In any case, I've never taken any money for doctoring.

Most people do it purely for the money.

I do it as a friend, and I won't do it *unless* as a friend. If somebody comes to me and I like the material and I see how I can make a contribution, I'll do it. But I don't take any money for it. And I won't work on a script behind the back of another writer. Many times, I've turned work down because the first writer on the project was a friend of mine.

Can you tell me which are the better-known films you doctored?

There was one giant hit I was involved with in the 1960s—just as a friend. And there were other films of more or less merit. But I don't want to give titles. As I say, I don't take any money, and I don't want any credit.

In Hollywood, taking no money and no credit, that must be regarded with great suspicion.

I'm sure everybody thinks I'm crazy. Ask David Brown. I don't care what they think. I have to live with myself. When I turn in a script—this must have happened a dozen times over the years—and they say, "Well, here's my notes," I have been known to say, "I don't want to do any of your notes." They say, "Well, you've got to do our notes . . ." I say, "No, I don't. I'll give you your money back. Let's tear the script up. If you don't like what I do, I don't want your money." The one thing I make clear is, give me my script back.

That brings us to Tucker.

Thank God for *Tucker.* That saved my sanity.

How were you brought in on Tucker*?*

Curiously, I got a phone call from Francis Coppola, who I had met only once on an airplane. He told me all about [the 1940s automobile visionary Preston] Tucker, whom I had never heard of. I told him I hated cars. "I would like to work with you, Francis," I said, "but I *really* hate cars." He said, "Will you meet with me and George Lucas, and talk about it?"

Why was Coppola so insistent about having you?

I don't know. I assume it is because I had worked with Frank Capra, and he wanted it to be a Capraesque picture. George said, "The film is not about cars. It's about Francis. Why don't you go live with Francis in Napa for a few weeks and then let me know?" I did that, and then I realized of course the film was about Francis, and told them I'd love to do it. I had to endure all the car bull-

"That saved my sanity": Jeff Bridges in *Tucker,* directed by Francis Coppola.

shit for the character—who was Francis. That part [of the concept] didn't come off too well because of the casting.

I was told by producer Fred Roos that all along they were thinking of Jack Nicholson in the starring role.

They talked about Jack Nicholson. I just assumed it was going to be Harrison Ford. When we got to that point, both proved too expensive.[*]

Did Coppola, himself an excellent writer, make script contributions?

Extremely valuable contributions. [He might say,] "There's a hole here, we need to fill this in. . . ," or "I've found this actual Tucker promo; see if you can weave it in . . ."

In a way, Coppola makes modernist movies, but on the other hand, he's a throwback to an old-fashioned way of screen storytelling.

Absolutely. He's a wonderful person. It drives me crazy that the idealists willing to take risks get knocked on their asses, while the safe guys—who do the movies that make all the money, and who have all the power—get none of the aggravation.

Tucker was a wonderful experience. Suddenly, it was back to the old days, working closely with Francis and being on the set, watching him direct and talking about scenes. Not a line was changed. I was there for rehearsals and had to leave for a while; then I came back when he was shooting; I tiptoed up to the script supervisor, because Francis is so notorious for improvising, and

---

[*] Jeff Bridges ended up playing Tucker.

said, "Just break it to me gently—what did he do with the script?" She said, "I've been working with him for *x* number of pictures, and I've never seen this happen before. An actor will ask, 'Can I try the line this way?' and he'll think for a minute, then answer, 'Well, why don't you do it the way it's written?' " I went up to Francis and said, "Francis, you're ruining your reputation. Why are you doing this?" I'm sorry, this sounds self-serving—I should have told it in a different way—but he said something to me that not many people in this town understand: "A hundred hacks can rewrite another hack, and nobody'll know the difference; but one good writer cannot rewrite another good writer because their rhythms are different."

They don't know that in Hollywood. They don't know about rhythms. They know how it says on page 26 of all these books about how to write a screenplay that you have to have a turning point. I myself don't know what the hell a turning point is. When I heard about a turning point in a meeting for the first time, I said, "What the hell are you talking about?" They told me that in the books on how to write a screenplay, they all say that on page 26, or whatever, you have to have a turning point.

The making of *Tucker* was marvelous. I loved what Francis did with the script. We knew it was a gamble—that a lot of people wouldn't get it; that we were doing some things deliberately, bad thirties acting and speeded-up [action]. But it is exactly what we set out to do. I love that movie.

Who is the credited cowriter, David Seidler?

Out of nowhere—I was in Venice or some place—I got a call from my secretary that this guy Seidler was suing for credit. I had never *heard* of him before. I didn't even take it seriously; I just dictated a little note about how I wrote the script. When I got back, I found out that he had been given cowriting credit. I was never allowed a rebuttal to the Writers Guild.

It turns out that ten years earlier, he had been hired as a research guy [on the project], and he had asked Francis, "Do you mind if I put the whole thing in screenplay form?" Francis said, "No, of course, go ahead, kid." His script started with Tucker at six years old and included every detail of the man's life until the day he died. Since it was a real-life story, obviously there were going to be incidents similar to those in my script—like Abe Lincoln: if ten writers write different scripts about Abe Lincoln, in all of them there's going to be a wife named Mary and a Civil War, and Abe's going to get shot in the end. This business of giving Seidler credit shocked me. The worst part of it is, when the film was coming out, I was helping out with publicity and speaking somewhere to some class of would-be screenwriters, and all they were interested in was how did the other guy steal the credit? Could *they* steal a credit? How?

At the opposite end of that type of crazy situation is Jay Presson Allen and *Funny Lady*, where I couldn't persuade the Guild to give her the credit she deserved, or films like *Won Ton Ton* and *Players*—where, no matter what, I wasn't permitted to take my name off the screen. Believe me, I was pissed off about the credit grabbing on *Tucker*. I'm still pissed off. That is one instance where every word of the script *is* mine.

I'm struck by how few writers who were here when you first came to Hollywood, in 1956, are still around and active.

Almost none. I don't know why. There's no sense of community out here, at least for me. I don't know if there ever was in Hollywood that marvelous sense of community which there was in New York when I was starting out. I miss that terribly. Probably it's me. I don't belong anywhere. I have not integrated myself into the movie community or the theater community or the writer community. I don't stay put long enough, I guess. I have realized only recently that everybody here in California thinks I live in New York, and everybody in New York thinks I live in California. Usually I'm not in either place. I've got this house mainly as a home for my books.

You never actually moved to California?

Never. At first I always lived in the East. I'd come out here to do the work and go back. Now I do the work and head for another country.

You made the decision to work in movies, but—

I still didn't want to live here.

Why is that?

The usual answer. I prefer cities where I can walk on the streets and see people. Where, if I feel like going out at three in the morning for a sandwich, I can do that. All the cliché reasons. And when I'm not working, I'm traveling. That's my other life. As a consequence, I really have become the outsider— that little boy who didn't have patches on his overalls. I realized not long ago that my life has come full circle.

Around the time of Goodbye, Columbus *you were flirting with becoming a director. What stopped you?*

I haven't had a hit since then. If I had a hit, I would have had the clout to go in and say, "If you want my next one, I direct it."

If Goodbye, Columbus *was your last hit, how have you survived financially?*

There have been hot streaks where I've had enough to live on and spent it all, but fortunately, I've always been able to command a good price. My son worries about me all the time. But my analogy to him is: Just imagine that I'm a yacht salesman. All I have to do is sell one yacht every three years, and I'll be fine. I'm not selling chewing gum.

I have been writing a movie of *And the Band Played On,* the book about AIDS by Randy Shilts. I should say I wrote it as a movie, but it will be produced by HBO for cable. The intention is that it become one of their event pictures. Incidentally, my name is on the project as coproducer, and I made it clear I didn't want that to be in name only, only if I could actually function in that capacity. I did the script for virtually no money—which I donated, and I don't have the money to donate. I wanted it to be a pure experience.

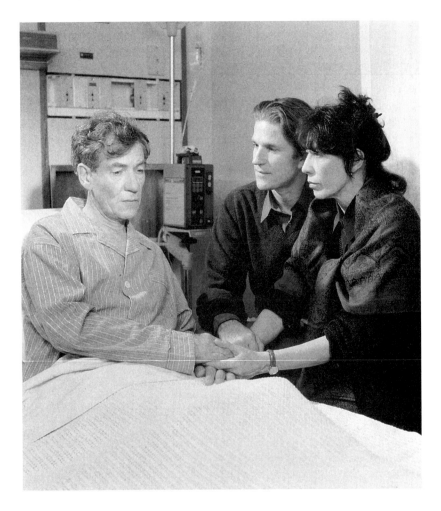

"A pure experience": from left, Ian McKellen, Matthew Modine, and Lily Tomlin in the telefilm *And the Band Played On*. Adapted from Randy Shilts' book.

What I thought would take two months of time has taken almost two years of my life, so far. One director came and went—I won't go into all the ugliness—then another director. I worked with the new director day and night, rewriting. Then another director came along and another director.* One director wouldn't even talk to me. The irony is, this is one thing I have done for

---

* *And the Band Played On* was eventually directed by Roger Spottiswoode.

altruistic reasons, as an indictment against greed, ego, and bureaucracy, and I have gone through a nightmare of greed, ego, and bureaucracy while doing the picture. It's taken so long [so far] that I have to flagellate myself to go back to work on it. But it will happen.

I've got a number of spec scripts that I really want to do, all of them in various stages. Wherever you look in this house, you'll see a pad and a pen—in the bedroom, the toilet, wherever. If I get an idea, I immediately write it down. Each project is in a cardboard box, and I just throw the idea in the box. When I get some time and the inclination to work on this one instead of that one, I do. It's hard to say which is going to be first.

If they don't sell, I'll definitely switch careers. I would go into novels now if I could afford it. As a novelist, I have no track record. I've written two based on the movies of *A Hole in the Head* and *Love with the Proper Stranger,* and I've written one nonfiction book about an Indian holy man that Viking published [*Baba* (New York: Viking, 1971)]. Any of these spec scripts, if they don't work, would make a good novel. I'll just do doctoring and write novels, because novels are yours. Good or bad, they're *yours.*

If it's not going to be fun, there's no point writing scripts anymore. I can't even watch today's movies—how can I write them? I would rather be living with the cannibals in New Guinea than sitting here writing scripts in this monastery. Although the euphoria, when you're doing well and you're in that extradimensional place—nothing can top that—that's a high that no drug, sex, or food can beat. Just as nothing beats the agonies when it's going awful.

Stirling Silliphant:
The Finger of God

Interview by Nat Segaloff

An admiring television producer, speaking to *Time* magazine in 1963, called writer Stirling Silliphant "almost inhuman. He is a writing machine. Any man who has been in this business for as long as I have can only see him as one of the fingers of God."*

Little has changed since the mid-1950s. For over four decades, Stirling Silliphant has been one of the most prolific—and, more importantly, most *produced*—screenwriters since Ben Hecht. The Writers Guild of America lists over two hundred television and screen credits for him, most of them solo, many of which he also produced. He has written six novels and scores of newspaper and magazine articles. And this isn't even counting the dozens of completed scripts for feature films, movies of the week, and television pilots that were abandoned after he delivered completed scripts to mercurial producers but that were never used. "I have two careers," he once lamented. "I write for the studio and I write for the shelf. I have at least 15 scripts on the shelf that will probably never be made into films."†

Born in Detroit, Michigan, on January 16, 1918, Silliphant at age seven moved with his family to Glendale, California. At Glendale Hoover High School and later at the University of Southern California, where he graduated magna cum laude, he wrote part-time for the *Los Angeles Post* and *Los Angeles Times*. After graduation, he left journalism to take a publicity job with the Walt Disney studios. In 1942, he moved to New York to do publicity for 20th

---

* The other four "fingers"—writer-producers responsible for the top five network shows— were Paul Henning of *The Beverly Hillbillies,* Nat Hiken of *Car 54, Where Are You?*, Rod Serling of *The Twilight Zone,* and Reginald Rose of *The Defenders* (*Time* [August 9, 1963]).

† *Women's Wear Daily* (December 18, 1974).

Century-Fox, becoming an assistant to Fox's then-president, Spyros Skouras. World War II service as a lieutenant junior grade attached to the Naval Air Service, handling special events and public relations, interrupted his studio career, but he returned to Fox at the war's end to become its East Coast advertising-publicity director. He finally left in 1953 to produce independently *The Joe Louis Story* for United Artists release.

Impatience with the producing process led him into scriptwriting. After some early success, he encountered a different kind of frustration: development deals. When three of his screenplays were bought but not filmed, he railed in the trade papers about the waste "that destroys your whole reason to work."* After a script of his finally *did* get made—the pilot episode for television's *Naked City*—it pulled him away from features and into television.

For the rest of the decade, Silliphant contributed to virtually every television anthology produced at that time, winning high regard for his crisp style and caring, human themes. He was also fast, often turning out scripts in a matter of days. Truth to tell, the inspiration was often economic; in the 1950s, a half-hour teleplay fetched only $500 to $750 instead of today's standard of nearly $14,000.

Yet Silliphant admits he savors his achievements less and less as the industry changes; by his own count, the slick stuff gets made more readily than the personal work. Like all Hollywood writers, he wears his scars like a map of hell: he is still bleeding from the network sabotage of his deeply felt *Fly Away Home,* a 1981 pilot for a year-long television series about the Vietnam experience told from both sides.

Nevertheless, Silliphant is amazingly free of rancor; perhaps the sheer size of his résumé cushions the disappointment. For example, from 1960 to 1964, while he was writing most of *Route 66,* he was also heavily contributing to the series *Naked City* and accepting freelance assignments (*Checkmate, Mr. Lucky, GE Theater,* etc.). He soon became known as someone who never turned anything down—a dangerous reputation despite the income it generated.

In 1965, he made a renewed bid for feature films with *The Slender Thread,* a drama about suicide, whose financial failure almost knocked him back into the PR racket. Fortunately, a new agent came along and with him the opportunity to adapt a short mystery novel about a black detective who works with a white sheriff to solve a murder in the racist South, *In the Heat of the Night.* The rest is, well, like something out of a movie.

For the next twenty years Silliphant was connected with some of Hollywood's most successful pictures, such as *Charly, The Poseidon Adventure, The Towering Inferno, Shaft, The New Centurions,* and *The Enforcer,* as well as some of its most notorious: *Over the Top, When Time Ran Out,* and *The Swarm.*

---

* Stirling Silliphant, interview, *Film Daily* (December 23, 1965).

He also entered—and quickly dominated—the movie of the week and television miniseries (*Mussolini: The Untold Story,* James Michener's *Space, Travis McGee,* etc.). It's safe to say that the last twenty years have seen movies descend from the relevant period of the late sixties and early seventies into a less personal, more commercial direction. But in an industry that craves naive, movie-bred youth, the worldly Silliphant remains in heavy demand.

This hasn't been accidental: hyphenate (writer-producer) that he is, Silliphant engineered it. In 1988, he and his family emigrated to Bangkok, Thailand, which he gleefully reported is "well distanced from the eel pit which is the Hollywood I have forever and always departed." Productive as ever, he is balancing a twelve-volume writing commitment to Ballantine Books (the John Locke sailor-of-fortune adventure novels) with screenwriting (*The Flying Aces* for the Showtime cable network, a remake of *Forbidden Planet,* and adapting Truman Capote's *The Grass Harp,* among other recent jobs), as well as a full social schedule. Typical of his efficient, almost compulsive, work ethic, (and with travel in either direction being impractical) he suggested conducting this interview around the world via fax machine. Whatever the number of questions or however specific were the answers they required, Silliphant would invariably respond within a few hours with the kind of detail and openness that demonstrates why he has remained at the top of his craft for four decades.

Silliphant began writing during what is now wistfully called the Golden Age of Television when *Naked City, The Defenders, East Side/West Side,* and other topically relevant programs captured admiration, if not always viewers.

"I think a lot of the memory of that period is overrated," he once averred. "A lot of the shows are what I call tenement dramas. If you were to look at them today you would find them particularly naive or pretentious or overly socially conscious."* But Silliphant is selling his legacy short. A screening of dozens of these supposedly pretentious programs reveals, instead, a moving use of language and an openness to honest human feelings that today's glib, plot-driven television dramas almost entirely avoid. Have audiences forgotten how to feel? Or has exploitation replaced compassion?

Silliphant's sympathies clearly reside with emotion. His *Route 66,* for example—for which he wrote an almost unimaginable 73 out of 114 hours over four seasons—chronicles the nation's changing sensibility. The concept was simple—two guys tool through the country in their sports car—yet the interpersonal discoveries they make along the nation's blue highways is worlds removed from the glossy *Dallas, Dynasty, L.A. Law,* or *Beverly Hills 90210* that light the airwaves today—all set, it should be noted, in major cities.

---

* Jurgen Woolf and Kerry Cox, *Successful Screenwriting* (Cincinnati: Writers Digest Books, 1968).

Stirling Silliphant in Bangkok, Thailand. (Courtesy of Stirling Silliphant.)

Silliphant, too, has made journeys, both physical and spiritual. He has been married four times, and he and his second wife, Ednamarie Patella, had two children: a daughter, Dayle, born in 1949, and a son, Loren, born in 1951. In 1969, Loren was shot and killed by Chester Allen Johnson, a convicted murderer who was unaccountably at liberty awaiting yet another murder trial at the time. On July 4, 1974, Silliphant and Tiana Dulong (Thi Thanh Nga) of Saigon were married at Chasen's Restaurant in Beverly Hills. (Their son, Stirling Jr., was born in 1976.) A former student of the martial artist Bruce Lee (for whom he created a famous scene in *Marlowe*), Silliphant follows Buddhist precepts, "within," he explains, "the limits of a still-remaining pragmatic Western orientation."

Like all great storytellers, Silliphant combines spellbinding narrative skills with the ability to remain focused on the dramatic objective. Because of his mammoth output, a title-by-title discussion of his career would fill a book; therefore, this interview concentrates on his significant feature films, early versus recent television work, and a general discussion of craft.

(Silliphant died on April 29, 1996 in Bangkok, Thailand. This was his last interview and has not been changed to reflect his death.)

Stirling Silliphant (1918–1996)

1953   *The Joe Louis Story* (Robert Gordon). Producer, uncredited contribution.

1955   *5 Against the House* (Phil Karlson). Script.

1956   *Huk!* (John Barnwell). Script from Silliphant's novel.
Nightfall (Jacques Tourneur). Script.

1957   *Maracaibo* (Cornel Wilde). Script from Silliphant's novel.
The Lineup (Don Siegel). Script.
Damn Citizen (Robert Gordon). Script.

1960   *Village of the Damned* (Wolf Rilla). Co-script.

1965   *The Slender Thread* (Sidney Pollack). Script.

1967   *In the Heat of the Night* (Norman Jewison). Script.

1968   *Charly* (Ralph Nelson). Script.

1969   *Marlowe* (Paul Bogart). Script.
A Walk in the Spring Rain (Guy Green). Script, Coproducer.
The Liberation of L. B. Jones (William Wyler). Co-script.

1971   *Murphy's War* (Peter Yates). Script.
Shaft (Gordon Parks). Executive producer.

1972   *The Poseidon Adventure* (Ronald Neame). Co-script.
The New Centurions (Richard Fleischer). Script.
Shaft's Big Score (Gordon Parks). Executive producer.

1973   *Shaft in Africa* (John Guillermin). Script.

1974   *The Towering Inferno* (John Guillermin). Script.

1975   *The Killer Elite* (Sam Peckinpah). Co-script.
When Time Ran Out (James Goldstone). Co-script.

1976   *The Enforcer* (James Fargo). Co-script.
Midway (Jack Smight). Uncredited contribution.

1977   *Telefon* (Don Siegel). Co-script.
The Swarm (Irwin Allen). Script.

1978   *Circle of Iron* (Richard Moore). Script.

1979   *Meteor* (Ronald Neame). Uncredited contribution.

1986   *Over the Top* (Menahem Golan). Co-script.

1987   *Catch the Heat* (Joel Silbert). Co-script.

1996   *The Grass Harp* (Charles Matthau). Co-script.

Television credits between 1955 and 1965 include *Route 66* (73 episodes), *Naked City* (35 half-hour episodes; 4 hour episodes), *Alfred Hitchcock Presents* (11 half-hour episodes), *Markham* (6 half-hour episodes), and scripts for *The Mickey Mouse Club, Zane Grey Theater, Suspicion, Chicago Manhunt, Perry Mason, West Point, Ford Theater, Jane Wyman Fireside, Studio 57, Tightrope, Man from Blackhawk, Alcoa-Goodyear Theater, General Electric Theater, Checkmate, Brothers Brannigan, Mr. Lucky, The June Allyson Show, Rawhide, Chrysler Theater, Maya,* and *Longstreet.* Silliphant was also executive producer for the *Maya* and *Longstreet* series.

Scripts, and in some cases production of television pilots, miniseries, and movies of the week, include *Wings of Fire, A World of Love, The New Healers, Movin' On, The First 36 Hours of Dr. Durant, Rodriguez, Pearl, Hardcase, Golden Gate, Fly Away Home, Travis McGee, Welcome to Paradise, Space, Mussolini: The Untold Story, The Three Kings,* and *Sidney Sheldon's "A Stranger in the Mirror."*

Novels include *Maracaibo, The Slender Thread* (under the pseudonym P. J. Merrill), *Pearl, Steel Tiger, Bronze Bell,* and *Silver Star.*

Academy Awards include an Oscar for Best Adapted Screenplay for *In the Heat of the Night.*

Learning the Craft

You've said that while you were working in publicity for 20th Century-Fox, you decided it was time to either write or be unhappy for the rest of your life. If you wanted to be a writer, why did you start out by being a producer?

I never intended to be a screenwriter; since childhood I had aspired to become a novelist and/or a poet. But I found films interesting, since I made my living publicizing them. When I met Joe Louis and learned that I could acquire the rights to his life story, it never occurred to me to write the film, only to produce it [*The Joe Louis Story*]. I hired Robert Sylvester, a friend of mine who was a columnist for the *New York Daily News* and a big fight buff, to write the screenplay. Only when Bob failed to give me some of the scenes I felt were essential to the film, did I step in and write them myself. Later, when I watched the completed movie, I saw that the several scenes I had written were far and away the best ones in the flick—at least to my considerably prejudiced opinion. But, even more, I had discovered the pain of having to sit there and WAIT—as a producer—for the writer to deliver. What the hell, it struck me, why not be the guy everybody's waiting for, rather than the guy who's going crazy waiting?

You've said that you were pressured—even threatened—not to make the film.

Yes, the flack from "friends" of mine, Southern exhibitors, was an eye-opener. They called long distance to tell me I was out of my mind to make my feature debut with a "race" movie. And what was that scene where Manny, Joe's trainer [John Marley], is sitting there with Joe's BLACK daughter on his lap? That's got to go—or it'll never play in OUR theaters.

Was this why one of your backers dropped out?

From the beginning, I never was fully funded. But I went ahead and shot anyway—even while I was still out drumming up money. We got a life-saving infusion halfway into the shoot from one of the few black businessmen who came through for Joe. This gentleman was Harlem's leading abortionist, and obviously business was good uptown.

What was your first screenwriting attempt?

Maracaibo. The year was probably 1952. I was East Coast publicity director for 20th Century-Fox, detesting my job despite the fact that, even in those days, I was being paid five hundred dollars a week, had a department of forty people, assorted assistants, and TWO secretaries. I heard from somebody in publicity at MGM in New York that their studio was looking for a script for Joan Crawford. I got a copy of some of our Fox scripts to see what the physical layout of such work looked like. Then I wrote a romantic story, the Joan Crawford role built around a Pulitzer Prize–winning poetess seeking love in Cuba and in the oil city of Maracaibo, Venezuela. I wrote the script in two weeks, working all night, every night, doing my Fox publicity job in the daytime. Then I rushed the finished script over to MGM to a sort of godfather of mine, Oscar Doob, who was Metro's VP in charge of advertising-publicity, and submitted it to him to send along, if he thought it was worthy, to his studio. He told me he'd be happy to read it, but he knew nothing of the studio looking for a Joan Crawford script; where had I heard that rumor? "From friends in your publicity department," I replied. Right then and there, he called the studio in Culver City. Result: nobody but nobody was either looking for or wanted a script for Joan Crawford, at least at MGM.

So there I was, script in hand, no market. A week later, while at lunch with Roger Straus [of the Farrar, Straus publishing house], I told him the story and joked about my gullibility. "Let me read the script," he suggested. I sent it to him, and the following day, he called to tell me he thought it would translate into a pretty fair novel. Did I know how to write a novel? "Well," I said, "three weeks ago I didn't know how to write a screenplay, so I might as well see if I can't also find out how to write a novel."*

About then, while preparing to produce *The Joe Louis Story,* I quit my job at Fox and moved to Cuba. I rented a house on the beach, a place well outside of Havana—Playa Tarara—and there, working nights only (the days

---

* The screenplay of *Maracaibo* was filmed by the actor-director Cornel Wilde in 1958.

were spent scuba diving), I turned the aborted film script into a novel [*Mara-caibo*] which Farrar, Straus published in 1954, and which my then-agent, Ned Brown, of MCA sold to Universal for what to me in those days was a small fortune—either $37,500 or $47,500. I have the feeling it was probably the lesser figure, but since I could live in Cuba on that much money for three or four years, I had suddenly become RICH. So this is a long answer to your question, how did I learn? I just jumped into the water and swam. I started out writing everything but the sprocket holes, but over time I learned to simplify.

Throughout the 1950s, you were involved with some exciting feature film-makers, particularly Phil Karlson [5 Against the House*], Don Siegel [*The Lineup*], and Jacques Tourneur [*Nightfall*]. Tourneur—uneven though he was—remains a fascinating stylist. He would have been prepping his classic* Curse of the Demon *[1957] while making your film in 1956; was he dis-tracted?*

All I remember of this gentleman was that he seemed much too gentle-manly to be a director. He flits elusively in the remote back country of my recall as a courteous person. He simply showed up on time at Columbia, took my script—which, incidentally, had Anne Bancroft in it—and went out and methodically shot it. If he was distracted—prepping *Curse of the Demon*—I was never aware of it.

The Lineup *is unusual in that it came four years after the debut of the TV series, whose pilot, like the film, was directed by Don Siegel. The few times I spoke with Siegel, I found him modest and gentle despite his reputation as a director of fierce action; his made-for-TV* The Killers *was deemed too rough to be aired. Since you virtually bookended his feature-directing career [for* The Lineup *in 1957 and* Telefon *in 1977], what portrait can you give of the man?*

Your fix on Don Siegel as modest and gentle was also mine. I LOVED the guy, no matter how visceral his action scenes were. I found him immensely competent, in total control of his craft. If Don ever had any doubts about what he was up to, I was never aware of them. If you had fought in a platoon in Vietnam, Don would have been the kind of lieutenant you'd have hoped you were lucky enough to have [had leading] your scared ass.

I was with him in San Francisco on location when he shot *The Lineup*. I remember being somewhat apprehensive about his reaction to my script when it was first given to him. I had created an off-the-wall character—played by Robert Keith, Brian's father — an agent for Eli Wallach, [playing] one of the country's top hit men.

The idea of a killer having an agent appealed to me immensely, since the connection to Hollywood was immediately symbolic. And as Wallach pro-ceeds through my script, blowing people away in successive killings, each time he'd return to the waiting line, the eager agent, Keith, would ask him the inevitable question: "Well, what were their last words?" Keith was an avid collector of such closing statements. Eventually, his insistence on knowing last words provokes his client to shoot him—Wallach is fucking fed up with this philosophic shit. Back in the fifties, this was hardly your average screen-writing, if I can be somewhat immodest; and so I was shaky about Don's reaction. Well, he fucking went out of his mind—hooted with laughter—and shot it all with relish.

You were getting into features about the time the moguls who built the industry—Mayer, Cohn, Warner, Zanuck—were beginning to fade. Do you have any memories of Hollywood at this time in general? And since you made 5 Against the House, Nightfall, *and* The Lineup *at Columbia while Harry Cohn was still alive and screaming, what can you tell me about this legendary son of a bitch? He supposedly personally insisted on casting Kim Novak in* 5 Against the House. *Even with his advanced heart condition, was he still running things when you made your films there?*

I only met Harry Cohn once—in his office. He was courteous and businesslike, but that could be because I was the only goy in the shop and young and wide eyed, and he knew instinctively he could have me for breakfast on the worst day of his life—and so he spared me.

And, yes, he did order us to cast Kim Novak in *5 Against the House.* But who cared? She couldn't act, but the role didn't require a Shakespearean capability. All she had to do was to slink and roll those eyes. And, yes, Mr. Cohn was definitely running things when I was there. But I preferred that hands-on, rough-and-tumble control to today's push-button executions from offices in distant skyscrapers. Today you never quite know who ordered your death. With Harry around, you never had any doubt.

Did you originate these projects, or were you called in on them? How did a producer get to be a producer in the 1950s, and once you switched over to writing, why did you not always produce those films, too?

I did originate *5 Against the House,* taking money I had earned from Universal for the sale of my novel *Maracaibo* to purchase screen rights from Jack Finney for his *Good Housekeeping* novel [5 Against the House (Garden City, N.Y.: Doubleday, 1954)]. *Nightfall* came to me via Frank Cooper, then my agent. *Damn Citizen* I got from Ned Brown at CAA [Creative Artists Agency]. Years later, *Telefon* was a rewrite at MGM—at the direct request of Don Siegel, I assume, because our relationship on *The Lineup* had been so rosy. So, clearly, the only project in which I had the clout to insist on being the producer was *5 Against the House.* Later, when I had more to do with originating projects [i.e., A *Walk in the Spring Rain, The Slender Thread,* the three *Shaft* movies, etc.], I always functioned as producer, thereby cutting down any outside input to its least damaging components—the collaboration between writer-producer and director—a streamlined working partnership which I enjoyed in almost all of my TV work.

Writing for Television

No writer today could be as prolific as you were, because he must go through pitch meetings, sponsor approval, treatments, network supervisors, etcetera. *What was the assignment process like in the sixties and seventies?*

Things in TV were immeasurably different than they are today. In the sixties and seventies, for one thing—and this is KEY—the network commitment to a producer was for a far greater number of episodes than the networks now allot. Half-hour shows usually scored a thirty-six-episode season. Hour shows seldom less than twenty-four episodes. For this reason, when a producer turned up a writer with whom he resonated, he was more likely than not to ask, even beg, that writer for multiple commitments. Apparently, I was such a writer when I was freelancing.

For example, the series *Tightrope,* starring Mike Connors, produced by Clarence Greene and Russell Rouse. I believe I wrote four episodes for *Tightrope,* and the producers wanted me to write even more; but I wasn't free after those four. Obviously, when I was doing my own shows, I wrote multiple episodes simply because it was easier to write them than to waste time meeting with other writers and having to wheedle, coax, persuade, rewrite, *etcetera*—an exhausting process—and a constant battle against other egos and creative rivalries. Thus, for *Route 66,* I ran up an almost ridiculous score. Similarly, for the half-hour *Naked City* season.

When we got to the hour-long *Naked City,* I couldn't maintain that pace since I had to write *Route 66* simultaneously. And *Route 66* was a far more demanding show, since it was actually, if truth be known, a dramatization of my personal four-year psychiatric exhumation of all the shit that was bubbling inside me—and it's hard to assign THAT one to another writer.

I have always felt that the most original writing I have done in the filmed medium was done in the period 1960 to 1964 when I wrote the majority of the one-hour *Route 66* filmed-on-location shows for CBS. These shows caught the American psyche of that period about as accurately as it could be caught. I wrote all of them out of an intense personal motivation; each was a work of passion, conviction, and, occasionally, of anguish—for example, "The Stone Guest," a bitter, antimarital statement.

Even in its pilot episode, Naked City *presents fully formed characters that don't hold to stereotypes. What were some of the challenges of this unconventional location-filmed series?*

There were, as you know, *two* pilots. I wrote the first one for the thirty-minute show [1958–1959] and the second one, "A Death of Princes," for the one-hour show [1960–1963], which was essentially totally recast.

Arriving at the main characters was a joint creative effort between me and my partner, Bert Leonard, who had acquired the rights to *Naked City* from

novelist and former newspaperman Mark Hellinger's estate. It seemed so simple—a gruff precinct boss; a young, idealistic detective; and a street-cop partner with flattened ears and a busted nose. When I wrote them, they didn't
seem like stereotypes. Today they simply wouldn't do.

*Are you the man who gave the world the phrase "There are eight million
stories in the Naked City—this has been one of them"?*

The line was first used in Mark Hellinger's black-and-white film noir *Naked
City,* directed by Jules Dassin [1948]. In the film, since the city was less popu-
lous at the time Mr. Hellinger produced it, the closing line was "There are *five*
million stories in the Naked City—this has been one of them." By the time we
geared up, New York had grown—hence, we notched the count up to eight million stories.

Each week, as I faced the daunting task of coming up with a new episode,
Bert and I would have lunch and kick ideas around. I remember saying to him
on several occasions, "Bert, if there *are* eight million stories in the Naked
City, why in the fuck can't we come up with even *one?*"

*You also wrote a number of shows for Alfred Hitchcock. Other writers have
said that Hitch was not exactly obsessive about the TV programming that went
out under his name.*

Except for one meeting with Hitch to discuss my scripting a one-hour *Suspicion,** "Voice in the Night," I never, over the seasons I wrote for the show,
met the man. My meetings were always with Joan Harrison, his series producer. Joan would simply call me up and tell me she was sending me a story to
read, and if I liked it, to come in and we'd talk about it. I don't recall ever having written an original for the show—only adaptations—and all based on stories given to me by Joan. She got them from all kinds of places and sources.

I can tell you, without any question, had it not been for Joan, Hitch's show
wouldn't have stayed on the air ten minutes, for he had less to do with it than
any of the several writers Joan used as her backstop for the scripts which she
then produced. It wouldn't surprise me to learn that Hitch probably didn't
even screen 90 percent of the episodes, or that he never read a single script.
Believe me, it was Joan and Norman Lloyd who made that show. Hitch was
their bookend. *Nada más.*

Now, my single meeting with Hitch: Joan told me the master was actually
going to direct one of his TV shows—this one his very favorite story—"The
Voice in the Night," to be the flagship episode for his one-hour *Suspicion*
series. Joan drove me to his home up Bellagio Road, one of those canyon
streets off Sunset Boulevard where you drive in through a gate.

Hitch was charming. Congratulated me on the scripts I'd done for the half-
hour *Alfred Hitchcock Presents* shows, personally made me a scotch and soda
and sat me down with my yellow pad.

---

*   *Suspicion* was a one-hour anthology spin-off from *Alfred Hitchcock Presents* for NBC.

I wouldn't trade the hour that followed for anything I can think of at the moment—except possibly—no, not even that. The man was BRILLIANT. He fucking dictated the script to me—shot by shot, including camera movements and opticals. He actually had already SEEN the finished film. He'd say, for example, "The camera's in the boat with the boy and the girl. The move in is very, very slow—while we see the mossy side of the wrecked schooner. Bump. Now the boy climbs the ladder. I tilt up. I see him look at his hand. Something strange seems to have attached itself. He disappears on deck. Now the girl starts up, and I cut to the boy exploring the deck. I'm shooting through this fore-ground of—of *stuff*—and I'm panning him to the cabin door. Something there makes him freeze. He waits. Now the camera's over here, and I see the girl come to him. Give me about this much dialogue, Stirling." He holds up his hand, thumb and forefinger two inches apart. I jot down—"Dialogue, two inches." As I say, the whole goddamned film—shot by shot, no dialogue—just the measurements of how much dialogue and where he wanted it. He left its content to me, since there is no dialogue in the entire short story. It's all introspection and the memory of horror, and the writer didn't want to spoil it with dialogue. Lotsa luck, screenwriter. "Give me two inches of dialogue right here."

I went away and wrote what I still consider a rather neat piece of work; but lo and behold, Hitch decided to shoot a theatrical movie, and his presence was denied to us. Arthur Hiller directed [the episode].

Route 66 *has been called a* Pilgrim's Progress *of the 1960s. Certainly, the notion of two guys [Martin Milner as Tod Stiles and George Maharis as Buzz Murdock] tooling around the country in a Corvette tapped into the national wanderlust. Despite these continuing characters, though, it was essentially an anthology series. Were you ever frustrated by having to bring two stars into a story that could have gone on just as easily without them?*

I never felt impeded by or burdened with our two main characters; and yes, we could have done many of the stories without them—as witness the fact that for almost two seasons I had to write without having George Maharis with us any longer.* But the stories somehow worked BETTER with Marty and George involved. In a sense, THEY were the viewer—bringing the audience into a new town, meeting new people, becoming involved, having the involvement either affect or not affect their own search for identity. Rather than feel they were a drag on the stories, I can tell you clearly that I would have been lost without them and their reactions and interplay.

Series regulars often lament that it's the guest stars who give the better performances; they had time to study the script.

---

* In November 1962, while *Route 66* was still in production, after a case of hepatitis, Maharis pulled out, and was replaced by Glenn Corbett until the series ended in 1964. The Maharis episodes aired through March 1963.

Of course, the guest stars got the juicy parts—as witness Anne Francis in "A Month of Sundays" or Julie Newmar in "How Much a Pound Is Albatross" or Tuesday Weld in "Love Is a Skinny Kid" or Bob Duvall in "Bird Cage on My Foot." But look also at George Maharis's cry of anguish when, at the end of "A Month of Sundays," Anne whispers, "I was alive, wasn't I? I lived." And she dies and George screams—over the honky-tonk carnival sounds behind him—"*No!*" Without George and the impact of Anne's death upon *him,* the story would not have been as affecting.

The series did attract some of the best actors from both New York and Hollywood. I remember Joan Crawford called us personally and asked if she could appear in an episode. I wrote a show just for her—"Same Picture, Different Frame." But we must remember that we had one of the most brilliant casting talents in the business working on the show: Marion Dougherty. And she was working out of New York, where her judgment was based on performance, not fan mail.

With the exception of the Joan Crawford episode, I never wrote for any specific actor or actress. The characters came out of the writing—the casting then came out of the character. For example, I wrote an episode called "Kiss the Maiden All Forlorn," which required a debonair actor of clearly established class—and Marion signed Douglas Fairbanks Jr. for the part. Bert Leonard flew him from London to the location in Texas.

From the raw agonies of drug withdrawal ["Bird Cage on My Foot"] to lupus ["A Month of Sundays"], you addressed ideas that were quite advanced for early-sixties television. One would imagine they also frequently challenged the Standards and Practices Code of the National Association of Broadcasters [NAB]. Just how free were you and Bert Leonard?

We did indeed deal with ideas which were out there on the cutting edge at the time, and with few exceptions, we never had a moment's problem with CBS. With two notable exceptions: "Don't Tread on Me," an episode written by Leonard Freeman, who was producing for us that season; and an episode called "The Newborn," which I wrote. Leonard's story savaged the John Birch Society, and it turned out that somebody high up in the General Motors hierarchy—Chevrolet bought half the show for the entire four years—must have been a Bircher, because all hell broke loose. Jim Aubrey flew out to meet with Bert and me, and demanded we withdraw the episode; but Bert pulled the contract which CBS had signed, granting us total creative freedom—the network's power was only that of not exhibiting the episode—they had to pay for it whether they approved it or not. So we won that one.

In the case of my script "The Newborn," I wanted to see how George and Marty could help an Indian girl about to have a child in the desert of New Mexico. How do you help a woman bear her child when you're miles from medical facilities and have nothing but the Corvette? The problem centered around the umbilical cord: how do you sever it without a knife—shoelaces, obviously—and what do you do about the placenta, etcetera, etcetera. Well, the network went APE when I devoted about six minutes of prime time to this area. They insisted we cut out all that "nastiness." We refused, once more waved our contract, and I fired off a memo accusing CBS types of having been born without navels. We ALMOST won that one. WE didn't cut anything out, and CBS put the episode on; but THEY cut out the disputed footage, and we ran end titles for about four minutes.

If you were using Route 66 *to work through some facets of your own psychiatric journey, are there elements of this that you feel comfortable discussing?*

This is the truest thing I will ever tell you—again, referring to that episode "Kiss the Maiden All Forlorn." Why did I write it? Because my sixteen-year-old daughter announced one morning she was going to become a Catholic nun—the Order of Blessed Virgin Mary—in Peoria. Gulp! And she did. I had to deal with this. It was not easy. So I researched the subject. Until that moment, I had never, never talked to a nun. I wouldn't have known what to say to one. Their outfits intimidated me. But by visiting several orders and LEARNING, I found that the church was not out hustling prospective sisters. You really had to have a *calling* to arrive at the decision my daughter had arrived at.

This gave me new understanding and lent credibility to the script which— had I written it from the outside, rather than out of my own anguish at having to surrender a daughter to an institution I had always regarded with distrust, still bearing in mind the screams of those who died during the Inquisition, of all the hundreds of thousands of Jews who went to their deaths, unprotected by Rome—would have not had the power this finished episode had. Without going into too much personal detail, there were few stories I wrote for *Route 66* during those four years which did not spring out of my own life struggle.

Didn't you once say, referring to the fifties and sixties, that half the stuff on television was written by the same guys? Clearly, you were one of them. These days, thousands of writers are starving in Hollywood. What happened?

True enough, back in the fifties and sixties, thirty or so of us were writing 85 percent of prime-time TV. I don't know if I can explain why—it just WAS. I never stopped freelancing, even while I was writing *Naked City* and *Route 66*. The phones never stopped ringing, and because once I had a relationship with a given show or a given producer, I was lucky enough to be asked to deliver multiple episodes.

So the combination of having my own shows, plus the then-common practice of producers trying to grab the hot writers for multiple assignments, plus the much-larger-than-now numbers of episodes per season—all these elements made it easy for me to pile up the kind of score I did.

For some reason—maybe it was those earlier years in publicity, trying to convince bored movie editors at the New York papers to: "Please, for Christ's sake, Bosley [Crowther], give me a break this Sunday, can you give us the right-hand column and a four-column cut for this piece of shit opening at the Roxy next week?"—for some reason, I seem to have a talent for pitching stories and telling just enough to whet the producer's appetite without telling him too much and revealing I haven't yet worked the fucking story out to whatever its ending might be. I don't recall EVER going to a pitch meeting—in those days, not now—from which I didn't emerge with an assignment or a multiple deal before I'd written "FADE IN."

Your reputation is now that of an adapter, yet the bulk of your early work was writing originals for TV. With the exception of Rawhide, Perry Mason, Mr. Lucky, Man from Blackhawk, *and one or two others, you pretty much wrote for anthologies. This means that you could originate your own characters, rather than slip into characters that some other writer had created.*

True. Except for those particular shows you mentioned, I wrote almost all my television for series in which I was involved as co-creator for anthologies. On the subject of writing originals or adapting the work of another writer, let us also put a pin into that one, since it is an important area.

I much prefer writing originals. Number one, they come out of my own experience and feelings. Number two, you don't have to waste time reading somebody else's work. Number three, you seldom get a really fine piece of material to adapt, since the best-written material is usually not able to be adapted. How would you like to take a crack at Proust's *Remembrance of Things Past,* for example? It is my contention that adapting the work of another writer is far more trying and requires infinitely more professional ability than writing one of these so-called original screenplays.

For me, the proof is that virtually all of my television writing, which I consider in many instances to have been my best writing for the medium, has been original; the stories, the people, the thematic element—all these came from within the cosmos of my own life experience in one way or another. The attitudes and beliefs expressed began in my own psyche. How much simpler to write out of one's self than to address an alien piece of material and find in it those elements which impelled the producer to acquire the property in the first place, then to try to dramatize those properties for the actor and the camera, and yet still try not to submerge within this foreign stew your own personal feelings and beliefs.

Looking back over the originals I wrote for the big screen, I see a definite pattern: the majority of them were never produced.

I suppose this is why—when I undertook the John Locke series of paperback novels—I announced IN ADVANCE of publication that none of them would ever be available in terms of its motion picture rights. I further buttressed that position by writing each of the three novels so far for this series in a style which would make it virtually impossible for any living screenwriter to be able to fashion a script from the work. In short, I determined to be totally out of the reach of studio group-think and to write books I damn well wanted to write for MYSELF.

It is my theory that few people at the networks have the capability of reading, let alone making a judgment call on something they may have been forced to read. These are not literary folk. Hence the "original" works best for them because the writer pitches a story concept, and since these concepts are virtually all the same, simply reworked, the buyer is familiar with the product and, feeling comfortable, green-lights the freshly regurgitated pap.

Writing for Features

Village of the Damned (1960)

You seldom shared writing credits, so how did it happen with Wolf Rilla and George Barclay? Would this credit have been arbitrated under WGA [Writers Guild of America] rules?

I never met Wolf Rilla or George Barclay. What happened in this instance was that I completed writing the script based on a wonderful science fiction novel, *The Midwich Cuckoos,* by John Wyndham [London: Michael Joseph, 1957], one of England's top science fiction novelists.* MGM's New York office was so high on the book that they airmailed me microfilm of each page of the manuscript as the author finished writing it, so that I could get a jump start on the script. My producer was Milo Frank. We offered the script to Ronald Colman, who accepted. Unhappily, this fine gentleman died before we could advance the production.

At that point, an incredible thing happened. The then-head of MGM, Robert H. O'Brien, who was Catholic, apparently actually read my script and flipped—NEGATIVELY. The idea of human females being impregnated by ETs and bearing laser-eyed young 'uns sent him into a religious cartwheel: What the fuck were we trying to say here? Were we making a mockery of the Virgin Mary? Or something to that effect. Bottom line: *Village of the Damned* got canceled so fast Milo didn't have time to pack his briefcase and leave the lot. As for me, I was so pissed I left features for a while and went over to TV. That's when I went into business with Herbert Leonard and did the first year of *Naked City* for ABC—this was the original half-hour series.

---

* One afternoon the entire British town of Midwich falls asleep for several hours. Months later every fertile woman in the town delivers a blond, hauntingly intelligent child who may have been fathered by extraterrestrials who visited the earth. Only the scientist George Zellaby (George Sanders) is able to gain the trust of these hybrid progeny who can read and control human thoughts. Apparently, other cities around the world have suffered similar visits. Distracting the children by concentrating on the image of a brick wall, he destroys the monsters—and himself—with a bomb hidden in a briefcase.

In any event, the script hung in limbo for months; then suddenly it surfaced in England as an MGM English project, and that's when Rilla and Barclay were brought in. They did little if anything to change my script; but in those days, our WGA didn't have power over English writers, and there was nothing we could do about their credit grab, which to this day I regard as a form of larceny on the part of these two British highwaymen.

The Slender Thread (1965)

When Anne Bancroft kissed Sidney Poitier at the 1964 Oscars, it drew comment from, among others, Jack Gould, the TV critic for the New York Times, *who noted that it was the first interracial kiss on network TV. Was this an element in later casting Poitier and Bancroft together in* The Slender Thread?

I didn't see the 1964 Oscars and therefore did not see Bancroft kissing Poitier; hence, this transracial contact had nothing whatsoever to do with the casting of these two fine actors. We picked each one because we felt there was no one around who could better portray what I had written for each.

This remains a riveting picture. It's moving to see Sidney Poitier when he could still play a vulnerable character. Is it significant that race is totally ignored—the two never meet—or did you and tyro director Sidney Pollack consider it when, at the end, Poitier rejects the idea of meeting Bancroft face-to-face?*

Yes, race was totally ignored. That's what appealed to me: that neither hero nor heroine could SEE each other; therefore, they did not and could not bring to their brief relationship any prejudices or preset standards of evaluation. Their mutual humanity is purely that: the relationship of people without the impact of race, religion, or societal pressures; people free to relate to each other on the simplest level of humanity, self-preservation. For this reason, at the end I elected to have Sidney NOT want to see the woman. Because he KNEW seeing her would diminish the magic which they had experienced, divorced from each other except for their connection by phone—their linkage heart to heart. The character elects to savor the triumph—to preserve it, unspoiled, in his memory.

You do a tricky number with point of view in this film: it's Bancroft's story we're seeing, yet it's shown through Poitier's eyes. It shouldn't logically work, but it does.

You are perceptive to understand the altered perspective of this screenplay, i.e., a woman's story seen through the eyes of a man who never, in point of fact, sees her, only senses her. You are quite right—it shouldn't work—and in

---

* In *The Slender Thread,* Sidney Poitier is a volunteer on a Seattle telephone hotline, trying to locate a caller, played by Anne Bancroft, who has just swallowed an overdose of sleeping pills.

some instances in the film, I'm not sure it did; but it worked well enough in total to validate the attempt to try something different.

The Slender Thread *was your first film credit after many, many TV shows. What pressures did you, as an established TV writer, face returning to features?*

As a TV writer, I was blissfully unaware. In TV, I was a comet, blazing across the heavens. In features, "Who he?" So the film was vital to me; it had to make its mark or ELSE. But it didn't, in one sense, and in another, it did.

We previewed in Encino, a valley suburb north of Hollywood, and as I watched the film and "felt" the audience, I knew I had failed. The picture was NOT giving off sparks. When it ended, I remember sitting alone in the theater while the Paramount execs, including the always ebullient and affable Howard Koch, were out in the lobby trying to strong-arm the rapidly fleeing patrons into filling out reaction cards. A fella with a big smile and red hair suddenly appeared in my row, as though he had materialized from the ceiling. He sat down next to me. "A bomb, huh?" he suggested. "Yep," I agreed. "A fucking bomb. From start to finish. I doubt that any single person in America will ever bother to buy a ticket to this flick." "You have to get another screenplay assignment before the word gets out," he counseled. "Yeah?" I asked. "And how do I do that?" "I'm Martin Baum," he said. "I represent Sidney Poitier."

I KNEW Marty Baum represented Sidney, and that he was one of Hollywood's most prestigious agents. "So you're Marty?" I asked. "Yeah," he said. "And I want you to know something: Sidney doesn't blame you for this picture." "Maybe Sidney doesn't," I said, "but I do. I wrote and produced the thing." "Well," he said, "I find that refreshing, that *somebody* in this town can admit he blew it. Look, I'm going to get you a job—fast. It has to be fast—because the minute word gets out about this turkey—forget it."

It couldn't have been more than two days later that Marty called and told me to meet him within the hour in the office of [the producer] Walter Mirisch. I met Walter, whom I have loved these many years for what happened next. Walter handed me a thin, little, Doubleday crime novel entitled *In the Heat of the Night* [by John Ball (New York: Harper and Row, 1965)]. "Sidney Poitier brought this in to us," Walter said to me, "and we plan to develop it." I truly owe that opportunity to two men only: to Sidney Poitier and Martin Baum.

In the Heat of the Night (1967)

This film affords us a good opportunity to discuss exposition. It is fully twenty-two minutes before we hear Sheriff Gillespie [Rod Steiger] called by name. As for Virgil Tibbs [Sidney Poitier], only once does he actually say, specifically, "I'm a police officer"; all the other times, he either flips open his badge, is introduced by Gillespie, or says nothing. Was this an effort to keep it

"Controlled and deliberate craftsmanship": Sidney Poitier (left) and Rod Steiger in *In the Heat of the Night,* directed by Norman Jewison.

from becoming a running gag instead of a constant reminder of his notable presence in the Deep South?*

This may be the most "controlled" and "deliberate" piece of craftsmanship of all my work. Usually in writing, I let emotion and feeling dominate, lead me down unknown and for me still-unexplored pathways. But what we have here is a mystery story—a whodunit in its original form, John Ball's Doubleday novel.

As a longtime fan of the mystery genre, I found the story more compelling in its opportunities to exploit the situations of the contending characters than I could generate any kind of enthusiasm for what is essentially a very thin and pale little mystery yarn with little surprise or suspense. The centrality of the story for me lay clearly in the wonderful concept John Ball had of putting a

---

*   A businessman is killed in a small southern town, and immediately the police arrest a black man on suspicion of the murder. As it happens, the black man is a crack homicide detective who is passing through town. Uneasily working with the reluctant sheriff amidst smothering racism, the detective solves the crime, whose motive, it turns out, was simple robbery.

city-trained BLACK homicide detective in a rural, southern cracker small town where everybody and anybody is a potential enemy—even the sheriff. I determined to tell this story and this story only.

The film is notable for its narrative parsimony. Tibbs seldom explains exactly what he's doing in his investigation; we have to pay close attention, and even then, it doesn't always lay itself out. In general, how much does an audience need to know, and can you lose them if you tell too much?

In discussions early on with Norman Jewison, the director, we agreed that if the crime story were plotted as the alphabet, from A to Z, how much of it could we pull out and play offscreen without ever seeing or making any reference to [it]? We kept A and jumped to F, then from F jumped to L and from L to P—then from P to Z—and then we tried to see how we could still pull more exposition out of that fragmentary crime-story structure. We applied this principle to every scene—wherever we could detect any explanation or exposition, we stepped on it.

The result of this withholding of information was to compel the viewer to invest attention in the least detail. Maybe there was a clue in the look Gillespie gave Virgil—maybe not. But we'd better watch and see.

An example of what you so aptly call "narrative parsimony," the opening few minutes of the film, best illustrates this deliberate technique.

The film does not actually begin—in its narrative thrust—until several hundred feet in. A cop is cruising—he sees various fleeting images—he has an encounter with a smart-ass at an all-night diner, he finds a dead man, he calls the sheriff. The sheriff, hoping to avoid any and all problems in this community to which he, too, is a stranger—I'll come back to that point in a moment—mumbles and fumbles at the scene of the crime. Then Virgil Tibbs is arrested as he waits in the small railroad terminal for a night train—brought into the office of the sheriff, where he is treated as the killer nabbed in the attempt to escape—and we extend that scene in which Steiger toys with this dumb nigger to the last second, at which point, Steiger asks, "And what do you do up in Philadelphia, boy?" To which Poitier replies that he's a police officer—and that up there they call him MR. TIBBS.

Well, at that moment the film EXPLODES into life and doesn't stop until the final moment, at the train station, when the sheriff reaches for, and Tibbs surrenders to him, Tibbs's bag—two human beings have bonded.

My point is that we protracted that moment of initial impact as long as we could—right down to the precise frame of film at which point we felt we might be teasing the viewer TOO long. So this was from the beginning the intent of my screenplay, and anything which did not advance that dynamic was ruthlessly rejected.

Now—about the book versus the script—if you will look through the book, you will see some amazing differences. The sheriff is a minor character in the novel. The central character is a patrol cop, played by Warren Oates, who falls in love with the daughter of the murdered man—I seem to recall he was a musician come to perform a concert in the town. I relegated the cop to a minor role and concentrated on building Bill Gillespie's character. I made him a southerner but from a different state, so that he was as much an outsider to the town as Sidney Poitier's character was. They had this alienation from the others as a common bond, which led to what is one of my favorite scenes in the film, the scene between Sidney and Rod in Rod's house where they start to let down with each other—then Rod flares up—and the race thing closes in again. I have heard that everybody claims to have written that scene—Haskell Wexler, the director of photography; Rod Steiger; and, Lord knows, even the generator man. I can assure you that I conceived it and wrote it. Rod did switch a couple of words around, but to an actor of his talent, I made no objection.

Your attitude toward the film, despite its Oscars, has been reported as ranging from dismissal to disgust.

I have been quoted and misquoted on this point for two decades. What I was referring to was the fact that the film had never been appreciated for its craftsmanship or for its unique and polished style of holding back, holding back, but was judged on the level of its black-white content. I felt then, and still feel, that such a judgment is overly simplistic; and for that reason, and that reason alone, I made the statement that getting plaudits for *In the Heat of the Night* was like waving the American flag or pushing Mom's apple pie. It was just too damn easy to manipulate people with issues which for the moment have flagged their attention. It was impossible NOT to like *In the Heat of the Night* at that time. Today's phrase is *politically correct.* I hated to be politically correct, since I felt there was no validation for the work in itself in such a posture but only a knee-jerk reaction on the part of a populist major-ity opinion on what happened by chance to be the subject matter of the film.

Norman Jewison was terribly hurt when he was denied the Oscar, even after the film he directed won so heavily. Can you recall what the Oscar fever and its aftermath were like?

About Norman Jewison, both the talent and the man, he is superb in both departments. I adore him—did from the beginning, always will. He was a magnificent sport when the Academy passed him over.[*] I can only tell you that those of us who went up to get our Oscars felt little personal triumph, because Norman—who made it all possible—wasn't up there with us. For that matter, neither was Sidney. But then the Academy had to decide: Sidney or Rod. It couldn't be both.

And, yes, I CAN recall that night. Every second of it. Mostly my disbelief when I heard Claire Bloom call my name. And then I was whizzing down the

---

[*]   Although *In the Heat of the Night* won Oscars for Best Picture and for four other cate-gories, the Best Director statuette went to Mike Nichols for *The Graduate,* one of the few times that Academy members have split the Best Picture and Best Director awards.

aisles, past all those smiling faces—wondering why are THEY smiling?—and as though fast-forwarded, I was in front of the mike and mesmerized by the backdrop of faces and tuxedos and great boobs of all the dazzling ladies who'd spent all day getting their hair done—all looking up at ME and awaiting something more than "I want to thank, etcetera." Not having expected to win—would you, competing against *Bonnie and Clyde* [1967] and *The Graduate* [1967]?—I had prepared absolutely nothing. I do remember mumbling something about "We members of the Writers Guild are not allowed to write on spec—and so I have nothing prepared." That seemed to do the trick—the audience gave me a warm, sweeping feeling of love and support—and I may or may not have said thanks to Norman and Sidney and Walter and especially to Marty Baum, who got me the job. At least I *hope* I said that. Then I was whisked off with my Oscar, far heavier than I had imagined—but then when had I ever imagined I'd be holding one?

Charly (1968)

You had to devise a tangible arc of intelligence and emotion and make the science fiction in this film so real that we continue to care about the character. The incredible experiment referred to in the story is like a Hitchcock Mac Guffin. How did you lick it?

In this script, a mentally retarded man is given brain surgery which raises his intelligence and perception to genius level—at least for a brief time—before there is regression and a return to his original condition.

Okay, *what* surgery? If it exists, why aren't surgeons sawing away night and day at the unfortunate mentally deficient? I didn't want to write a science fiction piece. I wanted and Ralph Nelson, our director, wanted and Cliff Robertson, our Charly and the man who refused to sell the film rights after his successful 1961 TV performance in *Flowers for Algernon,* Daniel Keye's short story on which the film is based, wanted—all of us wanted to make this a film dominated by the sense of real life, of reality. So I had to understand for myself—even if I never used any of the research—how the brain works. Imagine my astonishment, after digging into towering stacks of medical works and after meeting with numerous neurosurgeons and other experts, to discover that nobody really knew too much about the human brain. That is, knew for *sure.* And the more research I did, the more I found that each successive writer had somehow slightly poached on the work of a previous writer, and that ultimately, if you traced this pyramid to its foundations, everybody was borrowing from a few seminal sources.

For this reason, I arrived at the wondrously devious answer to my problems—when in trouble, punt. I dismissed everything I had learned and summed it all up in a simple scene between Claire Bloom and Cliff in which she asks the poor chap—still in his moronic stage—something like "Would you like to be smarter,

"One of my favorite films": Cliff Robertson and Claire Bloom in *Charly.*

Charly?" "Oh, yeah," he agrees, "smarter." "Well," she says, "there is this opera-tion." He asks, "Will it make me smarter?" She replies, "We hope so, Charly."

Go fight City Hall! You can't tear into THAT one because there's nothing to tear into. We just zap it at you. See, we got this operation. It's worked on a mouse. Now we're gonna test it on Charly. And that was that. By staying AWAY from everything I learned about neurosurgery—which was that there still remained more questions than answers—I solved my problem.

Charly is one of my favorite films because it is simple and human and unpretentious. And Cliff's performance was deeply moving. As you know, he won the Academy Award for Best Actor.

Marlowe (1969)

Raymond Chandler's novel about Hollywood, The Little Sister *[Boston: Houghton Mifflin, 1949], was set in 1949. The film was made in 1969. Updat-ing it by twenty years, you simplified the plot*—no mean feat—and moved*

---

*   Philip Marlowe (James Garner) agrees to locate the missing brother (Roger Newman) of a movie starlet (Sharon Farrell), and stumbles into a blackmail plot, gangland-style icepick mur-ders, and a shady psychiatrist (Paul Stevens).

the story from its original post–World War II setting into a faster-paced, modern movie milieu. How else did you adapt it for the screen?

I read the book a dozen times to learn it by heart and discover where, if at all, Chandler failed to communicate a point. I also studied the author himself to assimilate everything about him—his attitudes toward life, his feelings about his characters—and put myself onto his stage, where he went, moving along in his footsteps. I also refocused the characters to heighten dramatic tension or to reveal more of Marlowe in his relations to the minor characters.[*]

Was it you who discovered Bruce Lee for the role of a mob henchman, Winslow Wong, who tries to scare Marlowe off the case?

By the time of *Marlowe,* I had seen so many parodies of a thin guy with a weasel face and a fat guy with a black suit come into offices to threaten people that merely seeing such types enter a room would send me into gales of laughter. "So," I thought, "let's send in one of the world's greatest martial artists and have him demolish Marlowe's office." Since Bruce had the physical capability of doing the whole enchilada in one continuous ballet of directed violence, I didn't want to cut into it. Director Paul Bogart agreed, and of course, I rank this scene as one of the foremost martial arts scenes ever to appear in an American film. I brought Bruce in for the cameo because I had been studying with him for a couple of years at that point in time, and because he was, to me, probably the single most important man ever to be part of my life, brief as the time was—only a span of some four years—but every instant of our time together lasts in my memory.

It's apparent that Bruce Lee was responsible for your conversion to a more spiritual life. How did this happen, and what kind of a man was he—not the hype but the truth?

I owe my spirituality to Bruce Lee. In my lifetime, I never met another man who was even remotely at his level of consciousness. I'll give you just one example.

Early on in my workouts with Bruce in *jeet kune do*—"the way of the intercepting fist," in Cantonese—he observed that while my defensive moves were blindingly fast, my offensive moves were perfunctory. I tried to explain to him that as a member of the three-man foils fencing team at USC for three years and as a West Coast fencing champion in foil, I scored 90 percent of my touches via counterattacks. An opponent would make a move, and I'd counter it while he was still engrossed in attempting to deliver it—and skewer him where he stood. "Bullshit," Bruce replied. "That's a technical rationalization. There's something in YOU, something deep in your psyche, that stops you

---

[*]   Stirling Silliphant's comments about *Marlowe* are adapted from Stephen Pendo, *Raymond Chandler on Screen: His Novels into Film,* (Metuchen, N.J.: Scarecrow Press, 1976), by permission of Stirling Silliphant.

from attacking. You have to rationalize that the other guy is attacking you, so then it's okay to knock him off. But you don't have the killer instinct; you're not pursuing him. *Why?*" Well, Bruce and I worked on this for weeks. Finally, I volunteered that my father—pure Anglo—had never once in his life held me in his arms or kissed me. In fact, I had never in my life touched a man or had any body contact with another male. No, I was not homophobic. I just—hadn't—ever—done it. I remember that afternoon so vividly. Bruce and I were sweating—we were naked from the waist up—wearing those black Chinese bloomer pajama pants only. Bruce moved in closer.

"Put your arms around me," he ordered.

"Hey, Bruce," I said, "you're all sweaty, man."

"Do it!" he demanded.

So I put my arms around him.

"Pull me closer," he said.

"Jesus, Bruce!"

"Closer!"

I pulled him closer. I could feel the *chi* in his body—a vibrant force which literally throbbed from his muscles. His vitality passed between us—and it was as though a steel wall had just been blown away. He felt GOOD. He felt ALIVE. When I opened my arms and he stepped back, he was studying me.

"You have to love *everyone,*" he said, "not only women, but men as well. You don't have to have sex with a man, but you have to be able to relate to his separate physicality. If you don't, you will never be able to fight him, to drive your fist through his chest, to snap his neck, to gouge out his eyes."

Well, this stuff ain't for kids, I'm here to tell you. But over the years, I shared as much of my life with Bruce as time permitted us. I had many such lessons. They came from the guy—but they came from higher planes as well—and because of Bruce, I opened all my windows.

The Liberation of L. B. Jones (1969)

This was William Wyler's last film, and it looked as though he was not fully in control of his skills. How did you work with him on it?

You may not quite be able to grasp this statement, but for me, *The Liberation of L. B. Jones* is my favorite of all the motion picture scripts I've written until this year when, in my opinion, I surpassed *LBJ* with an adaptation of Truman Capote's novella *The Grass Harp,* which my partner, Charlie Matthau, the director—and Walter Matthau's talented son—is now trying to get financed for production. [It was produced by Fine Line Features, 1996.] Why this personal favoritism of *LBJ?* It may, I confess, have to do more with the issues involved than the work itself.

When I wrote *The Liberation of L. B. Jones* [based on the novel *The Liberation of Lord Byron Jones,* by Jesse Hill Ford (Boston: Little, Brown, 1965)] I was up to my gills with the prevailing wisdom that race relations in the USA were now okay. It was painfully clear to me that this was a dangerous professing of amelioration when in fact the only thing that had changed, deep down, in the white hearts of my countrymen was their delusion that they had at last accepted any person of a different skin color or ethnic background as a fellow human being.

For *LBJ,* in its own dark heart, is saying only one thing: "Fuck all of you, all you white bastards, all you black bastards, fuck you for hating each other, for hating yourselves!" The film is unremitting, inexorable, without pity or compromise or solution. It simply states that hatred prevails.

True, Mr. Wyler was nearing the end of his brilliant career—and the end of his life span—but Willy cared passionately about this film. After I had finished my screenplay and the changes he requested, he still wanted more. He wanted me on the set. He wanted to bounce ideas. At the time, I was becoming involved in another project—Lord only remembers what it could have been—so I told Willy I would not be available. In my place I recommended the man who had written the novel, Jesse Hill Ford, a dear friend of mine and a Southerner, who had LIVED the story. Jesse had based it on a true incident in a town in Tennessee.

Although Wyler was past his prime on LBJ, *he was certainly still revered. What were the things he asked of you? What attracted this refined man to such a coarse subject?*

I can't really clue you in about William Wyler, since *The Liberation of Lord Byron Jones* was produced by Ronald Lubin, and I was engaged solely as the screenwriter. Nor did I have any presence on the location, though Jesse quite faithfully did. I guess my passion for the finished film is based on the fact that the picture was uncompromising. It offered no solutions, no hope—it simply said, "This is what happens when two sides hate each other." I value the film because in the period when it was made, it was decades ahead of all the other "safe, Hollywood black-white themes." It was far closer to today's Spike Lee's *Malcolm X* [1992]. In short, closer to the truth. We dared to say that racial hatreds run *DEEP* in America—for that matter, all over the world—witness Germany as I write, witness Bosnia, etcetera, etcetera, etcetera. We scorned the happy ending—the ray of hope. This is why, to me, *LBJ* is one of the works of which I am the most satisfied. It is sans bullshit.

A Walk in the Spring Rain (1969)

This is an unusual film in that it portrays middle-aged people as still having their own lives and dreams, realized and unrealized, often separate from their children. It's more than an autumnal romance and a far cry from the other scripts you were doing at the time. What drew you to it?

I was drawn to *A Walk in the Spring Rain*[*] by my disappointment with my daughter. For reasons I have never been able to resolve with her, once I divorced her mother she kept our relationship frozen in the past, back in her little-girl period. This is what many parents do with their children, feeling disappointment when the child becomes a teenager, intent on his or her own life; but the parent keeps trying to recapture the vanishing childhood and creates friction with the child struggling to emerge into youth. With my daughter, the roles became reversed; and she kept trying to relate to me in past terms, rather than in terms of the reality of my now-liberated new life. So when I read *A Walk in the Spring Rain* [by Rachel Maddux (New York: Doubleday, 1966)], I jumped on it because here was a story of a selfish daughter who EXPECTED her mother to assume certain responsibilities simply because she was her mother. It has always struck me that these familial relationships should be based on love and caring and letting go, not on obligation.

About the time of A Walk, *you turned fifty—an age of reflection. The year of its release, your son was killed, and all your announced projects—"The Inheritors," "All the Emperor's Horses," and "America the Beautiful"—were cancelled. The answer to this question may not be anybody's business, but your life must have changed immeasurably during this period.*

The period you refer to—the murder of my son Loren, the loss of my house to fire, the failure of my projects with Joe Levine's company—was, I suppose, looking back now, a period of redefining myself; but I would urge you not to put too much stock in that possibility, because truthfully, I am redefining myself virtually every day of my life and am continually striving to change events, as well as my self. If anything, all these reverses may have impelled me more toward Buddhism and the certainty that everything—I mean everything—is transient and that to arrive at any state of even comparative happiness, you have to open your hands and let go of whatever it is you've been clutching, because whether you let it go willingly or are forced to, whatever you're holding is already moving away from you. If you let this certainty trouble you, you have a problem. If you accept it as the basis of all existence, you can actually be calmed by the loss of people and things.

Murphy's War (1971)

The whole film is low key and downplays any sense of exhilaration. Was this view of the futility of war nurtured by the Vietnam era or was it a creative decision based on something else less current?

---

[*]   Accompanying her professor-husband, played by Fritz Weaver, on a sabbatical in the country, Ingrid Bergman plays a woman who becomes attracted to a local handyman played by Anthony Quinn. Complications arise when their children—his son, her daughter—stake their own claims on their parents' lives.

Murphy's War, in my opinion, fell through the cracks. It is a far better film than either the public or most critics ever perceived. It was a curious project. Indeed, our purpose was to make a flat-out statement about the absurdity, the meaninglessness, of war. So we went for minimal sound, minimal dialogue, a kind of intense fumbling toward death, toward the showdown between enemies who have no further reason for enmity except the blind stupidity and vengefulness of the Peter O'Toole character. And this is why, at the end, in a high angle shot director Peter Yates closed out the film with the sub sinking, the barge sinking, and the river surging above both, covering them for all eternity. Over this he shot a ragged flight of jungle birds, wheeling off, the only survivors of this pointless encounter between men and their machines.

The New Centurions (1972)

You turned Joe Wambaugh's amorphous book [The New Centurions *(New York: Dell, 1970)] into a movie that was still episodic and yet had form, character arcs, and pace. In particular, you drew whole scenes out of a bit of dialogue from somewhere else.*

Let's be specific: In the book, we see *the incident where Kilvinsky goes into a woman's house to tell an intruder to leave, later revealing to his befuddled partner that there was no intruder—the caller simply had the DTs. In the film, Kilvinsky [George C. Scott] tells that story in his anguished phone call to Fehler [Stacy Keach] before killing himself. Then, at the end of the film, you show the encounter between Fehler and a woman [Anne Ramsey] in a similar incident—only this time, it's real, and Fehler is killed. By pairing the anecdote with the act, you create irony and closure where neither existed in the book.*

That coupling was quite deliberate because I was looking for a linkage between Kilvinsky's death and Fehler's death. And it seemed to me that SEE-ING Kilvinsky go into the house and play out the intruder-who-wasn't-there scene was not as dramatic—since the intruder *wasn't* there—as letting Kilvinsky tell it out of a wistful final moment of recalling the past as he is about to terminate for all time his own future.

Joe Wambaugh's dialogue in *The New Centurions* is so excellent, so realistic in terms of its coming out of his experience in the LAPD [Los Angeles Police Department], that I quite simply combed through it searching for bits which, in turn, suggested scenes. I found this a most rewarding search.

As to the mechanics involved in recognizing moments which may illuminate the story or its characters, I have no way of explicating that process. It comes solely from having done it for so many years that my trial-and-error sensors have become acute—and because of my own life experiences, I seem to make instantaneous choices from any number of options. In a way, it's the same process as the ancient Polynesian navigators used: years of remembering the scent of drifting flowers, observing the stars, watching and feeling the currents and waves, gave them the feeling of where in the Pacific they were—without sextants, compasses, or satellite navigation.

If we cite The New Centurions *as a good example, can you help me learn what goes into introducing a character without turning him into a stereotype?*

Nothing more than dialogue—the character's dialogue—and his line of action and reaction. Both what he says—or doesn't say—and what he does define him as an individual. If you do not keep his dialogue and action line pure—once you've set the character—he will evade you and confuse the viewer.

I always try to find the unexpected when I introduce a character. For example, if a guy who's behind in his rent has to get back into his West Side tenement and the fucking landlord is out front, hosing the sidewalk—and waiting—what does our guy say as he breezes in? Assume the landlord says, "Hey, Eddie, you forgot what today is?"—meaning the goddamn rent is due RIGHT NOW—what does Eddie say as he continues into the tenement? Well, if it's one kind of character, he might say, "Yeah, isn't it the 926th anniversary of the Battle of Hastings?" "Jesus," we have to say, "who is *this* guy? He looks like a bum, but what's this shit about the Battle of Hastings?"

Shaft in Africa (1973)

Blaxploitation movies of the early 1970s were often criticized for their stereotypes of African-Americans, yet they also provided entrée for black actors and filmmakers into the hitherto closed film industry.[*]

One of my great miscalculations. I felt that black Americans might have, deep within their psyches, some basic and lasting connection with their antecedents, their ancestry—as was ultimately demonstrated by the success of David L. Wolper's miniseries *Roots* [1978].

I persuaded Jim Aubrey, then heading up production at MGM, to let me write and produce a story dramatizing the slave trade in Africa. I was convinced that black America would flock to see Shaft "stick it to 'em" in darkest Africa and single-handedly throw a wrench into this miserable traffic in human beings. So we shot in Ethiopia and in Paris, and we made a slick, Hollywood product—lacking all the raw street vigor and honesty of the first *Shaft*. The film was a disaster. I was wrong about black America. They avoided the movie by the millions. At that time, any connection with Africa was not yet in fashion. This was before all the African historical revisionism and the now trendy African thing, right up to this week's fashions out of Paris, definitely showing an African-style influence.

---

[*]   Silliphant was executive producer of *Shaft* and *Shaft's Big Score*, both directed by Gordon Parks, with Richard Roundtree as the novelist Ernest Tidyman's black detective. In *Shaft in Africa*, directed by John Guillermin and again starring Roundtree, Shaft helps an African nation thwart modern-day slave trading.

As an example, whenever director Martin Ritt—Sounder, Edge of the City—*was criticized as a white man making movies about the black experience, he would deflect it by growling, "Until a black filmmaker can get the money to do it, I will." Given your beliefs, how do you regard today's reemergence of African-American cinema—Spike Lee, Bill Duke, Carl Franklin, John Singleton, etcetera?*

I am not in the cheering section for African-American cinema, although I certainly would do everything to encourage it, only because I dream of a time when Spike Lee, should he choose to, could direct *Star Wars* [1977] or *Home Alone* [1990] or *Basic Instinct* [1992]. Or that Ron Howard could direct *Malcolm X* [1992]. I am agin' this apportioning of rights to any individual based on his race or religion. When a white writer can write a better "black" novel than James Baldwin and a black man can write a better novel than Proust— THEN, I say, we're finally getting somewhere.

Disaster Pictures (1972–1980)

Somewhere along the way, somebody insisted that disaster movies should be called group jeopardy pictures.

Let me begin by saying that the person in most peril from working on group jeopardy films is the writer.

You wrote the bookends on this genre: The Poseidon Adventure, The Towering Inferno, *and then* The Swarm *and* When Time Ran Out.

I was doing great with the first two—*Poseidon* and *Towering*. But the downward spiral was my getting involved in those two classic golden turkeys *The Swarm* and *When Time Ran Out.* I have never been able to bring myself to screen *When Time Ran Out,* so horrendous was the experience of being within a thousand miles of it. What respect I may or may not have earned from my sixteen-year-old son, over the years, has been in group jeopardy of fusing out because of my involvement with these final two gasps of the "GJ genre."

You've said that with all the stars, there's precious little time for anything else.

It's simple math. Take *The Towering Inferno.* Look at the ads Fox and Warners ran—a strip of star photos with shots of Paul Newman and Steve McQueen and Bill Holden and Faye Dunaway and Fred Astaire and Jennifer Jones and Robert Wagner and O. J. Simpson and Richard Chamberlain, etcetera, each labeled "the fireman," "the architect," "the builder," "the contractor," etcetera, actually labeling the stereotype in advance for the potential viewer. You do stereotypes and then change them a little bit, so they're kind of off the wall and stylish. But, essentially, if they are not recognizable stereotypes, people have trouble with them—they have to know who they are so they can follow the story.*

* These last two sentences from Woolf and Cox, *Successful Screenwriting.*

Shelley Winters and Gene Hackman in Ronald Neame's film *The Poseidon Adventure.*

Okay, we had seven major narrative thrusts to fold in—seven major separate personal relationships to be introduced, developed, strained, then re-
solved, along with their interaction with another group: Holden with Chamberlain, Holden with his daughter, Holden with Newman, Holden with
McQueen—seven of the bloody things. And then the eighth character, the

FIRE itself, which while I wrote I gave a name to—*MY* secret—but my favorite character in the script. I determined to let the fire WIN—make it the hero—but I always knew that in the end the good guys, the architect and the fireman, would have to triumph. Now—you have a script of 130 pages. You have eight major story-character blocks—8 goes into 130 around sixteen plus times. So you know, going in, that you can only put Holden on 16 pages of the movie in terms of foreground action or any kind of meaningful dialogue, unless you unbalance everything and give him 22 pages and cut Chamberlain to 10, etcetera. Yes, I call that FRUSTRATING because what you are not doing is writing. What you are doing is juggling.

That's only the beginning of your problems. You have to deal with the logistics of the physical action, and this becomes a matter of charting, not writing. If something blows up on the fifty-seventh floor, and in the scene before that, you had Paul Newman down on the thirty-second floor and the elevators can't be used—how are you going to get him up there? Simple, let him use the stairway. What if the stairway collapses on his way up? Okay, we need a scene about that. So before you can get the man up there to do his few pages, you now have to create a new scene out of the mechanical motivations of the action. Jesus, guys, where did we leave Steve McQueen in his last scene before we had to cut away to Fred Astaire looking for Jennifer Jones's cat?

Despite this, *The Towering Inferno* did emerge as a powerful and engrossing film, I have to admit, despite all my assaults against having my writing driven by forces beyond my control. I believe this happened because we really took after the shoddy builders, the contractors who gamble with human lives to save a buck, so there was underneath all the never-ending action—and despite the superficiality of the characters—a deeper dynamic, a humanistic point which lifted the film an inch or two above its own genre. Naturally, I was astonished when it was nominated for an Academy Award as one of the five best movies of the season. There was no way it could ever win, but at least, we all got to put on our tuxedos and eat the standard chicken dinner at one of the big-time hotels.

The Poseidon Adventure *caught a lot of people off guard and became a huge hit. What was your thinking when you adapted Paul Gallico's book [London: Heinemann, 1969]—you had to juggle so many stories—was it* Grand Hotel *underwater or something else?*

This one was far easier—all due to Paul Gallico. *Poseidon* was a straight-out story with some—because of Paul—well-written, flesh-and-blood characters. The narrative line is simple: A passenger liner turns hull up and is sinking by the bow, its time afloat unknown but hardly more than a matter of hours. A group of survivors has to work its way UP toward what had previously been the bottom and, if they can achieve that level, attempt to break through the hull before the liner sinks. The group more or less remains intact, despite arguments among them, chiefly a difference of opinion between the

Ernie Borgnine character and the Gene Hackman character as to which way is the only way to survival. So, no, it was far less *Grand Hotel* underwater than *Towering Inferno* was *Grand Hotel* in a burning high-rise.

The matter of making the characters empathetic was not a problem, because I had a simple and central conflict going between Borgnine and Hackman. In their conflict, they exposed their own fears—and therefore their humanity—and as this impacted on the several other characters, we inevitably had to see them as facets of ourselves. And how can you go wrong with an actress of the brilliance of Shelley Winters, whose chubby rump has to be pushed upward, and her face of complaint at such a rude contact; and then when she has to dive and swim a hazardous course underwater in her bloomers and dies in the arms of her husband before they can get to Israel— come on, that's really snatching candy from a baby.[*]

Unlike The Poseidon Adventure, The Towering Inferno *was an all-star cast from the word go. How do you balance all the egos with the challenges of just writing the best film you can?*

The only ego problem I faced from all the actors on *Towering Inferno* was an occasional, i.e., daily, contact with either Paul Newman or with Steve McQueen or—on blacker days—from both. There was never a problem when they were shooting separate scenes. Incidentally, I was on the location throughout the filming and therefore, unluckily, in harm's way. But you put Paul in a scene with Steve, and we have an entirely different dynamic at work. I was told, privately and separately, by both gentleman on one occasion or another, "Don't let Steve—or Paul—'blue-eye' me in this scene!"

This meant that if you'd written the scene where the punch line comes at the end and the director is likely to cover with a close-up, you'd get Steve socking it across with one of my better lines and laying that cold blue stare right at the camera. Where does that leave Paul—with some kind of vapid reaction shot? No, damn it, now Paul needs a last line. He needs that blue-eyed close-up. It wasn't easy. I think I handled it decently, because I love Paul and I loved Steve—and I just sort of danced around between them and tried to keep all three of us happy.

[The producer] Irwin Allen became quite eccentric toward the end of his life and career. Yet he may well have been Hollywood's last great showman. Can you offer some personal insight into the man?

He was one of a kind. He was a dear friend. He was often irascible but never toward me—he was endlessly demanding. He was a perfectionist. He knew

---

[*]   Notably, in Paul Gallico's novel (*The Poseidon Adventure* [New York: Coward-McCann, 1969]), Winters's character, Belle Rosen, dies long after her swim, yet only moments before the group's rescue. Moreover, Gene Hackman's character, Reverend Scott, gratuitously leaps to death after blasphemously daring God to swap his life for the others—not, as in the film, after shutting a steam valve that blocks their escape. These changes, which tighten both drama and character, typify Silliphant's skills.

Paul Newman and Steve McQueen competing for close-ups in *The Towering Inferno.*

filmmaking. He was—for a writer—a superb producer because he made available to you any and every tool money could buy or imagination could create. He had his designers bring models of buildings and rooms and elevator shafts and upside-down ship compartments into my office, so that I could write to the specifics of each location. He was available for meetings and conference. He was never late. He worked longer hours than anyone else on his productions.

But, yes, he was vain. He could be arrogant—because he knew what he wanted, even if what he wanted was sometimes not the best choice. He lacked, I say with regret, the kind of sophisticated taste which would have let him produce a film like *Chariots of Fire* [1981]. But then, who knows, he MIGHT have been able to do that, had he chosen. But he was a showman. He loved the circus. He loved prancing horses and gyrating clowns. But he stayed too long at the fair. He should have gone onward and upward after *The Towering Inferno*—sought new directions.

The Killer Elite (1975)

Sam Peckinpah didn't do justice to this picture; he was also reportedly tanked a lot of the time. What input—if any—did he have to your rewrite, and what general changes did you make from Marc Norman's draft?

Sam. Yeah, he was into the scotch malts at the time. We had a script meeting two weeks before shooting, during which Peckinpah pulled out a large throwing knife and began tossing it at a target on the wall between sips of brandy.

"You and I had better have a *mano a mano,*" I said. "I've heard bad stories about you. I understand you have a drinking problem."

"What cocksucker told you that?" Peckinpah growled, taking the brandy glass away from his lips.

"Well, it's obvious from the way you're drinking tonight that this is something you do every night. Now it's very distracting for you to be throwing that knife. Are you trying to tell me something?"

"No, no, no," Peckinpah said. "You're reading too much into this."

To which I said, "I'll give you a clue. I've been studying with Bruce Lee, and I know I can beat the shit out of you. So if you take a shot, you better keep working on me, because if you don't kill me, I'm going to get up off the floor and destroy you. I'll flatten your nose. I'll close your windpipe. I'll ruin your kidneys. Let's be clear. If you take a shot at me, it had better be terminal; because if it's not, I'm going to kill you."

Peckinpah stared at me, then gave an innocent smile. "Whoa, you're really filled with hostility," he said.

"No," I replied, "I'm filled with love. I just want you to know what will happen."

Peckinpah smiled again, put away the knife, and we went to work.

Sam's heart wasn't in *The Killer Elite* because he had a script of his own he wanted to shoot instead; but he was alone in this desire and so was forced to do *The Killer Elite.*[*] He had little input on my rewrite, because I didn't accept any, and since we had reached the point where I refused to come on the set, there was no need for either of us to be too polite to each other, nor for me— since I was working for the producer Marty Baum and fuck the director—to be even courteous. My changes in Marc's draft were to change London to San Francisco and an African political figure into an Asian political figure. It was basically a location rewrite. I added the martial arts stuff. I was able to obtain employment for most of my karate buddies by bringing ninja into play.

In your script, you wrote, "What follows is the kind of exciting hand-to-hand fight scene that only Sam Peckinpah knows how to stage." Do you often customize descriptions that way?

It's amusing that you mention my note to Sam Peckinpah. By all means, yes, indeed. I was blowing smoke up Sam's butt because he was a goddamned

---

[*]   This anecdote about Stirling Silliphant's experiences working with Sam Peckinpah on *The Killer Elite,* from Fine, *Bloody Sam* (see "Walon Green: Fate Will Get You," n. 2), is adapted with permission of Stirling Silliphant.

pain in the ass on this project. But Sam—that's another whole long story—aside, frequently when I was writing episodes for *Route 66* at the rate of one every nine days, I would shorthand the exposition by telling the director to, e.g., "give us a three-minute fight here which makes the fight in *Shane* look like a Girl Scout dance."

You've read today's big spec scripts—The Last Boy Scout, Basic Instinct, *etcetera. If* The Killer Elite *were to be scripted by one of today's hotshots, it would be loaded with parenthetical line readings such as: Tommi (defiant): "He wouldn't shoot a girl." Locken (too aware): "Oh, yes, he would." How do you feel about writers who try to direct the picture from the page?*

How do I feel? I fucking detest it. I spit in the milk of the mothers of the bastards who do it. It is so inexperienced of such writers. It reveals instantly their lack of knowledge of the hard process of filmmaking.

First of all, the director isn't even going to read such nonsense. And any actor who's not on his first gig and who has ever before held a real-life, by-God script in his trembling hand is going to black out all those instructions in his copy. When I first got to Hollywood, I attended acting classes for three years; then, I went back every few years—right up until I left town. I wanted to understand the acting process, so I could write for actors. Watching them, I learned how to streamline my dialogue—where to hesitate, where to rush—so that the writing itself would give the actor all the clues he needed to find his way under the skin of the character I'd written. Why should I tell him to speak a line "defiantly" when he might be more effective, out of his own life, playing defiance by seeming to be meek—or seeming uncaring—or all the other infinite shades of human reaction? So not only is such writing presumptuous, it is short circuiting. It is denying the potential for magic to happen.

Believe me, I had to LEARN this, because I used to write that way too—feeling like God, telling my actors HOW they were going to conduct themselves in the presence of the nuggets I was giving them—until I put myself on the same stage with the actors and realized how goddamned hard it was to BE an actor, and that the last thing he needed was some half-assed writer telling him HOW to do his job.

And I had great teachers. Once, in a *Naked City* at the top of act 2, I wrote two inches of dialogue for Lee J. Cobb that I felt should have been carved in marble on the Lincoln Memorial. Lee took me aside before the scene was shot and asked me if he could play the scene with NO dialogue. I was appalled. "Jesus, Lee, NOT say all this good stuff here?" "Let me show you something," he said, and he ACTED out my words with a few simple movements, not mime, just body language which spoke far more eloquently than my precious words.

It's fair to note that in Hollywood logic the bigger and more costly the project, the less artistic a director they dare entrust it with. Your early scripts were directed by the diversely brilliant likes of Norman Jewison, Sidney Pollack, Don

Siegel, Jacques Tourneur, Ralph Nelson, and Willy Wyler. Later, when the budgets soared and the canvases broadened, they were helmed by John Guillermin, Richard Fleischer, Jimmy Goldstone, Ronald Neame, and Menahem Golan—prolific workers but, it's safe to say, directors without cinematic personalities. Since you are a man of substance and a writer whose rich characters provide much drama to explore, how do you feel your work has been served in the transition—or am I being cavalier to these hardworking directors?

A sad comment but so true. I wish all films had to be brought in for no more than five million dollars, limiting the sums paid to all those making the film; so that the emphasis would be on the work, not on the deal. Not only would more films be produced, but their variety would be far wider than today's high-cost, high-concept productions, where special effects and Gee-Whiz scenes prevail over human relationships and quiet moments between friends in diners.

The Enforcer (1976)

The Enforcer is the third in Clint Eastwood's Dirty Harry series. You're not known for writing sequels, so how did you approach this?

This was one of the most enjoyable experiences of my career, and how I became involved is frightfully simple: I was living in Marin, California. I had a call from Clint Eastwood. I mean, from Clint himself. No lackeys, no executive secretary, no "Can you fly down to Hollywood, Mr. Silliphant?" None of that classic shit. It was Clint over to you, Stirling. "Hello," he said, "this is Clint Eastwood." You always have to, at moments like this, hold back your impulse to say, "And this is Mary Poppins." "I'm thinking about doing a third *Dirty Harry*," he said. "You have any notions?"

"Matter of fact," I said, "I do," because I actually did.

"Okay," he said, "I'll fly up, and we'll meet. Tomorrow, okay?"

"Tomorrow's fine," I said. "Where?" I asked.

"You decide," he said.

"Okay, you know that little restaurant over in Tiberon, by Seal Rock, hangs out over the water, you look across at Angel Island?"

"Twelve-thirty," he said.

I loved the guy the instant I met him. We had lunch, and I told him he needed a new partner for his third movie—one of the world's primary underclass—forget Afro-Americans, Hispanics, and Asians. "What does that leave us?" He grinned. "A woman," I said slyly. "The female of the species. Can you imagine the absolute horror—it's truly Conradian—of Dirty Harry being saddled with a WOMAN as a partner?"

His eyes began to dance as he played with the concept. Finally, he said he LIKED it. But—what was the story?

"Unimportant," I said. "We'll come up with some basic caper line, like the French do, but in this third *Dirty Harry,* the emphasis is on the character relationship, the slowly evolving relationship of trust which develops between you and your female partner, how it opens you up as a human being and you begin to shed all the sexist shit humans beings are burdened with and in the end, she gets blown away and you go fucking rampage crazy—big shoot-out at the end—and Dirty Harry's a different man than he was at the top of the show."

So I was hired and wrote the script, and Clint liked it—ALMOST. He felt it still needed more narrative drive, that maybe I'd put too much into the relationship and not enough into the bread-and-butter stuff that would pull in Clint Eastwood fans. So he took a script he had bought earlier, which was built around a terrorist group, and with a writer [Dean Riesner] with whom he had worked before—I shared credit only on screenplay but story credit went to these writers who had earlier come up with the terrorist story—and folded it into my script. [Tyne Daly, later of television's *Cagney and Lacy,* was cast as Harry's partner.]

I wasn't happy about this,[*] but I liked Clint so much and have so much respect for his sense of what works for him that I put aside my unhappiness. Yet, to this day, I wish we could have persevered with the original concept arrived at that day as we watched the seals in Raccoon Strait and the ketches tacking toward Angel Island. It might have been a memorable film.

Did you search for another "I know what you're thinkin'" or "Make my day" catchphrase for Harry?

No. As a dialogue writer, I've never been apt at such sound bites. I leave that catchphrase stuff to ad writers or spin doctors. I am too involved with the human voice—and people tend to speak more in the way Paddy Chayefsky wrote them, especially in *Marty* [1955], than they do in the Ping-Pong, smart-ass, attempting-to-be-trendy style of most of today's scripts. You take a flick like most of those made by Arnold Schwarzenegger, and you get such magnificent dialogue as—when he has just stabbed a bad guy into a door and leaves him hanging there—"Stick around." I got weary enough during the barrage of James Bond flicks with Richard Maibaum's one-liners: e.g., Bond to Bad Guy he's just heaved into a moat of piranhas, *"Bon appétit."*[†] There is NO WAY, even in my dullest moment, I would allow my brain cells to clot in that direction.

---

[*]   In the *Hollywood Reporter* (March 4, 1976), Silliphant said that Riesner was brought onto the project by Eastwood and the producer Robert Daley, after Silliphant had departed for other commitments, not out of anyone's dissatisfaction with the script.

[†]   The James Bond meister, Richard Maibaum, is interviewed in *Backstory.*

Over the Top (1987)

Sylvester Stallone is famous—no, notorious—for rewriting the scripts he's agreed to do. "Over the Top"* is so far from your intelligence, style, and knowledge of dramatic structure that I would like to know what happened after you wrote "Fade out."

As warming as was my experience with Clint Eastwood, my experience with Sylvester Stallone represents everything I detest about Hollywood. Stallone has one talent—that is to have soaked up all the bullshit which has accumulated in La La Land over the years, coated it with an ersatz patina of culture and love of fine art, and created from his bootstraps a genuine, authentic Monster. I have managed to expunge from my memory the where and how of my getting involved in this disastrous project, but no matter how many sponges I pass over the blackboard, I can't erase the underlying chalk which spells MY OWN FUCKING FAULT.

It was to be a quick rewrite of an existing script and the money was good and I was about ready to buy a new BMW in Munich—or some such nonsense—so I went along with the producer to the brick-walled house in which at the time Stallone was serving time. I was tempted to ask, where are the Dobermans? but I didn't. When I met Stallone, I was surprised to see how SMALL he looked. But, of course, I am a person, not a special camera lens. I will tell you that I found him at this first meeting charming, respectful, and intelligent. I dismissed at once everything negative I had heard about him. He told me a few ideas which he had which he thought might help in the rewrite, then encouraged me by saying, "It's your ball, Stirling. I don't have to tell YOU what to write. But if at any time you get stuck or want to bounce ideas around, call me."

A few days into the rewrite, I did find a need to talk to Stallone. I was seeking his reaction to some Indian stuff I was adding to the mix. I called him. Now I found myself in a Kafka novel. There was NO way I could get through. The entourage had closed in around their deity. What did I wish to talk to Mr. Stallone about? "It's about making him part-Indian," I explained "You see, before he goes to Vegas he needs to renew his strength—his soul. It's much like the Sun Dance performed by the Lakota. But, in this case, I'm inventing a really weird sort of Apache ritual involving a lot of rattlesnakes." CLICK! I persisted. I called the producer. I called a few art galleries where the rumors were he might be showing up. I called the restaurants he's known to haunt—if that is the proper verb. No Stallone.

---

*   Stallone plays a truck driver who attempts rapprochement with his estranged son while they drive across country to the deathbed of the boy's mother, who is the truck driver's former wife. Father and son eventually bond by the time of an arm-wrestling contest in Las Vegas, where, among other resolutions, the boy learns that it was his megalomaniacal grandfather, not his father, who drove the wedge into the family.

So I went ahead on my own. Goddamn rattlesnakes and all. I finished the rewrite in short order, turned it in. The producer loved it. I got my money. But never a word from Stallone. Until a while later, I get a letter from the WGA about writing credit, and I discover that the screenplay is suddenly by Sylvester Stallone and Stirling Silliphant, based on a story by a couple of honest and innocent other writers. Or could it have been that the submitted credit only listed one name as the screenwriter—HIS name?

The term *going ballistic* came into being at that moment. I prepared an appropriate letter of protest to the WGA arbitration committee and sent along the supporting materials, story notes, research, and finished script—and shortly thereafter, Rocky was knocked into second position. But what difference does it really make if the other guy puts his name ahead of yours when he's the bloody star? The finished movie was about as embarrassing as most Stallone films.

I can't possibly explain to you the hundreds of little cuts and jabs that were performed upon the screenplay I turned in. All the Indian stuff was out. Rattlesnakes? Forget it. The relationship between the truck driver and his estranged and dying wife had been turned into a comic strip. The "love" scenes between father and son somehow were trivialized. Much of my dialogue was changed, not so much in its narrative sense as in its literary sense. Wherever I might have written a piece of dialogue which had at its center some kind of feeling or concept, it seemed to have suffered a sex change. Or maybe it's just that Stallone can't get too far beyond "Yo."

My vehemence toward and distaste for Stallone is not personal, strangely enough. In person he can be, I understand, a warm and delightful friend. I believe my abhorrence is based rather on the fact that he has let himself become the ultimate example of Hollywood excess. It's the stretched limo, the need for the number one table at the trendiest restaurant in Venice, the private jet, the expectation that this is the best suite in the hotel—all the trappings which have nothing to do with the world. Only with the business—and all the thousands of remora who swarm around the sharks they create.

Of all your projects, you've said that Fly Away Home *[1981] was the most disappointing. Given the industry's gauntlet and your productivity, why does this one stand out?*

Fly Away Home was designed to be a one-year, twenty-two-hour novel for television about the Vietnam War from the Tet Offensive in 1968 until the fall of Saigon in 1975 when the last of the American invaders butted out.

ABC let us make the two-hour pilot, but whatever flicker of courage had caused the network to authorize me to develop such a bold and daring show suddenly was extinguished. I suspect that New York [where ABC has its headquarters] shot it down. The salespeople probably said to the West Coast, "You fucking idiots, what are you guys doing? What corporation is going to sponsor THIS thing?"

I can't even begin to tell you what a crushing blow it was to have this mini-series aborted in the way it was. It sent me into weeks of destructive behavior. I went public. I announced—imagine, I, a lone writer without resources or power—that never again would I work for ABC until certain executives were fired. And I named them. Well, three years later I was back at ABC; all the guilty had been expunged. Vengeance would have been sweet had their dismissals come as a result of my pissing in the wind. But, no, simple attrition did them in. They're gone—and I'm still writing and producing—so possibly there, and there only, can one isolate the triumph, meaningless as it may be. But the bitter bottom line is that what might have been a major contribution to the American psyche—airing the issues of the US involvement in Indochina—never came into being.

I think the thing that haunted me the most was the fact that for once in all my years of writing, I had actually written the last line of dialogue for a script which would have run 1,320 pages and covered a period of seven tumultuous years crosscut between Vietnam and the States—and never got to use it. The line was to be spoken by the news cameraman, the part played by Bruce Boxleitner, as, remaining behind after the Americans abandoned Saigon, he is photographing the first NVA [North Vietnamese Army] tank breaking through the fence at the Presidential Palace. He looks at the faces of the South Vietnamese, faces without expression, a series of cameos which tell you nothing—and everything. And he says, more to himself than to anybody, "Won't anybody say—'We're sorry'?"

Over and out. I never got to use the line. And to this moment, nobody—no American I have ever heard, certainly nobody in either our government or in our military hierarchy—has ever spoken those absolving words: WE'RE SORRY!

Craftsmanship

Which for you comes first—character or plot? Do you structure your work beforehand, or do you keep it in your head until it just comes out—or neither or both?

I DETEST that word *plot.* I never, never think of plot. I think only and solely of character. Give me the characters; I'll tell you a story—maybe a thousand stories. The interaction between and among human beings is the only story worth telling.

I suppose at the beginning of my screenwriting, I still had one foot in the old bear trap—still unable to escape from the constant reminders all writers get all the way back to Greek theater—about act 1, act 2, and act 3. It was not until I wrote more and learned from my mistakes—and until I lived more and learned from life itself that every moment is a lifetime, and that matters seldom have a remembered beginning or a conscious end. So when I write, I let the characters drive the story. If there are expositional or connective elements to be dealt with, I keep trying to push them back, deeper and deeper into the film, right to the very end—and at that point, to avoid the Agatha Christie inevitable roundup scene where all the suspects are called into the parlor, and we learn the butler did NOT do it, I try to end my story WITHOUT the explanation, that is, without the factual explanation, hoping that the emotional truth of what has happened to the characters will be resolution enough.

I must concede that if you're doing a typical piece of Hollywood shit where nobody can leave the theater until the good guy has blown the bad guy away, you have serious problems with my way of handling a story. The answer—for me, at least—is NOT to get involved writing the kind of film in which I have to solve a plot problem. Just a simple choice of material!

You've said that it takes you two to four weeks to write a first draft. Is this of a TV show or a feature?

The writing is the easiest part of it. The trying period is the period of conceptualization, followed by research. This prewriting time can take anywhere from six months to ten years. But once I know everything there is to know about my characters, the actual writing of the script switches to automatic pilot. It makes no difference whether the script is for TV or a feature—the writing period is the same: five pages a day, seven days a week. That's it. Nothing mystical. You just sit there and keep typing. When you've got your five pages, you're the hell out of there and go off to explore life away from the IBM. So, okay, that's 35 pages a week. If you're talking about a one-hour TV show, you should finish in two weeks. A two-hour MOW takes me three weeks, since these end up anywhere from 105 to 110 pages in length. A script for a feature, using this measurement, should take no more than four weeks—at the max. But here—in consideration of the fact that you can elevate the quality of dialogue and the visualization of the scenes themselves, their staging, their mood, their texture, given the fact that a director is going to have more money and can spend more time in shooting a feature than a TV chunk of sausage—I cut down my page count per day to three pages rather than maintain the 5-page-a-day pace. I round this out at 20 pages a week and allow myself between six and eight weeks for the first draft.

If a writer takes more time than that, he is bullshitting you. Of course, if you want to calculate working time from sitting down without the faintest idea of what you intend to write—until you finish whatever that thing may be—you could spend a lifetime and produce nothing. It shouldn't take the writer any longer to write his script than it takes the director to shoot it or the actors to act it.

Okay, do you still type on yellow paper as you once recommended? Or do you now have an amber monitor for your word processor?

No. I type on plain white paper with three holes punched into the left side of the sheet, so I can place the finished pages into a loose-leaf notebook and move them around if I decide to change my continuity or if I want to replace the scenes already written.

Also, I never write a script in continuity. I write my favorite scene first. I always ask myself, "What is the single most important, most moving, most dramatic scene in the film, the single scene people will still be talking about a week later?" I write that scene first, no matter where it might play in the finished script. And I put it into the notebook. Then I write my next-most-favorite scene and put it into what may end up being its appropriate position. And so on and so on, until I have to start connecting those fragments. The last thing I write are these connections, and I spend hours thinking of them in terms of images and locations.

I do NOT use a computer. I tried, really gave it my best shot, but it never connected for me. I felt too much separation between me and the screen—somehow the words up there lacked immediacy. I could not relate to them. I find that I am faster on the IBM Wheelwriter than any computer instructor I've ever known is on the computer. Believe it or not, I've held contests with the doubters and every time creamed them.

Do you have self-imposed rules for how a script should physically look, such as: no speech more than two fingers in length; always have some dia-logue on the first page, so the producer doesn't see all the description and think it's an art film; hit certain beats by certain page numbers; etcetera?

I have no self-imposed criteria for how a script should look. Or all the rest of the incantations which the guys who write the "How To" books recommend. All that stuff tends to be trendy and to drop by the wayside as time drums relentlessly by. Every script is different; laying these "rules" in is like coaching a guy on foreplay.

Your résumé alone dismisses this question—have you ever been blocked?—but what sort of discipline or ritual do you use to get yourself into the frame of mind for writing?

I believe there is a certain preparation the writer should make before he goes each morning or afternoon or evening to his computer or typewriter or yellow pad. It may be the Buddhist in me, but I truly believe that a sort of rite of cleansing is involved here. Certainly, you can't do your best work if your mind is cluttered with other matters. To clear my thoughts, I simply read a few paragraphs of Harold Brodkey. How was that again? Yep—Harold Brodkey.

I will take a paragraph at random, for example, the following which ends his story "Ceil":

In the tormented and torn silence of certain dreams—in the night court of my sleep—sometimes words, like fingers, move and knead and shape the tableaux: shadowy lives in night streets. There is a pearly strangeness to the light. Love and children appear as if in daylight, but it is always a sleeping city, on steep hills, with banked fires and ghosts lying in the streets in the dully reflectant gray light of a useless significance.

I do not believe there was any justice in Ceil's life.

And I will read it aloud to myself several times, dwelling on "pearly strangeness" or "the dully reflectant gray light of a useless significance."

How, after reading this kind of conceptualizing, can I possibly write a screenplay describing my hero as "young and lean" or a physical movement as "he hurries across the room"?

You see what now happens? The talent in you, if you have any, is challenged—and you go to your work DETERMINED to put poetry on the page—for in setting, stage directions, time, place, feeling, the writing in a script should be at the level of a Bergman script, written more as a novella than as a Hollywood blueprint for a director who understands not words but only MTV images and blue light and wet streets.

Terry Southern: Ultrahip

Interview by Lee Hill

From 1962 to 1970, Terry Southern was the screenwriter who most embodied the sixties zeitgeist. He was an icon who entered the film world with underground cult status as the writer, behind *Candy* (co-written with Mason Hoffenberg), *Flash and Filigree, The Magic Christian,* and *Blue Movie.* He was directly involved in the making of *Dr. Strangelove* and *Easy Rider,* two films that neatly bookend and encapsulate the apocalyptic obsessions of the hothouse decade. His contributions to the films *The Loved One, Casino Royale, The Collector, Don't Make Waves, Barbarella, The Cincinnati Kid, The Magic Christian,* and *End of the Road* varied from on-the-set script surgery and uncredited rewrites to hands-on coproduction.

Born in Alvarado, Texas, on May 1, 1924, Southern served in the US Army during World War II. He completed a bachelor of arts degree in English at Northwestern University in Chicago and attended the Sorbonne on the GI Bill. During the fifties, he perfected a personal brand of black humor and irony through his novels and the short stories and sketches found in the 1967 collection *Red Dirt Marijuana and Other Tastes.* It was a sensibility that allowed Southern to move through several worlds at once. He socialized with the Beats downtown and the *Paris Review* crowd uptown. Despite his hipster aura, he made friends easily. His close friends in his pre-Hollywood days included Kenneth Tynan, Henry Green, Lenny Bruce, and Alexander Trocchi.[*]

By the early sixties, Southern came to the attention of two other cultural heroes, the director Stanley Kubrick and the actor Peter Sellers (there is a little bit of Terry Southern in Sellers's interpretation of Claire Quilty in the film *Lolita*). The unique brand of epic satire in Southern's novels made him an

---

[*] Alexander Trocchi, the Scottish novelist and iconoclast, wrote *Cain's Book* (New York: Grove Press, 1960).

ideal candidate to complete the troika of sensibilities that made *Dr. Strangelove* arguably one of the greatest films ever made.

The wide distribution of *Dr. Strangelove* and the mainstream publication of *Candy* in 1964 fueled a highly successful eight-year stretch for Southern as a screenwriter. He abandoned the "Quality Lit Game" and embraced the possibilities of film with a passion unusual in literary circles. The response of the international film community was mutual. During this heady period, Southern worked with or was courted by, to name a few, the directors Tony Richardson, Alexander Mackendrick, Norman Jewison, Peter Yates, Jean-Luc Godard, Roger Vadim, Joseph McGrath, Mike Nichols, Richard Lester, Otto Preminger, and Jerry Schatzberg.

Dr. Strangelove, Southern now concedes, was his best experience working with a director. Southern was often hired to "do a Strangelove" on other scripts, but his skill as a screenwriter was broader than that. *Easy Rider* would lack much of its punch without the George Hanson character, inspired by Southern's love for William Faulkner's writing and the small-town lawyer, Gavin Stevens, who runs through Faulkner's novels. Hanson as played by Jack Nicholson provides the film's moral center. And despite its garish international-coproduction quality, *Barbarella* still amuses because of the *Candy*-like plotting and Jane Fonda's intuitive feel for the gentle joke in such Southern dialogue as, "A lot of dramatic situations begin with screaming." In Southern's two most underrated films, *The Loved One* and *End of the Road,* he had a role almost equivalent to that of codirector. The wild and overreaching structure of these metasatires holds up surprisingly well in the play-it-safe nineties, and both films are overdue for serious critical reevaluation.

In the seventies and eighties, Southern continued to write a screenplay a year, but none was produced.* Aside from his 1970 novel, Blue Movie, his most notable efforts during this period were his work on the 1981–1982 season of Saturday Night Live for the program's executive producer Michael O'Donoghue and *The Telephone,* a troubled 1988 collaboration with Rip Torn and Harry Nilsson, starring Whoopi Goldberg. Having had the privilege of reading scripts like "Grossing Out," an original commissioned by Peter Sellers, and his adaptation of Harry Crews' *Car* (New York: Morrow, 1972), I can only speculate that increasingly retrograde studio decision making in the nineties accounts for their unproduced status.

•   While a complete list of unproduced projects cannot be listed for space considerations, it should be noted that, despite Southern's lack of on-screen credits after 1970, he remained a prolific screenwriter. Aside from the projects mentioned in this section, he worked on, to name a few, a script about Hermann Göring for a Swedish producer, an original called "Honky Tonk Heroes" for Rip Torn, and "Floaters," a script for Kubrick's former partner James B. Harris.

Terry Southern in Salisbury, Connecticut, 1995. (Photo by William B. Winburn.)

One of his most recent projects, with the photographer Peter Beard, was a dark meditation on conservation called "End of the Game."* He also taught a new generation of screenwriters in a graduate seminar at Columbia University in the last years of his life.

Like the surrealist billionaire in his classic novel, *The Magic Christian,* Southern was a grand guy in person. Shy and reserved upon first meeting, he opened up when he relaxed. His expansive wit and generosity, along with a remarkable gift for mimicry, surfaced continually in our conversations. This

---

* "End of the Game" is based on Beard's book-length photo essay, which depicts the decline of the elephant safari in Kenya, and explores the pros and cons of conservation polices in the region, first published in 1965 (New York: Viking).

interview was conducted in person at Southern's home in Connecticut and by mail during 1993 and 1994.[*]

Terry Southern (1924–1995)

1955   *Candy Kisses* (short subject) (David Burnett). Co-story, codirection.

1964   *Dr. Strangelove; or, How I Learned to Stop Worrying and Love the Bomb* (Stanley Kubrick). Co-script.

1965   *The Loved One* (Tony Richardson). Co-script.
          The Collector (William Wyler). Uncredited contribution.
          The Cincinnati Kid (Norman Jewison). Co-script.

1966   *Don't Make Waves* (Alexander Mackendrick). Uncredited contribution.

1967   *Skidoo* (Otto Preminger). Uncredited contribution.
          Casino Royale (Val Guest, Ken Hughes, John Huston, Joseph McGrath, and Robert Parrish). Uncredited contribution.

1968   *Barbarella* (Roger Vadim). Co-script.
          Candy (Christian Marquand). Adaptation by Buck Henry from Southern and Mason Hoffenberg's novel.

1969   *Easy Rider* (Dennis Hopper and Peter Fonda). Co-script.

1970   *End of the Road* (Aram Avakian). Coproducer, co-script, actor.
          The Magic Christian (Joseph McGrath). Co-script, adapted from Southern's novel.

1988   *The Telephone* (Rip Torn). Co-script.

Southern makes cameo appearances as himself in *The Queen, Cocksucker Blues, The Man Who Fell to Earth,* and *Burroughs.*

Television credits include *The Emperor Jones* (1958, adaptation), *Stop Thief!* (1976, teleplay), and *Saturday Night Live* (1981–1982, staff writing).

Novels include *Flash and Filigree, The Magic Christian, Candy* (with Mason Hoffenberg), *Blue Movie,* and *Texas Summer.* Other books include *Red Dirt*

---

[*]   This interview was completed shortly before Terry Southern's death. En route to his screenwriting class at Columbia, Southern collapsed and was rushed to St. Luke's Hospital. He died on October 29, 1995, from respiratory failure at the age of seventy-one. In one of many tributes, Bruce Jay Friedman, a longtime friend and fellow writer said that, while most "writers coexist uneasily, this observation did not apply to Terry Southern, who, for all his dark, satirical genius, was the most generous of men."

Marijuana and Other Tastes, Writers in Revolt (coedited with Alexander Trocchi and Richard Seaver), *The Log Book of "The Loved One," The Rolling Stones on Tour—Log Book,* and *The Early Stones: 1962–1973.*

Academy Award honors include Oscar nominations for Best Screenplay Based on Material from Another Medium for *Dr. Strangelove* and for Best Story and Screenplay Based on Material Not Previously Published or Produced for *Easy Rider.*

Writers Guild honors include Best Written American Comedy for *Dr. Strangelove.*

Dr. Strangelove; or, How I Learned to Stop Worrying and Love the Bomb (1964)

What was the status of the Dr. Strangelove *script before Stanley Kubrick decided to hire you in the fall of 1962?*

When Kubrick and Peter George first began to do the script, they were trying to stick to the melodrama in George's book, Red Alert [published under the pseudonym "Peter Bryant" (New York: Ace Books, 1958)].* There was an outline. They didn't go into a treatment but went straight into a script. They had a few pages and in fact had started shooting, but in a very tentative way. Kubrick realized that it was not going to work. You can't do the end of the world in a conventionally dramatic way or boy-meets-girl way. You have to do it in some way that reflects your awareness that it is important and serious. It has to be a totally different treatment, and black humor is the way to go. That was Kubrick's decision.

When you first got together with Kubrick, did you start changing the tone of the script right away?

Yeah, after the first day, at our first meeting, he told me what the situation was. All those things that I've told you were his very words. "It's too important to be treated in the conventional way. It's unique! The end of the world is surely a unique thing, so forget about the ordinary treatment of subject and go for something like a horror film." He decided to use humor. The flavor that attracted him in my novel *The Magic Christian* could be effective in this new approach. He would talk about the mechanics of making it totally credible and convincing in terms of the fail-safe aspect and then how to make that funny. And the way you make it funny, because the situation is absurd, is by dealing with it in terms of the dialogue and characters.

I'm curious about the day-to-day working relationship with Kubrick as you wrote the film from the preproduction period through the actual shooting.

---

* Peter George, a former Royal Air Force officer, published *Red Alert* in 1958, and collaborated on a straight adaptation of his book with Kubrick during the early stages of the project.

Well, after my first day in London when he told me what he had in mind, I got settled into a hotel room not far from where he lived in Kensington. That night, I wrote the first scene, and then he picked me up at four-thirty the next morning in a limo. The limo was a big Rolls or Bentley. We rode in the back-seat with the light on. There was this desk that folded down. It was very much like a train compartment. It was totally dark outside. If it got light, we would pull the shades down. He would read the script pages; then we would rewrite them and prepare them for shooting when we got to the studio, which was about an hour to an hour-and-a-half drive depending on the fog.

Kubrick is notorious for his organizational mania.

Yes, he loved nothing so much than to go into stationery stores and buy gadgets and organizational aids.

You hear all these fantastic stories about how Kubrick lives. Did you visit his home much when you were in London?

Yes, several times. He has a castlelike structure, a grand old mansion, which has this two-projector screening room. It has electric fences and security devices. It has everything except a moat. He's super private because he lives for his children. He lives in comfort and luxury in almost total isolation.

Peter Sellers was going to play all four parts originally, including the Texan bombardier. I understand you coached Sellers on his accent.

The financing of the film was based almost 100 percent on the notion that Sellers would play multiple roles. About a week before shooting, he sent us a telegram saying he could not play a Texan, because he said it was one accent he was never able to do. Kubrick asked me to make a tape of a typical Texan accent. When Sellers arrived on the set, he plugged into this Swiss tape recorder with huge, monster earphones, and listened to the tape I made. He looked ridiculous, but he mastered the accent in about ten minutes. Then Sellers sprained his ankle and couldn't make the moves going up and down the ladder in the bomb bay. So he was out of that part. The doctor told him he couldn't do it. Then it was a question of replacing him. Stanley had set such store by Sellers's acting that he felt he couldn't replace him with just another actor. He wanted an authentic John Wayne. The part had been written with Wayne as the model.

Did Kubrick ever try to get Wayne to play the role?

Wayne was approached, and dismissed it immediately. Stanley hadn't been in the States for some time, so he didn't know anything about television programs. He wanted to know if I knew of any suitable actors on TV. I said there was this very authentic, big guy who played on *Bonanza,* named Dan Blocker. Big Hoss. Without seeing him, Kubrick sent off a script to his agent. Kubrick got an immediate reply: "It is too pinko for Mr. Blocker." Stanley then remembered Slim Pickens from *One-Eyed Jacks* [1961], which he [had] almost directed for Marlon Brando, until Brando acted in such a weird way that he forced Stanley out.

George C. Scott and Peter Sellers in *Dr. Strangelove,* directed by Stanley Kubrick.

When Pickens was hired and came to London, wasn't that the first time he had ever been out of the States?

Yes, in fact it was the first time he had ever been anywhere outside the rodeo circuit as a clown or the backlots of Hollywood. Stanley was very concerned about Slim being in London for the first time and asked me to greet him. I got some Wild Turkey from the production office and went down to the soundstage. It was only ten in the morning, so I asked Slim if it was too early for a drink. He said, "It's never too early for a drink." So I poured out some Wild Turkey in a glass and asked him if he had gotten settled in his room. "Hell, it doesn't take much to make me happy. Just a pair of loose shoes, a tight pussy, and a warm place to shit." One of Kubrick's assistants, a very public-school type, couldn't believe his ears, but went "Ho, ho, ho" anyway.

Finally, I took Slim over to the actual set where we were shooting. I left him alone for a few minutes to talk to Stanley. While we were standing there talking, Stanley went, "Look there's James Earl Jones on a collision course with Slim. Better go over and introduce them." James Earl Jones knew that Pickens had just worked with Brando. Jones was impressed and asked Pickens about the experience of working with Brando. "Well, I worked with Marlon Brando for six months, and in that time, I never saw him do one thing that wasn't all man and all white." Slim didn't even realize what he was saying. I glanced at James Earl Jones, and he didn't crack [a smile]. Slim replacing

Sellers worked out well because, unbeknownst to me at the time, the actor that was playing the copilot [Jack Creley] was taller and stockier than Sellers. Whereas Slim was about the same size [as the copilot] and more convincingly fulfilled the intention of this larger-than-life Texan.

To what extent did Peter Sellers' improvisation depart from the shooting script?

It was minimal. It wasn't like *Lolita,* where he improvised a great deal. His improvisational bits in *Strangelove* were very specific. One scene that comes to mind is when [Sterling] Hayden goes into the bathroom to kill himself, Peter's lines are: "Oh, go into the bathroom and have a brushup . . . good idea." Sellers changed that to: "Splash a bit of cold water on the back of the neck . . . ," which is more of a British thing. That was good.

What was Columbia's reaction to this subversive black comedy that the studio had helped to finance?

Columbia was embarrassed by the picture and tried to get people to see Carl Foreman's *The Victors* instead. At the time we thought we were going to be totally wiped out. People would call up the box office and be told there were no seats for *Strangelove* and asked if they would like to see *The Victors* instead. Gradually, the buzz along the rialto built word of mouth in our favor.

Wasn't there some falling-out between Kubrick and yourself over screen credit following the film's release?

Stanley's obsession with the auteur syndrome—that his films are by Stanley Kubrick—overrides any other credit at all. Not just writing but anything. He's like Chaplin in that regard. That's the reason why he rarely uses original music in his films. [Since I had] written this great best-seller, *Candy,* which was number one on the *New York Times* best-seller list for something like twenty-one weeks, my reputation eclipsed Stanley's; so I got total credit for all the *Strangelove* success in *Life,* the *New York Times,* and other publications. The credit I was getting was just so overwhelming and one sided that naturally Stanley was freaking out. He took out an ad in *Variety* saying I was only one of the three writers on the film, the other two being Peter, George, and himself. He just lashed out. But it was like an overnight thing. I wrote a letter to the *New York Times* explaining that there was no mystery involved, and that I was brought in to just help with the screenplay.

The Loved One and
The Cincinnati Kid (1965)

After Dr. Strangelove, *you worked on* The Loved One *and* Cincinnati Kid, *two films produced by John Calley and Martin Ransohoff. What can you tell me about those experiences?*

The Loved One was the most underrated film I've worked on. However, it has recently been released on videocassette and will finally be seen and, presumably, recognized. The cinematography by Haskell Wexler should have received an Academy Award. Everyone who knows anything about film agrees on that. The cast, which included John Gielgud and Rod Steiger, is one of the finest ever assembled. And working with Tony Richardson was extraordinary. He had just come off *Tom Jones* [1963], which won every award possible and made everyone connected with it a fortune—and yet such is the total sleaze and corruption of the studios that MGM refused to renegotiate his contract and made him abide by his pre–*Tom Jones* commitment to *The Loved One* for a minuscule fee. They thought they were being shrewd. Well, Richardson was so completely pissed off at them that he cast an American actor, Robert Morse, to play an English poet—at a time, when Tom Courtenay, James Fox, and Albert Finney, to mention a few, were available— and he barred [the producer] Martin Ransohoff from the set. We started each morning in the production office by opening a magnum of Dom Pérignon. The dailies were shown at the screening room of the Beverly Hills Hotel, with plenty of canapés laid on. In other words, their shrewd avarice cost them a pretty penny in the end.

Sam Peckinpah was the original director of *The Cincinnati Kid.* There is a sequence in the beginning where Slade, a wealthy southerner played by Rip Torn, is at home with his wife and two children. He is shown to be a sanctimonious family man. In a subsequent scene, he is shown in bed with his mistress. Well, it was obvious that the full irony of his hypocrisy, in this citadel of southern virtue, New Orleans, could only be attained by her being black. So that's how it was written, and that's how it was shot with Peckinpah of course in enthusiastic agreement. When the producer saw the dailies, he freaked. "We're not making a message picture," he said and replaced Peckinpah pronto with Norman Jewison, who said something like "Hey, you guys must have been nuts to try that!"

It may have balanced out though, because there's a scene in the movie where the Kid [Steve McQueen] is very depressed because his girl [Tuesday Weld] has just left, and he's trying to get his head together for the big game with the Man [Edward G. Robinson]. Norman said, "Okay, let's create an atmosphere of really devastating loneliness. Maybe Steve walking along an empty street. You know, putting an emphasis on his solitary situation. Think that will do it?" "Yes," I said, "if it's at night." That gave Norm pause. "A night shoot? Very expensive, Ter. Well, I guess we can manage it." "Well, if you really want to max it for loneliness," I said, "it really should be raining as well." "A night shoot in the rain? Holy Christ!" So there we were with a couple of blocks in midtown New Orleans cordoned off, at night, with rain machines letting it pour from the roofs of several buildings. Of course, the producer, Big Mart Ransohoff—the guy who had fired Peckinpah—freaked out completely. "Are you guys out of your gourd?" He kept shouting, "You're killing me, you're killing me!"

The British Film Boom

You spent a lot of time going back and forth to London during the height of the British film boom.

After *Strangelove,* I started working pretty quickly on an adaptation of [the novel by John Fowles] *The Collector* [Boston: Little, Brown, 1963].

Did you stay in England for that?

Yeah, although I quit before the shooting began. The two American producers [Stanley Mann and John Kohn] insisted on finding a way to save the girl [at the end of the story]. At the end of John Fowles' novel, the heroine dies of pneumonia after trying to escape in a rainstorm. Changing that didn't even seem like a possibility. It sounded like a stupid idea. I was not comfortable changing the ending, because of my admiration for Fowles' novel. I even wrote a letter to the *London Times* protesting this change, and it had some effect on the producers, which gave me a bit of satisfaction. Then they said, "We've been thinking about it. Maybe the real message is that art can triumph over an asshole like the collector." After showing his complete nerd-jerk-nowhere-man creepiness, I contrived to have her escape by outwitting the collector through her art [the girl is an art school student] and ultimately to prevail. So I wrote a couple of scenes where Samantha Eggar was working with a papier mâché sculpture in her cell. I set up a pattern whereby Terence Stamp would open the door of this room and look in very cautiously to make sure she wasn't trying to escape, because a couple of times when he opened the door, she tried to dart out. He would say, "I want you to stand where I can see you from the other side of the room." She created this papier mâché likeness in such detail that it deceived him. He would open the door and look across the room and see "her," when she was, in fact, just behind the door. Because the sculpture was so artfully done, he fell for it. The scene was like Hitchcock. Then she locked the door behind her and [locked] him in her former cell. Years later, she would be seen having a picnic on a lovely day. "It's so lovely here in this pastoral sylvan setting; I can understand why you like to come here," her companion would comment. The camera would then pull away to reveal they are having a picnic just a few feet away from the cellar door. By this stage, they had gone too far back toward the original premise for them to use the new ending that I proposed.

The making of Casino Royale *was a fairly acrimonious affair with all the directors from John Huston and Robert Parrish to Joseph McGrath. You spent a fair amount of time as an uncredited writer on the film.*

* Joseph McGrath, the Scottish director, who worked with Richard Lester on *The Running Jumping and Standing Still Film,* then directed for television, most notably the BBC series, with Peter Cook and Dudley Moore, *Not Only . . . but Also. Casino Royale* was to have been McGrath's

I received a call from Gareth Wigan, a famous British agent, who was representing me at the time. He had this call from Peter Sellers saying Peter wanted me to write some dialogue for him on this movie. Wigan said, "I think you can ask whatever you want, because the producer, Charles Feldman, wants to make it a blockbuster." There was a lot of heavyweight on that movie because of Orson Welles and Woody Allen. However, Woody Allen and Peter were such enemies on that film that I didn't really associate with anyone but Peter. An extraordinary thing happened. Because Woody Allen was having such a bad time on the picture, his agent came over to the Dorchester Hotel to speak to him one day. When he came into the lobby, he was dead sure he spotted his client Woody Allen at the newsstand reading a paper. The agent came over and said, "Hey, Woody, we're gonna fix that fucking Sellers, and he'll be off this picture." But it was actually Peter Sellers he was talking to. Sellers immediately realized that it was a case of mistaken identity and of course went right along with it, apparently giving a masterful impersonation of Woody Allen. He used to repeat this imitation with the grimace and glasses. The agent kept ranting for three or four minutes how Sellers should be fired and some specific things like "I've seen his contract, and I know how much he's getting, blah, blah, blah," and then he split. Peter was so irate—later he was amused—that he walked straight out the door and flew home to Geneva and announced he was taking a few days holiday. So this multimillion-dollar movie came to an abrupt halt. It was an incredible situation costing thousands a day. They tried to shoot around Peter in his big confrontation scene with Orson Welles in the casino. Welles was furious. They didn't even have all the actors in the master shot, just some stand-ins, and each day, they would shoot around whichever star didn't show up.

There were a lot of writers involved on that project. Can you remember which scenes you wrote?

Just the Peter Sellers stuff. I rewrote all his dialogue in the scenes he was in. I just rewrote with an eye to giving him the best dialogue, so that he would come out [of the film looking] better than the others. I earned an enormous amount for work which I essentially did overnight.

Where would you stay in England when working on a film?

I was staying at the Dorchester during *Casino Royale.* I stayed at a number of hotels. Writing on a contract for a major studio, you get the very best. I

---

feature film debut, but the producer Charles Feldman hired, fired, and then rehired him along with four other directors—Robert Parrish, Val Guest, John Huston, and Ken Hughes—and the results were edited together. Other writers, credited and uncredited, included Wolf Mankowitz, Michael Sayers, Joseph Heller, Ben Hecht, and Billy Wilder. McGrath's other film credits include *Thirty is a Dangerous Age, Cynthia,* and *The Bliss of Miss Blossom,* and, or course, the adaptation of *The Magic Christian.* Southern and McGrath later worked on an unproduced film version of William Burroughs' *Last Days of Dutch Schultz* and a spoof about the Cannes Film Festival.

would go back and forth on these over-the-Pole flights, where you would go from LA to London. I wrote a lot during those flights.

You spent a fair amount of time socializing with the Beatles, the Rolling Stones, and others in the scene associated with Robert Fraser's London art gallery.

I knew about Robert Fraser's gallery because friends of mine like [artists] Claes Oldenburg, Jim Dine, Larry Rivers, and others would show there. Robert Fraser was an extraordinary guy. Kenneth Tynan lived on Mount Street near the gallery. He used to take me to a lot of places like that. Fraser's gallery became very common knowledge in the industry. One day, Tynan said I had to meet this friend of his, Colin Self, who had done this extraordinary piece of sculpture which was like the *Strangelove* plane. They wanted me to pose with it at Fraser's gallery. That was my first actual trip there. While I was there, Michael Cooper,* the photographer who took some pictures, said, "You must come over [to my place] for drinks. Mick and Keith are going to be there." Robert used to have this very active salon at his flat. So I went over and got to know them in a very short time. Christopher Gibbs, the antique dealer and production designer for *Performance* [1970], was part of the crowd at Robert Fraser's. Then there was Tara Browne, who was killed in the car crash John Lennon wrote about in "A Day in the Life." Sandy Lieberson, who was an agent who optioned *Flash and Filigree* and produced *Performance,* was there a fair bit. He was involved with the American film industry in London. I wasn't around during the actual shooting of *Performance,* but I heard a lot of talk about it from James Fox and his father, [the film and theatrical agent] Robin Fox.

Wasn't your old Paris buddy [the novelist] Mordecai Richler still living in London then?

He was in fact living there and so was [the director] Ted Kotcheff. We had these great poker games.

Did you meet the Beatles around the same time?

I met the Beatles at exactly the same time, because Michael Cooper was doing several of their album covers. He had that market sewed up.

Do you remember how they decided to choose your face for the cover of Sgt. Pepper?†

---

*   Michael Cooper died in 1973, but his photographs of the period can be found in two wonderful books, *The Early Stones; 1962–1973* (New York: Hyperion, 1992) with text by Terry Southern, and *Blinds and Shutters* (London: Genesis/Headley, 1990), both edited by his former assistant, Perry Richardson.

†   In the upper left-hand corner of the *Sgt. Pepper's Lonely Hearts Club Band* album cover, Terry Southern wears big dark glasses, with Tony Curtis on his right, Francis Bacon just off to the left, and Lenny Bruce, Anthony Burgess, and W. C. Fields just above.

I was probably one of the few people they knew who wasn't an icon of a sort. Most of the other faces on the cover were historical choices. [Of all the Beatles] I am closest to Ringo. Ringo was a very good friend of Harry Nilsson. Through Ringo, I met Harry, who I became grand good friends with and later worked [with] on scripts like *The Telephone* for Hawkeye, a company that we formed.

Candy (1968)

Before Candy *was directed by Christian Marquand, you were involved in the adaptation as a coproducer as well as writer.*

Yes, the first plan for *Candy* was for David Picker, who was the head of United Artists at the time, to produce and Frank Perry to direct. Perry had just come off *David and Lisa,* [1963], so he was big. We were going to get Hayley Mills to play Candy. She was perfect. [However,] John Mills, her father, wouldn't let her do it. We were still in the process of trying to persuade him to let her do it when David Picker lost his position. Then, my good friend Christian Marquand, the French actor who was trying to break into directing

Marlon Brando and Ewa Aulin in the film *Candy,* based on Terry Southern's novel.

and was certainly competent enough to direct at the time, begged me to let him have the option for two weeks for nothing, so he could put a deal together. So I did, and sure enough, Marquand immediately put Brando in the cast because Brando was his best friend. They were lifelong friends to the extent that Brando named his first son after Marquand. So on the basis of getting Brando, he was able to add Richard Burton and having gotten those two, he was able to get everyone else. Then, he disappointed me by casting a Swedish girl [Ewa Aulin] for the lead role, which was uniquely American and midwestern. He thought this would make Candy's appeal more universal. That's when I withdrew from the film. The film version of *Candy* is proof positive of everything rotten you ever heard about major studio production. They are absolutely *compelled* to botch everything original to the extent that it is no longer even vaguely recognizable.

Buck Henry wrote the final screen adaptation. Did you know him at all?

I didn't know him at all at the time. I wasn't even aware that he had written a script of *Catch-22*. I just thought he was the creator of *Get Smart.*

Did you look down on TV writers at the time?

Well, how would you feel? I mean, situation comedy! What could possibly be creatively lower than that? It has nothing to do with TV versus film. It's just that situation comedy is mass produced and not something that has much to do with writing.

Barbarella (1968) and
Easy Rider (1969)

In the fall of 1968, you went to Rome to work on Barbarella.

Yes, I stayed there during the shoot at Cinecitta. I was living at the top of the Spanish Steps in a good hotel there. It was a good experience working with Roger Vadim and Jane Fonda. The strain was with Dino De Laurentiis, who produced the picture. He was just this flamboyant businessman. His idea of good cinema was to give money back on the cost of the picture before even going into production. He doesn't even make any pretense about the quality or the aesthetic.

Vadim wasn't particularly interested in the script, but he was a lot of fun, with a discerning eye for the erotic, grotesque, and the absurd. And Jane Fonda was super in all regards. The movie has developed a curious cult following, and I am constantly getting requests to appear at screenings at some very obscure weirdo place like Wenk, Texas, or a suburb of Staten Island. Around 1990, I got a call from De Laurentiis. He was looking for a way to do a sequel. "On the cheap" was how he expressed it, "but with *plenty action* and *plenty sex!*" Then, he went on with these immortal words: "Of course, Janie is too old now to be sexy but maybe her daughter." But nothing, perhaps fortunately, came of it.

Jack Nicholson in the jail scene in *Easy Rider*, directed by Dennis Hopper.

Wasn't it during the making of Barbarella *that you first began working on* Easy Rider*?*

Yes. Very early on it was called "Mardi Gras" to identify it. The first notion was that it would entail barnstorming cars, stunt-driver cars, which do flips and things—a troupe who play a few dates and places, and eventually get fed up with that, so they make this score—but that just seemed too unnecessarily complicated. So we just settled for the straight score of dope, selling it, and leaving the rat race. We forgot about the commonplace thing of daredevil drivers. Finally, we forewent any pretense of them doing anything else other than buying cocaine. We didn't specify that it was cocaine, but that's what it was. They go to New Orleans to sell it. Then, once they got their money, they ride to coastal Florida or some place like Key West where they could buy a boat cheap—not in New Orleans, because it would be too expensive. That was basically the story, which I then started to flesh out after our initial script meetings.

Did they actually do some kind of formal writing, or was it mainly in the form of tossing around ideas at story conferences?

Story conferences, mainly.

So, when you worked with Hopper and Fonda at your office and during the New Orleans shoot, you would just talk the story out and then go off and physically write the pages?

I did *all* the writing on it. They just had the idea in the beginning of the two guys making a score and using the money to buy their freedom from the rat race of America. Their pilgrimage on the road. That was all they had. No dialogue.

So you were the only one doing the actual, physical writing on it?

I did the *only* writing on it. Peter Fonda was the only working actor in the group. Dennis wasn't really into acting at this time. He was a photographer. He had acted a long time before and had been a child actor. He was in *Sons of Katie Elder* [1965]. Peter Fonda had been in several of these really low-ball series of biker movies for AIP [American International Pictures]. He had a contract for one more in a three-picture contract. Dennis had this idea they would do instead of doing one of their typical B-picture dumbbell movies: under the guise of doing a biker movie, they could maybe pull off a movie that might be more interesting, [and] Dennis would be able to make his debut as a director in one fell swoop. It seemed possible under these auspices, whereas he couldn't get arrested ordinarily. Under the setup where Peter Fonda owed AIP this picture, it would be possible to get this different approach in under the wire. He persuaded Peter to go along with this, "We'll get Terry to write the script!" I had this good reputation off of *Dr. Strangelove* and *Candy*.

How did Easy Rider *end up at Columbia?*

That was through this guy [the producer] Bert Schneider, who made a deal for the distribution rights. He wasn't involved during the production. He made some kind of deal with Dennis and Peter. Peter was the nominal producer. So that was the situation when they came by my place in New York. They said, "We want you to write this, and we're going to defer any money in exchange for splitting 10 percent three ways." For a variety of complicated business reasons, I wasn't in a position where I could defer; so they said, "You can get $350 a week for ten weeks in lieu of that." So I did it that way. So I never had a piece of the film, which turned out to be very lucrative.

Anyway, they told me the basic notion of two guys who were fed up with the rat race and commercialization of America. So, in order to get out of it, they're going to make this score and then head to Galveston or Key West, and buy a boat and take off. The story would involve a cross-country trip and the various adventures that could befall them. The idea of meeting a kind of a straight guy, which turned out to be the Jack Nicholson role, was totally up to me. I thought of this Faulkner character, Gavin Stevens, who was the lawyer in this small town. He had been a Rhodes scholar at Oxford and studied at Heidelberg, and had come back to this little town to do whatever he could there. So I sort of automatically gave the George Hanson character a sympathetic aura. I wrote the part for Rip Torn, who I thought would be ideal for it. When shooting began, we went to New Orleans and Rip was going to come, but he couldn't get out of his stage commitment in a Jimmy Baldwin play, *Blues for Mr. Charlie*. At the time, it seemed like there was a possibility he might. We could shoot his part in a few days, and he would still be able to make this theatrical commitment. It wasn't a big part. [The Baldwin play] was a Greenwich Village production and very little bread for him. He was doing it because he felt committed to it. Because he's very much that kind of guy. So he missed the role of a lifetime. And Jack Nicholson was just on the scene, always around. He was a good choice, because he had that sympathetic quality.

How did you feel after the release of Easy Rider, *when in interviews Dennis and Peter kind of downplayed the fact that you had written the screenplay. It seemed almost like an attack of amnesia on their part.*

Well, vicious greed is the only explanation. And desperation for some ego-identity material, because neither one had much of that. Whereas for me, I was filled with an abundance of praise and things.

You said you wanted to talk more about Easy Rider *because of a possible lawsuit regarding your rights to it.*

I don't want Dennis to do [*Easy Rider II*] without notifying me or anything, because in order to get their names [Hopper's and Fonda's] on *Easy Rider* I had to call the Writers Guild to say it was okay. For a director and a producer to be named on the writing credits is practically unheard of. Since there has been so much coercion, bribery, and so on by directors in the past, tacking themselves onto the credits, nowadays it's an automatic arbitration. And so, I received this phone call from Peter saying, "Well, we've got this print. I think we've got a nice little picture here. Dennis and I want to get our names on the writing credits, but in order to do that, you'll have to notify the Writers Guild to say that it's all right."

Did you think it was a fair request at the time?

It wasn't fair, but it didn't matter to me at the time because I was ultrasecure. I had *Candy* and *Dr. Strangelove*. I said, "Sure, that's fine." I didn't mind. So I spoke to the Writers Guild. They were a little surprised. They said, "Well, those guys aren't even members of the Writers Guild. They're not really writers, are they?" I said, "Yes, that's true, but you don't have to be in the Writers Guild to write something," although you are supposed to be in order to participate [in the profits, residuals, et al.].

A lot of people still seem to think Easy Rider *was this completely improvised film, but looking at the shooting script, I was surprised to find even the graveyard hallucination scene was completely scripted out. Why did Peter and Dennis take the lion's share of the credit on that film?*

Yeah, neither of them is a writer. It's often the case with directors that they don't like to share credit, which was the case with Stanley. He would prefer just "A Film by Stanley Kubrick," including music and everything. Aside from Kubrick, other directors I worked with rarely did anything on the script.

End of the Road (1970)

The director of End of the Road, *Aram Avakian, and you were co-conspirators and friends since meeting in Paris in the late forties?*

He had a kind of Renaissance-man quality so he just got interested in films.

He edited Jazz on a Summer's Day *[1959].* * *Was that his first gig?*

Yeah, he started work as an apprentice for Bert Stern, who was the director. Aram was invited to direct a film called *Ten North Frederick Street* [based on the John O'Hara novel]. *Ten North Frederick Street* was going to be his big chance. Something went wrong there. Then he met some producer who was powerful enough to get him another directing job. The movie the guy got him was called *Lad: A Dog,* in which the hero was a dog. You can *imagine* what a challenge that would be. Avakian did some work on the script. He used to come by and discuss things. It reached the state where at the end of the movie, the dog, Lad, was getting married. The story called for a kind of wedding between the dog, this Lassie-type collie, and some sort of very pampered dog of the same breed. Of course, Aram insisted that it shouldn't happen like that, and instead Lad should run off with a mongrel dog. Aram said if he could get away with that, the film would work. What happened was he got fired because the studio wouldn't go along with that.

End of the Road came about through a mutual friend, Max Raab, who was a very nice guy, whose line of business was women's clothing shops, a certain kind of casual wear. Very expensive, very high fashion. Raab wanted to get into show business, and he was very knowledgeable about movies. He said, "Look, you guys find a property, and I'll get hold of about $300,000."

I had just read this John Barth novel [*End of the Road* (Garden City, N.Y.: Doubleday, 1958)]. Aram had read it on my recommendation. We simultaneously agreed that it was a good story, and that it would make a good movie. So we got an option on it, wrote a treatment, and showed it to Max Raab—who hated to be called Max A. Raab, being very Jewish. (*Laughs.*) So he agreed. We got the money together and hired Steve Kestern, who had worked with Arthur Penn, as our production manager.

Dennis McGuire has a cowriting credit along with you and Avakian. What was his role?

He was some guy who, unbeknownst to us at the time, had an option on the Barth novel. We couldn't buy him out, so we had to cut him in on the writing fee.

Since he wasn't active in the writing of the shooting script, was crediting him a conciliatory gesture on your part?

---

* A documentary of the 1958 Newport Jazz Festival.

Yeah. In the late summer of 1968, we scouted locations around East Canaan in Connecticut and Great Barrington, Massachusetts. We found this fantastic old button factory in Great Barrington, which was perfect as a soundstage. That's how *End of the Road* got started. Oh yes, one of the interesting things was that we needed a good director of photography. We couldn't afford a regular one, so Aram had this idea of scanning commercials and getting a director of commercials who wanted to break into features. We started to look at these reels of guys who made commercials, and we noticed one who was much better than the others. We hired the director, who turned out to be the great Gordon Willis.

You were also fortunate to cast people like James Earl Jones, Stacy Keach, Harris Yulin, and Dorothy Tristan. The film has some very interesting effects and a startling opening montage.

We tried to give the film a full-on sixties flavor—student unrest and so on—which seemed inherent in the book. A very good book, and, I like to believe, a most faithful adaptation, with a little something extra in the form of Doctor D's [played by James Earl Jones] theories.

The Magic Christian (1970)

Your next big project was The Magic Christian. *That project had been in gestation for about four or five years before shooting started in February of 1969.*

The way it evolved was that Peter Sellers and Joe McGrath had been working together with Richard Lester on his *Running Jumping and Standing Still Film* [1960], so they got to be good friends. McGrath had been working as an assistant to Richard Lester. McGrath wanted to direct something on his own. He asked Peter what would be a good movie to direct. And that turned out to be *The Magic Christian*. Peter had bought a hundred copies of my novel to give out on birthdays and Christmas. Joe McGrath thought it was a match made in heaven, so Peter immediately started to develop the property. Peter had a contract with some studio which had produced his last movie. He told them *Christian* was going to be his next movie and he wanted Joe to direct. Did they want to finance it, or did they want him to look somewhere else? Their first reaction was "Yes, we'll do it!"

Was it your idea to give Guy Grand a son, which, along with switching the location from America to England, was the major departure from the novel?

Well, that came about because the producers wanted to get what they called some extra box-office appeal. Peter had seen me hanging out with Paul [McCartney], I think, and said, "Well, Terry knows the Beatles. Maybe we can get one of them." Ringo had said that he would like to be in the movie. So I said, "How about getting Ringo?" I've forgotten who came up with the specific

On the set of *The Magic Christian:* Terry Southern and a certain Richard Starkey, O. B. E., a pop star of some note.

idea of having one of the Beatles as Guy Grand's son, Youngman Grand, but I was willing to try it.

I understand you completed the script with Joseph McGrath, but that he and Sellers and company made changes while you were busy with End of the Road.

When I finally made it to the set of *The Magic Christian,* I spent a lot of time doing damage control. It was probably due to Seller's insecurity or a manifestation of that. Although he loved the original script and it was the key to getting started, he also had this habit where he would run into someone socially, like John Cleese or Spike Milligan, and they would get to talking, and he would say, "Hey, listen, can you help me on this script?" They would come in and make various changes, sometimes completely out of character from my point of view. I found these scenes, a couple of which had already been shot, to be the antithesis of what Guy Grand would do. They were tasteless scenes. Guy Grand never hurt anyone. He just deflated some monstrous egos and pretensions, but he would never slash a Rembrandt—a scene which they had in the movie. There's a scene at this auction house, where, just to outrage the crowd or the art lover, Guy Grand and his adopted son bribe the auctioneer to deface this great painting. Guy Grand would never do that. It was gratuitous destruction; wanton, irresponsible bullshit which had nothing to do with the character or the statement. It was very annoying. They shot the auction scene and agreed to take it out for a time, but it stayed in the final cut. Peter did come around to seeing it was tasteless.

There was no dissenting opinion on the film.

No, Joe McGrath didn't dissent. He could have dissented at the time they were making these changes, because he was the director. He had a more disciplined sense of comedy than Peter, if not Peter's flaring strokes of genius. McGrath didn't have that much control, and he was so in awe of Peter that he wasn't able to resist him.

Towards the end of production, you shot the final scene with Guy Grand and his son persuading various passersby to wade into a tank full of manure and help themselves to money floating at the top of the mess [—the tank was] at the base of the Statue of Liberty.

Peter insisted we had to shoot that scene under the [real] Statue of Liberty. The producers resisted because of the expense of the trip. They were ready to shoot it there in England. So Peter, in a fit of pique and rage, said, "Well, I'll pay for it!" and then they said, "No, we'll pay for it!" We were going to fly first-class to New York and shoot the scene. Then Gail [Gail Gerber, Southern's companion since the midsixties], of all people, noticed this ad saying the *QE2* [*Queen Elizabeth II*] was making its maiden voyage. She said, "Wouldn't it be fun to go on the *QE2* instead of flying?" Peter thought that was a great idea. He assumed that it wouldn't be any more expensive than flying first-class, but it turned out to be much, much more expensive. Flying was like

$2,500 a person; but going in a stateroom on the *QE2* was $10,000 a person, because there were all these great staterooms on the *QE2*. The dining room was beyond first-class. Like, really fantastic. Instead of eating in the ordinary first-class place, [we] had this special dining room. It was called the Empire Room. It was a small dining room with about six tables in it. That was another $2,000 right there. But the producers were committed to it.

Before we left, I'd introduced Peter to this Arabic pusher, who had given Peter some hash oil. Peter put drops of it on tobacco with an eyedropper, and smoked the tobacco; or if he had cannabis, he would drop the oil on that and smoke it. It was just dynamite. Like opium. Peter became absolutely enthralled. He couldn't get enough of it. It was very strong stuff. So we all went on this fantastic five-day crossing. The whole trip was spent in a kind of dream state.

So there was you, Peter, Gail, and Ringo?

Yeah, Ringo, his entourage, his wife, and some of the kids. We never saw the kids. They were usually with the nanny. There was also Dennis O'Dell, the producer, and his wife.

That trip must have cost, as Guy Grand would say, "a pretty penny."

Yeah, I saw the figures on it once. The crossing cost about twice as much as the shot. They didn't use the shot of the Statue of Liberty in the end.

In 1969 and 1970, you had three major films in release with your name attached to them. Was it a good situation to have that kind of momentum, or was that a complicated time because of controversies like End of the Road*'s X-rating?*

Yeah, that [X-rating] didn't seem to help. *Easy Rider* did get a nomination, like *Strangelove.* It also won the Writers Guild Award [in its category] for that year. You would think you would have more leverage in a situation like that. I am sure that you are sensitive enough to imagine how not having certain projects get off the ground could feel. If there were anything to be gained from indulging that feeling, I would certainly pursue it. It just seems like a silly thing to think about, because it's self-defeating.

Some Unproduced Projects

You were involved in A Clockwork Orange *with the photographer Michael Cooper around 1966. How did that project end up with Kubrick?*

When Michael Cooper turned me on to that book [*A Clockwork Orange*], I read it and said, "This is really good and so cinematic." I sent the book to Stanley, circa 1966, and said, "Look at this." He got it and read it, but it didn't appeal to him at all. He said, "Nobody can understand that language [Nadsat, the newspeak-type lingo Anthony Burgess created for his novel]." That was that. The whole exchange occupied a day. Still, I thought someone should make a movie of this book.

At one point, I was making so much money on movie projects that I needed someone to handle paying the bills. I got involved with this friend of mine, Si Litvinoff, who had produced some showbiz things in New York like off-Broadway theater. He did a couple of things for me as a lawyer. I showed him the book and told him how it would make a great movie. He said, "You have enough money. Why don't you take an option on it?" So I took a six-month option on *A Clockwork Orange* [by Anthony Burgess (London: Heinemann, 1962)] for about $1,000 against a purchase price of $10,000 and some percentages to be worked out. I wrote a script, adapted it myself. I thought I'd show the book around, but meanwhile, I would have the script too. After I finished the script, I showed it to some producers, including David Puttnam, who was working with various companies like Paramount. He was one of the people who read the script and saw the cinematic possibilities of it. In those days, you had to get the script passed by the Lord Chamberlain [then British censor of film and theater]. When we submitted it to him, he sent it back unopened and said, "I know the book, and there's no point in reading this script, because it involves youthful defiance of authority, and we're not doing that." So that was that.

About three years later, I got a call from Stanley, who said, "Do you remember that book you showed me? What is the story on that?" And I said, "I was just showing it to you because I thought it was a good book, but later I took an option on it." He said, "Who has the rights to it now?" What had happened was that there was a renewable yearly option. I had renewed once, and when it came up for renewal for another thou[sand], I didn't have the money; so I told Litvinoff I was dropping the option. So he said, "Well, I'll take it out." Then he held the rights. So I told Stanley, "As far as I know, this guy Litvinoff has it." He said, "Find out how much it is, but don't tell him I'm interested." I tried to do that, but Cindy Decker, the wife of Sterling Lord, my agent at the time, found out about this inquiry of Kubrick's; so she passed the word on to Litvinoff and his friend Max Raab, who had put up the money for *End of the Road*. He and Raab sold it to Kubrick and charged a pretty penny for it. Around seventy-five thou[sand], I think.

Did Kubrick use much of your script at all?

Well, when I learned that he was going to do *A Clockwork Orange,* I sent him my script to see if he would like it. I got back a letter saying, "Mr. Kubrick has decided to try his own hand." It wasn't really a relevant point because it was an adaptation of a novel. You're both taking it from the same source.

You and Kubrick also shared the rights to [the novel] Blue Movie. *When you decided to write the novel, you dedicated it to him.*

He had in a way given me the idea for *Blue Movie*. One night, around the time of *Strangelove,* somebody brought a hard-core porn film to show at Stanley's house. They put it on. Very soon into the screening, Stanley got up and left the room. We watched a little more of it, then stopped the film. Later

Kubrick said, "It would be great if someone made a movie like that under studio conditions." I thought Kubrick would be the ideal person to direct such a movie. When I came back to the States, I started writing a novel based on this concept and would send him pieces of the book from time to time. I still have a great telegram from him saying, "You have written the definitive blow job!" in the scene with the Jeanne Moreau–type, Arabella.

Was he ever interested in directing Blue Movie?

No, when he first mentioned it, I assumed that he *would* be interested in directing it. But it turned out that he has a very ultraconservative attitude to most things sexual. Around 1974–75, John Calley, who was then president of Warner Brothers, decided to make a film of *Blue Movie.* A number of other people wanted to do it but always with the idea of compromising the work by having simulated sex. Calley, however, was convinced, as was I, that the first production of a full-on erection-and-penetration movie using big-name stars and a talented director, made under studio conditions, would be a blockbuster of *Gone with the Wind* proportions.

Calley was friends with Julie Andrews at the time, and he and Mike Nichols, who had been signed to direct, were able to persuade her—for love, art, and a lot of money—to play Angela Sterling, the heroine of the story. A fourteen million dollar budget, quite adequate for the time, had been secured, and everything was ready. Ringo Starr had held an option on the book but was quite ready to step aside now that there was an actual production ready to roll. He didn't want any participation. He just wanted to see the book made into a movie. Enter the villain of the piece: Ringo's lawyer—who shall remain nameless—in absolute hysteria, ranting about how he, the lawyer, was "going to look like a schmuck if the picture gets made, and we don't have a piece of it." John Calley and I were prepared to give him a piece, but it turned out that Mike Nichols wanted to retain all points, so he could use them to make deals with actors. That proved to be a deal-breaking stipulation.

Had you written an actual shooting script for Blue Movie?

Well, as soon as I became convinced that the film was for real, I started immediately, without even getting into a contract. I eventually completed a script, but the deals didn't go through. We were as close to a movie being made as I ever experienced or have ever heard of. There didn't seem to be any possible deal-breaking element. When it fell apart, it was just a total freak thing.

Did you try to develop anything else for John Calley after that?

He liked a story I had written called "You're Too Hip, Baby" about a white jazz aficionado who lives in Paris and goes to see the blacks in the clubs in Paris.* He had the idea of a screenplay set in Paris, dealing with those charac-

---

* "You're Too Hip, Baby" originally appeared in *Esquire* (August 1963) and was later included in Southern's classic anthology, *Red Dirt Marijuana and Other Tastes* (New York: New American Library, 1967).

ters. That got as far as an outline, which I was paid for, but nothing further was pursued. When *Blue Movie* fell through, that was really the end of our relationship.

Calley was considered the hippest movie producer of the time because he was able to deal with the money guys yet maintain an active rapport with directors like Kubrick and Nichols.

Yeah. I doubt that Kubrick and Nichols would work with anyone else. I doubt if there were any other producers who were percipient, sensitive, and aware enough to be tolerated by Kubrick and Nichols.

Around 1972, you were at work on an adaptation of Nathanael West's A Cool Million *with [the director] Jerry Schatzberg?*

I had known Jerry Schatzberg since he directed *Panic in Needle Park.* [1971] He was the first person who expressed interest in *A Cool Million* [New York: Covici, Friede, 1934]. We finished a script, and he was trying to raise money.

Did he have anyone in particular in mind with the casting?

He was a good friend of Faye Dunaway's. So he had her signed up . . . not that he thought she was right for the film, but he thought she could generate interest. She understood that and went along with it because they were good friends. We didn't have any male actor. It was going to be someone like Timothy Bottoms as Lemuel Pitkin. The subtitle of the book is "The Dismantling of Lemuel Pitkin."

After The Magic Christian, *did you still see Peter Sellers on a regular basis, or was it only during the time of "Grossing Out" [c. 1980] that you became involved with him again?*

I saw him on a sporadic basis, which turned out to be pretty regular. There was nothing planned.

You and Peter started to work on "Grossing Out," a script about international arms dealing, after the success of Being There *[1979]. Did you work on* Being There *at all?*

No. Peter ran his lines by me one time.

Andrew Braunsberg, who produced Being There, *was going to do "Grossing Out."*

Yes. "*Grossing Out*" dealt with the Western nations selling arms to the Third World and exploiting these countries.

Was there a director lined up before Peter died?

No, but Hal Ashby expressed considerable interest. I had written a script.

You worked with Dennis Hopper on the "Junky" screenplay in 1977, [*] *and then there was the Jim Morrison screenplay, which* Hustler *publisher Larry*

---

[*]   *Junkie* was originally published by Burroughs under the pseudonym "William Lee" (New York: Ace Books, 1953). When the book was republished under Burroughs' byline in 1977, it was retitled *Junky.* The unproduced script that Southern worked on was always called by the revised spelling.

Flynt wanted to produce in 1983. How has your relationship with Hopper evolved since Easy Rider*?*

Well, he's [Hopper] always said, "We're going to make that up to you," regarding *Easy Rider.* And while we were working on "Junky," I heard him say, "We want to make sure Terry has a good contract because he didn't get his share out of *Easy Rider.*"

Wouldn't it have been easy for them to give you points after the fact?

Oh, yes.

What prevented them from doing that?

Well, I say vicious greed. That's the only reason.

What about "Junky"?

Well, "Junky" was something that Jacques Stern, also known as Baron Rothschild, who was a lifelong friend of Burroughs', optioned.* Then Hopper and Stern commissioned me to write the screenplay. Hopper was going to play the part of Bill Lee, the junkie narrator of the novel, as well as direct. It turned out that Dennis wasn't that interested in making "Junky," and Stern didn't have enough money to produce the film, although he did have enough to option the book and finance the screenplay.

Did you actually finish a draft?

Burroughs, James Grauerholz [Burroughs' secretary], and I wrote a draft, which we showed to Stern [about which we asked] him if he had any criticisms or suggestions. Stern was trained as a physicist and was ultralucid, but he was also a decadent drug user. He had some kind of paralysis which left him wheelchair bound. He was living in Gramercy Park, while we stayed in a hotel uptown. Jacques had a hypodermic-type device taped to his wrist. All he had to do was tap this device, and he would get a jolt of speedballs. Jacques would say to us at our meetings, "See if you can work up some heavy thoughts? I have to get off!"

When you guys were writing "Junky," what was Dennis' function? Was he helping you write it?

No, he was just hanging out and hoping to direct it, but at the time, he was just higher than a kite. That was his preclean stage.

Both the book and script jump around quite a bit from New York to the rehabilitation center to Mexico and then back to the States. It's somewhat episodic. [The book] Junky *treats drugs in a noncelebratory and nonjudgmental way. The book itself is a rare document.*

Yes. Burroughs wrote some things for *Lancet,* the British medical journal, like a critique of a British doctor who had one of these remarkably successful

---

* According to Ted Morgan's biography of Burroughs, *Literary Outlaw: The Life and Times of William S. Burroughs* (New York: Holt, 1988), Stern, a Harvard-trained physicist, raised $100,000 to hire Burroughs, Dennis Hopper, and Terry Southern to work on the ill-fated *Junky* adaptation in 1977.

addiction cures using a drug called apomorphine. It's like morphine but is used to reduce the body's dependence on heroin. Apomorphine provided some protection, so that you wouldn't get this terrible sickness when you try to withdraw.

I gather apomorphine was similar to the methadone treatment.

Yes. One of the first scenes in the script deals with this guy who is coming to sell a package of army surrets. These are 3 cc ampoules of morphine which were in medical kits for soldiers on the front, so that if you got wounded, you could shoot one of these up. That was one of the things sold in trafficking in the forties.

You never actually finished a final script.

No. If Jacques Stern had taken it more seriously as a real project, instead of as a way to work out his relationship with Bill, it might have worked. There was an atmosphere of ultraparanoia between Jacques and Bill.

The Telephone (1988)

How did Harry Nilsson get involved in writing scripts?

Nilsson was a very creative guy. He had this story about a reporter who works for tabloids like the *Enquirer* or the *Star,* writing outlandish stories like "Headless Man Seen in Topless Bar." So we wrote a script called "Obits." Harry was able to finance the writing.

The Telephone *was a collaboration with Nilsson that actually got filmed. I have always been curious about the story behind that.*

We had this idea about an out-of-work actor who gets so into hallucinatory-type improvisations that he even makes up phone calls to himself. By chance, we were in the basement parking lot of the Chateau Marmont, and getting out of the car next to us was Whoopi Goldberg. We had seen her work and thought she might be right for the part.

Who were you thinking of originally?

Robin Williams. We wrote it with him in mind. We made this strenuous effort to get the script to him or at least talk to him on the phone. One night, by chance, we ran into him at the Improv [a comedy-improvisation theater]. He hadn't gotten the script, and then after a long time, we found out his manager didn't want him to do the film at all.

How did Rip Torn end up directing The Telephone*?*

Well, we needed a director, and I had seen some things Rip directed on stage. It just occurred to me that he could do it, and I didn't think there would be much to do, because it all takes place in a one-room apartment. It turned out Whoopi was a great admirer of Rip. When he and Geraldine lived on Twenty-second Street in New York, Whoopi was an unwed mother on welfare and living in that neighborhood. She would be walking to the welfare office to get her check and sometimes pass them in the street.

Was the shooting of The Telephone *quick, or was it a long process?*

Well, what happened was these big asshole producers told Whoopi that "this is a Whoopi Goldberg movie . . . ," so she could do whatever she wanted to do. Thus armed, she was able to ignore the script and just wing it. She's a very creative woman, and her improvisations were often good, but she had gotten involved because she really loved the script, and now she was suddenly making all these changes. So anytime she and Rip would get into an argument about a scene, she had this upper hand. After she did her improvisations, Rip would say, "Okay, let's do one for the writer." This went on and on through the production. I was on the jury at [the] Sundance [Film Festival] the year *The Telephone* was finished and took Rip's cut of the film there. I was ambivalent about it. I was too close to the film to be objective, but a number of people ended up liking the released film. [The New World version] is still selling well as a cassette at my local drug store.

Bibliographic Notes

.

Marjorie Rosen interviewed **Jay Presson Allen** in the *Los Angeles Times* (May 11, 1975); Debra Goldman's article "Nuts" profiling Allen appeared in *American Film* (March 1988); and Justine Blau's interview "The Prime of Jay Presson Allen" appeared in *Columbia Film View* 3 (1988).

Allen is one of the people interviewed by Judith Crist in *Take 22: Moviemakers on Moviemaking* (New York: Viking, 1984).

A portion of my interview with Jay Presson Allen originally appeared, in different form, in the biography *George Cukor: A Double Life,* by Patrick McGilligan (New York: St. Martin's, 1991).

Allen is well represented in the multitude of books about Alfred Hitchcock. Hitchcock himself discussed the shortcomings of *Marnie* in *Hitchcock/Truffaut,* François Truffaut's book-length interview with him (New York: Simon and Schuster, 1967). Jay Presson Allen and Evan Hunter, who wrote *The Birds* for Hitchcock, conducted a colloquy on the director for the Writers Guild of America-East newsletter *On Writing* (March 24, 1993). A few of her remarks from that session appear here, with Allen's permission.

The producer David Brown tells his side of what happened behind the scenes of *The Verdict* in *Let Me Entertain You* (New York: Morrow, 1990), while *Making Movies* (New York: Knopf, 1995), the autobiography of Sidney Lumet, makes essential cross-references to Jay Presson Allen's career, as well as to Walter Bernstein's.

Nick Roddick chronicled Allen's career in the *Dictionary of Literary Biography,* vol. 26, *American Screenwriters* (Detroit: Gale Research, 1984 [hereafter cited as *DLB,* 26]).

George Axelrod has a cult following in the United States and abroad, and has been interviewed for publications on both sides of the Atlantic. Bertrand Tavernier's interview with Axelrod in French in *Positif* (February 1974) is one of the first and best; but

Richard Corliss also profiles him in "Midsection: The Hollywood Screenwriter," *Film Comment* (July-August 1978). (Corliss also assesses Axelrod's career in his definitive *Talking Pictures: Screenwriters in the American Cinema* [New York: Overlook Press, 1974].) A more recent feature ("Enter George Axelrod . . . and the Lady Reappears") was published in *Films Illustrated* (May 1979).

Axelrod has often been interviewed for newspapers. Arthur Gelb profiled him early on in "Young Man with a Smash Hit" for the *New York Times* (March 1, 1953); Cecil Smith interviewed him ("Playwright Axelrod Sings Blues; Can't Keep the Money He Makes") for the *Los Angeles Times* (May 6, 1956); Charles Champlin profiled his career in "Hollywood Memo: Let George Do It" for the *Los Angeles Times* (November 29, 1965), and again for "Fragments from a Sanskrit Lunch," also in the *Los Angeles Times* (October 16, 1967); and J. A. Engels interviewed Axelrod for his article "Axelrod: 'Too Old, Too Rich, Too Successful' " in the *Los Angeles Herald-Examiner* (September 3, 1977).

Joshua Logan wrote about Axelrod and the making of *Bus Stop* in his second memoir, *Movie Stars, Real People and Me* (New York: Delacorte, 1978); and Axelrod is among the people interviewed about working with Billy Wilder in *Billy Wilder in Hollywood,* by Maurice Zolotow (New York: Putnam, 1977).

Guy Flatley of the *New York Times* profiled **Walter Bernstein** in his "At the Movies" column (December 3, 1976). *Cinemag* (March 31, 1980) covered the production of *Little Miss Marker* with "Bernstein Remakes Runyon & *Marker." Cineaste 3* (1987) published Pat Aufderheide's "Language of Film and the Grammar of Politics: An Interview with Walter Bernstein." Aufderheide also reported on the making of *The House on Carroll Street* for *Film Comment*'s "Journals" section (January–February 1988).

Bernstein's years of blacklisting receive limited coverage in Victor S. Navasky's *Naming Names* (New York: Viking, 1980); but more recent oral histories that include his experience, in his own words, are *Red Scare: Memories of the American Inquisition,* by Griffin Fariello (New York: Norton, 1995); and *The Box: An Oral History of Television, 1920–1961*, by Jeff Kisseloff (New York: Viking, 1995).

The NPR Interviews 1994, edited by Robert Siegel (Boston: Houghton Mifflin, 1994), includes the transcript of a National Public Radio interview with Bernstein and Abraham Polonsky, reminiscing about their scripts for the *You Are There* television series of the 1950s. (A collection of Polonsky's blacklist-era television work, *To Illuminate Our Time: The Blacklisted Teleplays of Abraham Polonsky,* edited by John Schultheiss and Mark Schaubert, was published in 1993 by Sadanlaur Publications in Los Angeles.)

Bernstein's work with Martin Ritt is explored in Carlton Jackson's *Picking up the Tab: The Life and Movies of Martin Ritt* (Bowling Green, Ohio: Bowling Green State University Popular Press, 1995), which is also recommended for further reading on Irving Ravetch and Harriet Frank Jr.

An interview with Bernstein, of some length, appears in *Contemporary Authors,* vol. 106 (Detroit: Gale Research, 1983).

A portion of my interview with Bernstein appeared in McGilligan's *George Cukor: A Double Life.*

Horton Foote was interviewed by Nina Darnton for "Horton Foote Celebrates a Bygone America in *1918"* in the *New York Times* (April 21, 1985); Samuel G. Freedman also profiled Foote in "From the Heart of Texas," in the *New York Times* (February 9, 1986); and Myra Forsberg reported on the making of *Convicts* in "Southern Memories Shadow the Makers of *Convicts*" for the *New York Times* (December 3, 1989).

Elizabeth Gordon profiled Foote ("Oscar-winning Writer Foote Explores His Family's Past") in *Film Journal* (May 1986); and Louise Tanner interviewed him for *Films in Review* (November 1986). The playwright-screenwriter was interviewed by Tom Teicholz in *Interview* (September 1985). Foote participated in "Dialogue on Film" published in *American Film* (October 1986); and Margy Rochlin spotlighted his career in "Tender Crimes" also in *American Film* (January–February 1987). *Literature Film Quarterly* has profiled Foote twice: T. Barr and G. Wood assessed his work in "A Certain Kind of Writer" No. 4 (1986); and G. Edgerton contributed the article "A Visit to the Imaginary Landscape of Harrison, Texas: Sketching the Film Career of Horton Foote" No. 1 (1989).

Foote is among the writers quoted on screenwriting in *Screenwriters on Screenwriting,* by Joel Engel (New York: Hyperion, 1955). Foote is also cited in Kisseloff's *Box.*

Foote's career is detailed in numerous reference books on theater and film. Joseph R. Millichap discusses Foote's film work in *DLB,* 26; and Foote is interviewed at length in *Contemporary Authors,* n. rev. s., vol. 34 (Detroit: Gale Research, 1991).

"Tomorrow" and "Tomorrow" and "Tomorrow," edited by David G. Yellin and Marie Connors (Jackson: University Press of Mississippi, 1985), chronicles the evolution of William Faulkner's short story "Tomorrow" into television and film, incorporating the original story basis, teleplay, the motion picture script, and an interview with Foote.

Foote's three most famous screenplays—*To Kill a Mockingbird, Tender Mercies,* and *The Trip to Bountiful*—have been published with an introduction by the writer (*Three Screenplays* [New York: Grove Press, 1989]).

Walon Green is discussed in recent biographies of Sam Peckinpah, including Garner Simmons's *Peckinpah, a Portrait in Montage* (Austin: University of Texas Press, 1982); Marshall Fine's *Bloody Sam* (New York: D. I. Fine, 1991); and David Weddle's *If They Move—Kill 'Em!: The Life and Times of Sam Peckinpah* (New York: Grove Press, 1994). Nat Segaloff also interviewed Green for *Hurricane Billy: The Stormy Life and Films of William Friedkin* (New York: Morrow, 1990), in which a portion of the *Backstory 3* interview originally appeared.

An in-depth interview with **Charles B. Griffith**, "Charles Griffith and the Little Shop of Corman!" by Mark Thomas McGee, appeared in *Fangoria* 11 (February 1981).

Recommended for background on Griffith's career is Samuel Z. Arkoff's memoir *Flying through Hollywood by the Seat of My Pants,* with Richard Trubo (New York: Birch Lane Press, 1992); and Roger Corman's *How I Made a Hundred Movies in Hollywood and Never Lost a Dime,* with Jim Jerome (New York: Random, 1990). Griffith is interviewed and quoted extensively in the Corman autobiography, shedding light on hidden facets of his years writing low-budget pictures.

There are many books about Roger Corman and AIP that include discussion of Griffith's contribution to the Corman mystique. Among the most comprehensive and reliable is *Fast and Furious: The Story of American International Pictures,* by Mark Thomas McGee (Jefferson, N.C.: McFarland, 1984).

Donald Spoto interviewed **John Michael Hayes** for his definitive-to-date *The Dark Side of Genius: The Life of Alfred Hitchcock* (Boston: Little, Brown, 1983). In Hitchcock's authorized biography, *The Life and Times of Alfred Hitchcock,* by John Russell Taylor (New York: Pantheon, 1978), the author ungraciously described Hayes as "not too strong on construction (Hitch could supply that) but great in the creation of lively, funny, sophisticated dialogue and smoothly believable characterization." Taylor's book, in contrast to Spoto's, is stingy with comments about the screenwriter's contribution to Hitchcock's oeuvre.

Hayes is interviewed in *Contemporary Authors,* vol. 108 (Detroit: Gale Research, 1982); and his career is chronicled by Willard Carroll in *DLB,* 26.

Ring Lardner Jr. has written occasional pieces of journalism over the years, often reflecting on his own life and career. An article, adapted from his speech to the American Jewish Congress about the thirtieth anniversary of the HUAC hearings, appeared in the *New York Times* (March 18, 1978); and his obituary for the producer Hannah Weinstein in the *Nation* (March 24, 1984) touches on his pseudonymous television work during the cold war era. His "Foul Ball" article in *American Film* (July–August 1988) describes John Sayles's filming of *Eight Men Out,* about the 1919 Chicago White Sox scandal, in which Sayles plays Lardner's father, the sportswriter Ring Lardner.

An article in the *New York Times* (January 13, 1987) reported on Lardner's revisit to the Soviet Union after fifty-three years and his second thoughts on the Communist Party.

Lardner is a key player in many books about Hollywood politics and the blacklist period. Among the most authoritative are Navasky's *Naming Names;* Nancy Lynn Schwartz's *Hollywood Writers' Wars* (New York: Knopf, 1982), about the background and struggle to organize the Screen Writers Guild; and Larry Ceplair and Steven Englund's definitive *The Inquisition in Hollywood: Politics in the Film Community, 1930-1960* (Garden City, N.Y.: Anchor/Doubleday, 1980). Lardner is also included among the subjects in Fariello's more recent *Red Scare* and Kisseloff's *Box.*

Lardner is one of William Froug's interview subjects in the indispensable *The Screenwriter Looks at the Screenwriter* (New York: Dell, 1972). Lardner is interviewed by Kenneth Geist in Richard Corliss's anthology *The Hollywood Screenwriters;* and his career is assessed by Corliss in *Talking Pictures.*

Lardner wrote the nonfiction *The Lardners: My Family Remembered* (New York: Harper and Row, 1976), which, though not expressly about himself, contains fascinating autobiographical material about his own life, as well as about his family.

Lardner is interviewed in *Contemporary Authors,* n. rev. s., vol. 13 (Detroit: Gale Research, 1984); and his life and career are sketched by Joyce Olin in *DLB,* 26.

Mick Martin's interview with **Richard Matheson** ("Matheson: A Name to Conjure With!") appeared in *Cinefantastique* 2 (1974); Paul M. Sammon wrote about Matheson's films and interviewed him for "Richard Matheson: Master of Fantasy," in *Fangoria* Nos. 2, 3 (October, December 1979); and Lawrence French contributed "Richard Matheson on *Twilight Zone* and *Jaws* 3-D,*" also in *Fangoria* 1 (1982), focusing on the writer's relationship with Steven Spielberg. Tom Milne wrote "Richard Matheson, or the Inhuman Condition," chronicling Matheson's career for the *Monthly Film Bulletin* (April 1981).

Matheson was profiled ("Master of Things That Go Bump in the Night") by the *Los Angeles Times* (February 26, 1978), and by Sean Mitchell ("This Man Can Make Your Blood Run Cold") for the *Los Angeles Herald-Examiner* (July 21, 1983).

Matheson is interviewed in *Contemporary Authors,* vols. 97–100 (Detroit: Gale Research, 1981); he is profiled by Roberta Sharp in *Dictionary of Literary Biography,* vol. 44, *American Screenwriters* 2d ser. (1986); and Raymond Carney writes about his literary career in *Dictionary of Literary Biography,* vol. 8, *Twentieth-Century American Science Fiction Writers* (Detroit: Gale Research, 1981).

A republished edition of Matheson's breakthrough novel *The Shrinking Man* (Boston: Gregg Press, 1979) contains an excellent introduction by Joseph Milicia, as well as the director Jack Arnold's storyboard drawings for the film version.

Books about Roger Corman and Steven Spielberg routinely cite Matheson's contribution to their work.

Wendell Mayes is interviewed in *Contemporary Authors,* vol. 103 (Detroit: Gale Research, 1982); and Tamita C. Kelly discusses his career in *DLB,* 26. Mayes was also one of Billy Wilder's collaborators interviewed for Zolotow's *Billy Wilder in Hollywood.*

Irving Ravetch and **Harriet Frank Jr.** have only rarely given interviews for publication.

Before the media explosion over the telefilm *And the Band Played On,* **Arnold Schulman** had escaped undue publicity. A definitive article about the long, troubled history of the HBO production ("*As the Band Played On:* Searching for Truth," by Betsy Sharkey) appeared in the *New York Times* (September 5, 1993).

Schulman was not interviewed for Joseph McBride's exhaustive *Frank Capra: The Catastrophe of Success* (New York: Simon and Schuster, 1992); nor was he interviewed for *On the Edge: The Life and Times of Francis Coppola,* by Michael Goodwin and Naomi Wise (New York: Morrow, 1989), where his name is misspelled; nor was he interviewed for *George Cukor: Master of Elegance,* by Emmanuel Levy (New York: Morrow, 1994).

A portion of my interview with Schulman appeared in McGilligan's *George Cukor: A Double Life.*

The article "Silliphant Proving Screenwriters on Par with Those 'Auteurs,' " by Thomas Pryor, focusing on **Stirling Silliphant,** appeared in *Variety* (July 23, 1975). Silliphant was also featured in the "Dialogue on Film" section of *American Film* (March 1988).

Silliphant's interview is one of those featured in Froug's *Screenwriter Looks at the Screenwriter;* and his career is reviewed by Randall Clark in *DLB,* 26.

Silliphant's script for *A Walk in the Spring Rain* was the subject of the book *Fiction into Film,* by Rachel Maddux, Stirling Silliphant, and Neil D. Isaacs (Knoxville: University of Tennessee Press, 1970), which published the screenplay, along with Rachel Maddux's original novella and critical commentary on the novel into film.

Key interviews and articles published at the height of **Terry Southern**'s fame, 1964 through 1970, include "A Creative Capacity to Astonish," by Jane Howard in *Life* (August 21, 1964); and an interview about *The Loved One* and *The Cincinnati Kid,* by the future screenwriter-director Curtis Hanson in *Cinema* (August 1965). More recent pieces include an illustrated feature in *Interview* magazine (February 1990); Lee Hill's "The Vox Interview with Terry Southern," *Vox* (Canada) (September 1990); and Mike Golden's "Now Dig This: Interview with Terry Southern" in *Reflex* (September 1992).

Additional background on *The Loved One* appears in Southern's *Journal of "The Loved One"* (New York: Random, 1965), with photos by William Claxton; and Tony Richardson's *Long Distance Runner: A Memoir* (New York: Morrow, 1993). Southern is interviewed "On Elvis, *Strangelove,* Barbeque, and *Barbarella*" in *The Catalog of Cool* edited by Gene Sculatti (New York: Warner Books, 1982). Michel Ciment's *Kubrick* (New York: Holt, Rinehart and Winston, 1983) features long interviews with the enigmatic director, mentioning Southern. Alexander Walker's *Hollywood, England* (London: Michael Joseph, 1974) is arguably the definitive account of the sixties British film boom, in which Southern was a key figure.

Beginning in the 1950s, Southern was an advisory editor to the *Paris Review* and a frequent contributor to the *Nation*. His work also appeared in *New Story, Zero, London Magazine, Queen,* the *Realist, Grand Street,* the *Evergreen Review, National Lampoon, Spin,* the *New York Review of Books, Saturday Review, Esquire,* and the *New York Times,* among others. Southern's highly amusing accounts of working on an abandoned Doors film ("Dennis Hopper/Terry Southern") and *Dr. Strangelove* ("Strangelove Outtakes: Notes from the War Room") have appeared in *Grand Street* Nos. 36, 49 (1991, 1994).

Southern is one of the subjects explored in Corliss's *Talking Pictures.* Jerry McAninch wrote about his fiction in *Dictionary of Literary Biography,* vol. 2, *American Novelists since World War II* (Detroit: Gale Research, 1978).

The published script of *Easy Rider* (New York: New American Library, 1969), edited by Nancy Hardin and Marilyn Schlossberg, is in fact a "cutting continuity"—not the actual screenplay, but a transcript of the edited version of the film. But Grove Press has recently announced an ambitious reissue program of Southern's work to include the original screenplays of *Dr. Strangelove, Easy Rider,* and *Barbarella.*

Notes on Interviewers

Joseph A. Cincotti is at work on a book about the history of New York University's film school.

Dennis Fischer, whose interview with Curt Siodmak was published in *Backstory* 2, is a Los Angeles–based schoolteacher. He writes regularly for science fiction and fantasy film magazines. He has contributed chapters to books on such subjects as *Star Trek,* kung fu, the *Alien* movies, and Bela Lugosi. His book *Horror Film Directors: 1931–1990* was published by McFarland in 1991. He is working on a book detailing the careers of science fiction directors.

An award-winning journalist and film critic, **Susan Green** has written for *Premiere, Travel & Leisure, Baseline* (an on-line entertainment news service), and the *Vermont Times,* among other publications. In addition, she worked on two projects—a 1985 book and a 1986 documentary film—about Bread and Puppet Theater. A Vermont resident, she has taught college-level journalism and film history courses.

Lee Hill is a writer and editor who has written on a wide number of arts topics for various Canadian publications. His book on *Easy Rider* has just been published by the British Film Institute. His interview with Terry Southern is excerpted from a biography in progress.

Rui Nogueira has been an essayist and critic for many film magazines, including *Cahiers du Cinéma, Positif,* and *Sight and Sound.* He is author of *Melville on Melville,* a contributor to numerous film dictionaries and encyclopedias, and is presently completing *Sherman on Sherman,* an interview book with the director Vincent Sherman. Nogueira lives in Geneva, Switzerland.

Nat Segaloff has written five books, among them *Hurricane Billy: The Stormy Life and Films of William Friedkin,* and is coauthor of the blacklist play *The Waldorf Con-*

ference. A former newspaper journalist, he now writes, produces, and directs television documentaries including *Biography* for the Arts & Entertainment Network. He lives in Los Angeles.

Barry Strugatz is the co-screenwriter of *Married to the Mob* and *She-Devil.*

The photographer **William B. Winburn** lives in Brooklyn.

General Index

Index of Films, Plays, and Books

Compositor: Impressions Book and Journal Services, Inc.
Text: 10/12 Times Roman
Display: Helvetica
Printer: Edwards Bros.
Binder: Edwards Bros.